The Growth Idea

A Study of the Weatherhead East Asian Institute

The Growth Idea

PURPOSE AND PROSPERITY
IN POSTWAR JAPAN

Scott O'Bryan

 University of Hawai'i Press • Honolulu

© 2009 University of Hawai'i Press
All rights reserved
Printed in the United States of America
14 13 12 11 10 09   6 5 4 3 2 1

Library of Congress Cataloging-in-Publication Data
O'Bryan, Scott.
    The growth idea : purpose and prosperity in postwar Japan / Scott
O'Bryan.
        p. cm. — (Studies of the Weatherhead East Asian Institute)
    Includes bibliographical references and index.
    ISBN 978-0-8248-3282-7 (hard cover : acid-free paper)
    1. Japan—History—1945–   2. Economic development—Japan—
History—20th century.   3. Japan—Economic conditions—1945–1989.
4. Japan—Social conditions—1945–   I. Title.
    DS889.15.O28 2009
    952.04—dc22
                                    2009012187

University of Hawai'i Press books are printed on acid-free
paper and meet the guidelines for permanence and durability
of the Council on Library Resources.

Studies of the Weatherhead East Asian Institute
Columbia University
The Weatherhead East Asian Institute is Columbia University's center for
research, publication, and teaching on modern and contemporary Asia
Pacific regions. The Studies of the Weatherhead East Asian Institute were
inaugurated in 1962 to bring to a wider public the results of significant
new research on modern and contemporary East Asia.

Designed by University of Hawai'i Press production department

Printed by The Maple-Vail Book Manufacturing Group

To my parents and grandparents

Contents

Acknowledgments

This project owes its earliest and biggest academic debt to Carol Gluck, whose guidance and enthusiasm were an inspiration throughout my graduate student career. Also at Columbia University, I thank Henry D. Smith II, Anders Stephanson, Barbara Brooks, and Hugh Patrick for their challenging advice and kind support. Conrad Totman and James Crowley also helped train me, and I thank them for their generosity. Nakamura Masanori kindly served as my sponsor at Hitotsubashi University. Sugiyama Mitsunobu and Amemiya Shōichi showed warm interest as the project took shape in Japan, and I thank them for their encouragement. Thanks are also due to Awaya Kentarō, Asai Yoshio, Itō Mitsuharu, Minami Ryōshin, and Watanabe Osamu. My warm thanks go to Chris Hill and Sarah Thal, who read the very earliest drafts of this work. Elizabeth Tsunoda, Laura Hein, and William Tsutsui all took time to share their thoughts when this project was only beginning to take shape. Bill has continued to be a supportive interlocutor since those early days. I also thank Mark Metzler for his intellectual exchange. My appreciation goes to the members of the Southern Japan Seminar, with special thanks to Jan Bardsley, Steven Heine, and John Tucker. Takeshi Daimon has generously provided research space at Waseda University. At Indiana University, I sincerely thank for their intellectual companionship and encouragement Nick Cullather, Robert Eno, Tom Keirstead, Mark Roseman, Richard Rubinger, Jeff Wasserstrom, and George Wilson. I feel a special debt to Michael Robinson for his intellectual openness and his personal support and to Robert Fish for his counsel. Margaret Key and Hiromi Yampol provided thorough research assistance. The many people who have made thoughtful comments on material from this project that I have presented in conference, seminar, and university settings in Japan and the United States also receive my thanks. The anonymous reviewers for the University of Hawai'i Press provided generous and rigorous feedback on the book manuscript, and I am indebted to them even as I may have failed adequately to account for all of their critiques.

I acknowledge the generous graduate and research support of Yale University; Columbia University and its history department; the United States Fulbright Commission; the U.S. Department of Education; the Heyman Center for the Humanities, Columbia University; the Leonard Hastings Schoff Publication Award of the Office of University Seminars, Columbia University; the Cecil and Ernest Williams Research Fund at the University of Alabama; Indiana University and the Department of East Asian Languages and Cultures; the East Asian Studies Center of Indiana University; and the Weatherhead East Asian Institute of Columbia University.

I thank the staffs of the Starr East Asian Library, Columbia University; the Hitotsubashi University Library and the library of the Institute of Economic Research at Hitotsubashi; the libraries of the Institute for Socio-Information and the Economics School at Tokyo University; the libraries of the Japan Productivity Center and the Economic Planning Agency; the U.S. National Archives, College Park; the Waseda University Library; and the Herman B. Wells Library at Indiana University.

I acknowledge and thank Iwai Shōko, Kobayashi Minako, and the Shakai Keizai Seisansei Honbu (Japan Productivity Center for Socioeconomic Development) for kind permission to use their images. My sincere gratitude goes to Patricia Crosby at the University of Hawai'i Press and also to Madge Huntington at the Weatherhead East Asian Institute, Columbia University. I also thank Barbara Folsom, whose editing and advice during the final stages of preparing this manuscript were invaluable.

Earlier versions of some of the material in Chapter 2 of this study originally appeared in *Japan Studies Review* 6 (2002) and is used with permission.

*　*　*

Following Japanese practice, the surnames of Japanese precede given names in this book. However, the names of Japanese who have published in English are cited with the given name first.

Abbreviations

CPB	Cabinet Planning Board
EPA	Economic Planning Agency
ESB	Economic Stabilization Board
ESS	Economic and Scientific Section
IRNE	Institute for Research on the National Economy
JPC	Japan Productivity Center
LTES	Long-Term Economic Statistics
SCAP	Supreme Commander for the Allied Powers
SRIJ	Statistical Research Institute of Japan
SSC	Special Survey Committee of the Foreign Ministry

The Growth Idea and Early Postwar History

The Meaning of "Loss"

As the end of the twentieth century neared and Japanese marked the completion of the first ten years of the Heisei era, public commentaries and scholarly examinations alike came to speak of the 1990s as Japan's "lost decade." Taken together, Japanese vernacular opinion and that of both native and foreign specialists on Japanese society all have routinely portrayed the ten-year period beginning in roughly 1991 as one of wasted years, a retrograde decade during which the Japanese people somehow lost ground, national power waned, and Japanese society foundered on the shoals of earlier national success. In not a few such accounts from the American perspective there lurked a barely disguised, but historically familiar, undertone of secret relief and satisfaction that Japan had, in the end, finally been brought down a notch. The least careful of these analyses created an unfounded impression of historical compression in which the troubled 1990s represented, not a significant but temporary period of national transition following upon a remarkable half-century of achievement and change, but rather the wholesale demise of the entire long, miraculous dream of postwar Japanese power, material might, and national competence. In their numerous additions to the perennial *Nihonron* (On Japan) genre of socianational treatise, Japanese, too, have produced their share of grim accounts of the 1990s as nationally aimless years when progress, they seemed to imply, abruptly ceased. Nor did the major publishing houses and their stable of celebrity commentators have a monopoly on such sullen diagnostics. As any observer of contemporary Japan could attest, "whither Japan?" anxiety surged strongly to the surface of public consciousness during the last years of the century, expressed in one way or another in the national press, on TV, and in the public pronouncements and private conversations of business people, politicians, teachers, and students alike.[1]

Such panoramically bleak and historically foreshortened representations of "lost" national years can seem rather odd when viewed in the context of the actual entirety of the complex, jostling record of the ten years beginning in 1991. Considered in the conventional sense in which nations are cast as unitary subjects operating on a world stage, a great deal of continued Japanese dynamism and global influence in fact marked that period of supposed Heisei-era gloom. Whether in terms of cultural production and influence, health and individual physical welfare, the transnational flows of people and capital into and out of Japan, continued corporate power, environmental leadership, or a comparatively high level of continued wealth—just to name a few domains of national prominence—Japanese displayed levels of creative activity at home and around the world that seem to stand in contrast with the "lost decade" thesis and stark etiologies of a sick Japan.

What paradigmatic set of assumptions, then, could be so persuasive that it would seem legitimate to speak of the complexity of collective experience in Japan during that decade's time in terms of being somehow gone? Inverting this initial question helps make clear the need to identify the discursive and material representations of loss's opposite—gain, achievement, acquisition, victory—at work inside the architecture of assumptions supporting such readings of the recent Japanese past. What lay at issue beneath declarations of Japanese failure were the accepted yardsticks at century's end of the success of nations.

From this perspective, a universe of expectations about the primacy of material achievement, described in the specific technical terms of national macroeconomic growth, comes more clearly into focus. Here growth means, foremost, increase in the total size of the gross domestic product (GDP) of the national economy, and it is against this ideological backdrop that "the 1990s," a time labeled one of "recession" (low-growth, no-growth, or even at certain moments decline in the size of the overall size of the GDP), now could be dismissed in terms of failure. It was the so-called bursting of an economic bubble in 1991 that economists tell us marked the beginning of the decade of failing growth. It was then that an interlocking inflation of stock-market and real-estate values that had begun some five or six years earlier came to a sudden end. Incessant reference to the burst bubble since the early 1990s itself quickly became shorthand for several interrelated troubling social and economic developments.[2] Primary among these was a sudden absence of macroeconomic growth: GDP at best went flat and remained more or less in what was considered that pathological state for the next decade.

This deep current of social expectation about GDP growth, whether always overtly spoken or not, was of course not new to the post-bubble 1990s. The statistic of GDP (or the earlier more common variant, gross national product, GNP) had by that time already served long years as the premier national measure of things in Japan and in the broader global state system. And yet, there was a time when the knowledge formations and vocabularies of macroeconomic growth, its prescriptions and instrumentalized practices, were not yet so fully naturalized. Even as late as 1961, Ryū Shintarō, the famous economist and social critic, could point out the sheer novelty of what he described in a popular *Asahi* newspaper column as the "glorification of growth, growth" *(seichō, seichō o raisan shite)* that had come in recent years to grip the nation.[3] As his repetition of the word "growth" suggests, Ryū, whose analytical career had passed through its formative stages under very different conceptual conditions during Japan's colonial and increasingly corporatist 1920s and 1930s, wrote his 1961 *Asahi* columns more in mocking alarm than in the sort of celebration of growthist success that we have been conditioned to expect by our narratives of the postwar decades. He warned that, in his view, the obsession with rapid growth as such was based on shaky material foundations, rife with misconceptions and potentially detrimental to national fortune. But more telling was the mere fact that Ryū felt compelled, in the midst of a moment of national reconception in the early 1960s, to call at least brief attention to the fact that growth as a new organizing principle of political-economic perception seemed to have rather suddenly supplanted earlier conventions. Indeed, Ryū argued, the very word "growth"—*seichō*—had begun to drown out mention of all the familiar concepts—words such as *keiki* (health of the economy), for example—by which the economy had formerly been understood.[4]

It is difficult today to imagine a world of political and economic policy, social scientific practice, economic enterprise, and even personal behavior, whether in Japan or elsewhere, in which the idea of ever-expanding material and financial accumulation (and the provision of new forms and increasing amounts of services) was not fundamental to our view of how societies and nations should work. Yet, despite its apparent temporal transcendence, growth—as an array of statistical measures, a body of theoretical models, a set of assumptions about the operations of the nation, a social and political goal to be accomplished, and a charge assigned finally to the state—has a history. This book attempts to write just such a history of the formative years of the growth ideal as it took shape in Japan during the first decade and a half after the Second World War. It is not my intent to write the entire intellectual and political history of the concept of growth as this played out in Japan from 1945 up to today, but rather to trace the early postwar history by which the pursuit of growth came, by the beginning of the 1960s, to occupy such a dominant position in Japan and much of the rest of the world system and continues to do so in its own ways even today.

Growth as Concept

In a commonsense way, the fixation on economic growth that Ryū Shintarō saw all around him would seem to have had good cause. GNP was growing at an annual rate of over 10 percent in 1961 and, for the prior five years, had grown at an average of 9 percent annually.[5] The flush of optimism this expansion engendered was reflected in national policy: Prime Minister Ikeda Hayato's new Income Doubling Plan, which had just been passed in December 1960, projected average economic growth rates of over 7 percent every year for the next ten years and committed the government to promoting that outcome. Indeed, by the end of that decade, the Japanese economy had become the world's third largest in terms of size of the GNP, surpassed only by the United States and the Soviet Union.

The story of this rapid economic growth dominates histories of Japan, coloring not only our descriptions of the post–World War II decades but also, retrospectively, much of the literature on the whole span of modern and even early modern Japan. Historians and social scientists for many years searched earnestly in every historical nook and cultural cranny for explanations for this national "performance." Indeed, the story of the second half of the twentieth century is often told as if it were synonymous with the trajectory of high-speed growth. Defining both popular perceptions and scholarly research programs for decades beginning in the 1960s, growth became in great part what we knew about Japan. The rates of expansion themselves were remarkable, of course; and indeed, a great deal of scholarship has been written explaining this explosive growth on the material and social levels.

My argument is that to these important studies of the economic changes of the twentieth century we might also usefully add perspectives that account for growth as an idea, one that emerged alongside the rapid economic expansion itself of the postwar period. This book is thus at heart a conceptual history of growth in its postwar forms. Its central thesis is that the preoccupation with high growth of the postwar years in Japan was not merely a reflection of the material fact of increased economic circulation, which while remarkable in its rate was surely not in itself unique to that period of history, but was an artifact of the twentieth-century rise of growth as an object of social scientific knowledge and as an analytical paradigm that came to govern political-economic practices in nations around the world. Economies, after all, seemingly rooted as they are in the material "thingness" of making, selling, and consuming, are not objects that enjoy an existence distinctly prior to the theories by which we attempt to conceive them. While not merely imagined, nonetheless they are, to borrow the term of Timothy Mitchell, "made" in the interplay between the real and cultural realms as quite sophisticated abstractions whose parameters and processes shift according to the rules projected by our modes of knowing them.[6] It is thus not the anatomy of growth per se that interests me, but growthism—the conceptual frameworks, modes of economic imagination, and political programs by which Japanese understood rapid material change and simultaneously attempted in national terms to give it meaning and shape its direction.

This book explores three broad, intersecting themes in the history of the postwar growth regime as these unfolded between 1945 and the early 1960s. The first relates to the ways in which changes in social science contributed to Japanese forms of postwar growthism. This social-scientific dimension relates in part to new epistemological developments within the ascendant discipline of economics, the technical revolutions that enabled a new breed of technocrats to shape a shared vocabulary of growth for a national public. I specifically trace the history of national income accounting, the analytical procedures by which the new statistic of GNP and related macro-benchmarks were calculated, and show how these techniques rose to the forefront of economic understanding and policy making in Japan in the 1950s. As such aggregative empirical methodologies reshaped postwar social science, bureaucrats and scholars transformed GNP from an obscure academic exercise into one of the key conceptual instruments by which macroeconomic growth was imagined and pursued.

Such technical innovations fueled social-scientific fascination with applying what increasingly came to be called "growth theory" to the practical problem of understanding the real physiologies of growth and to promoting it within the national context. In this cause, scholars and bureaucrats revisited an older modern interest in the possibilities of planning. Immediately after the end of the war, many argued that planning could be redeemed from its failed wartime past and made to work for a new Japan. They thereby helped renew a vision of technocratic guidance that had increasingly, in various guises, formed a central component of national social and economic policy during the twentieth century. By the 1960s, the general acceptance of the ideal of planning as fundamental to the optimal working of postwar economies resulted in a new wave of apologia for the principle of planning now specifically cast by some in terms of growthist ends and modes of analysis.

The second dimension of the rise of growth thought and practice that I examine is the political harnessing of the growthist ideal to articulate, by the middle of the second decade after surrender, a domestic vision of national postwar purpose. Since the Meiji period, analysts from a variety of perspectives had consistently compared Japanese capitalist development to supposedly universal models and declared it insufficient and "deformed." With Japan now defeated and the empire ended, reformers resurrected these older forms of what I call negative national exceptionalism. Combining prewar Marxist critiques with postwar modes of macroeconomic understanding, they mobilized long-standing fears of "backwardness" to argue for a growthist vision of national reformation in part informed by a panoply of new macroeconomic methodologies.

The idea of a structural reshaping of long-standing political-economic patterns in Japan seemed to dovetail with the postwar mantra of full employment that found voice in national economies around the globe as the new macroeconomics of the British economist John Maynard Keynes began to alter the theories and practices of the discipline in fundamental ways. In Japan, prominently placed economists after the war seized on the ideal of full employment to support a progressive program to foster the rise of a more vigorous middle class in Japan and, hopefully by extension, to support institutions of democracy more thoroughgoing than those of the prewar and wartime pasts. Historians and economists have marshaled great evidence for the contribution of the external or international aspects of Japanese material success during the postwar years—the fact that a significant portion of the rapid increase in total output can be explained by an intense Japanese orientation toward exporting high value-added products to the rest of the world. Yet it is also true that conceptions of rapid macroeconomic expansion were in part based on the convictions of its most ardent technocratic promoters about the important contributions that overall expansion of the GNP could make to their goal of fashioning a domestic society of prosperity and equity.

The third overlapping dimension the book presents relates to efforts made by growth publicists over time in the early postwar years, and more overtly after the end of the Occupation period, to expand Japanese notions about what level of material and social prosperity their nation might be able to achieve in a reshaped postwar world. Visions of prosperity that became more fully articulated by the beginning of the very high-growth era of the 1960s did not emerge fully formed immediately after the war. Massive wartime devastation and the most basic need simply to rebuild a society in near ruins placed material and conceptual limits on what could be imagined for the future of the nation. Such apparently wretched prospects, however, render all the more remarkable the many attempts that Japanese did make after the war to grope their way toward social and economic goals that were considerably refashioned toward more expansive notions of national and even personal prosperity. The intertwined sets of ideas that constituted this prosperity vision, often underwritten by new theories of the workings of national economies, found increasingly stronger expression once the recovery emergency of the late 1940s had receded. The full-employment ideal itself, and the accompanying belief in the need, more than had been true in earlier eras, for the government to provide stronger welfare and insurance supports for Japanese citizens as workers, both were critical parts of the conceptual framework of postwar prosperity.

But so, too, was a new willingness to accept enlarged understandings of the role of consumption in the national economy. Both public and private organizations strove to supplement a cultural canon of frugality and thrift—long evoked throughout Japanese history and a constant refrain during the war—by promoting the idea that certain forms of private consumption were newly appropriate in the drive toward a prosperity economy of growth. Largely heretical as these views would have seemed in earlier times in Japan much as elsewhere, by the 1950s many began to cautiously envision a consuming society on the basis of theoretical and statistical evidence observable in the field of contemporary economics.

Economists alone were not responsible for the incremental changes that took place in Japanese understanding and acceptance of consumption, however. International social-scientific support for rethinking the place of consumption in the economies of the postwar world did not operate in some rarified theoretical vacuum. The wave of iconoclastic views of consumption, demand, buying, and spending that surged forth from mid-century economics was in fact mingled with a host of real-world developments. Producers everywhere around the world sought new lines of business in consumer goods as the need for armaments shrank after the end of the Second World War; beginning in the 1950s, an increasing cultural focus on household domesticity characterized societies in one way or another in all the former wartime belligerents; wages and disposable income generally rose as labor unions around the world fought for their share of relative postwar prosperity; and, although less marked everywhere else than in the United States, the apparatuses of marketing and advertising expanded in complexity and reach during the postwar decades.[7]

Even during these changing times, any unguarded exuberance for consumerism in postwar Japan would have had to confront a formidable arsenal of critique, one armed with culturally and politically venerable languages of sacrifice, frugality, and saving.[8] Those who suggested a reconsideration of the role of consumption did so in a complex cultural, economic, and political environment that simultaneously included postwar versions of movements supporting the causes of savings and temperance that had been a constant feature of earlier decades of national life. Indeed, none among those seeking to adjust national conceptions of consumption for a new age ever advocated the idea of unfettered consumerism: careful, appropriate rationality, in their view, ought to govern the nature of consuming, no matter whether by government, business, or individual citizen. Yet, these cautions aside, Japanese society by the 1960s was one in which private consumption played a much larger role than it had earlier in the century, in terms of personal experience and behavior, cultural acceptance, and material fact. Efforts by economists operating in a variety of spheres to sanction these changes represented an important part of this history and were closely linked to larger conceptions of national prosperity.

This strand of the book's findings helps to insert Japan into the larger history of consumerism that has proved so riveting to scholars in many disciplines and national fields over the last two decades. By thus helping to historicize our understanding of Japan as one of the richest and most complex of consumer societies it also contributes to an increasingly vibrant conversation within Japanese historiography about the competing visions in Japanese modern history, on the one hand, of cultural and personal continence in regard to the desire and increasing ability to consume and, on the other, of the good life as defined in ever more materialist terms.[9]

My concern throughout the treatment of these themes is to contribute to a broader historicization of the pervasive, but increasingly dated, concept of never-ending growth that over the course of the first postwar decade and a half began to be articulated in ways familiar to us today, and that stubbornly continues in the early twenty-first century to undergird our most basic beliefs about societies and the global economy. To be sure, I attempt to do so by tracing the technical and political trajectories by which the concept was naturalized in the specific instance of Japan. Yet even as Japan became the premier icon of the postwar growthist ideal, neither the faith in rapid growth as a prescription for postwar peace nor the ascendancy of economics and econometric techniques that provided its technical support was unique to Japanese experience. This constellation of developments reflected, rather, a mid-century romance with technocracy common to industrial nations the world over and to the multilateral organizations formed after the war to manage global markets and development. Charting the ways in which growth as theory and practice emerged in the specific context of Japanese capitalism, the book is offered also as a contribution to our understanding of the larger transnational history of this technocratic ideal.

The fixation on growth in Japan as it came to be expressed in the mid-twentieth century shared continuities with earlier modes of economic thought that industrializing societies cast in nationalized terms of material power and competitive advantage. It also in part represented a renewal of an older emphasis on the "wealth of nations" that, first in the eighteenth century, had emerged as a preoccupation of the canonical strands of European political economy that would later so shape the modern and contemporary forms of the economics discipline. As can be seen in early modern ideas and practices, Japanese too had explored the implications of their own desire to promote the material prosperity of the realm. In the case of an otherwise obscure figure like Sada Kaiseki, some in the immediate post-Tokugawa years even suggested that promoting virtuous cycles of consumption of domestic products would accelerate economic circulation and thus the wealth of the country.[10]

But, in important ways, growthism as it came to be practiced by the early 1960s in Japan, as in industrialized economies the world over, was a distinctly postwar phenomenon. Technical revolutions within the social sciences, particularly the discipline of economics, the rising power of economic knowledge within both the academy and the public sphere of policy debate, the conceptual trauma visited by the Great Depression on orthodox views of how economies worked and ought to be managed, and the techniques of macroeconomic management with which leaders first experimented in the prosecution of total war all had the effect of creating a new level of awareness of what began to be called the "macroeconomic growth" of nations as the key objective of an activist vision of economic administration, the focus of scholarly research programs, and the most significant gauge of national power. To talk about growthism in the early years of its formation is not to claim that it alone caused economic growth. Rather, it is to begin to tell the history of the ways in which growth as a concept came to govern national and global agendas, not just for the early postwar decades, but indeed for the remainder of the twentieth century and beyond.

While part of a common mid-century history, national inflections particular to Japan affected the rise of growthism there in the late 1940s and the 1950s. One of the purposes of this book is precisely to shed light on the contextual conditions of possibility in which growthism initially took shape in Japan, and to suggest as well some of the reasons for its eventual strength there. In the course of the narrative, the book will propose at least three interwoven explanations.

The first relates to the dramatically altered geopolitical context of the postwar years. As Japanese searched for new purpose after the war, they did so as members of a nation not only thoroughly defeated but one that had suffered the swift demise of a far-flung empire on which they had premised conceptions of national power for a full half-century. The postwar period everywhere was characterized by a trend toward decolonization, as old metropole powers slowly came to terms with the moral and political force of nationalist movements around the globe. In the case of Japan, however, the relinquishment of imperial lands was an entirely forced one and, at least in legal terms, almost instantaneous. It was partly in response to such radically revised and newly confining circumstances that Japanese eventually imbued the growthist ideal with such bedrock national meaning. Following a period of uncertainty after the death of the old verity that the state secures the nation by securing territorial empire, a new axiom supposed that the state, though certainly more circumscribed than before, can help to secure national power by ensuring conditions for domestic industrial strength and rapid growth.

The second factor contributing to the Japanese instance of postwar growthism was an exceptionalist view of Japanese political economy that held that peculiar structural "dualities" could be addressed once and for all only by a national mobilization to expand rapidly the total size of domestic economic production. Elements of both the right and left wings of the political spectrum after the war supported this view of the special applicability of a growth remedy for uniquely Japanese socioeconomic diseases. This diagnostic formula, moreover, drew in its own way on older modes of Japanese exceptionalism that had long informed modern nationalist thought, even as it did so in this case by positing that an unhealthy state of affairs defined the Japanese case. It thus revealed telling continuities between the conceptual tropes of the postwar growth nation and those of earlier years.

The third broad factor that helped to amplify the power of the growth idea in Japan in its most formative years relates to growth as a technocratic pursuit. Accompanying (even underwriting) a belief in growth as telos with identifiable laws of progression was a new panoply of tools for counting, measuring, predicting, and managing it. Together these contributed to a view of postwar economic practice as now truly scientific. Such an idea was particularly attractive in post-defeat Japan. Identifying the goal of growth as a universal good and the techniques for understanding it as the marks of rationalized statecraft, bureaucrats and policy makers in Japan now seemed to have an acceptable replacement for the bankrupt national languages of imperial power, racial mission, and cultural purity of the colonial and wartime pasts. Practitioners also embraced the view that growthist technocracy provided an apolitical means to governing that could escape what many now dismissed as the irrational, ideological management of the state that had existed in earlier years.

Historicizing Economic Knowledge

While on the whole the topics and sources of this book relate to the domain of economics, the term "economics" here is multilayered. It refers not only to the scholarly discipline as pursued on university campuses, though this was at times important, but also to the public practice of policy, to the pursuits both of labor and capital in the operations of the market, and to a rising parlance of GNP-ism among a national public. My interests thus lie both in knowledge developments internal to the discipline of economics and in the more publicly cast expression of economic thought as it affected conceptions of the nation, cultural ideals, and the connections between individual subjects, private lifestyles, and national fortunes. I often draw on books and journals intended for scholarly audiences and on technical publications of key economic agencies and research organs of the government. At the same time, I also make use of national newspapers, journals of opinion, books for the mass market, and the popularly packaged reports and white papers, particularly of the Economic Planning Agency and its predecessor institutions, that regularly garnered wide readerships during the first postwar decades and exerted unrivaled influence on public perceptions of economic change. I examine as well a variety of other documents and official organs produced by planners, reformers, and related advisory, research, and promotional institutions that particularly contributed to the strands of growthist thinking after the war as I have laid them out. The U.S. National Archives files from the Occupation period provided some insight into the early American role after the war in promoting a postwar vision in Japan of macroeconomic regulation of the nation, though, even in this case, institutional histories and document collections from the Japanese side yielded a great deal of the relevant detail.

This study focuses much energy on epistemological change, the invention of new high-modernist abstractions, and political interpretations of history; but people matter here, too. A cast of seminally important individuals figures prominently throughout the chapters that follow. It was on their senses of national mission, social-scientific dedication, and political faiths that the conceptual and institutional developments I narrate in great part depended. Their autobiographies and memoirs, the histories they wrote, and interview recollections of their activities during the 1940s, 1950s, and 1960s all also provided rich material for the stories I tell. While politicians and journalists do appear, this history features economists, working in a variety of settings, most prominently. "Economists" here refers to professionally trained academics (commonly called *keizaigakusha*), but also to economic bureaucrats in central state institutions (generally known in the Japanese context as "bureaucratic economists," *kanchō ekonomisuto*) who daily assumed more public roles on the national scene after the Second World War. A significant number of such government economists, as well as prominent academic economists who frequently served together with their government counterparts as official advisers, attained considerable public stature in the late 1940s and the 1950s, and they played critical roles in employing new analytical methods and shaping public opinion and state policy. It is this new breed of what I call "public economists," whether bureaucratic or academic, that most often in this study commands my attention.[11]

This book does not focus on just one specific institution as somehow explanatory of the postwar growth "system." I have drawn the sources for this study from a variety of official and academic institutional settings, and many organizations and voices combined in the history I trace to articulate growthism as I am defining it here. All the same, it is also true that some agencies loom far larger in my story than others. In particular, the Economic Stabilization Board of the early postwar period and the later Economic Planning Agency (EPA), which grew by the mid-1950s out of that earlier organization, represented some of the most significant institutional settings in which growthist paradigms were shaped and disseminated.

The Economic Stabilization Board wielded unprecedented powers during the Occupation years of recovery, and in many ways no other one political-economic agency of the Japanese state overshadowed it during its existence. The later EPA was also centrally important to the functions of the Japanese state and to the shared perceptions of officials and the private sectors of economy and business. Unlike the ministries and agencies with which it worked to formulate its plans and forecasts, however, the EPA possessed no explicit administrative authority by which to pursue its goals. Criticisms of the agency as ineffectual and removed from the practical issues of real governance are common in the historical record. Detractors frequently attacked it as a "thesis ministry" and dismissed its plans as nothing more than "paper" lacking any real power of implementation.

Yet despite its lack of administrative authority, the EPA wielded considerable power in the realm of public opinion during the the formative years of the growth idea. Although those with higher hopes for more authentic government coordination of the economy did attack EPA planning at the time, many of the critiques of it as a "thesis ministry" were, in fact, a product of a later time, when high growth ended in the 1970s and the charmed aura that had surrounded the agency faded in the wake of failures to predict fundamental changes in the economy.

The diminished stature of the EPA later in the century stood in contrast to earlier decades.[12] From the time of its creation in the mid-1950s, the agency had been known as one of the government's "Big Three Economic Agencies" (along with the Ministry of International Trade and Industry and the Ministry of Finance) or, alternatively, when counted along with the Foreign Ministry, even as one of the "Big Four" organs of the government as a whole. This was perhaps in some measure due to its historical association with its indubitably powerful predecessor institution, the Economic Stabilization Board. But the high estimation of the place of the EPA also issued from its role in setting the terms of national debate on the economy. It was uniquely charged to take the pulse of the entire economy and positioned to make comprehensive statements on its future directions. The EPA served as a clearinghouse for conceptual and methodological developments in economics, transforming these into coherent representations of national fortunes for the mass media and a public readership. While some portion of the outcomes of rapid expansion in economic output might have occurred without the plans of the period, these and the other documentary products of the EPA remained significant in their influence in determining what was "known" about the economy and therefore the objects of attempted state remediation. EPA plans and white papers certainly provided what economists refer to as a "signaling effect," in which their economic projections helped form expectations about continued prosperity that influenced government, business, and consumer behavior. Less remarked, however, is the way in which they functioned to introduce and shape the conceptual instruments by which growth as an organizing principle of national affairs was conceived.

This book participates in an enlarging body of literature that takes as its subject the historicity of economic knowledge and that simultaneously works to broaden our view of the multiple discursive fields in which "the economic" operates. This scholarship is often conversant with the theories and treatises of the discipline more formally defined,[13] but also in the ways these stand in iterative relations to political practice and wider cultural fields, over time becoming deeply dissolved into the perceptual ether of national publics. The writings of Keith Tribe, Philip Mirowski, and Deirdre McCloskey all in their own way represent seminal demonstrations of the inherent status of economics as discourse, one that generates its own modes of rhetorical construction and that produces reality effects that are less than direct "reflections" of the material facts of economic action.[14] Other histories as diverse as those of Ian Hacking on the replacement of causal determinism in nineteenth-century Europe with new laws of statistical chance, of Martin Weiner on long-standing tensions in England between commercial values and pastoral ideals, and of William Leach on the many spheres in which experts and publicists sanctioned a new order of consumer society in late nineteenth- and early twentieth-century America all explore the vernacular life of economic ideas on cultural terrain.[15] These works have all provided inspiration, confirming and expanding on the initial impulses and concerns that fed my thinking as I reflected on my initial archival research and as my arguments took shape.

The book that has resulted has particular affinities with an especially fruitful strand of scholarship interested in the history and sociology of numeracy and statistical modes of description. While some of the work done by the narrative that follows is rooted in the administrative practices and institutional history of numerical production, one of my accompanying concerns is with the power of those statistics to name and assign order. The book thus shares with a broader historical scholarship on statistical modes of knowing an interest in the ways in which "practices of quantification have also their own logics."[16] Two books have been particularly important to me in this regard. In *The History of the Modern Fact*, Mary Poovey retraces the history of knowledge practices in Europe that from the sixteenth to the nineteenth centuries increasingly accepted numbers as the most appropriate representation of fact. That numerical modes of knowledge seemed to allow for transparent description, immune from questions of interpretation, contributed to a near obsession by the nineteenth century with counting—with assigning numbers to observed particulars. Silvana Patriarca's *Numbers and Nationhood* ties this counting impulse to a history of nationalism, showing the ways in which statistical data deployed by patriots created a spatial portrait of a unified Italy. Social and demographic numbers thus helped project a geographical body for a nation not yet existent, one that would encompass all the varied territories and political units arrayed over the Italian peninsula.[17]

I wish, however, to extend the insights of histories such as those of Poovey and Patriarca by lengthening the temporal frames applied to the developments they narrate. The question of how practitioners of the sciences of wealth and society sought to generate and represent their particular forms of knowledge does not end, as the accounts of Poovey and Patriarca essentially do, with the nineteenth century. The increasingly formalized discipline of economics, in particular, turned to statistical epistemologies with renewed fervor in the twentieth century, often by supplementing older forms of induction with mathematical practices and modeling. This book is occupied in great part with tracing the expressed intentions and self-conscious goal setting of economic practitioners across an early postwar arc of time. It attempts to do so, however, by also keeping an eye toward how the twentieth-century modes of statistical innovation that these public economists employed conditioned their descriptive practices.

One of the critically influential forms that reinvigorated statistical obsessions took during the twentieth century constitutes a central topic of this book. Though at the outset of this project I could only dimly have imagined such a subject playing an important role in the history I would write, the sources I began to uncover during my research slowly suggested a story of postwar growthism that was intimately linked to an explosion in new, powerful statistical methodologies by which social scientists were beginning to conceive economies at mid-century—and by which growth would eventually come routinely to be spoken. As I discovered, the very concept of a GNP, a number derived by accounting techniques that saw an entire national economy as if it were a household economy writ large, represented a very recent invention. Its sudden appearance in the historical record in Japan during the late 1940s and early 1950s seemed to bear more than coincidental relevance to the questions I was interested in exploring. It was thus through rather unexpected but happy card-catalogue discoveries that I began to see the seemingly rarified story of statistical technologies, if you will, as a key to understanding the history of growth as I wanted to tell it.[18] On this score especially, it is my hope that this study adds to our understanding by supplementing our anatomies of growth as material fact with an account that highlights the very recent provenance of the tools themselves by which economic practitioners of the time demonstrated such fact—and by which the economic-historical anatomist could in retrospect reconstruct and explain it.

The Mid-Twentieth Century and the Postwar-ness of Growthism

The many significant dimensions added during the twentieth century to what were seen as the ends and means of economic thinking came, moreover, at certain moments. The emergence and eventual apotheosis of the social-scientific object and political ideal of macroeconomic growth was, in Japan, centered on a period running from the mid-1940s to the beginning of the 1960s. These are the years, therefore, covered most explicitly in my narrative. At the same time, this post-1945 history represented only the most visible portion of a complex international story of theoretical innovation, empiricist practice, and instrumentalizing application that in fact links that initial postwar decade and a half with technical developments begun in the 1920s, 1930s, and wartime 1940s. My narrative also accounts for these early traces of the thinking that would go on to inform postwar growthism by circling back where appropriate to earlier twentieth-century moments of invention.

The conceptual genealogy of growthism can be seen, therefore, as one aspect of an array of technocratic developments, fueled by modernist desires for managing societies, that tie the years both before and during the Second World War to those after. At what might be called the lowest power of temporal magnification, it is useful to think of a period called the mid-twentieth century as a distinct era, one stretching roughly from the end of the First World War through the 1960s and defined, among other things, by epistemological developments within the sciences of society and the economy that seemed to confer more far-reaching abilities to ascribe to them the truth claims of science, deepening faith in the possibilities of rationalized planning, and a political-economic modernism that played out in a host of large-scale experiments with reshaping metropole, colonial, and postcolonial states, societies, and geographies. At the same time, it is also crucial that historians be sensitive to the many layers of change even within such a mid-twentieth-century period.

Such a view of novelty within continuity is fundamental to my conception of the place of the Japanese instance of growthism in the broad transformations of the mid-century era. The descriptive and predictive practices on which GNP growthism rested shared many impulses with the various forms of modern developmentalism—whether enacted at home or in colonial holdings—that had marked Japanese history. But as their full influence began to be felt in the postwar years, these practices also introduced significant new elements to national economic and political imaginaries, elements that have often been taken for granted as nothing more than natural epiphenomena of material change itself or as identical to other forms of economic statecraft.

This fact has implications for our received understandings of the vaunted "postwar Japanese system" of political economy, however one may wish to describe this mythical abstraction that so occupied the interpretive energies of scholars, journalists, and policymakers in Japan and around the world during the late century. Long-standing debates on the nature of Japanese postwar political economics—both those that have focused on the history of industrial policy and found either a "strong state" or a "weak state" the key to Japanese forms of capitalism and those concerned with the postwar legacies of wartime mobilization and new institutions of coordination as these arose between capital and the state—certainly have relevance to this book and, at some moments more than others, constitute a conceptual "deep context" to the arguments as these unfold.[19]

Readers will find, however, that it has not been my intent to reexamine these particular older debates on their own terms in any programmatic way. As I hope is clear by this discussion, I am in fundamental sympathy with histories that emphasize the transwar dimension of political-economic institutions in Japan, particularly in regard to experiments with industrial policy and a panoply of schemes of financial and material resources allocation that emerged fitfully beginning in the late 1920s and more forcefully during the wartime 1930s and 1940s.[20] Yet, by the same token, it is a mistake to portray all postwar conceptions and approaches as nothing but static carryovers from interwar, colonial, or wartime experience. I concur with arguments that emphasize the continued importance of colonial and mobilization planning approaches and of industrial policy during the postwar years. Yet I also maintain that any history of postwar change misses a great deal unless it takes into account the ways in which Japanese were drawing in those years on an expanding palette of social-scientific knowledge and applying some of this in a postwar language of growth that was new. Postwar growthism thus did not supplant industrial policy practices of longer standing but supplemented them, existing side by side in ways that eventually made the postwar years different from those before.

Finally, a brief summary of the chapters that follow will give a sense of how the themes I have discussed in this introduction fit into the overall trajectory of my narrative of the formative years of growth as an idea that redefined national conceptions of purpose and prosperity. Chapter 1 treats the concerted movement by former wartime planners to resuscitate and redeem the ideal of planning for the postwar era. Though their definitions were often diffuse, partisans revived their faith in planning, which had been tainted by war, defeat, and empire, by self-consciously recasting it in terms of a new democratic and scientific humanism.

Chapter 2 revolves around the significant changes that were at work within the discipline of economics worldwide in the mid-twentieth century and the effect that these new lines of theoretical and methodological inquiry had in Japanese social-scientific thought. The chapter specifically traces the rise of a host of statistical epistemologies that formed the basis of the accounting conventions out of which was produced the statistic of GNP, a highly charged measure that by the 1950s became a central component of macroeconomic growth analysis and perception in Japan and around the world.

In Chapter 3, I continue the discussion of changes within economic knowledge that supported an increasing macroeconomic focus on growth. Though rarely translated into policy in any idealized form, Keynesianism and its emphasis on the ideal of full employment seemed to offer a possible vision of abundance applicable even to a Japan still grappling with the problem of postwar reconstruction.

The book goes on in Chapter 4 to trace the rise of growth theory within the academy and economic agencies of Japan in the 1950s and illustrates how its analytical power prompted historians and economists to reevaluate both Japan's national past and its national future in terms of that theory's conceptions. It also argues that Japanese technocrats seized in perhaps surprising ways on the growthist view of planning as they believed it was practiced in the United States to argue for the importance of central economic blueprints for growth.

In Chapter 5, I show how public economists leveraged the postwar ideal of full employment to argue that structural inequality and what they saw as Japan's age-old population problem could finally be overcome through a macroeconomic focus on rapid domestic growth. This chapter concludes with a look at how hopes about the possibility for a society of abundance intersected with new economic conceptions of the importance of spending and demand in national economies to prompt some to suggest that new kinds of private consumption might also have their place in the Japanese economy of growth.

CHAPTER 1

A New Mobilization

The Redemption of the Planning Ideal

t was the initial policy of the Allied Occupation to leave the responsibility for economic rehabilitation to the Japanese government.[1] The task
that lay ahead for Japanese, however, was enormous. The economy was
in a state of near collapse by the time of surrender, and the wartime privations of daily life had reached new extremes. Food rations had dwindled
in the final winter of the war, and bad weather, along with shortages of
fertilizer, equipment, and labor, resulted in a disastrous harvest in 1945.
Agricultural output had plummeted so precipitously by August 1945 that
mass starvation seemed imminent. Production of consumer goods such as
clothing and household wares had long before come to a virtual halt. The
ranks of the unemployed swelled as soldiers, administrators, and civilians
returned from the former empire and as workers at home were idled by the
shutdown of military production.

The destruction of the war had laid waste to great swaths of the industrial capacity of the country, and production was at a "complete standstill."[2]
Intensive wartime production had left decrepit what industrial facilities
remained. Because foreign trade had all but ceased and internal infrastructure almost completely broken down, raw materials were hard to come by.
Financial markets were in disarray, causing severe shortages in the capital
that industry needed to rebuild and retool. Exacerbating all of this was galloping inflation: by December 1945, prices had risen nearly six times above
their level at the time of surrender four months before.

In the face of this desperate emergency, Japanese government policy
was confused and adrift. The burden of the war effort in the final months
of the conflict had strained resources to the breaking point, and in the
desperate fight for survival, civilian and military bureaucrats had done little
comprehensive planning for what the world might look like after the war.[3]
"We were dazed," then president of the Bank of Japan, Shibusawa Keizō,

later recalled, "truly numb."[4] Beyond the constraints imposed by dire circumstance, laying plans for postwar policy had presented official Japan with an ideological dilemma during the endgame period of the war, for it meant confronting what was becoming increasingly difficult to deny: Japan would be defeated. The final swiftness of the surrender, moreover, had caught key ministries such as Munitions and Finance and other official agencies unprepared for conversion to a postwar economy.[5] Arisawa Hiromi, a left-leaning economist who participated broadly in postwar policy formulation, notes that there was no independent response by the government to the issue of reconstruction as the Occupation forces began arriving in Japan, while an early economic study panel on which Arisawa served declared that the government merely "idly looked on" as the wartime system collapsed.[6]

This policy vacuum was in part the product of the dramatic geopolitical changes brought about by defeat. The Japanese bid for economic autarky had failed, and with the end of empire, Japan lost over 50 percent of the area under its control. The dream of an integrated bloc economy—through which the architects of empire had hoped to secure a ready supply of raw materials and captive markets for manufactures—was foreclosed forever. The entire framework on which Japanese economic theorizing, planning, and policy making had rested for the better part of a decade and a half had collapsed.

On top of all this, Occupation policy at the time of surrender was an unknown quantity. The Potsdam declaration of July 1945 had called for seemingly wide-ranging changes in the political and economic structures of Japan. Yet the exact nature of the reforms was still unclear by the end of the war. The months during which Occupation policies on reparations, the dissolution of the *zaibatsu* industrial combines, the purge of economic leaders, and deconcentration of capital holdings were hammered out further unsettled the climate for effective action by the Japanese government on economic recovery.[7]

Big business, for its part, did little better than government. Dazed by the far-reaching changes in corporate Japan that the Occupation seemed determined to enact and financially dependent on war contract outlays from the government, business leaders failed to fill the policy void with their own formulations of a recovery plan. Industrialists were, it was heard at the time, "marking time in vain."[8] Management in Japan had "lost its confidence," argues Inaba Hidezō, a wartime researcher in the Cabinet Planning Board, and did "nothing to establish its own autonomy."[9] Although businessmen retained power for a time in the postwar successors to wartime industry control associations, Elizabeth Tsunoda notes, these were banned by the Occupation in the spring of 1947.[10] Only the surging labor movement, embarked on new wage systems and a union-controlled production movement, met the immediate postwar period with a positive program.

All of this stood in marked contrast to earlier years. During the 1930s it had seemed that everyone had a plan: colonial development plans for Manchukuo, five-year plans for increasing industrial strength at home, and eventually grand schemes for the construction of a "new economic order" that would meet the needs of the defense state while avoiding the excesses of both capitalism and socialism. Empire, war, and the perception from the end of the 1930s of an epochal clash of world civilizations all seemed to demand grand experiments in managing economic structures and flows. These projects were accompanied by the rise of far-flung institutional structures of planning and an emerging class of technical researchers and analysts, or as expressed in a common sobriquet, *chōsa man* (research men),[11] to run them.

The contrast between the lack of economic road maps, official or otherwise, in the immediate postwar period and the brisk trade in planning proposals during the more confident days of the 1930s and 1940s was made even more stark by those who, revisiting the earlier discourses on planning, argued the need for rationalized management of the postwar economy. Many of the most prominent of these spokesmen had in fact participated in wartime mobilization planning in institutions such as the Cabinet Planning Board, the Greater East Asia Ministry, and the South Manchurian Railway Company. Others concurred as well. A broad array of voices from the academy, the press, and major economic agencies variously argued that the economy must be "systematized" *(soshikika)*, "rationalized" *(gōrika)*, and "planned" *(keikakuka)* along "scientific" *(kagakuteki)* lines. Though few were equipped with a plan, many were convinced of the need for planning.

This desire for a rationally ordered governance of economic life was expressed in the context of a broader discourse emphasizing technical knowledge and the predictability and manageability of economic phenomena. Such ideas, based as they were on faith in a growing class of technical experts, in specialized knowledge, in the formalized analytical techniques of the social sciences, and in a more interventionist state, were the legacy of earlier discourses of the modern past. Their lineages most obviously may be traced back to the experience of total war, but also earlier, to the post–World War I era, and perhaps even to the 1890s, when a new class of self-styled experts first turned to defining a host of "social problems" and promoting various state initiatives to solve them.[12]

The postwar articulation of the managerial state built on these heritages, however, in two significant ways. The first was the rise of more elaborately articulated and more vigorously practiced techniques of empirical quantification. The explosion of statistical knowledge in economics after the war was accompanied by more highly formalized and coordinated institutional structures within which data were officially produced and then deployed toward a variety of new macroeconomic ends within the system of growthism.

The second way in which older notions of rationalized management of the economy were extended after the war is more particularly the subject of this chapter. Revived hopes for planning amid the postwar confusion were tempered by what were widely perceived by both the left and the right as the blunders of the wartime controlled economy *(tōsei keizai)*. Planning, moreover, had been closely associated with wartime aims. The rhetoric of "nation" now having been discredited, discursive attention shifted from the state to the people, from the public to the private. This reorientation presented a challenge to unproblematic implementation of state-led development after the war. Planning advocates therefore hastened to articulate a revised vision of planning more appropriate to a "new," open Japan. The solution to the botched wartime system, advocates argued, was to develop a renovated controlled economy that was both scientific and democratic.

It was easy enough, of course, to employ what often seemed no more than woolly sentiment in the service of older schemes for central economic controls. Postwar political necessity and the demands of the ubiquitous mantra of "democracy" were both at work here. Yet, by the same token, the rhetorical reshaping of planning into a "democratic" instrument signaled a significant shift, supporting changes under way in economic thought that would contribute in the next decade to the ideas and practices of growthism. Indeed, the strategically linked themes of technocracy and democracy—combined in what might be called a vision of "humanistic technocracy"—in many ways served as the two principal ideological keynotes of postwar social, political, and economic thought.

Postwar Dilemmas of Planning

Although little official action was taken during the war to lay out postwar policy guidelines, during 1945 individuals in and around the bureaucracy began in their own small ways to set their sights on the postwar economy. One of these was Ōkita Saburō, a young analyst in the Greater East Asia Ministry (later the Foreign Ministry) who quietly began organizing a group in the spring and summer of that year to study options for postwar policy. What began as a modest study group soon grew into an important committee. The ambitious report it produced, *Nihon keizai saiken no kihon mondai* (Basic problems in the reconstruction of the Japanese economy, March and September 1946), represented the most significant early effort by government officials and economic specialists toward documenting current conditions and setting a rough framework for reconstruction.[13]

To the elite members of this Foreign Ministry committee, the war provided many lessons, but chief among them seemed to be the rising importance of economics in the modern world. It was clear to them that economic weakness had been the cause of Japan's ultimate failure in total war, while economic strength lay at the heart of the Allied victory. Yet economics now determined not only the outcome of modern war, the committee argued, but also the possibility of future peace. Indeed, the experiences of the previous several decades had shown that all manner of political, diplomatic, and social problems plaguing the modern world were at heart economic in nature. Though such emphasis on the determinant character of the economic realm surely reflected the beliefs of resurgent Marxists, it found equal voice in this case among capitalists as well as labor, among conservative bureaucrats as well as liberal professors. Growing recognition of the underlying economic causes of political problems, as the Foreign Ministry committee pointed out, had in fact prompted the creation of the new national and multilateral systems to manage the world economy that were the hallmark of the postwar age. As debate about how to bring about recovery swelled, it seemed to the experts on the committee that economics in the postwar world would be newly endowed with pivotal meaning.

An electrical engineer by training, Ōkita Saburō joined the Communications Ministry in 1939 as an analyst of foreign electrical industries. After moving to the Greater East Asia Ministry, however, he was engaged in mobilization research and gradually transformed into an economic analyst. Ōkita had been dubious about Japan's prospects for victory from the very start of the war, and he began secret discussions in the spring of 1945 with the prominent political economist Taira Teizō about forming a group to study options for postwar policy. Taira was secretary of the Research Section of the South Manchurian Railway Company and had been one of the leaders, along with Ryū Shintarō, Gotō Ryūnosuke, and others of the Shōwa Juku (Shōwa Institute), an offshoot of Prince Konoe Fumimaro's national policy think tank, the Shōwa Kenkyūkai (Shōwa Research Association) of the late 1930s. The Juku had sought to educate college students and young graduates on the problems of Japanese political economy and the China question. Ōkita had first met Taira after becoming a student at the Juku in 1939, soon after he joined the Communications Ministry.[14]

With Taira's help, Ōkita began organizing like-minded economists and other specialists into a study circle. Given the ideological climate at the time, however, it was not possible to speak openly about the aims of the group, and Ōkita took pains to avoid reference to the "postwar" or "reconstruction." Under the pretense that enemy submarines would soon cut off the home islands from the continent, therefore, the group was initially dubbed the Research Group for Self-Sufficiency of the Japanese Mainland.[15] The invitations to the first meeting were also vaguely worded so as not to run afoul of the military police. After the notices were sent out, Ōkita and some of the other organizers paid visits to those invited to explain personally the true nature of the committee.[16] Such were the obstacles to planning under the military regime.

Although only a modest gathering of ten people began deliberations on the first day, this informal group grew into a significant and officially supported ministry committee soon after the surrender. The initial meeting had been scheduled several weeks in advance for August 16—one day, as it turned out, after the emperor's announcement ending the war. The members therefore decided on that first day to rename their group more appropriately the Committee for Research into Postwar Problems. Meetings were held in the South Manchurian Railway Company Building at the head office of the Greater East Asia Ministry, and funding was secured by Ōkita's boss, Sugihara Arata, head of the Ministry's Bureau of General Affairs (and then of the Research Bureau in the Foreign Ministry), and Tajiri Akiyoshi, vice-minister of GEAM. Once the Greater East Asia Ministry was abolished in late August 1945, Ōkita followed his boss to the Foreign Ministry, and the Committee continued its work there, now as a Special Survey Committee (hereafter SSC, Tokubetsu Chōsa Iinkai) under the Bureau of Research and Analysis. The ministries of Finance, Agriculture and Forestry, and Commerce and Industry lent mid-ranking officials and administrative personnel to the effort, and the number of participants increased steadily, growing to almost thirty principal members as well as tens of lesser participants.[17]

The SSC was remarkable for the wide range of opinions and disciplines represented within it. In addition to the contingents from the various ministries, it also brought together members of the academy, industry, and the press. The many economists in the group included leading Marxians such as Ōuchi Hyōe, Arisawa Hiromi, Inaba Hidezō, Wakimura Yoshitarō, and Uno Kōzō, most of whom had been associated with the socialist Rōnō (Labor and Farmer) faction during earlier Marxist debates over Japanese capitalism and had been arrested for their leftist views during the campus roundups of the late 1930s. Other leftist and liberal experts on political economy also participated, some of whom, such as Tōbata Seiichi and Rōyama Masamichi, had been members of the Shōwa Kenkyūkai (Shōwa Research Association, itself an organization that had displayed a wide amalgam of ideas, from leftist to ultranationalist thought). The growing area of "modern" (kinkei) neoclassical and marginalist economics in Japan was represented by Nakayama Ichirō, a professor at Hitotsubashi University, who was also familiar with Keynesian theory. Technical experts from agriculture and engineering were also members, as were industry leaders such as Ishikawa Ichirō, chairman of the Federation of Chemical Industry Associations and later the first head of Keidanren (Federation of Economic Organizations).

This surprising range of backgrounds was a reflection of the postwar policy vacuum on one hand and the opening of intellectual possibility after years of stricture under war and domestic repression on the other. With militarists now largely discredited, the immediate postwar inaugurated an

age of inclusiveness. Most notably, the end of the war saw the resurgence
of the left, a development reflected in the unmistakable prominence in the
SSC of economists from that end of the political spectrum. This opening
of debate also provided opportunities for new, young voices: Ōkita and his
cohorts, who together had conceived the SSC, constituted its secretariat,
and drafted its report, were all men around thirty years old, and they would
go on to play prominent roles in shaping the lineaments of postwar economic policy.[18]

For many, the sense of possibility after the war engendered—even in
the face of stark privation—an almost ebullient spirit of hope. This was,
perhaps, especially true of those on the left. Arisawa Hiromi, a Tokyo University professor of economics who had been arrested in the Professor's
Group Incident of 1938 for being "red," relished the difficult task facing
Japanese, calling it one of "joyous construction" *(tanoshii kensetsu)*.[19] Such
optimism, combined with the fluid political landscape and an overriding
sense of urgency, worked to bring an early spirit of cooperation to the job
of reconstruction. "In those days postwar political divisions were still in
their formative stages," Ōkita himself later explained: "Although our Committee contained members with widely differing political views, each member participated freely in the debates and discussions...and everyone was
eager to build a new society from the ashes of the old."[20] Another leftist
SSC economist who had been jailed for a time during the war, Ōuchi Hyōe,
recalled with historical flourish that the economic experts on the committee had "engaged in discussion with all of the élan of the patriots of the
Meiji Restoration."[21]

The SSC met some forty times between August 1945 and March 1946.
It released more than ten thousand copies of the 145-page final report in
March, and a somewhat revised version appeared in September of that same
year.[22] Though greatly influenced by leftist concerns, *Basic Problems in the
Reconstruction of the Japanese Economy* was by no means a blueprint for radical
revolution. Indeed, in its moderate tone and cool examination of world
trends, the report often seemed to go to great lengths to include something
for everyone, projecting a portrait of a mixed economy founded on heavy
industry that at the same time provided new guarantees for public welfare.
The SSC was not a cabinet-level committee, however, and no mechanism
existed directly to translate its findings into policy.[23] As the first comprehensive survey of postwar conditions and recovery options, the report did,
at the same time, carry considerable weight. This was particularly true in
regard to the question of reparations, which figured so largely at the time.
In its emphasis on heavy industry and manufacturing exports, the report
implicitly countered the punitive reparations stance of the Pauley Mission
of the American Occupation, arguments for an internalist development
strategy over export-based recovery, and calls for restricting the economy

to a light-industry orientation. As Laura Hein points out in her work on postwar energy policy, moreover, the report continued to influence strategic planning well into the Occupation period.[24] Arisawa Hiromi, the author of the famous priority production program of that early powerful organ of the Japanese state, the Economic Stabilization Board, intended that policy to be a means to carry out the principles laid out in the SSC report.[25] Likewise, the five-year Economic Recovery Plan of the Economic Stabilization Board, ill-fated though it was, also drew on the SSC view of a rehabilitated industrial economy. More generally as well, as has been pointed out by Nakamura Takafusa and others, the industrial vision the report presented tallied remarkably well with the trajectory of development eventually traced by the postwar economy.[26] Finally, *Basic Problems* brought together many of the names that would go on to shape economic planning and policy in the decades to follow.

Whereas the antidotes to war sought in the post–World War I era had centered on the essentially political concerns of moderating international power politics, regulating territorial demands, and ensuring national self-determination, post–World War II arrangements were designed to manage the smooth functioning of the world economy, primarily by promoting a liberal trading regime and convertible currency exchange. Surveying these developments after the war, the SSC saw growing recognition of the paramount importance of economic problems in politics and interstate relations. The Bretton Woods system and early Allied measures for managing defeated and war-ravaged nations reflected the conviction, the SSC report declared, that domestic and international peace would now more than ever be a function of economic stability.[27] All of this suggested an epochal change from people as subject to people as master of the economic realm: "These trends imply that human society is moving from the era when it was blindly influenced by economics to an age when human beings desire to control economic phenomena deliberately."[28]

Economic questions had figured prominently in world events leading up to 1945. The crisis of capitalism during the 1920s and 1930s—and the accompanying crisis of economic thought it triggered—had placed the theoretical and practical problems of economics front and center within the halls of power in the industrial nations of the world as perhaps never before. Social dislocations within national economies had spawned radical political movements, while turmoil over exchange rates and the gold standard, over trade wars and economic blocs, had destabilized interstate relations.[29] Finally, the Great Depression had threatened to cut the stays of the capitalist system the world over. All of these—and the terrible war to which they seemed to have contributed—appeared to be lessons in failure: the failure not only of capitalism itself, but also of the science of economics, whose charge it was to know the laws by which economies operated.

Japanese national experience revealed little better and some much worse consequences. Looking back over the previous two and a half decades or so, the observers on the SSC found the landscape of Japanese history littered with controversial and failed economic policies. The interlocking crises of the 1920s—the post–World War I panic of 1920, followed by the so-called Ishii financial panic and bank failures of 1922; the inability to deal with the hardships and inequities of the countryside; the worsening balance of payments; yet another financial panic in 1927; the reversion to the gold standard that took effect just as the Depression hit; and the Depression itself—contributed to a sense of national emergency that at least in part encouraged intellectuals and political leaders to search for external solutions to these domestic problems. Though for a time the unbalanced fiscal policies of Finance Minister Takahashi Korekiyo succeeded in reviving the depressed economy in the early 1930s, they also fueled the thirst of the military for ever-increasing weapons budgets, a trend that the succeeding finance minister, Baba Eiichi, was willing to accommodate. The creation of Manchukuo in 1932 spurred a growing discourse defining the continent as the "economic lifeline" of Japan. By decade's end, this notion had widened in scope and ambition to become the ill-fated dream of an economic bloc and eventually a "co-prosperity sphere."

The sense of economic policy failure was perhaps strongest in terms of the prosecution of the war itself. The grand strategies of isolation and autarky for which the war was fought aside, many SSC members were convinced that Japanese leaders had failed at the tactical level as well: the military had expanded the war on the continent beyond the ability to finance and equip the conflict, then plunged the nation into war with the United States just as economic output was beginning to wane. Some on the committee understood this from firsthand experience. In his research position at the Greater East Asia Ministry, Ōkita had calculated in 1941 that Japanese steel production had begun to decline that year. The inexplicable decision to launch a war with the United States at such a time so shook the young analyst that in 1942 he and several of his colleagues took their findings to Kazami Akira, chief secretary and then justice minister in the earlier Konoe cabinets, in hopes that he might urge the former prime minister to influence the course of events.[30] "These young men were overcome with sorrow, as they knew from their research that the war must inevitably end in defeat," Kazami later wrote. "With tears in their eyes," according to Kazami's account, "they stressed the impending destruction of the country." Although Kazami had relayed their prophetic message, the fate of the nation remained unaltered.[31]

SSC member Inaba Hidezō had similar wartime experiences of the willful refusal of military leaders to acknowledge the economic limits to the fighting strength of the nation. He later recalled the outrage with which military officials greeted the emergency mobilization plan he had helped to write at the Cabinet Planning Board in 1940. Refusing to accept the board's starkly pessimistic appraisal of Japanese resource strength in the event that war was initiated with the Anglo-American powers, one army representative from the Army-Navy Liaison Office (Rikkaigun Kankeikan), "suddenly slamming the table," exclaimed: "'You mean to tell me that the Cabinet Planning Board impudently intends to sit there and make up this slipshod data and then force us to accept it? Where do you Cabinet Planning Board people get off thinking you don't have the responsibility or shouldn't have to muster the determination to come up with the strength the nation needs to fight its way resolutely out of even the worst circumstances?'"[32]

Finding solutions to the economic dilemmas of the twentieth century, the SSC thus argued, loomed as the crucial task of the postwar period. Moreover, rapid technological change, terrifyingly represented by the specter of the atom bomb, only compounded the need for "cooperation among countries." In its vision of increasing cooperative management of economic and technological change, in fact, the SSC's report went so far as to predict the slow demise of the autonomous nation and the rise of "the concept of a world federal state."[33]

The view of economics as the key to the postwar world drew strength from several interrelated developments identified by the SSC as emerging out of the conflict just ended. The first was growing economic globalization. Changes in communications and transportation, sped by wartime innovations, were bringing nations and regions into closer relations than ever before and "linking the world into a single entity." Whereas after World War I national economies had still been considered independent units, "set outside the world economy," they now had to be considered as integral parts of the world economy as a whole. Thus, a range of what had formerly been considered domestic issues—employment and national welfare levels, for example—were becoming, the SSC pointed out, international concerns.[34] It could now be expected that extranational influences would be brought directly to bear on the management of domestic economies. No longer a matter of the flows within and between autonomous economies alone, economics had become internationalized.

Dramatic changes in the power structure within the world economy also underscored the new relevance of international economics to domestic questions. Here again, the SSC compared conditions following World War I with those after World War II: characterizing international relations during the earlier period as horizontal in nature, the SSC saw the current situation as organized according to "what may be called vertical relations," in which, "standing on the summit...are the United States and Britain": "It appears in short that the world economy has moved into a systematic structure in which the United States and Britain as its partner will play a central role."

Though the Soviet Union stood outside this new system, the SSC could still argue at this early date that it "nevertheless at least supports [it]."[35] The aims of the nations at the top of this vertical structure would, more unambiguously than ever, affect the directions of the world economy.

Within this vertical structure stood the new multilateral mechanisms intended to ensure the health of world capitalism and to promote the recovery of the Axis nations and Europe in general. The SSC report pointed to the International Monetary Fund, the International Bank for Reconstruction and Development, and United Nations organizations such as UNRAA (United Nations Relief and Recovery Agency) as pillars of a structural framework for world economic management that was unique to the post–World War II period. Through these U.S.-based financial institutions, world trade, exchange, and development would be newly integrated, strengthening the close international linkages that would be the cornerstone of the postwar global economy.[36]

Taken together, these closely related developments were understood as a shift toward what one SSC member elsewhere described as international economic "systematization" (soshikika).[37] This term, and a litany of related phrases, became common parlance in the burgeoning public debate on recovery after the war, and many of these—the term "systematic structure" used to describe the vertical relations of the world economy, but also "organized" or "controlled capitalism"—appeared throughout the SSC report.[38] Systematized "contemporary market economics," SSC economist Wakimura Yoshitarō optimistically declared soon after the release of the SSC report, would bring the "harmonization of the sovereignty of every nation with the organizational power of world economic systems."[39]

The SSC endorsed the principle of international planning that systematization seemed to represent. By ensuring free interchange, "planned management of the world economy" promised to contribute to world prosperity; by preventing the wrenching economic distortions and rivalries that followed World War I, it promised to contribute to world peace. Paradoxically, the freedom from old restrictions on trade, foreign exchange, and prices that planning through multilateral financial institutions entailed did not suggest a return to a free-trade world economy, but "a step toward a more sophisticated, globally rational system."[40]

As the international economy would be marked by planning and rationalized management, so too, it seemed, would the economic life of individual nations. "There will be no return," the SSC declared, "... to the past days of laissez-faire."[41] Yet while absolute laissez-faire may have had few defenders after the war, the automatic continuation of wartime control practices was not a foregone conclusion either. Common notions notwithstanding, the history of extensive government intervention in the economy was not so old. Its emergence from the end of the 1920s, moreover, had been fraught with unending political struggles for leverage and control all along the way. In addition, the excesses and failures of wartime planning seemed to present clear arguments against undue government participation in the workings of the market. Any program for state regulation of the economy—whether indicative planning, corporatist controls, or command powers—would, therefore, require ideological justification.

It is frequently taken as an article of faith that the defining characteristic of the Japanese economy has always been some form of state guidance, control, or planning. The concomitant view holds that, as part of a program of "catching up" to the Western powers, there existed a deep ideological commitment to central planning and intervention in the economy among intellectuals and policy elites from the very first days of the modern period. Yet claims that these early years were marked by state-led industrial development are often backed by only hazy references to the shibboleth of those years, *fukoku kyōhei* (rich country, strong army). While government did lead the way in advanced industrial development—investing in spinning mills and iron works—beginning early in the Meiji period and while state involvement continued in, for example, the iron industry and the nationalization of railroads, a closer look at the history up to the 1930s does not validate common ideas about the extent of central direction of the economy. Nor did official and scholarly opinion uniformly support an activist program of government intervention in the workings of the free market. A commitment to promoting, where possible, basic and defense-related industries through various cooperative efforts, licensing preferences, capital subsidies—and after treaty revision in 1911—protectionist tariffs, was unquestioned. These practices, however, which together fell under the rubric of *shokusan kōgyō*, did not amount to national goal-setting through state planning nor to direct guidance of the private sector as it first came to be known in the late 1930s.[42]

Discussions of Japanese "government" or "state" interventionism usually refer, whether explicitly or not, to the activities of the bureaucracy. Much has been made of the political and social status enjoyed by the bureaucracy throughout Japanese history, and it is commonly credited with leading the way in Japanese industrialization. Tetsuo Najita uses the term "bureaucratism" to describe an ideological consensus with roots in the *bakuhan* political system of the Tokugawa period that has both defined the nationalist mission of the bureaucratic class and conferred upon bureaucrats high prestige within Japanese public life. Chalmers Johnson concludes that, despite their lack of reigning authority, it has been the bureaucrats who have ruled Japan.[43] Though the premise of government by bureaucratic diktat may lend easy support to the idea of extensive state intervention in the operations of private capital, the two issues should not be conflated. It is well to bear in mind that one may hold true without the existence of the other. The unmistakable role that bureaucratism has played in nation building and the forging of national subjects does not at the same time support notions of state economic interventionism as historically transcendent.

Modern state direction of the economy is commonly traced from the early Meiji period, when the young government set about actively developing industrial manufacturing. Yet, as Thomas C. Smith has argued, "there was no conviction among the Meiji leaders that industrial development should in principle be achieved through government enterprise." State industrial policy during Meiji was not a reflection of deep commitment to intervention per se. It was, rather, a product of necessity. Private capital, while of considerable quantity within the top tier of old merchant families, was not sufficient to meet the requirements of industrial development. Government agencies were often quite clear that, were the requisite funding available, private initiative would be preferable to government management. "Although it is the natural task of private interests to undertake an enterprise like this," explained the Department of the Interior in a proposal for a government woolen mill in 1876, "the project must be carried out by the government. How can our people at present undertake such a large and exacting enterprise that will require a very large investment?"[44]

While state functions generally increased and the bureaucracy grew early in the twentieth century, the central government was not involved in extensive planning or control functions as they came to be practiced by the civilian and military bureaucracies beginning in the late 1920s. As the contributors to *The Japanese Economic System and Its Historical Origins*, edited by Tetsuji Okazaki and Masahiro Okuno-Fujiwara, convincingly demonstrate, the generally greater market orientation of the Japanese economy occurred in the decades before the 1930s, from which point the development of closer ties between the government and the private sector began.[45] Especially after the establishment of the Diet and then the Sino-Japanese War of 1894–95, "industrial administration was almost nonexistent," writes Johnson.[46] Government assumed no more than a facilitator role in the development of private enterprise.

The succession of economic jolts during the 1920s found the government lurching from one emergency policy to another, with little consensus on what its proper role in managing the intractable recession of that decade should be.[47] As Elizabeth Tsunoda has demonstrated, the first government steps toward setting up a positive economic program at the end of the decade were in fact made at the urging of big business.[48] Drawing on their experience of corporate and industrial rationalization, spokesmen for business pleaded with the government to provide "resourceful leadership," writes Tsunoda, in order to achieve a level of overall coordination that had thus far escaped private enterprise working on its own. Casting the government as a corporate *honsha* (head office), industrialists encouraged the state to perform economy-wide planning functions corresponding to those of central management in a *kontsuerun* business conglomerate.[49] By such corporate rationalization writ large, the leaders of big business hoped to avoid the strangulations of "excessive competition" and to set the economy on a forward course.

The initial bureaucratic response was, in retrospect, remarkably circumspect. "In general, our future industrial development should await the inspired efforts of the industrialists concerned," advised Commerce and Industry Minister Nakahashi Tokugorō soon after the formation of the Commerce and Industry Deliberation Council in 1927 to explore solutions to the problems threatening business. While the creation of the council is commonly cited as the beginning of Japanese industrial policy, Nakahashi's comments underscore the novelty of government intercession and the profound ambivalence it engendered in bureaucratic circles: "I think the current trend toward dependence on government is becoming too pronounced, and we must proceed cautiously."[50] Bureaucrats were increasingly chided by industrialists for their aversion to assuming a larger role, yet they possessed little knowledge of the problems besetting big business; in the end, they turned to business for rationalization expertise. By the early 1930s, the moniker "rationalization" had come to stand for government economic policy—ever more active in directing the larger processes of national economic activity—in general.

Yet even during the war, at the supposed height of its control, direct state manipulation of the private economy was more circumscribed than commonly imagined. The mobilization laws of the late 1930s gave—on paper at least—unprecedented powers to government agencies. Yet the Materials Mobilization Plan of 1938, perhaps one of the most recognizable expressions of the state's wartime authority, was chiefly aimed at regulating only the import and export of vital raw materials from colonial holdings. It is true that, in addition to the materials plan, a series of sectoral plans—for foreign trade, capital control, and labor—were devised to try to take the place of market mechanisms of distribution that control laws had supplanted.[51] Yet even as the war on the continent was expanding, no mobilization blueprint was drawn up for the economy as a whole. From 1941, the chief organs of economic rationalization were the industry control associations, and these were in the private hands of *zaibatsu* functionaries. Government coordinating activities throughout the conflict, moreover, were riddled with division between and within the military, big business, and "new" bureaucrats. By the time of the Cabinet Planning Board Incident of 1940, in which that agency was gutted by those wanting to expand the war, business had effectively defeated state initiatives to assume near-absolute management authority over private industry. This marked a period of reduced cooperation between state and industry and left mobilization efforts for most of the remaining years of the war with no central coordinating body. Only in November 1943 did military planners, through the creation of the Munitions Ministry, attempt to centralize all economic leadership functions. In the end, this move only succeeded in adding yet another layer of bureaucracy over the existing control association structures and came far too late in the war effort to make a difference.[52]

For much of modern Japanese history, then, intervention was not the norm. The real expansion of bureaucratic control over the economy came, in fact, only after World War II under the Occupation regime. The bureaucracy grew in size and power so that, according to Johnson's familiar argument, control functions that had been shared by business and government during the war now became the sole prize of bureaucratic agencies. New institutions such as the Economic Stabilization Board rose to replace wartime analogs (the Cabinet Planning Board in this case), and their capabilities often went beyond even those of wartime institutions. The Economic Stabilization Board, for instance, soon assumed all ministerial planning functions, as well as control over both commodities and trade through the Temporary Materials Supply and Control Law of 1946.

Scholars have well established that many of the particular methods and institutional strongholds of economic guidance after World War II were legacies of total war mobilization.[53] At the same time, the expansive role assumed by state agencies after the war did not emerge unproblematically and wholly formed out of the "wartime system." Nor, given the relatively brief and troubled history of state planning, was the question of interventionism in the immediate aftermath of defeat a settled one. While wartime bureaucrats, with "an abiding commitment to top-down, long-range planning," in John W. Dower's words, may have "stepped lightly across the surrender and continued to administer the postwar state,"[54] they did not do so without exerting considerable, very public efforts to make the case for planning in the postwar period. Hastening to explain the rapidly unfolding institutional changes after surrender, bureaucrats, economists, and other expert commentators revisited the historical record of planning. In the process, they laid the ideological groundwork for reinvigorated practices of central economic management.

Planning as Science "without Compulsion"

The anxiousness to justify a significant state role in postwar economic management is nowhere more evident than in the SSC's *Basic Problems in the Reconstruction of the Japanese Economy,* the most significant statement of expert opinion in the immediate aftermath of defeat. Belying conceptions of planning as preordained, the report goes to considerable lengths to lay out the rationale for a planned economy; indeed, a commitment to the promotion of planning colors the entire survey. Here it is possible to witness the first attempts to work out the principles and practices of planning for the postwar period.

The lessons that the SSC's report drew from the recent history of world capitalism provide a road map to justifications for planning. Pointing to international systematization as the harbinger of related trends on the national level, the SSC concluded that national capitalisms would be marked by mechanisms of regulation and planning just as would the world economy as a whole. Capitalism had reached an impasse, suggested the SSC, in which "unexplored markets no longer exist" and "free competition motivated by pursuit of profits would only lead to confusion and stagnation," to over-competition and monopoly. In contemporary "State capitalism," therefore, national economies would be "organized" to prevent these ills.[55]

Such hopeful notions of an ordered domestic economy were frequently based on an idea of evolutionary necessity: capitalism, the SSC averred, had "at last" entered a new "era"; the trend toward planning that emerged during wartime was "inevitable" and would increase "as a natural stage of social evolution." Even in the United States and Britain—presumably the last redoubts of free-market liberalism—freedom, the SSC prophetically predicted, would be "a 'freedom' restricted by planning."[56] Indeed, with the New Deal, the United States must have appeared to Japanese observers as a model of sorts for new planning techniques. The Soviet Union, too, victorious in war and not yet a symbol of apparatchik bureaucratism, provided a potent example of economic guidance. Planning, in short, seemed the worldwide wave of the future.

The belief that an evolutionary stage of planning was inexorably approaching was, it goes without saying, informed in no small part by historical materialism. As has been pointed out, many of the leading economists on the committee were Marxian in training and outlook even if they were not allied with the most radical aspects of Marxist thought. Yet one did not have to subscribe to some abstract theory of stages to find evidence in recent events that planning seemed destined here to stay. For one thing, the mobilization experiences of wartime combatants—those at home, of course, but also more positively those of the victorious Allies—gave credence to the predictions of planning evangelists. It was clear, moreover, that by inviting institutional oversight of the workings of national economies, international systematization would provide a boost to planning. International exchange rules set by the International Monetary Fund would require that nations regulate their foreign trade and might also indirectly prompt state controls over production and prices. The International Bank for Reconstruction and Development would similarly require that borrowing countries meet certain conditions that would implicitly shape redevelopment policies. These international institutions would also promote domestic planning in more concrete ways, for by dispensing capital and reconstruction loans to central governments, they would encourage an active government role.[57]

The statecraft of planning, the SSC argued, was not merely a vague promise for some distant future, but indeed the very means by which to extricate the nation from immediate economic crisis. The present emergency and conversion to a peacetime economy were, in SSC member Arisawa Hiromi's words, "shaking the very foundations of capitalism" in Japan.[58] A wavering response threatened prolonged chaos. Only the "conscientious and wise" implementation of a "comprehensive and specific year-to-year...plan" would assure rapid reconstruction: "The entire productive structure of the Japanese economy is like a huge wheel that has stopped turning, and without systematic, planned, well-coordinated measures," the SSC warned, "it will be very difficult to set it spinning again."[59]

Given the paralysis of big business, the job of coordinating the national response would fall by default, exponents believed, on government. John W. Dower argues that the turmoil that followed defeat afforded rich opportunity for business initiative. As he shows, this was certainly true for small manufacturers who, like the firm that transformed bomb shells into *hibachi* grills, found enterprising ways to turn munitions into consumer items.[60] As touched on earlier, however, big industry, beholden to government for capital and fearful of postwar changes, was generally paralyzed in the wake of defeat. Given the penurious conditions in the economy as a whole and the relative dominance of these industrial giants, no amount of clever retooling by subcontractors alone would be enough to put the "wheel" of the economy in motion again.

The particular characteristics of the Japanese economy also buttressed the demand for a systematic response by the government. Now without colonial holdings, the nation had few natural resources. It was poor in relation to its new international partners, poorer still after the devastation of defeat. Rebuilding the economy would therefore require the "planned utilization" of what few economic capabilities the country could muster, advised the head of the Economic Stabilization Board, Wada Hiroo, in July 1947.[61] "The nation...will not be able to afford any waste of its economic capacity," the SSC similarly explained: "Production will have to be confined strictly to that of necessities...from the standpoint of the interests of the whole nation." Again later in its report the SSC baldly announced that "the waste of economic power that would result from allowing laissez-faire play to market forces will not be permitted."[62]

Envisioning as it did a reconstruction based on heavy industry, the SSC also pointed to what it identified as peculiarities in the industrial structure of the Japanese economy to bolster its call for state planning. The SSC credited the *zaibatsu* industrial combines with having played a special role in Japanese economic history. They alone had had the means to erect worldwide commercial networks, to invest in production and managerial research and development, and to promote heavy industry. Their postwar dissolution, the SSC maintained, would require government to step in to fill these critical functions. SSC members also worried that postwar reforms aimed at deconcentrating wealth would hamstring industry's ability to accumulate the capital required for large enterprises. Here again, government would find it necessary to intervene, extending credit and subsidies. Domestic industries, newly exposed after the war to competition from foreign (read "Allied") industrial powerhouses, would require protection from a nurturing government. And finally, government would be required to assume a large role in managing the balance of payments problem, promoting where necessary technological gains to boost export values.[63]

The principles of planning laid out by the SSC received stimulus from the Occupation. As the SSC itself trenchantly indicated, the Japanese government was, after all, being asked by Occupation authorities to file plans "one after another"—plans for the supply of foodstuffs, for the control and distribution of imports, for unemployment relief, for agricultural self-sufficiency, for public finance reform.[64] At the same time, however, the American position on planning was complex, changing, and often contradictory. Many of the civilian members of the Economic and Scientific Section of the Occupation who had been associated with New Deal programs and war mobilization agencies, such as Edward Walsh, head of the Antitrust and Cartels Division, Harry Alber, head of the Price and Rationing Division, and Sherwood M. Fine, economic adviser to General William F. Marquat, head of the Economic and Scientific Section, were more amenable to assertive government intervention in economic reconstruction. They had to contend, however, with hard-liners who defended the principles of the free market. Even within the Economic and Scientific Section, often the greatest promoter of expanded public powers in the economy, most officials instinctively recoiled at the suggestion of anything that sounded like socialist central planning.

The SSC report itself came in for criticism on this score. Norbert A. Bogdan, an economic adviser to the Occupation's Economic and Scientific Section who the previous month had submitted a review of the SSC's finding to MacArthur, met with Ōkita and several other SSC members in June 1946 to discuss the March version of the SSC report. Chief among Bodgan's criticisms was that the report undercut its essentially free-enterprise orientation by seeming also to argue that, in the language of the record of this meeting, "the state take all the initiative." Bogdan worried that the committee's belief that because the people determine the state it is appropriate for the state to take the lead came too close to "Soviet-style democracy" and "risked the danger of a return to an absolutist state." It would be necessary, Bogdan declared, according to the minutes of the meeting, to distinguish between emergency measures and permanent policy. The fine line that economic officials in the Occupation often drew, however, between Soviet-style statism and New Deal–inspired interventionist policies, themselves the objects of odium among free-market purists at home, was underscored when later in the meeting Bogdan urged the SSC to replace language calling for "unemployment relief" with a stronger recommendation for an active government effort to offer the idle employment through public works projects.[65]

In general, while the charge of "planning" was always less fearsome to New Dealer types, even hard-liners such as General Marquat of the Economic and Scientific Section looked past their antipathy to anything that smacked of socialism when believing that strong state initiative would rationalize recovery efforts. The Occupation leadership's desire for an assertive, organized recovery program was complemented by a shift on the part of the Occupation's Government Section away from its early desire to overhaul dramatically the Japanese bureaucracy because of the key role it played in the "totalitarian regimentation of the people's lives." Whereas the Government Section's early reform proposals sought to cleanse the bureaucracy of its undemocratic elements, the measures it eventually took were determined more by technical principles of efficiency than by the political goal of democratization.[66] The Occupation thus vowed, on one hand, to improve efficiency by cutting the civil service rolls while on the other hand it encouraged the government to expand its involvement in the administration of reconstruction and recovery. In the end, the latter impulse proved to be stronger, and the size of the bureaucracy increased. Excluding military personnel, the ranks of national government employees rose to well over 1.5 million by 1949, a threefold increase over what had already been considered an alarming level in 1931. The number of top officials within the bureaucracy, moreover, the *chokunin* imperial appointees, suddenly swelled under the Occupation from a previous high of 1,900 to 3,744 by 1948.[67]

Along with increasing size, Occupation policies had the effect of bestowing greater powers on the bureaucracy. Authorities in the Economic and Scientific Section of the Occupation became increasingly frustrated by what they perceived as foot-dragging on the part of the Japanese government in response to the economic crisis. Moving away from its initial hands-off stance, the Occupation stepped in to demand that the government assume greater powers of direction. In August 1946, the Yoshida government created the Economic Stabilization Board to draft and oversee recovery plans. Sherwood Fine in the Economic and Scientific Section continued to hope, however, that the Economic Stabilization Board would assume even more direct enforcement over the day-to-day processes of the economy than government bureaucrats themselves were willing to assume.[68] MacArthur himself wrote Prime Minister Yoshida in March 1947 announcing the Occupation's position that government planning must supplant "free enterprise."[69] Furthermore, he ordered the Stabilization Board in the summer of 1947 to expand its coordinating role, taking on all ministerial planning functions.[70] The Occupation similarly endorsed a host of other powerful agencies. It assented, though reluctantly, to nationalization of the coal industry; watched the Coal Agency within the Stabilization Board grow to control virtually all domestic fuel supplies and then allowed it to implement the Temporary Materials and Supply and Control Law, giving it command powers over all commodities; and pushed the creation of tens of public wholesale and distribution corporations called *kōdan,* which were modeled on U.S. wartime government corporations that had handled imported rubber and petroleum. The confusion of controls implemented at the behest of the various administrative sectors of the Occupation proliferated so wildly that General Marquat, head of the Economic and Scientific Section, was forced to institute a Controls Coordinating Committee.[71]

While the Occupation was careful not to endorse a command economy, the effect of its activities was to provide a positive context in which arguments for planning such as the SSC's could be made. Increased bureaucratic guidance of the economy confirmed Japanese analysts in the lessons they drew from world history, the wartime record of Japan, and the postwar drive toward international systematization. Even after more hard-line business-oriented personnel were recruited from the United States to implement Dodge's retrenchment policies in 1949, the trend toward broadened government functions in the workings of the private economy continued. The Foreign Exchange and Foreign Trade Control Law and the Law Concerning Foreign Investment of 1949 and 1950 respectively, for example, both sponsored by the Americans, gave great latitude in these areas to administrative officials and remained in effect for decades after the Occupation had ended.

Critics and reformers expressed their demands for rationalized governance of the economy through appeals to the beneficent powers of science. Postwar planning above all had to be "scientific" *(kagakuteki).* This emphasis on scientific rationalism extended to all of the attendant administrative and analytical practices of planning as well. In fact, reformers in the immediate postwar years scarcely made a recommendation for an economic measure that did not insist on the need for a rigorously "scientific" approach. Advocates constantly urged that all recovery policies be guided by a scientific understanding of current conditions. Bureaucrats enjoined researchers to carry out their investigations into everything from the stagnation of production to national consumption patterns, government expenditures, and the effectiveness of wartime mobilization "scientifically."[72] The SSC's treatment of economic institutions included suggestions for "modern scientific management systems" and "scientific personnel management" in government administration. The science of economic statecraft, moreover, would require "specialized and concrete knowledge," insisted the SSC, as well as a "new type" of economist who possessed both technical and economic expertise, and systems by which to "scientifically forecast" economic trends.[73] Ideally, the dictates of science were to govern all aspects of economic governance.

This postwar preoccupation with applying the methods of science to the economic realm was a continuation of earlier enthusiasms. Industry had long been concerned with the newest technologies, techniques, and, to the extent that any business enterprise must strive to achieve the greatest output with the least input, the question of efficiency. The first programmatic use of the language and what were touted as the methods of science in Japanese industry, however, can be traced to the Taylor-inspired "Scientific Management" (*kagakuteki kanrihō* as rendered in Japanese) movement beginning in the 1910s.[74] Though often ill-defined, the movement grew. By the early 1920s, universities offered courses that borrowed heavily from American techniques as popularized by Frank Gibney's *Motion Study* and Frederick Taylor's *Shop Management,* while "efficiency engineers" attended training sessions funded by local businesses. By 1930, the ideological emphasis on "scientific" principles at the heart of Taylorism was being applied to an expanded drive for rationalization not only at the level of the shop floor, but of entire industries. The industrial rationalization movement now offered science as the antidote to the undisciplined principles of self-interest that critics charged were the cause of economic woes: a "visible hand" of rationalized control must replace the faulty mechanisms of laissez-faire capitalism.[75] But by the end of the 1930s, as the cartel-like cooperative mechanisms and economic concentration aims of industrial rationalization were attacked as failures, renovationist critics prescribed various statist arrangements to rationalize the national economy as a whole.[76] The dizzying assortment of so-called New Order voices—popular publicists of corporatism such as Ryū Shintarō, military planners promoting materiel mobilization techniques, and "reform" bureaucrats such as Okumura Kiwao advocating a comprehensively planned economy—were animated by a shared belief in scientific control and the superiority of elite administrative specialists over political mechanisms of governance.

Although the industrial rationalization movement was temporarily laid low in the immediate postwar years, the newer goal of scientifically regulating the disequilibria of the economy as a whole was a key source of inspiration for exponents of planning in the SSC and the Economic Stabilization Board. Yet even as postwar advocates drew on the wartime ideal of scientific planning, they found little to praise in the actual history of war mobilization and the controlled economy. The analysts in the SSC were unequivocal in their denunciation: "It would appear that Japan's wartime controlled economy will go down in history as a truly dismal failure."[77] Zen Keinosuke, the first chief of the Economic Stabilization Board, similarly described the "failure" of the controlled economy.[78] Such condemnations of the inability of the wartime system to get the job done, so to speak, were almost ubiquitous as observers came to terms with the reality of defeat and occupation.

Sufficient grounds certainly existed for censorious accounts of war planning.[79] Internecine struggles among civilian bureaucrats, military planners, and big business meant that government operatives never managed to fashion themselves into a unified, coherent administrative system. Even after the consolidation of powers in the Munitions Ministry in late 1943, civilian planners with Manchurian experience found their efforts hampered by battles with military officials assigned to the ministry.[80] For most of the war, contends Richard Rice, these political factors represented a greater obstacle to mobilization than the unquestionably severe economic limitations under which Japanese conducted the war.[81] Multiple layers of regulation meant that controls on prices, imports, raw materials, transportation, and the like were not systematic, and these were implemented only reactively as conditions deteriorated. Planners relied for their data on the industry groups they were attempting to control. The famous materiel mobilization plans themselves were not the comprehensive blueprints commonly imagined, but were instead highly compartmentalized and fragmented: these were, in Cabinet Planning Board member Inaba Hidezō's words, "extremely crude affairs."[82]

What troubled postwar critics most was what they saw as the scientific deficiencies of mobilization. "The failure of the wartime controlled economy," declared Zen Keinosuke, head of the Stabilization Board in a speech before the Diet in 1947, "was that it was not based on science."[83] The SSC concurred, blaming the collapse of the wartime economy on the fact that the "soldiers" who were in charge were the "most feudal and unscientific among all Japanese."[84] Inaba Hidezō, a planning participant at the time, later criticized top-level decision making during the war as little reflecting the economic realities facing Japan. Policy was determined less by reasoned resolution than by the arbitrary judgments of willful individuals.[85]

Such criticism of unscientific methods was not unique to the problem of planning. Time and again, critics in the immediate aftermath of the war announced that it was only through science that a new, reconstructed Japan might be achieved. This constant intoning of the need for science on the part of politicians, bureaucrats, labor leaders, and social-science scholars was everywhere counterposed with what these critics maintained was the irrationality of earlier times. Ōtsuka Hisao, historian of Western Europe, political-economic theorist, and social critic, pointed to an "only fleeting respect for the concept of rationality, the very backbone of modern science" among Japanese as partly to blame for the absence of a "modern

man" in Japan.[86] Economist Yanaihara Tadao criticized Japanese colonial-
ism as "unscientific" because it had been subject to "irrational" ideologies
of emperorism and ethnic chauvinism.[87] Ōuchi Hyōe, the leftist economist
considered one of the "four wise men" of the time in the economics department at the University of Tokyo, saw the very decision taken by Japan to go
to war as having resulted from a lack of science: Japan had committed its
historical "crimes," he said, because it suffered from the "social disease of
self-conceit," an affliction that in turn arose because "there was no scientific
reflection *(kagakuteki hansei)* in regard to Japan's own capabilities."[88] Kimura
Kihachirō, a socialist political party leader, similarly saw Japan's war as one
of "exceeding ignorance and recklessness" and urged that reconstruction
be founded, by contrast, on "wise scientific judgment."[89]

A weak scientific consciousness was adduced to explain, in fact, not only
the road to war, but the reason for defeat as well.[90] Here the emperor himself weighed in, albeit in a private manner. In a letter to Crown Prince Aki-
hito, twelve years old at the time, Hirohito wrote that the war had been lost
because military leaders had stressed spirit over science.[91] Hirohito's analysis,
of course, recalled the familiar formula of "Western science, Eastern spirit"
long employed by nationalist ideologues. Though formerly celebrated as a
source of strength in Japan's righteous clash with the West, the mythic Japanese spirit was now castigated as the nation's greatest weakness. That such
an unlikely pair as Kimura and the emperor should both pin the disaster
of the war on the failure of objective rationalism in Japan underscored the
potent allure of the postwar mantra of science. Through their etiologies of
the war, commentators hopefully—and with nearly one voice—cast the new
age to come as the antithesis of that former time. If the age of militarism
had been characterized by feudal attitudes and the rule of rash spirit, then
the postwar period would see the ascendancy of reasoned intellect.

In an important sense, the accusation of unscientific recklessness referred
to a failure to act in accordance with objective fact. But at a deeper level,
critics found a fundamental faultiness in the relation between practice and
human nature. "The controlled economy lacked humanity," according to
the second half of Stabilization Board head Zen Keinosuke's tidy diagnosis.
Wartime planning was a perversity of natural impulses: "We concluded that
by simply passing an ordinance a controlled economy would be achieved and
gave not an iota of consideration to whether or not a regulation was in harmony with human nature." While the notion of an essential human nature
was inherently a vague one, Zen, formerly director of the Industrial Patriotic
Association, identified one impulse in particular as having been particularly
and inexcusably flouted by wartime control practices: the capitalist drive for
profits. "Controls were enacted," lamented Zen, "that eliminated profits and
impugned the fair pursuit of corporate profits as criminal."[92]

As head of the recently instituted Economic Stabilization Board, which by 1947 had assumed unprecedented authority over national economic activity, Zen occupied a position that made it uniquely incumbent upon him both to account for the planning of the past and to justify current government controls. His entreaties for government guidance with a human touch, therefore, were logically tied to the democratic sentiment of the day. Whereas ideologues had long claimed that human feeling among Japanese was most naturally expressed in the native traditions of familialism and communitarianism, now humaneness would be achieved, it was argued, through democracy—democracy in politics, in industry, in education, in the relations between the sexes. State planning, too, would be subject to the same transformation. Bureaucrats could no longer lord it over society, enacting "fanatical" controls, Zen warned. They would have to implement a "new controlled economy" characterized by "democratic administration" and cooperation with the private sector.[93] Others, too, urged bureaucrats to open up. Economic plans ought not to be "simply a piece of prose cooked up in the heads of a small group of bureaucrats," wrote one observer, but should "amply reflect the opinions of specialists from various perspectives."[94] In July 1947, Wada Hiroo, the socialist successor to Zen at the Stabilization Board, echoed his predecessor by suggesting in a speech before the Diet that a renovated "control structure" that was "democratic" was the solution to the disarray of the distribution system and the means to assure a minimum standard of living.[95] The SSC also maintained that the "planned and fairly strict state control of the economy" must be predicated on a democratic government.[96] The economic statecraft of the postwar period was thus to be a true science, one harmonious with "human nature" and that hewed to the demands of democracy.

The dilemma of the "new controlled economy" was how to reconcile state intervention with the goal of democracy. Some level of controls was needed, most agreed, for the projects of reconstruction and recovery. Yet their continuation, even remade more in line with postwar aims, risked a return to the war days of overweening bureaucratism. "On the one hand, the responsibility for the war clearly must be placed on the bureaucracy as well as on the military and the zaibatsu," a *Chūō Kōron* editorial maintained in August 1947:

From the outbreak of the war through its unfolding to the end, we know that the bureaucracy's influence was both great and evil. Many people have already censured the bureaucrats for their responsibility and their sins. On the other hand, given that under the present circumstances of defeat it is impossible to return to a laissez-faire economy, and that every aspect of economic life necessarily requires an expansion of planning and control, the functions and significance of the bureaucracy are expanding with each passing day.

The "dissolution of the bureaucracy" was unimaginable, the editorialist went on, for the economic emergency and the growing complexity of economic activity demanded the technical expertise that only the bureaucracy possessed.[97] Many critics of meddlesome government intervention feared "the entrapment" of the economy in a "whirlpool" of complete control such as had reigned during the war.[98] There were those who believed that only through absolute freedom from controls would the promise of the new era be achieved, and those who posited controls as necessary given the special circumstances of the time. Yet irrespective of their position, critics laid out their arguments according to a common rhetoric that vilified, not fascism, authoritarianism, or totalitarianism per se, but bureaucratic tyranny as the evil antithesis of democracy to be avoided.

The notion of a true postwar science of the economy was often an ambiguous one. Critics who in the immediate postwar years assailed the wartime experience were hard put to provide a positive definition of what would replace past practices. A reader today might be forgiven for concluding that the unspoken (perhaps unconscious) motivation behind the indictment of the war years as "unscientific" was more often than not visceral disgust at the failure to win; the "unscientific" nature of the war effort thus followed from the very fact of defeat itself. Calls for science often evaded the hard task of defining the relation between science and democracy. Throughout the writings of commentators on the economy, however, ran the general sense that economic science was somehow a requisite of democracy. In the eyes of Ōuchi, the economic doyen of Tokyo University, what was needed to fulfill MacArthur's democratic promise was a "scientific government" and a "scientific daily life of society."[99]

In their linking of science and democracy, reformers imagined a postwar Japan that would be simultaneously technocratic and humanistic. It would be technocratic in that practice would be based on conclusions duly arrived at according to the procedures of science. Administration of the economy and policy making in general would be insulated from the political machinations and therefore the myopic decision making of the past. Postwar technocracy, moreover, would embrace a "comprehensive view of things" over against the narrow points of view of personal or institutional interest; and it would broaden both temporal and geographic perspective by promoting correct understandings of the movements of history and the trends in other nations and across the globe. Postwar Japan would be humanistic in that it would accomplish all of this as a natural expression of national aims. Provided the economy were truly measured, ordered, and managed scientifically, then it would be possible to "systematize economic activities without compulsion *(kyōsei o mochiizushite)* [in order] to have them comply with the needs of society automatically."[100] Objective technical competence would reign over slanted political irrationality, the democratic well-being of the nation over narrow competition between bickering interests.

Although liable to criticism on its own terms, this almost utopian vision of the possibilities for depoliticized technical manipulation of the economy, this faith in the ability to make social goals easily reflect the logic of scientific necessity, was understandable given the lessons critics had drawn from their war experience. Failure in wartime had occurred, they believed, because science had been ignored. Yet for all their effort to set postwar humanistic technocracy apart from the bureaucratic technocracy of the New Order past, exponents spent remarkably little time addressing the forms and structures by which past excesses were to be avoided. Few detailed prescriptions can be found in the sources of the time for preventing a benign humanistic technocracy from devolving into the very sort of antidemocratic bureaucratism that critics so often fulminated against.

Inaba Hidezō and Technocratic Redemption

The ideal of humanistic technocracy, it seems, offered the possibility of redemption. It recast planning, not as an instrument of war, but as a tool with which to manage a peacetime economy, and thus offered the possibility that postwar planning could avoid wartime mistakes. Hoping to make good on this second chance, self-styled reformers set to work organizing like-minded experts within the bureaucracy and in the private sector. The SSC itself, while helping to create the intellectual supports for such work, at the same time became a reflection of these renewed planning energies. Many of those who took to the mission of redemption with the most fervor were middle-to-low–level bureaucrats who had learned the planning trade while constructing mobilization blueprints for the war. Inaba Hidezō, whose bitter wartime experiences on the Cabinet Planning Board filled him with the desire to realize what he felt was the true potential of planning, was one such young official. His efforts were representative of those who cast about after defeat to reconstruct the means to guide the national economy rationally.

Inaba had graduated from the philosophy department of Kyoto University in 1931. He eventually went to work as a researcher in the Cooperation and Harmony Society (Kyōchōkai), a public foundation that was established after World War I to conduct research on social issues and promote communitarian values and cooperative relations between labor and capital and that was a predecessor organization to the important Central Labor Council (Chūō Rōdō Iinkai) of the postwar period.[101] At the Cooperation and Harmony Society Inaba investigated the plight of small metal-casting firms in

Japan, then later moved on to study labor issues in Europe. When the Cabinet Planning Board (hereafter CPB) was created in 1937 as a central economic council for pursuing the government's new program for the "expansion of industrial capacities," he was invited to join the staff, an unusual occurrence as he had never taken the civil service examination. As the CPB was preparing emergency mobilization plans in 1941, however, Inaba was accused by the military of being a Marxist and was arrested along with other reform bureaucrats such as Wada Hiroo who were similarly to become famous in the postwar period. Though he remained in jail for close to three years, Inaba was later found innocent of the charges. Just thirty-eight years old at the end of the war, he became a prominent figure in postwar planning, partly on the strength of the moral caché that came with having been identified as an enemy of the wartime state. He participated on a wide variety of advisory councils as well as within the bureaucracy itself (in his work on the SSC and then in the powerful Economic Stabilization Board) and became a prolific commentator on economic policy.

According to Inaba's account of his arrest in the CPB incident, he and the others were targeted not so much because of their leftist inclinations, but because the forecasts they made at the CPB did not support military leaders' designs to broaden the war. The CPB had predicted that output would begin to fall dramatically if Japan entered a war with the United States and Britain. The deprivations forced on civilians, the CPB planners had warned, would also be intolerable. The army and navy reacted vehemently against the CPB's conclusions, accusing the planners of willfully understating Japan's war potential. The CPB stuck to its conclusions but was soon the object of the so-called Cabinet Planning Board Incident shake-up that dramatically reduced its influence. As the nation marked its 2,600th-year anniversary in November 1940, Inaba wondered whether, given the deterioration of Japan's economic position, there was any cause for celebration. "I wanted to prevent the worsening of the situation, to secure the basis for a more stable future for the nation. I couldn't stop wondering if there wasn't some way to accomplish this."[102]

Inaba's arrest in January 1941 came as a shock, and the years he spent in jail, much of the time in solitary confinement, afforded him ample opportunity to reconsider the events that had led up to his incarceration.[103] He was ready to admit the difficulties of reliably prognosticating the economic future. Likewise, he allowed that he himself had reservations about the absolute accuracy of the CPB's figures. But he had no doubt about the overall thrust of the CPB's report: "The figures we produced probably had a margin of error of twenty percent. But even if the margin were over twenty percent, no, even over fifty percent, there was no way we were greatly mistaken in our basic understanding of current conditions." In jail, Inaba reflected on his own responsibility for the inability of the CPB to influence policy. He worried over the impending doom of the country and burned with the desire to have the CPB's forecasts recognized by those determining events.[104]

Haunted after the war by the idea that there might have been more he could have done through his economic analysis to have reversed the fortunes of the nation, Inaba immersed himself in the project of redeeming planning. His first act after surrender was to begin collecting economic documents being destroyed by government officials who anticipated a punitive occupying force. He was not, as it turned out, alone. Ōkita Saburō also later recounted surreptiously hiding away records that the personnel of government ministries and agencies had been ordered to burn as the war came to an end. This wholesale destruction of official economic records "was a very stupid thing to do," Ōkita later wrote, "but at the time people were shocked at losing the war and afraid of the occupation forces, who were a completely unknown quantity."[105] Ōkita's account of his own attempts to save state records in fact mentions a chance encounter with the similarly appalled Inaba hurriedly rescuing documents himself:

> The documents being burnt in courtyards and other places included
> mobilisation documents, production capacity surveys and many basic
> economic materials, many of which would help our work in planning
> the postwar economy. Consequently I went along to those places where
> documents were being burnt and secretly brought some home. One
> day, while engaged on such work, I ran into Hidezō Inaba [sic] and
> discovered he had come on the same mission as myself.[106]

For Inaba's part, as he set about rescuing what records of the recent past he could, he was determined to dedicate himself to the study of Japan's economy and to contribute thereby to the rebuilding of the country. With the hope of garnering lessons for the future, Inaba formed the Institute for Research on the National Economy (hereafter IRNE) (Kokumin Keizai Kenkyū Kyōkai) in October 1945 and began comparing economic performance during the war with the projections made in the plans of that time.[107]

Although the IRNE started with a mere five members, working in the borrowed corner of a company office, it soon exploded in size and scope of mission. In addition to his own efforts to rescue wartime records, Inaba soon received urgent requests from the Ministries of Commerce and Industry and Agriculture and Forestry, which were being besieged with demands for data by the Occupation, to help them collect and organize documents. At the same time, he received a steady stream of entreaties for work from dislocated economic researchers who had formerly been employed in various wartime institutions, particularly the South Manchurian Railway Company. Inaba moved to bigger quarters, set up research offices in both the Commerce and Industry and the Agriculture and Forestry ministries, and expanded his payroll to over fifty analysts by the spring of 1946. Meanwhile, document collections flowed in from former mentors and colleagues.[108]

A key clearinghouse for economic data, the IRNE played a central role in the revival of sophisticated economic analysis and planning. As bureaucrats, scholarly experts, and corporate statisticians scrambled to set up structures for data gathering and policy formulation, a fluid environment prevailed in which experienced, though young, economic analysts such as Inaba moved freely in and out of public agencies, ministerial advisory groups, and independent economic organizations. Inaba's relations with other important rehabilitated leftists such Wada Hiroo (also jailed in the CPB incident) helped place him at the center of the government's planning efforts, and he soon came to hold simultaneous positions within his own IRNE and the growing economic bureaucracy of the postwar period.

While the IRNE continued its work on industrial output indices, raw material estimates, industrial production, and reparations in the fall of 1945, Inaba decided that he no longer wanted to be only a passive analyst but an active participant in making his recommendations a reality. He joined the government's Coal Committee, which shortly became the kernel of the Priority Production Program for economic recovery. He also became a member of the SSC at the end of 1945, at Ōkita Saburō's invitation. His work in these organizations expanded his contacts with prominent economists such as Arisawa Hiromi and Ōuchi Hyōe. Inaba's writings began to appear in the growing economic press. His warnings in a 1946 monthly report of Nissankyō, the predecessor industrial association to the famous Nikkeiren, that production would collapse when stockpiles were exhausted, contributed to intensified attempts by central authorities to jump-start industry. In the fall of 1946 he took a position as a nonpermanent employee of the Economic Stabilization Board, then later became a vice-secretary of that increasingly powerful body. In 1947 and 1948 he worked with Arisawa Hiromi to formulate the Economic Stabilization Board's Five-Year Economic Recovery Plan. Though the plan was eventually rejected by Prime Minister Yoshida Shigeru, who anticipated the soon-to-come retrenchment policies of the Occupation, the Economic Recovery Plan represented the first concrete postwar attempt to redeem the long-range planning techniques of resource allocation and industrial production that had been of such importantance during the war.[109] A belief in the necessity of "reasonable and appropriate planning targets and rational and attainable yearly plans themselves" for a democratic Japan animated Inaba's activities throughout his participation in these efforts.[110]

Many of the evangelists of planning after the war were men such as Inaba and Ōkita who had done so much of the grinding number-crunching work on which war mobilization planning had been based. They were the ones who often had been most acutely aware of the desperate and "feudal" folly of Japan's ever-expanding war. As this cadre of technical experts, many of them just returned from colonial institutions, took stock after the end of the conflict, they clung to the belief that technocratic guidance of the economy could work for the postwar world. Planning had not failed them, in their view; rather, politics had failed planning. The "true tragedy" of wartime guidance of the economy was that it had been taxed beyond the limits of Japan's ability to fight. Arguing that the miserable experience of the wartime economy should "serve as a guide to a better planned economy for tomorrow," these men stepped in to help fill the policy vacuum after the war to mobilize a new vision of humanistic technocracy.[111]

CHAPTER 2

The Measures That Rule

A s scholars, bureaucrats, and other economic leaders rehabilitated economic planning after the war, many pointed out that it was statistical knowledge that would drive the analytical apparatus they would use to regulate the "systematized" economy. Without the mass production and manipulation of accurate empirical facts, it was broadly argued, scientific governance of the economy would remain an empty promise. One of the attractions of these appeals to quantification and positivistic economic research was the support they lent to the idea of planning as an exercise beyond ideology. The postwar question seemed one, not of political agenda, but of technical competence: the redemption of planning would require a new level of commitment to the collection of objective data. In short, it was clear to leaders across a broad spectrum of academia, government, business, and labor that if the "systematized" economy referred to newly rationalized institutional arrangements, statistical fact had to be its foundation and its lingua franca.

The postwar statistical movement was part of a broader reorientation of economic theory and practice toward highly quantified techniques of measurement and analysis that had been under way for several decades. Keynesian theory and the rise of new highly empirical aggregate methodologies combined, in response first to the crises of national capitalisms during the 1920s and 1930s, then to total war, to nurture a growing discourse within economics that placed nearly unprecedented emphasis on statistical fact and on applied analysis of macroeconomic phenomena. This statistical revolution of the mid-twentieth century, particularly as represented in the techniques of national income and gross national product accounting, spurred the construction of new aggregate pictures of national economies. Economic analysis became increasingly concerned with the composition of and structural relations between such macroeconomic facets of national economic life as employment, aggregate demand, and national income. Marking a significant departure from much of past practice, furthermore, this analysis was conducted with specific instrumental ends in mind. Through the state's technical manipulation of the macroeconomy, it was hoped that the periodic crises that had historically plagued capitalism the world over might be moderated or avoided altogether.

Japanese experience followed a similar pattern. Though the magnitude of statistical production had risen throughout the early part of the twentieth century, calls for a more vigorous data system became more insistent in the face of persistent economic ills during the 1920s. Statistical research then increased dramatically in the 1930s and 1940s with the advent of planning for empire and war. Yet, even so, the quantity of reliable economic data remained small by postwar standards, and the material was rarely subject to rationalized coordination. During the first years of crisis after the war, the Japanese government, prodded by Occupation authorities, responded to demands for a more vigorous statistical system by beginning the construction of an encompassing institutional framework for the accumulation of economic fact. By the early 1950s, statistical production had become a formalized and regularized function of the state as never before, and national accounting practices lay at the heart of this expanded analytical regime.

The macroeconomic statistical techniques that quickly came to dominate postwar economic analysis accompanied, and in many ways constituted, the technical conditions of possibility for the rehabilitated discourse on scientific rationalism explored in the previous chapter. Indeed, one is hard put to explain the postwar growth system without taking into account the epistemological changes that were transforming the discipline of economics at the same time. The desire to promote national economic power and industrial output in some form in Japan was not new in the postwar period. Nor was rapid economic expansion. Yet the fixation on growth as it appeared by the beginning of the 1960s was indeed a distinctly postwar phenomenon. The statistical and macroeconomic revolutions in Japan, as elsewhere, provided the technical means by which to measure national growth in powerful new ways. And they did more than enable better ways of tallying economic strengths and weaknesses; they also provided the conceptual instruments by which rapid aggregate growth of the nation might be first conceived and then pursued.

The Empirical Revolution in Twentieth-Century Economic Knowledge

The linchpins in the complex of statistics reshaping the discipline of economics after the war were the macroeconomic measures of national income and gross national product. In fact, the empiricizing movement, felt first in the United States and England, that would eventually transform economics from a generally descriptive discipline to a quantitative one was in large part motivated by the need to accumulate large data sets to support research into these new aggregate techniques. But while it was only during the postwar period that the "national accounting" techniques by which these aggregate statistics were calculated came to dominate economic analysis in Japan and elsewhere, significant antecedent developments can be traced at least to the 1920s. It was then that, participating in a wider trend in the economics discipline, calls for a new order of quantified economic research were voiced by Japanese academics, business leaders, and bureaucrats alike. And it was during those earlier decades that the first experiments in the macroeconomic computation of national income were conducted in Japan.

The history of attempts to measure economic wealth in Japan is a long one, reaching as far back in the documentary record as the land allotment surveys and population registers of the Taika Reforms in the seventh century. Numerical measures were always valued as important to the problem of statecraft, but the desire to quantify economic and social phenomena increased sharply in the mid-nineteenth century in Japan as it did in other nation-states of the time. To a long-standing urban culture of numbers was now added a rising interest in Western European texts on statistical methods and statistical compendia of the nations of the world.[1] During this age of geopolitical uncertainty and administrative experimentation, Japanese scholars avidly translated English, French, and German works on statistics, a field that was burgeoning in these nations due to precisely the same geopolitical and national concerns that drove the interest in Japan. Intensifying competition within the international state system of the nineteenth century lent new urgency to measurements of national wealth and power.[2] After the Meiji Restoration, new government organs were created to carry out statistical research, and by the last decade of the century, a small but growing infrastructure of statistical inquiry had taken shape.[3]

Various calculations of production had existed in Japan prior to the first experiments with measuring the totality of national wealth.[4] Measures of industrial output, including mining, iron foundries, shipbuilding, railroads, machine manufacturing, and so on were carried out in the newly instituted Construction Ministry beginning in 1870, and expanded to include other agricultural and commercial statistics as the bureaucratic system evolved.[5] None of this, however, amounted to national accounting. Production statistics (*bussan chōsa*) tended to be simple tabulations of output totals in various agricultural and industrial categories.[6] Chief among the concerns of leaders of the 1870s and 1880s was the acquisition of data by which to compare the industrial and military status of the nation to the Euro-American world powers. But this quantification of production was tallied on an industry-by-industry basis, recording simple tonnage produced, length of track laid.[7] No attempt was made to determine the total production or income of the national economy as a whole.

Commercial and political rivalries had driven interest in comparative measures of total national income in England and France from the seventeenth century. Income estimates were made in other nations during the nineteenth century as part of the desire to express economic power and "relative degrees of civilization" in statistical form.[8] The first estimate of national income in Japan was made in 1902 (for the year 1900) by a scholar named Nakamura Kinzō. His report, titled *Teikoku jinmin no shotoku* (Income of the populace of the empire), was based on net output figures for various industrial categories, and it estimated national income at 1.8 billion yen. Just several years later Yamashita Tetsutarō, also an academic, estimated national income for the year 1904 by using the final expenditure method of calculation.[9]

These early calculations were unsophisticated compared to the national accounting procedures that would later become commonplace. Both Nakamura and Yamashita made one-time estimates of income for one calendar year. Their calculations were simple production aggregates, not related to one another through formalized accounting procedures.[10] The practitioners of these income calculations, moreover, were individual academics working on their own research agendas. Estimates were not official. Government played no part in their computation, and few channels existed by which these statistics were employed in shaping the large designs that leaders imagined for the economy, or in policy making in general. During these early years, most economists, and economic bureaucrats in general, considered national income estimates to be a fringe statistical endeavor seen as an interesting exercise, perhaps, but not one with a potential for practical application.

As industrial capitalism expanded in Japan around the time of World War I, bureaucrats and scholars hoped to boost the accumulation of economic data. Calls for reform of the statistical system had been heard from as early as the turn of the century, but the rapid transformations in the teens and twenties gave greater weight to arguments that economic knowledge was not keeping pace with changes in the economy.[11]

The desire to expand the production of economic statistics was part of a larger shift toward empirical and mathematical approaches taking place elsewhere as well. The highly mathematical nature of the preponderance of economic research today—the dominance of statistical modeling, game theory, and the like, and the econometric fusion of empirical data and policy analysis—makes it easy to forget that these mathematical and statistical aspects of economics are a relatively recent phenomenon, one that has particularly dominated the field only since the end of World War

II.[12] The so-called statistical revolution in economics—the transition from a largely deductive to a quantitative science—got its start in the 1920s and 1930s. Antecedents, of course, had existed. Attempts to apply mathematical techniques and empirical data to economic theory can be traced back to the earliest history of European political economy, and the use of basic economic measures by the state in Japan, too, had a long history. Yet, in the words of one prominent postwar economist, statistics until this time had remained "the poor and largely passive relation of economics."[13]

Regnant neoclassical economic theory came under attack from many quarters in the first several decades of the twentieth century for being, as one scholar later put it, "'academic' (in the pejorative sense of the word),... 'theoretical' (again pejorative), abstract, ahistorical, [and] hypothetical-deductive."[14] From around the 1920s some economists in the United States, led most visibly by members of the institutionalist school, began attempting to move their profession toward a more empirical approach by which the theories devised through traditional deductivist strategies might be statistically supported or falsified. In the United States especially, this impulse to ground theory empirically, to measure actual economic behavior, was accompanied after the 1929 stock market crash by an urgent sense of the practical need for stronger efforts in data collection. In general, a shift was under way everywhere in industrialized countries from a view of economics in terms of theories of natural laws to one based on operational theories.[15] Rather than looking at the economy as operating according to universal laws, new empirical research was designed to gauge the effect and probability of economic phenomena through the use of large-scale statistical research and emerging procedures such as model and simulation analysis.

In Japan, this empiricizing trend found fertile ground among those calling for statistical reform in the face of rapid economic change. A push for better quantification of economic phenomena was manifest in a variety of developments. A Central Committee on Statistics was formed within the cabinet at the end of the Taishō period to make proposals on changes to official statistical systems. As factory and social insurance legislation came under consideration, the committee spearheaded the first government collection of data on labor conditions and standards of living.[16] A decades-long campaign for reform of the population survey system culminated during this period in the more sophisticated national census *(kokusei chōsa)* of 1920, which has been called "the first modern census" in Japan.[17] Although fairly comprehensive production statistics were collected for agriculture and forestry by the 1920s, the same had not been true for many other areas such as mining, construction, and manufacturing. In 1929, the recently created Ministry of Commerce and Industry, the ancestor of the later Ministry of International Trade and Industry, revamped its statistical system for factories, making its reporting "somewhat closer to an industrial census."[18] The move to quantify economic analysis in Japan was not confined to official circles. During the efflorescence of historical debates over Japanese capitalism in the late 1920s, Marxist economists attempted to back their claims to scientism by marshaling great amounts of statistical data. In 1930, the annual convention of the International Statistical Society (Kokusai Tōkei Kyōkai) was held in Tokyo and served as an apt symbol of the increasing focus in Japan on economic fact, measurement, and analysis.[19]

It was during the period of statistical expansion during the 1920s that organs of government first turned to the problem of national income. The first agency to do so, the Cabinet Statistics Bureau, made three estimates: the first in 1928 for the year 1925; then one in 1933 for 1930; and the last around 1939 for 1935.[20] The Cabinet Statistics Bureau also published income estimates for years in between its full official calculations. These were calculated by assuming that national income rose and fell commensurately with the level of assessed income subject to taxation.

Some of the most extensive national income work, however, was being done by scholars. Hijikata Seibi's *Kokumin shotoku no kōsei* (The composition of the national income), published in 1933, estimated national income by combining production figures for industry and agriculture with calculations for the commercial sector based on wages, salaries, and corporate profits.[21] Cited as the "classic" work of Japanese national accounting before the institutionalization of the practice in the postwar period,[22] Hijikata's research was the first to go beyond computation of income for one particular year. Rather, he produced a statistical series across more than ten years from 1919 to 1930.[23] Further, he presented more than a simple aggregate income, including in his calculations the breakdown of total income across industry categories.

Hijikata's expansive approach to national accounting—both in terms of temporal scope and structural analysis—represented a broadening of earlier concerns. While previous single-year soundings of the total size of the economy had been shaped by a desire to compare relative national strengths, Hijikata hoped by his structural, time-series data to be able to understand the recent ups and downs of the economy and its structural shifts. This was a vision of national accounting as a tool for gauging the economy in terms of its interrelated sectors, one that would mark the national accounting system as it developed in the postwar period. The rationale was that "the relation of the parts to the whole" would be "examined from the point of view of income." At heart, Hijikata believed that it "was impossible to ignore" the usefulness of national income in "judging the importance of fiscal policy within the entire economy."[24]

Hijikata's work reflected the rising desire among analysts in the 1920s to better grasp the large mechanisms of the economy's swings. It underscored the eruption of controversy beginning in the early 1930s over the appropriate role for government fiscal policy in management of the economy. The cumulative effects of the long economic crisis of the 1920s, the Wall Street Crash of 1929, and the disastrous return to the gold standard by Japan in early 1930 seemed to demand a reappraisal of how government policy ought to respond to economic ills. With Finance Minister Takahashi Korekiyo's repudiation of his predecessor Inoue's contractionary policies beginning in 1931, the issue of *zaisei* (fiscal policy) became the subject of hot debate and remained so through the late 1930s.[25]

Takahashi instituted what variously came to be known as *zōtai zaisei* (expansionary fiscal policy) or *fukintō zaisei* (unbalanced fiscal policy). By rapidly increasing government expenditure, he hoped to finance expanding military activities on the Chinese continent, and secondarily, to reinflate the sagging economy. Many critics, however, were made uneasy by "Takahashi fiscal policy." Responding to a stagnant economy with red-ink budgets had not been tried before, and it went against ideals of balance held so dear in economic thought of the time. Not surprisingly, the military, for its part, supported Takahashi's ballooning budgets; without them, fighting on the mainland and military buildup in general would be impossible. Others, however, worried that such imprudent policies would drive the Japanese economy to further ruin.

The chronic problems of the Japanese economy and the emergence of fiscal policy into the limelight worked to focus new attention on national income research. Hijikata's work received much acclaim, but there were also other new national accounting projects begun by scholars and private groups in the wake of the "Shōwa Depression." The Mitsubishi Economic Research Bureau produced estimates based on Hijikata's work, which it included in its English-language *Trade and Industry: Present and Future* of 1936, and the business group Nihon Keizai Renmei released a report in 1938, compiled from available estimates, that featured income figures for the years 1931–39.[26]

A similar trend was under way in other countries as the idea gained strength in the 1930s that a clearer understanding of national production and expenditure was required in order to deal with the great worldwide economic challenges of the day. Especially in the United States and Britain, the magnitude of the crisis of capitalism in the 1930s stimulated a new, deeper interest in improving national accounts. In fact, it was in those countries that the real explosion of theoretical developments and empirical research was taking place. In the United States, this work was pioneered by well-known figures such as Wesley Clair Mitchell at the independent National Bureau of Economic Research and by newly minted New Deal agencies. Complementary work was done in Britain in the Economic Advisory Council. Diagnosing what ailed industrial capitalism seemed to demand a rigorous focus on the statistical measurement of all facets of national economic activity and a practical understanding of the aggregate components of the national economy. It also was apparent that new measures for economic recovery could be assessed only by linking quantified analysis of actual conditions with national economic policy making as never before.[27]

More than just an incentive to step up data collection efforts, the Depression and the expansion of government programs in its wake in the United States and England also acted as spurs to national accounting research in more direct ways. Although economic orthodoxy demanded small and balanced government budgets, the increasingly important role of government expenditure in the national economy as a whole was becoming hard to deny. This new awareness was, by the late 1930s, greatly influenced in Anglo-American circles by a growing cadre of economists inspired by Keynesian ideas, who argued that government outlay would be required to make up the shortfall between national spending and national production. Keynesians argued that the economic stagnation of the 1930s was a result, not of insufficient production, but of insufficient demand. It was supposed in classical economic theory that supply always created its own demand, a formulation known as Say's Law. Economists believed that the circular flow of payments set in motion by the provision of goods and services would always find its way from consumers and investors back to suppliers in such a way that it would be adequate to the cost of producing more goods and services. Problems of insufficient demand, and by implication long-term unemployment, were not theoretically possible according to this thinking, and therefore received little attention—this despite the fact that economic reality often seemed to defy such basic tenets of classical faith.

The scale of the economic crisis in the 1930s, however, impelled many thinkers to challenge formulations such as Say's Law. Simon Kuznets' national accounting techniques were part of new attempts to understand how economic conditions not accounted for in orthodox thinking (i.e., massive, long-term unemployment) might be explained and remedied. The statistical categories he created in GNP (and its companion calculations of national income), and his concurrent work in devising the consumption, savings, and investment components of national income, were designed as tools for measuring total aggregate demand (national purchasing power) in relation to the total value of production. Keynes himself was at the forefront of related innovations in England that allowed analysts to understand the relation of government income and expenditure to total national income and expenditure.[28] These national accounting tools made it possible to indicate a dearth of demand in relation to supply. It followed by implication that an infusion of income, through increased government spending for example, might overcome shortfalls in national spending and borrowing. One could hope thereby to increase the purchase and production of goods, breaking the economic deadlock and boosting employment.

The power of these new accounting techniques thus gave a shot in the arm to emerging Keynesian arguments for countercyclical fiscal intervention in the economy by the government, for as John Kenneth Galbraith has felicitously explained, "it was one thing to resist Keynes' theory; it was something else and much harder to resist the Kuznets statistics."[29]

Total War and the Rise of National Accounting

It was not economic hard times, however, but war that truly propelled national accounting into the policy arenas of the industrial powers. This was true in Japan, where, as the influential economist Ōuchi Hyōe later declared, the awareness among economic analysts of the central role that national accounting would play in the economy of the future "originated in the demands of war and a planned economy."[30] As the militarization of political and social life increased during the 1930s, practitioners of national income research became preoccupied with the question of Japan's preparedness for war.

Although they contained little new income research, a spate of works appeared that made use of available data, from the Cabinet Statistics Bureau and the Mitsubishi Economic Research Bureau for example, to draw conclusions about Japan's ability to fight.[31] Perhaps the most important of these was *Sensō to Nihon no keizairyoku* (War and the economic strength of Japan) of 1937, by the famous Marxian apologist for Japanese imperialism Takahashi Kamekichi. Most writers insisted that national income and other data indicated, despite persistent doubts, that the Japanese economy was adequate both financially and materially to the demands of a protracted military conflict.[32]

The matter of fiscal policy arose here again as well, only now more specifically in terms of war financing. In *The Economic Strength of Japan*, Asahi Isoshi used national income estimates to calculate the tax burden of Japanese citizens relative to those of other major powers. Asahi argued that the proportion of taxes to total national income around the time of the "China Affair" in 1937 was half that recorded during the Russo-Japanese War and considerably less than the ratio in other powers. He thus held that the Japanese economy yet had great room for increased expenditures to pay for the war.[33]

As Japan's war on the continent dragged on in the beginning of the 1940s and hostilities with the Anglo-American powers seemed imminent, the problem of war financing took on paramount urgency. In response, the cabinet passed Basic Guidelines for Fiscal and Financial Policy (Zaisei Kin'yū Kihon Hōsaku Yōkō) in July 1941 as part of Prime Minister Konoe Fumimaro's effort to formalize a so-called New Economic System *(keizai shintaisei)*. Under the guidelines, the government attempted to employ national income-like techniques to devise capital allocation plans *(shikin keikaku)*. National income work, accordingly, was moved that same year from the Cabinet Statistics Bureau to the Finance Ministry.[34] Taking up the Cabinet Statistics Bureau's earlier efforts, the Finance Ministry made calculations of national income based on the value of production output for years beginning in 1939. As the war tide turned against Japan, however, income figures were no longer made public. The last income report to appear was released in 1942.[35]

As part of its planning to secure sufficient financial resources for the war effort, the Finance Ministry also began calculations to determine what was called national economic resource strength *(kokka shiryoku)*. Intended to indicate the total production power of the economy, these statistics were based in part on national income calculations. In addition, they also included public revenues, industrial capital, foreign investment, and national consumption. They were used to help devise a series of financial plans, including those governing public debt issuance, general operating revenues, expenditures for Manchuria, and national savings. While these plans were being crafted within the Finance Ministry, moreover, the president of the Bank of Japan, Shibusawa Keizō, also perceived the need for statistics on total "national economic power." He created the National Economic Resources Research Institute (Kokka Shiryoku Kenkyūjo) within the bank to further theoretical explorations into economic and financial planning such as those being conducted by Finance Ministry bureaucrats.[36]

Despite the flurry of interest from the 1930s in various forms of national accounting, however, the government began cutting back its economic data collection as the war grew in intensity. Okuno Sadamichi argues that "the long wartime system proceeded to suffocate and stifle statistical work." Reliable data became scarce as "statistical research and its practical application were halted" and "statistical institutions simply reduced or eliminated."[37] Wartime bureaucrats ended a range of statistical research projects on agricultural and commercial inventories, corporations, and labor. Soon, basic data sources ceased to be published.[38] The Japan Statistical Yearbook, for example, which had been published by the Statistics Bureau of the Office of Prime Minister every year since 1882, ended publication in 1941.[39] Two dynamics were at work here. First, as the economic strains of pursuing all-out war intensified, resources for pursuing statistical work were rerouted. Second, Japan's diminishing prospects during the war gave an incentive to both government and business not to reveal the inconvenient truth that the Japanese economy was in deep trouble. As a result of "substantially curtailed" data gathering beginning around 1937, national income estimates produced after 1936 generally were inferior to earlier efforts.[40] By the last years of the war, the statistical system in Japan was so debilitated that national accounting work played little reliable role either in management of the economy in general or in the prosecution of the war.

Just as statistical systems in Japan were foundering, however, national accounting was being put to vigorous use by the governments of the United States and Britain. The great swell of theoretical and applied work in those countries from the early days of the Great Depression was now turned toward mobilization for war. The practical power of new national accounting knowledge was soon made clear to doubters, and new institutional arrangements developed under which this work began to be carried out.

GNP is an assessment of the total annual production of goods and services, a figure related to its companion, gross national income, which is the income derived from that output (minus depreciation). By applying the new forms and values for computing national accounts developed by Simon Kuznets and others (planners, for example, in new British government organs such as the Central Statistical Office), it was possible for the first time to determine the size of the war effort that might be mounted and to plan war mobilization strategy accordingly. Knowing with practical accuracy the total value of what was produced in the economy as a whole enabled forecasts of the amount of increased production that might be gained for weapons manufacture. The construction of national accounts according to the new methods devised in the United States and Britain made possible efficient resource planning so as to limit bottlenecks, idle capacity, and domestic consumption. It also proved a valuable tool for ensuring that sufficient financial resources were made available to the war effort. Given the almost uniformly disastrous experience of inflation in combatant nations during World War I, the issue of budget planning during this war loomed as large in the Allied Powers as it did in Japan. The title of Keynes' *How to Pay for the War* (1940), so instrumental to the inauguration of official national accounting during the war in Britain, made clear the urgency of the problem of financing the war in the eyes of the eminent economist.[41]

In the United States, these techniques were famously employed in the Victory Program of the War Production Board, in which a schedule for weapons, tank, and ship manufacture was planned and subsequently met. Similar programs in Britain led one scholar to comment that "it is a symptom of the recognition given to the significance of this type of analysis for economic policy that in the days of greatest physical danger work of, at first sight, so academic a character should have been so vigorously pursued."[42] Although it may seem improbable that a statistical technique such as GNP accounting would be identified as a strategic wartime advantage, John Kenneth Galbraith appraises the economist most responsible for its present form, Simon Kuznets, as "one of the least recognized of the pillars of Allied power in World War II."[43] Elsewhere, it has been noted that knowledgeable opinion after the war held that "the power of national economic accounting in the war effort [in the United States] was greater than that of the atomic bomb."[44]

The portrait that emerges from a comparison of the wartime experience of Japan to that of the Allied Powers should not be interpreted as one of a recalcitrant Japanese statistical system in comparison to a vanguard of U.S. or British economic research. It was true that the richest production of theoretical and empirical work was being conducted in the United States and Britain. And some temporal differences between the penetration of the concepts at question here into economic and official practice in, say, the United States and Japan did emerge, especially during the war years. These, however, were small and, in the longer run of the history of statistics, of minor consequence. Compared to the great majority of the nations of the world, in fact, Japanese estimates of national income had begun early: Nakamura Kinzō's 1902 calculations placed Japan as only the ninth nation for which estimates had been attempted at all.[45] The inconsistent application of new national accounting methods during the war, furthermore, was not unique to Japan: German leaders, too, did relatively little efficaciously to employ them in their war effort.[46]

The more relevant point here is that national income accounting, as it came to be used during the war especially in the United States and Britain, was a revolutionary practice everywhere at the time. Although wartime national accounting work by the Allied governments reflected relatively early recognition of its practical power in planning, official calculations even in those countries were not instituted without controversy. The story of the inauguration of official national income reports in England is a case in point. Professional economists working as advisers to the British government in 1940 urged the authorities to begin work on the sort of national income and expenditure calculations that John Maynard Keynes had undertaken in his influential *How to Pay for the War* (1940). Still, "finance ministers either dismissed national income estimates as the idle speculations of academic minds and as having no practical utility whatsoever, or, at best, referred to them merely as interesting information, for the accuracy of which they could not vouch."[47] Mistrust on the part of the economic authorities toward national income estimates was overcome only by the dire threat posed by the war. Largely on the strength of appeals made by John Maynard Keynes himself, the chancellor of the exchequer, with "difficulty," was finally persuaded of the importance of national income accounts to war planning. Now charged with the responsibility for calculating national income, the British government published its first income report along with the 1941 budget. "This was indeed a great revolution," R. F. Harrod has written in his biography of Keynes: "The Treasury had hitherto confined itself to figures for actual, known transactions. This account included estimates, and certain figures had to be obtained by the method of difference from other estimates...."[48]

The profound effects of the Depression in the United States stimulated a spirit of experimentation there that somewhat tempered suspicion of national accounting. Even so, official income reports were not instituted on an annual basis in the United States until 1947. This was the same year in which the Economic Stabilization Board in Japan first set to work calculating national income, thereby inaugurating postwar official national accounting in Japan, a fact that counters any idea of an overwhelmingly advanced American statistical system.[49]

Despite the growth of research in national accounting and its increasing use in official contexts in the industrialized nations from the 1930s, then, the practice was still quite experimental. Instrumental interest in it had intensified with the challenges posed by depression, government expansion, and war; but, in Japan as well as the United States and Britain, no mechanisms existed for regularized production of national income statistics.[50] As yet few formal systems had been created for linking national accounting to the policy apparatus of the state. Moreover, varying systems for calculating national income competed with one another. Hijikata Seibi pointed out that there was "no end to theories of income" in general and that "even less clear" was the "concept of national income" in particular.[51] Economists, moreover, also used other statistics for gauging national economic power, statistics such as national wealth *(kokufu)*, which measured the total capital stock of the nation, and later the wartime measure of national financial and productive power *(shiryoku)*. No consensus on standardization of methods had emerged. Different measurement criteria, term definitions, and accounting methods among researchers gave rise to "large discrepancies" between results, calling into question the reliability, and certainly the comparability, of these calculations.[52] Yano Tsuneta, author of a statistical almanac on the Japanese economy, warned in 1929 that most results up to then had been only "rough estimates" and that figures that could be trusted were "quite hard to come by." Although a fairly early evaluation, Yano's critique nevertheless reflected the state of national accounting knowledge in most countries at least until the Second World War.[53]

The drive for greater data production beginning in the 1920s did little to quench the thirst for empirical knowledge of the economy that had risen especially sharply during the 1930s. The early pioneer of national income research, Hijikata Seibi, made much of this problem, arguing that a lack of industrial production data handicapped attempts to calculate income by "objective methods."[54] This acute feeling of a continuing dearth of empirical knowledge was not confined, however, to those on the cutting edge of income research. Rather, it was a common theme among business leaders and academics, among bureaucratic analysts and military planners who dreamed of some form of rationalized guidance of the economy as a solution to Japan's internal and external problems. Elizabeth Tsunoda notes that, as part of their effort to encourage greater official coordination of the economy, business leaders pressed the government to "'publish numbers energetically.'"[55] "Citing Herbert Hoover as precedent," writes Tsunoda, the business magazine *Daiyamondo* argued in 1930 that "'all economic transactions yield numbers as the measure of their reality,'" and it "urged government to take responsibility for confirming the accuracy and objectivity of industrial statistics."[56]

The gap between the supply and the demand for data in Japan only grew worse during the war. The materials mobilization laws that became the keynote of government policy from 1937 on were considerably handicapped by a lack of statistics. Obata Tadayoshi, vice-chief of the Cabinet Planning Board, later said about those wartime years: "Considering the situation from today's vantage point, we were just groping in the dark.... The statistics we used as a base were haphazard from the beginning.... The fact is, I never really knew how much oil was in Japan. That was the shape we were in."[57]

But perhaps more significant for planners in Japan was their frustration with a lack of progress in understanding the theoretical and practical aspects of analytical tools such as national accounting. Ōuchi Hyōe, a leftist economist who was to become one of the most influential analysts of the postwar period, was located in the Bank of Japan during the war at the time the National Economic Resources Research Institute was undertaking its work there on national productive power (*kokka shiryoku*). He later lamented that although the institute apparently made some modest progress in its work, it "was never able to produce the sort of research that had been hoped for."[58] Not only were resources being shunted away from such economic analysis, planners were also cut off from knowledge of developments elsewhere during the war. Ōuchi specifically mentions the inability of Japanese researchers to acquire materials from abroad as a cause of the disappointing wartime results.[59]

This portrait of national statistical systems in general and of the inchoate development of national accounting in particular seems at odds with the general view of state control over the economy in Japan during the war. It has by now become a common theme that, believing they needed to prepare for "total war," Japanese military and political leaders sought to institutionalize state planning for national mobilization. They set up new bureaucratic arrangements to that end, beginning with the creation of the Cabinet Resources Bureau (Naikaku Shigenkyoku) in 1927. New organs of information gathering and deployment then emerged under the Resource Survey Law (Shigen Chōsahō) of 1929, and this research and planning apparatus grew in scope as the 1930s wore on. Direct state intervention in the economy reached new heights in 1937 and 1938 with the creation of the Cabinet Planning Board (Kikakuin) and a spate of mobilization laws that on paper gave control of every facet of national economic life to the government. Recent literature on "total war" and the "mobilization system" portrays a massive defense state armed with penetrating systems of data gathering, surveillance, and control.[60]

How is the image presented here of faltering statistical practices inadequate to the tasks at hand to be reconciled with what the literature on the wartime (and the postwar period, for that matter) tells us about the growth of economic bureaucracies and the steady expansion of government direction over the economy from the late 1920s? In one sense, similar ideas to those laid out here can be found in the existing literature. Once the war was over, analysts wasted no time, for example, in declaring that Japan's wartime controlled economy had failed miserably, and this theme was taken up early by scholars. The burden of total war and the irreconcilable political tensions within Japan's defense state indeed resulted in the utter collapse of coordinating systems during the war.[61] (The contention precipitated by wartime planning was not, in fact, unique to Japanese experience. Lest the earlier discussion of the uses of national accounting in the United States during the war paint an inappropriately rosy picture of unqualified success, it bears noting that wartime economic gains in the United States can be seen much less as a product of smoothly rationalized planning than of the mere fact of the overwhelming economic bounty at the disposal of the war effort there.)

The question, however, goes beyond facile charges of political failure. Rather, the crux of the problem was that the quintessentially modernist vision of totalized planning that came to be championed by military planners, reform bureaucrats, and even many in the business community in Japan exceeded the limitations not only of empirical knowledge but also, as Ōuchi's lament about unfulfilled hopes for wartime national accounting attests, the technical boundaries of economics as a discipline: the statistical and analytical tools needed to implement many of the designs that leaders envisioned for the economy were often lacking.[62] This problem was broader than national accounting alone. A range of powerful statistical techniques—probability-based methods such as sampling and correlation analysis, for example—that allowed researchers practicably to grasp the characteristics of large statistical universes were just being developed and did not become common practice in Japan until after the end of the war.[63] In many ways, the great hopes placed in technical knowledge and planning during the 1930s and 1940s were more a dream than a reality.

More important, the planning and guidance of the economy that took place from the 1930s on were not yet much informed by what came to be called "macroeconomic" theories and practices that would dominate the postwar period.[64] Keynesian theory, the statistical revolution, and national accounting were fundamentally reshaping economic thought, but they were far from orthodoxy and had little institutional grounding. Aggregate demand, employment, and national income were not the intended objects of manipulation. And while national accounting was beginning to play a role in broad analysis of the flows and structure of the national economy, it had not become the central tool of economic analysis and policy making that it would after the end of the war.

Borrowing language that Alan Brinkley uses to make a different point about the United States, "planning" was not yet a matter of the "Olympian manipulation of macroeconomic levers," but was about the "direct intervention in the day-to-day affairs of the corporate world."[65] Economic intervention by the state, while carried out on a unprecedented scale in Japan during the war, was directed at the microeconomic level: the National General Mobilization Law of 1938, for example, gave the Cabinet Planning Board the authority to set wages and prices, to direct capital flows and control corporate profits, to shut companies down and merge others. These powers were sweeping, but they were not oriented toward the macroeconomic means and ends that were beginning to reconfigure conceptions of national economies.

National accounting in the 1930s and early 1940s, furthermore, was not about growth per se. It did not inform a system geared to the expressed purpose of producing growth in the economy or to reproduce and extend knowledge of growth as a defined theoretical field of inquiry. While the very conception of what economic policy ought to be would be fundamentally transformed after the war in great part on the strength of national accounting, planning before 1945 was at heart about resource allocation—that is, material distribution and controls—again, an essentially microeconomic orientation. The allocation aims of planning, moreover, were reflected in the statistical research that supported it, research such as the materiel census *(Rinji kokusei chōsa)* of 1939.[66] The conceptions of macroeconomic policy into which national accounting calculations might be fit, whose purposes they might serve, were just beginning to take shape. Although they were starting to alter thinking about national economies, the techniques to foster growth through the manipulation of the grand macroeconomic flows of a national economy had not yet been institutionalized. Indeed, there was little conception of such administrative purposes at all beyond the vague desire that national output should increase.

Despite the difficulties experienced in the actual practice of planning and the controlled economy during the war, discourses on the technical manipulation of the national economy generated during the 1930s survived into the postwar period. As we have seen, analysts and leaders trying to forge a vision of a rebuilt Japanese economy at the end of the war quickly revived the dream of rationalized planning and guidance. Critical to success this time, they believed, would be a vigorous, broad system of statistical research, at the center of which, it turns out, national accounting would come to occupy a defining role. Unfulfilled hopes for national accounting notwithstanding, recalled Ōuchi later, there were some technocrats during the war who, hunkered down in their Finance Ministry offices and elsewhere, sensed the "inevitability that national income would become the central problem of the national economy in the postwar period."[67]

Numbers for a New Japan: Stuart Rice and the Japanese Statistics Commission

Faced with the near destruction of the Japanese economy, those who began to think about recovery returned to familiar ideas about rationalization and scientific management. A science of economic statecraft was seen not merely as the way out of the immediate crisis but also as the wave of the future. Yet as the war ended, statistical systems had all but ground to a halt in Japan. Statistical bureaus had been gutted, figures were scarce or suspect, records had been destroyed. It was clear to many that any hope for successfully rationalized management of the postwar economy would be predicated on a renovated statistical system.

Calls for fortified statistical practices in Japan were heard immediately after the war from a variety of voices—business leaders, economists, government officials, and, not least, the Allied Occupation. In a sense, this theme was heir to the empiricizing drive that began in the 1920s, only now more rigorously bound to the discourse on rationalization than ever before. Defeat and the prostrate condition of the nation in its wake, however, gave special significance to the old problem of statistics. Just like the problem of planning itself, statistical production was now viewed through the prism of the wartime experience.

For some, such as academic economist Nonomura Kazuo, the collapse of statistical production in Japan by the end of the war put no less than the fate of the entire reconstruction effort and Japan's future status as a world-class economy at stake:

Complete and fully furnished statistical records by which one is able to gain a general view of the entire national economy first become available in each nation as its economy becomes capitalist. The fact, then, that China does not yet possess national economic statistics is one indication of the low, backward status of its economy in the world. By this same logic, the fact that basic statistical records from the wartime until today that would provide a view of the entire national economy of Japan and its future direction have not been put before the Japanese people indicates the stagnation that Japan's capitalist economy has experienced since the prewar years and is an index of the importance of the perilous reconstruction our defeat in the war has necessitated.[68]

Here the problem of statistics stands in for two distinctly postwar anxieties about the status of the Japanese nation. First, Nonomura makes statistics represent successful capitalism. In light of both the cautionary tale of the "precapitalist" economies of the colonial world and the specter of surging postwar communism at home, the wartime collapse of statistical undertakings in Japan seemed an especially troubling sign for the fate of Japan's capitalist economy. Second, Nonomura's comparison with China is telling. Pointing up anxieties over the now ambiguous place of Japan in the order of nations, Nonomura was concerned that Japan distance itself from nations with "low, backward status" economies. By virtue of scientific sophistication—here represented by statistical knowledge of the economy—the argument seems to say, Japan might take a first step toward its postwar "escape from Asia."

While Nonomura's comments revealed unease over the grander questions of geopolitics and political economy, most commentators demanding quick reform of statistical systems were concerned with the more immediate problems of gaining control over day-to-day economic affairs and of planning for recovery. Ōkita Saburō, the government economist who figured prominently in the drafting of the final *Basic Problems* report of the Foreign Ministry Special Survey Committee in 1946, and who then set out to write a broad overview of the economy on the model of England's just released White Paper, later complained that such postwar planning had been especially difficult given the "extremely limited" availability of statistical data.[69] Nonomura, too, complained at the time that the scarcity of data was much to blame for the confusion of economic policy immediately after the war: "The fact that a complete solution to the problem of the character of the Japanese economy in the postwar period has not been achieved, despite the fact that many issues relating to the problem have been raised and that many theoreticians have been mobilized for this purpose, has surely been exacerbated by what it is fair to say is the complete vacuum of records and statistics for the period from the wartime to the present."[70]

The virtual cessation of statistical production during the war was made worse by the fact that much of the data that had been tabulated had been destroyed. Some were lost in Allied bombing raids. More vexing to analysts, however, were the great amounts destroyed at the end of the war by panicky personnel in the various ministries, as we saw in the previous chapter described by those who had attempted to rehabilitate planning after the war, such as Inaba and Ōkita. Ōuchi Hyōe also refers to the wartime destruction of statistical materials, writing that even when the Japanese government did produce statistics, "it didn't save them."[71]

Japanese planners were not the only ones dismayed by the state of statistical knowledge of the economy after the war. The most powerful voice demanding quick action on this front was the Allied Occupation. As soon as the Occupation forces arrived, they began putting requests for statistical records to the Japanese government "in rapid succession."[72] While it was Occupation policy that economic recovery would be the responsibility of Japanese themselves, both the day-to-day administration of the Occupation and planning for reforms required that Occupation authorities have detailed data. Yet "whether it was the Bank of Japan, the Finance Ministry, or any of the other various administrative agencies, none of them had any records at all" with which to respond to Occupation requests, explains Ōuchi Hyōe.[73] Arisawa Hiromi recounts that GHQ officials requested Japanese census data, but when they saw the disparities between different census results, declared that "'Japanese statistics were no good.'"[74] Exasperated by the inability of the Japanese side to respond to its demands, GHQ increased its pressure on the government to quickly implement measures to remedy the problem.

Complaints about these immediate problems were just the first points of attack in a broad critique of wartime statistical practices articulated by commentators from all quarters. The most serious problem was not simply the dearth of data but the manipulation of statistics that critics charged had routinely taken place at all levels. Criticisms of wartime statistical abuses by the government had been voiced since the first few years of Japan's long conflict with China. Pointing to what he charged was the government's programmatic use of statistics to suit war purposes, Takano Iwasaburō, the well-known head of the Japan Statistics Association (Nihon Tōkei Gakkai) and former chief of the Ōhara Social Issues Research Institute (Ōhara Shakai Mondai Kenkyūjo), was outraged by what he saw as the willful destruction of the Japanese statistical system. The government regularly manipulated data and even purposely made up false figures, Takano claimed, to make the nation appear stronger or to cover up the extent of losses. Often, it simply neglected to release data that had been collected. In 1933, Takano enlisted Ōuchi Hyōe, also a member of the Japan Statistics Association, to draft a protest letter to the government on behalf of the group.[75]

The association's letter had little effect at the time, but by some dozen years later the criticisms it contained had become commonplace. It was clear that statistical systems had catastrophically failed. Available data could not be trusted, and much of it lay untabulated, moldering in storage. The Statistical Research Institute of Japan (Nihon Tōkei Kenkyūjo), which counted among its members many economists who had experienced the wartime system, later recounted that military and ministry planners during the war rarely presented actual data in their reports to the Diet. Rather, they obfuscated, attempting to hide troubling conditions by such subterfuges as using a percentage of the prior-year level. Planning groups in various agencies competed for materiel, capital, labor, and shipping by inventing statistics out of whole cloth: "They duped each other," writes the Tōkei Kenkyūjo. And if Japan's loss in the war could be blamed on maladroit administration of the war effort, the group argued, then the proximate cause surely was that leaders had "ignored statistics."[76]

The Statistics Commission (Tōkei Iinkai), created in the cabinet in 1946 to reform statistical institutions, located the crux of the problem in what it dubbed a "system of secrecy" during the war that sent statistical production into "disarray." "By hiding important statistics from the eyes of the nation and avoiding the widespread use and criticism of statistics by the people, the stimulus for statistics reform was lost and national statistical consciousness was dramatically lowered," the Statistics Commission argued in a 1947 report to the Diet on the aims of a proposed statistics reform law. The strain on materiel and labor power during the war, furthermore, meant that there was little reflection on the need for systemic improvements. The result was general "confusion, the weakening of institutions, and the lowering of the quality of the people doing statistical work." The commission exhorted the government "to quickly adopt resolute reforms" to respond to the urgent need for viable statistics.[77]

It was clear that statistical institutions required revamping after the war to meet the immediate challenge of the economic emergency. Commentators also averred that fundamentally reformed statistical systems would be required as the backbone of the new systematized economic order that they were convinced would characterize the postwar period. Among the earliest, most forceful arguments linking the planned economy to statistical reform was that made by the Special Survey Committee of the Foreign Ministry in its *Basic Problems in the Reconstruction of the Japanese Economy* report of 1946. The Survey Committee pointed out that, regardless of ideological orientation, statistical knowledge would be indispensable to the technical management of national development:

No matter whether Japan adopts a capitalist or socialist system in the future, it is an absolute requisite for the nation to have well-prepared statistical data. A socialist economy would naturally be premised on a planned economy, and a planned economy would be managed on the basis of well-prepared statistical data. Even capitalism is now in an age of controlled and organized nationalistic capitalism that will require a complete set of statistical data in its management. This is exemplified in the fact that both the Soviet Union and the United States are attaching importance to the availability of well-prepared statistics.[78]

Kawashima Takahiko, director of the Cabinet Statistics Bureau, also drew on the examples of both the United States and the Soviet Union to argue for a "new state system of statistics" *(shin naru kokka tōkei seido)*. He marveled at the pioneering use in those countries of "governing statistics" *(keiei tōkei)* for the "comprehensive management of the entire nation and all of society."[79]

The importance of robust statistical knowledge for scientific planning was also one of the central tenets among the bureaucrats and academics who gathered in early 1946 in the Cabinet Deliberation Office in study groups that would soon form the kernel of the Statistics Commission. Even before the study groups formally convened, Yamanaka Shirō, chief of the Cabinet Deliberation Office, was engaged in research on the statistics problem at the behest of GHQ. In a March 1946 paper that foreshadowed the premises of later Statistic Commission discussions, he wrote that "comprehensive, scientific analysis" of the economy would have to be founded on "accurate statistical records of current conditions." New statistical investigations of the money supply, food stocks, and important industries such as coal and fertilizer were required to "determine the skeleton of a unified economic recovery plan." "Protocols for the arrangement and processing of statistics" and for the "organization of a prompt statistical reporting network," Yamanaka wrote, were necessary to ensure the continued smooth functioning of the planning system beyond the immediate emergency. Yamanaka called for what amounted to a vast statistical complex to accomplish all of this. He envisioned legions of economists pumping out research for the Economic Stabilization Board and the "broad mobilization" of universities and other outside research organizations in the private sector toward that effort.[80]

Industrial policy makers also placed renewed emphasis on quantification, declaring they would throw their energies into promoting statistical analysis as part of their postwar rationalization campaign. In August 1949, the Ministry of International Trade and Industry announced new directions for its corporate administration policy, the centerpiece of which would be "enterprise rationalization." Describing the new policy as a "shift from administration of materiel to administration of enterprises," the Ministry stated that "analysis of comprehensive statistical research on the actual conditions of corporations" was the "paramount condition" for its success.[81] Rationalization also required the quantification of corporate operations themselves. The Special Survey Committee recommended the introduction of new statistical practices in order to achieve

> among other things the systematized control of corporate accounts
> and office work so that entrepreneurs are able to know at all times the
> exact state of their business statistically and quantitatively and to identify
> at once any waste or shortcomings in the business operation. For that

end, the system of office work will have to be modernized, for example, by the improvement of accounting systems from plural bookkeeping to a card system. . . . Auditors . . . equipped with improved statistical information . . . should be able to examine and criticize company affairs freely and thereby provide impetus for putting companies' matters in better shape.[82]

Finally, rationalization meant statistical improvements in production technology. To become competitive, proponents believed, Japanese businesses would have to increase the quality of the goods they produced. Here again statistical methods were prescribed by top management, engineers, and foreign advisers alike, this time as the remedy for the "shoddy" workmanship for which Japanese industry was supposedly notorious. William Tsutsui argues that statistical quality-control techniques became the focus of technical groups such as the Union of Japanese Scientists and Engineers after the war.[83] Niki Shōichirō, an officer in the union, wrote in 1949: "'We were deeply impressed by our recent finding that in Britain and the United States statistical quality control developed enormously during the war. . . . Why can we not have such refined techniques? . . . Every Japanese will remember the fact that during the war our industry produced innumerable planes which couldn't keep aloft long enough to meet any enemy plane to fight with.'" W. Edwards Deming, the now legendary American statistician who gave "highly mathematical and technically sophisticated lectures" on quality control in Japan during the early 1950s, was only the most visible symbol of a flourishing statistical quality-control movement among Japanese production engineers.[84]

In the breathless postwar days of a "New Japan," putting statistical systems on the right track was even declared the key to the heady goals of peace and democracy. Indeed, in the eyes of the Statistics Commission, the failure to adhere to scientific statistical procedures in the past had not merely contributed to Japan's loss of the war, but had been the very reason Japan had embarked on its disastrous war strategy in the first place. In explaining the aims of proposed legal reform of the statistical system to the Diet, the commission wrote that "we cannot blind our eyes to the fact that the country adopted mistaken policies and brought the ravages of war to the nation because there was . . . a dearth of accurate statistics essential for an objective assessment of the international and domestic situations."[85] The argument was, of course, debatable. One might charitably read the commission's denunciation of wartime policy as promoting a progressive idea of technocratic statecraft: more complete knowledge of "actual" conditions leads to more enlightened state policies. Yet a less laudable logic lies just below the surface here, for the commission might also be taken to have been arguing that Japan's wars in China, Southeast Asia, and the Pacific were ill-considered, not because they were wrong, but because they didn't make statistical sense.

Oblivious to the ambiguous implications of its particular critique of the wartime past, the Statistics Commission presented an optimistic vision of the postwar future in which statistics reform constituted a "fundamental undertaking for constructing a new Japan." The work ahead to "realize true democratic government, by the people and based on the constitution" made the construction of "an accurate statistical system" all the more urgently necessary.[86] In his work with the commission, Ōuchi Hyōe similarly pronounced statistics the "most important means to achieve democracy."[87] The commission declared that the nation should "establish...a scientific consciousness of real conditions, based on statistics, to serve as a signpost guiding us toward a reconstruction based on peace." A reconstructed Japan could then secure the "correct understanding and trust" of the Allied occupation and the international community at large through statistical proof—"with no deception"—of its peaceful ways.[88]

The almost ubiquitous discourse on statistical quantification immediately after the war sprang from the desire for ordered management of national economic life. Bureaucratic and scholarly critics had gushed in earlier decades over the potential benefits of statisticalized knowledge. Yet never had faith in statistical measurement been so widely held or economic and political institutions been so motivated to implement new techniques. This was true in no small part because of the harsh lessons of the war. The drive for economic quantification was fueled by the belief that Japan had chosen a mistaken path during the war due to incomplete knowledge, an "ignorance of the trends of world history," in leftist Kimura Kihachirō's sweeping terms.[89] Statistical data—"accurate," "trustworthy," "scientific"—would be the coin of the "systematized" realm of the postwar period economy; at the same time, it would be the means by which past errors might be overcome and future errors avoided.

Against this backdrop of idealized calls for statisticalized management of the economy, Japanese government officials and leading economists set about to create a coherent, national system of data production. It quickly became clear, as one of the early study groups on the issue explained, that while the eventual goal of statistical reform would be "the various statistics themselves," the first order of business must be to "make arrangements for the agencies that will produce the actual statistics."[90]

Although there was relatively little planning by Japanese institutions for the postwar period, the first moves in response to the collapse of statistical practices came before the war had ended. Shibusawa Keizō, then president of the Bank of Japan, was one of those convinced during the war, despite the relatively small success of the National Economic Resources Research Institute, that economic planning in the postwar period would only succeed if backed up by advanced statistical techniques such as national income accounting. After the war, he decided that the National Economic Resources Research Institute would be spun off from the bank and set up as an independent body "to further research on the national resource strength problem," in the words of Ōuchi Hyōe. Receiving withering criticism of Japanese statistical practices from GHQ, however, Shibusawa (who was shortly to become finance minister in the Shidehara cabinet) soon urged the reorganization of the Institute into the Statistical Research Institute of Japan (Nihon Tōkei Kenkyūjo, hereafter SRIJ) and assigned it the broader task of considering how the Japanese statistical system in general ought to be rehabilitated. The new SRIJ was headed by Ōuchi and, as experts gathered in Tokyo after the war, quickly attracted the leading Japanese lights of advanced economic analysis. "Our spirits were high," recalled Ōuchi. A mishap with the funds appropriated for the SRIJ, however, and then a shift in priorities at the Bank of Japan (which had been providing financial support) resulted in dramatic cutbacks in the size and mission of the research group.[91] Still, the organization, ill-fated as it was, and the pooling of talents that it prompted, indicated the breadth of the movement for statistical reform.

Under intense pressure from GHQ to do something about the lack of viable data, the Shidehara cabinet (October 1945–April 1946) directed the Cabinet Deliberation Office (Naikaku Shingishitsu) to investigate solutions to the problem.[92] Beginning in May 1946, representatives from the various ministries gathered in the Deliberation Office for informal meetings about the statistics dilemma. Little real progress had been made since the end of the war, however, and in the spring of 1946, the new prime minister, Yoshida Shigeru, turned to Ōuchi Hyōe (who was now the chief at SRIJ and who just days before had turned down Yoshida's offer of a cabinet position) to take the lead on reforms. Meanwhile, the study groups in the Deliberation Office had asked SRIJ to join forces with them in their deliberations. This combined study group became the basis for a preliminary committee that by December 1946 had led to the formation of the Statistics Commission in the prime minister's office.[93] With Ōuchi as the head, the commission was the first parliamentary committee on bureaucratic administration in Japan, and it was given a broad mandate to review current statistical practices and draw up an overall blueprint for national statistical institutions.[94] The commission was not a temporary organization designed only to institute structural and procedural reforms. Rather it was meant to be a permanent body that would administer the statistical operations of the government on an ongoing basis.

Meanwhile, not content to wait for a Japanese response to the statistics crisis, the Supreme Commander for the Allied Powers (SCAP, referring to

General Douglas MacArthur and his Occupation headquarters) sent a message to the Department of the Army on October 31, 1946, requesting that it send a team of top economists to guide reform of Japan's statistical system. A task force of what would eventually be seven members, headed by Stuart A. Rice, deputy chief of the U.S. Bureau of the Budget and head of its Divison of Statistical Standards, began arriving in Japan in December 1946. (The team also included W. Edwards Deming, the statistician who would later become famous for his lectures in Japan on statistical quality control.)[95] Rice's position at the Office of the Budget as well as his chairmanship of the United Nations Committee on Statistics made him a major figure on the cutting edge of statistically driven approaches to economic governance.

Easily the least recognized of the many American missions to Japan during the Occupation, the Rice Mission began its work just as the Statistics Commission was getting under way. Rice and his staff met with the commission often and supported its efforts, ensuring that it had ultimate authority over statistics policy in Japan. They gave advice on institutional arrangements and modern statistical techniques, including gross national product and national income; industrial censuses and industrial production indices; price indices; financial and fiscal reporting; surveying and sampling methods; and so on.[96] The mission also counseled statistics chiefs in the ministries. At a January 1947 reception for the Rice Mission held by the Yoshida Shigeru administration, the director general of the Economic Stabilization Board, Zen Keinosuke, praised the advice of Rice and his staff as "the most fundamental factor in the task of correcting the deficiencies of Japan's statistics."[97]

One of the primary themes consistently sounded by the Rice Mission was the need for Japanese to implement rationalized coordination of all official statistical work. Although the mission did at times warn against absolute Soviet-style top-down approaches, echoing the calls by many of those Japanese themselves most concerned about statistical reform, it repeatedly placed at the top of its lists of recommendations the need for Japanese to develop what it called a "statistical system" (quotations in original) within which "the collection of official data" should "be centralized to the maximum practicable degree" at the cabinet level. Especially troubling to the members of the Rice Mission were the facts that in earlier periods government agencies had "traditionally left to 'control organizations'" so much of the work of collecting statistics, and that there continued to be little understanding of the need for systemic coordination and for the comparability of statistics across functionally related segments of the economy.[98]

But Rice's message was not limited to questions related to the statistical methodologies to be used by the analytical elite within the government nor to official institutional arrangements. As expressed in April 1947 in the final summary report of the mission, titled "Modernization of Japanese

Statistics," and throughout the mission's other interim pronouncements, his vision of reform was based on a grander desire to help "democratize Japanese society" by transforming the very consciousness of the Japanese public.[99] Rice ascribed what the mission considered the low quality of statistics in Japan "chiefly to a national deficiency in 'statistical mindedness,'" and he saw the promotion of "habits of thought" among Japanese that were "more factual" as one of the Mission's most important tasks.

The American people and their government, by contrast, were, in the estimation of Rice, "probably more 'statistically minded' than any others in the world." The statistical outlook with which even ordinary Americans viewed the universe was evident everywhere and, he claimed, was the basis of "democratic ideology": "The average democratic American wishes 'to know the facts,' to 'look at the record.' ... His stocks go up or down by 'points.' His favorite team establishes a 'batting average.' American business ventures and Government programs are based on statistical information, the accuracy and objectivity of which are demanded and relied upon by all concerned." Through the confident, fairly crusading terms with which Rice lauded America's love of the numerical, he portrayed statistics as the key to the entire American way of life and, indeed, as an explanation for the ascendancy of American "national power."[100]

Japan, on the other side, came in for bluntly deprecatory criticism. Rice allowed that Japanese had implemented many aspects of "western statistical practice," but asserted that these often were not accompanied by an appreciation of "the modes of thought which lie behind them and give them meaning." The failures of past statistical practices in Japan, Rice went on, had risked making the collection of statistics there "either a meaningless imitation of western custom or a reflection of belief" that the statistics themselves "have some undisclosed magical value."

Rice's solution was a broad campaign to instill statistical awareness in the Japanese people from the earliest years of public education. Arguing that "the basic observations and concepts from which statistical science has been evolved are elementary and are easily grasped by normal school children," he called for curricula throughout primary and secondary education systems that would promote "the value of objectivity and accuracy by noting the penalties of 'wishful thinking,' guesswork and inaccuracy." Skills of "counting, measurement, variability, classification, frequency, distribution and central tendency or average" would help instill "intellectual honesty," he continued, "as a basic virtue." At a time, moreover, when debates in the United States about whether statistics ought to be considered a separate discipline in its own right within the university, or studied as an integrated aspect of all social-scientific inquiry, Rice made the case that statistical training in Japan should be a part of the higher education of all economists, sociologists, social workers, and specialists in public administration. He also suggested that new study-abroad programs for statistical training would be an important way for Japanese to compensate for their "war-time isolation" and to participate in the "statistical progress" of the United States and other nations. In-service training programs for government employees, instituted in tandem with the universities, would further help bridge the troubling gaps in statistical knowledge among those in official positions until a new generation of university graduates began to enter public service.[101]

Rice returned to the States in January 1947, although his deputy, Peyton Stapp, stayed on until April and other mission staff remained even after that in the Occupation's Economic and Scientific Section. His relatively short visit and his almost strutting critique of past practices in Japan did little to dampen enthusiasm for what many of his Japanese hosts perceived as Rice's generous efforts in their country. His report was received warmly and read widely by scholars and those in government.[102] His strong articulation of the importance of statistics boosted the morale of economists, and his friendly support of the Statistics Commission gave the reform group great momentum. At Prime Minister Yoshida's reception for Rice at the end of the American's trip, Statistics Commission chairman Ōuchi Hyōe marveled that such an event was taking place at all. An even greater surprise was that members of the Japanese Statistics Commission themselves had been invited! "It is an extreme rarity that statistics be held in such high honor in Japan. Particularly since the beginning of the war, such a situation has been absolutely nonexistent," he pointedly remarked.[103] The relationship forged during the Rice Mission between the statistical operatives of the two nations would continue in following years as influential visits by American advisers to Japan and by Japanese study groups to the United States—to discuss topics ranging from national income accounting to statistical quality control and corporate planning—continued during the 1950s and early 1960s.[104]

Taking up work begun by the Economic Stabilization Board, the newly formed Statistics Commission in the Prime Minister's Office completed the drafting of a Statistics Law, which was passed by the Diet with little problem in March 1947.[105] The law was designed to formalize the authority of the Statistics Commission to direct official statistical research, stipulate the public reporting and preservation of statistics, hold researchers and research subjects to strict standards of accuracy, and improve the quality of statistical personnel throughout the government. In the past, official statistical research in Japan had been characterized by little intragovernmental coordination. Few standards had been established and redundancy was common. The compatibility, consistency, and relevancy of data sets from variant research were therefore low.[106] The Statistics Law inaugurated two reforms in particular to impose standards and ensure a new level of comprehensiveness in statistical studies: creation of the "designated statistics" *(shitei tōkei)* system and expansion of local statistical organs *(chihō tōkei kikō).*[107]

Under the designated statistics system, the Statistics Commission acted as a coordinating directorate and information clearinghouse for statistical research nationwide. It designated what "important" official national statistics would be regularly collected, when, and by what specific private organs or by what local or national governmental agencies. Designated research bodies were required to adhere to strict public reporting requirements, and the commission had the authority to review the planning, methodology, amendments, and budgeting of any designated statistics project. It could, moreover, carry out inspections of designated research projects in progress. Even more sweeping, statistical organizations carrying out research that fell outside the purview of the designated statistics system (but stipulated by a separate ordinance) were required to report their projects, their aims, methodology, and so on to the commission, which was authorized to make alterations to research proposals and even cancel projects it deemed inappropriate. This reporting system was intended to allow the commission to keep abreast of all relevant national research and its relation to the designated statistics, to exert a degree of influence over lesser projects nationwide, and to reduce redundancy.[108]

The second reform, the rapid expansion of local statistical organs, was designed to create an integrated network of official statistical production that was truly nationwide in scope. By formalizing the data links between the smallest localities and the national government, the cabinet hoped to broaden the areas of statistical study in localities, to increase use of local statistics at all levels of the statistical system, and to improve the speed at which statistical knowledge was transmitted. Prefecture-level statistical personnel who had previously been funded by each separate ministry were unified into one national staff and their numbers bolstered. The government was to pay the expenses of designated statistical personnel in each locality: a minimum of two persons in each town and village and an appropriate number in each city based on population. Finally, the work of this network of local staff would be supervised by the Statistics Commission. The Occupation declared, however, that the cabinet's attempt to actually place national government staff in the prefectural offices as statistical chiefs ran counter to the principle of local rule. In the end, prefectural statistical chiefs were employed by the prefecture but funded by the national government.[109]

The number of nationally supported statistics personnel at all levels of local government rose dramatically with the passage of the Statistics Law. In the prefectures, the number of these statistical staff members increased from 1,101 at the start of 1947 to 4,365 by the end of that year. An additional 1,200 statistical staff were provided for at the city level and 10,310 at the town and village levels. While the total nationwide increase of 15,875 people was only somewhat more than half of what had originally been planned by the cabinet, it still represented a dramatic jump in the short span of one year. These numbers rose and fell over the next several tumultuous years, but the basic commitment to the vertical integration of the national statistical system did not change.[110]

The success of this ambitious national network clearly would require a new class of technically expert bureaucrats and outside agency personnel. Rice was not alone in calling for a far-ranging campaign to improve statistical education. Japanese commentators, too, criticized the woeful preparation of the bureaucratic and military personnel responsible for economic affairs in decades past. The Special Survey Committee wrote in the *Basic Problems* report that it was "necessary to appoint capable persons to the posts in charge of statistics," the implication being that this would be a significant departure from past practice. It argued for the broadening of statistical knowledge in general, noting that "the habit of placing importance on statistics must be cultivated through various means." One such means was the schools, in which students could "acquire an ability to handle things surrounding them in terms of statistics." Another was the encouragement of "statistical publications, especially popularly accessible statistical magazines" that would contribute to the "generalization of knowledge about and use of statistics."[111]

The Statistics Law addressed the quality of personnel by stipulating education and training requirements for researchers engaged in official statistical work. If an employee did not already have at least two years of experience in statistical research, then completion of university or technical school degrees in mathematics or statistics, or else special retraining at institutes specified by the Statistics Commission, was required.[112] One such statistical training institute for government employees had existed earlier in the Prime Minister's Office but had been discontinued during the war. In 1947, it was rehabilitated and expanded, and the curriculum revised. A second institute also was launched that same year in the Education Ministry, and a third outside institute was accredited by the government.[113] The curriculum at training institutes was set by the commission and consisted of a hundred hours of instruction in general economics and in statistical theory and practice.[114] While perhaps not in the end as ambitious as Rice's vision of popular statistical education, the campaign to increase statistical knowledge for the first time achieved the implementation of government-wide training requirements for those responsible for official statistical work.

General education reforms fell under the jurisdiction of the Education Ministry, but the Statistics Commission did also indirectly support local experiments with model statistical education programs in elementary and middle schools and also planned at one point to institute a system of two-year statistical colleges. Experiments with model statistical schools became quite successful, and their numbers increased rapidly, from 55 schools in three prefectures in 1949 to 250 schools in fifteen prefectures by 1952.[115] The

Statistical Association of Hiroshima Prefecture, an organization founded in 1950 to encourage the exchange of statistical knowledge among local statistical officials and to promote statistical awareness among private citizens, announced with great pride in 1951 that it would be spearheading the opening of ten model statistical schools, a program that was to be expanded gradually throughout the prefecture, the association ambitiously declared, "until all school children are given statistical knowledge." In fact, at this early stage of its existence, the Statistical Association of Hiroshima reported to officials in the Programs and Statistical Division of SCAP the creation of an already active program for promoting statistical awareness among citizens, including publication of its monthly newsletter, "Tōkei-no-izumi" (Wellspring of statistics), public lectures, and a contest to guess the correct number of "the domiciled population" of the prefecture.[116]

The Statistics Commission also oversaw revolutionary improvements in the technical infrastructure of the government's statistical apparatus. The Japanese government could not hope efficiently to produce statistical data on the new scale envisioned by reformers without powerful calculating machines like the ones used in the United States and Britain during the war. Calculating machines from the United States had been used in the Finance, Railroad, Commerce and Industry, and Agriculture and Forestry Ministries from before the war. Import restrictions during the war, however, meant that old machines were not replaced, and most were now unusable, either worn out or war-damaged. Without the machines, tabulations had to be done by hand. The error rate was high, and often there were simply not enough qualified personnel to do the job.[117] Where machines were still in use, they were older, smaller models, offering nothing like the scale of computation possible on newer machines. Okita Saburō later recalled the laborious calculation process during his work on the Economic White Paper of 1947: "In those days statisticians did not have the large capacity computers that econometricians use today, but were forced to use primitive calculating machines which looked like old-fashioned cash registers in miniature. You punched the numbers and cranked the handle, and somehow it performed the four mathematical functions. We cranked the handles of those calculating machines night after night."[118] The U.S. machines were expensive, however, and money was scarce. The Statistics Commission was so desperate that it even sent Arisawa Hiromi around to various corporations that still had working calculating machines to ask if they might lend some to the Cabinet Statistics Bureau for a time.[119]

Finally in 1949, as Japan prepared to participate in the World Census of 1950, the commission was able to secure the funding and coordinate the purchase of a host of new IBM and Remington Rand machines for the various statistics agencies throughout the government.[120] In this case, the rise of a vast government data machine was reflected quite literally in the machines upon which so much of statistical analysis was coming to depend. The new calculating equipment was the first step in the construction of what by the early 1960s would be a technology-driven data system.

The Statistics Commission was abolished in 1952 in the midst of bureaucratic changes instituted after the Occupation ended, and its functions were subsumed under the Administrative Management Agency (Gyōsei Kanrichō). By the time of its succession by the Administrative Management Agency, the commission had presided over the unprecedented institutionalization of many of the statistical practices so insistently called for by critics immediately after the war. Some critics, to be sure, were disappointed in the commission's achievements. A source of particular chagrin for Ōuchi Hyōe, Kawashima Takahiko (director of the Cabinet Statistics Bureau), Arisawa Hiromi, and others was their failure to erect a more thoroughly centralized statistical system centered on the Cabinet Statistics Bureau (later the Statistics Bureau of the Office of the Prime Minister).[121] This had seemed to them to be the appropriate response to the ill-coordinated statistical work of wartime, and indeed the many pronouncements and recommendations of the Rice Mission had seemed to support such centralizing impulses. The ministries, however, put new emphasis on strengthening their own statistics bureaus after the war. These were expanded or created where they had not existed before, and seasoned statisticians were put in charge for the first time.[122] This development, coupled with fierce bureaucratic sectionalism, tempered the power of the commission and in general worked against centralization. The proliferation during the Occupation period of new agencies with their own statistical mandates, such as the Economic Stabilization Board and the Price Board, further diffused statistical work. The Rice Mission, too, contributed to this trend, arguing against absolute "Soviet-style" centralization. The commission itself also accepted that a degree of decentralization should be built into the system. As the commission's numerous reform struggles with the ministries attest, however, it still found itself on the more centralizing side of the ledger than were the other bureaucratic arms of the government.

Still, although the dream of absolute centralization cherished by some had been modified, reformers largely had achieved their hopes for a true national "statistical system" (tōkei taikei).[123] Calls to rehabilitate the nation by means of numerical fact had been at heart about a desire for a "systematic" organization: a seamless, comprehensive, standardized web of statistical production incorporating the economic and social life of the entire nation. An institutional framework for such a system indeed had emerged—contentious perhaps, but greatly more complex and interconnected than ever before. The Statistics Commission and the Administrative Management Agency after it, though embattled by the ministries, exercised unequaled oversight over the operations of official statistical systems.[124] The strengthened Cabinet Statistics Bureau and the statistics bureaus in the ministries and the ESB created an institutional breadth and scale unseen before the end of the war. Under the Statistics Law, moreover, the official function of the state as a producer and manager of statistical knowledge was now codified, legislated as it had not been earlier. The designated statistics system both reflected and promoted an explosion in new fields of study as the economy came to be defined by an ever-increasing variety of sophisticated, formalized statistics. And perhaps most striking, national statistical systems reached into the furthest reaches of local government to a degree not achieved by earlier arrangements. By the early 1950s, Japanese planners and bureaucrats—under the watchful eye of the Occupation—had constructed an elaborate new "system," run by a class of expert officials who would manage the economy, and society as a whole, through the science of statistical fact.

GNP as "One of the Most Vital Means"

As the Statistics Commission created a postwar statistical infrastructure, macroeconomic statistics such as national income accounting began to emerge as governing analytical tools within the new system. As the war drew to its awful close, a few economic leaders, such as Shibusawa Keizō at the Bank of Japan, desperately tried to set up new mechanisms for large-scale statistical study of the economy. Yet it was not Shibusawa's National Resource Institute, nor even the Finance Ministry itself, but the U.S. government that prepared the first postwar estimations of national income in Japan. In October 1945, the Intelligence Branch of the U.S. State Department made a quick calculation. Then, in 1946, during its investigation of the efficacy of the Allied bombing of Japan, the United States Strategic Bombing Survey calculated Japanese national income for the years 1942 to 1945, relying in part on data on the last years of the war still held by the Bank of Japan.[125]

This initial research, made under the most difficult of circumstances, was part of the Occupation's scramble to assemble whatever data it could on the Japanese economy. Such investigations by the Occupation revealed the near complete disarray of economic governance in Japan. In marked contrast to their grand blueprints for colonial development and early war mobilization schemes, Japanese bureaucrats had made few plans for the postwar period, either in terms of basic policy approaches or organizational strategies. Thus the wherewithal to undertake research on the order of a national accounting survey for the most part was absent within the Japanese government immediately after the end of the war; Shibusawa's efforts were generally the exception that proved the rule.

Despite the wartime hunches of Shibusawa and Ōuchi Hyōe that national accounting would find a prominent place in postwar period economics, talk of the technique was rarely to be found among Japanese economic leaders immediately after the war. While not an especially technical document, to be sure, the Special Survey Committee's *Basic Problems* did not mention national accounting. As Kawai Saburō, a member of the Cabinet Deliberation Office and the Statistics Commission after the war and, later, head of the Administrative Management Agency's Statistics Section, points out, neither, more surprisingly, did the reports of groups such as the Institute for Research on the National Economy (Kokumin Keizai Kenkyū Kyōkai), which in the period before the formation of the Statistics Commission set out what sorts of statistical information would be crucial to economic stabilization policy. "Production statistics; transport; inventory; foodstuffs; prices; household income and consumption; employment; monetary and finance statistics as well as inflation indicators are all there, but the word 'national income' doesn't appear anywhere at all," Kawai notes.[126] Similarly, the four subcommittees (population, production, labor, and finance and prices) formed within the Statistics Research Group (Tōkei Kenkyūkai), the early study group within the Cabinet Deliberation Office that directly led to the formation of the Statistics Commission, did not include a "national income" committee.[127] Even within the commission itself national income accounting did not immediately figure in planning discussions, this despite the participation of economists such as Ōuchi and Arisawa Hiromi who had some knowledge of the practice during the war years. This is partly due to the fact that the commission's work was initially more focused on setting out the institutional framework of statistical research. Moreover, since even basic data production had faltered, grand statistical instruments such as national income might have seemed beyond the reach of the government's statistical agencies at the time.

The absence of Japanese efforts to estimate national income in fact resulted from more than a lack of data or manpower. While various forms of national accounting had attracted increasing attention both before and during the war, it had not yet come to occupy a governing role in either Japanese economic theory or policy making. In truth, as Arisawa later recalled, the absence of national income accounting during this early period was probably due to the simple, if somewhat tautological, fact that "no one" among Japanese planners "was thinking about it yet."[128]

In the United States, however, things were quite different. The rising prominence of national income during the war did not end when the fighting ceased. By now it was clear to many analysts in the United States that national accounting was a powerful tool that could be applied, not only to the special circumstances of wartime mobilization, but to the general problem of measuring and, it was hoped, regulating the broad swings of the national economy. National income reports by the U.S. government became an annual affair in 1947. Increasingly united with an approach to economic governance that was broadly identified with Keynesianism, national accounting techniques were coming to redefine economic thinking, the subject of a later chapter. Here it is enough to note that the theoretical and empirical questions that American economists and policy makers asked were increasingly dominated by the econometric agendas of national accounting. A scholar of the subject, Paul Studenski, summed up the effect of this rise of national accounting, writing that the "whole structure of economics was being changed by this new analytical method."[129]

American administrators were animated from the very first days of the Occupation by the belief that a dearth of statistical data threatened their success in Japan. And high on the wish list of the ESS staff at GHQ were figures on national income. As the Occupation went about its calculations of Japanese national income in 1945 and 1946, it also quickly turned to a review of Japanese capabilities for their own production of these statistics. The effects of these efforts were felt even in the year or so before the Rice Mission arrived to formally review statistical practices. Based on recommendations for a framework for research on the macroeconomic conditions of the nation made by C. Patrick,[130] chief of statistics in GHQ, a new Kokumin Shiryoku Kikakushitsu (National Economic Resource Planning Office) was established within the Finance Ministry in February 1946. By the following year, the Kikakushitsu unit boasted a staff of twenty. In addition, the Kikakushitsu housed a technical committee on National Economic Resource statistics. Headed by Yamaguchi Shigeru, a Hitotsubashi University professor, the committee was staffed by economists and statisticians whose job it was to make recommendations on national income practices and applications. These modest institutional measures were accompanied by a concerted effort on the part of Patrick in GHQ to encourage the production and publication of national income data. Based on recommendations she had made in 1946, figures calculated that year in the planning office of the Bank of Japan on per capita income in Japan were included in the first-ever Economic White Paper in Japan, released by the Economic Stabilization Board in 1947.[131]

A serious attack on the problem of a coordinated system of national income calculation, however, did not materialize until the arrival of the Rice Mission at the very end of 1946. The statistics of gross national product and national income were part of the Rice Mission's mandate from the beginning, for they had been identified as areas needing immediate attention by SCAP when in October 1946 it put out the original call to the United States for a team of statistical experts. In fact, among all statistics the mission investigated these two "in particular," arguing that they were "fast becoming one of the most vital and powerful means by which economic policies [were] instituted and measured in the major nations of the world."[132] The importance the mission placed on national income accounting in Japan was underscored by a lengthy report on the issue prepared by mission member Michael Sapir that evaluated past and current income accounting efforts in Japan and laid out guidelines for future practices. In Rice's final mission report of April 1947, he reiterated the importance of national income in the eyes of the American experts, a point reflected in the prominent position it was afforded among the specific statistics he discussed.[133]

Rice and Sapir urged the Japanese government to step up their training of statisticians in the concepts and methods of national income and GNP. They argued that only the unity and consistency of statistical output would ensure the success of national income accounting and emphasized to their Japanese colleagues the need to reform the survey statistics—such as population, wages and income, production, employment, consumer income and expenditure—that fed into income calculations. The mission also reviewed methods used in the past to calculate national income in Japan and instructed its Japanese counterparts in agencies throughout the government as to the standards and definitions employed in computing national income in the United States.[134] Such concentrated attention on national accounting reflected the quickly growing belief among the elite of American economics that these statistics would be the linchpin of postwar economic governance.

Consistent with his belief that a new level of centralized rationality needed to be brought to Japanese statistical systems, Rice advised his Japanese counterparts to assign national accounting functions to one central authority. As a result, national accounting work was moved in June 1947 from the National Economic Resource Planning Office of the Finance Ministry to the young Economic Stabilization Board, which in its later incarnation as the Economic Planning Agency remained the institutional home of national accounting for the remainder of the century. By October of that year, a National Income Research Office (Kokumin Shotoku Chōsashitsu), with forty-two technical staff, had been created within the ESB to be exclusively devoted to the computation of the statistic. This new office also housed a technical committee to carry out basic work on standards and practices.[135]

The assignment of national income accounting to the ESB came at an important moment in the history of that organization. It had begun its operations in August 1946 as a fairly weak planning and coordinating organ virtually ignored by the ministries. As a consequence of its Priority Production Plan to jumpstart the economy in spring 1947, however, ESB was authorized to implement the Temporary Materials Supply and Demand Control Law (Rinji busshi jukyū chōsei hō) of the previous September. It thereby won virtual complete control over the flow of all major commodities in Japan. This strengthening of the agency was encouraged by SCAP, which directed that it should assume all ministerial planning functions. Suddenly at the center of economic policy making and implementation, the ESB exploded in size: by May of that year, it had two thousand employees, up from just some three hundred the year before.[136] Thus the assignment of national accounting work to the ESB institutionally situated it at the heart of the government's economic policy apparatus.

Thus far, this discussion of the state of Japanese statistical enterprises by the end of the war has been weighted toward the efforts of those in and around the government. Yet, in academic circles as well, the crisis of Japanese statistics and of the discipline of economics in general did not fail to elicit equally spirited declarations of the need for renovation. A growing empiricism and concern with economics as an applied science among Japanese academics supported the rise of new statistical techniques such as national accounting. This postwar empiricist movement encouraged broader experimentation in new techniques, the accumulation of the massive data sets required by macroeconomic analysis, and an instrumental approach to current policy questions. It was greatly influenced by developments in the United States. The dazzling practical power of quantitative approaches to economic problems there, combined with the postwar geopolitical hegemony of the United States, made the American field of economics the new metropole of theoretical production.[137] This trend was later strengthened by education programs such as the Fulbright scholarships, which underwrote the study of Japanese students at centers of economic research such as Harvard, University of Chicago, and the like.

One figure whose thinking was decisively shaped by American empirical research was Tsuru Shigeto, whose knowledge of developments in the United States predated the end of the war. Tsuru, who would eventually become the president of Hitotsubashi University, had received his undergraduate and doctoral educations during the 1930s at Harvard University, a hotbed of research on aggregate quantitative approaches and national income. He remained at Harvard as a lecturer until his repatriation as an enemy alien after the beginning of the war with the United States. With the end of the war, Tsuru became a leading voice in the empiricist movement in Japan, aided the work of the Rice Mission during its days there, and was instrumental in the founding in 1950 of *Keizai kenkyū,* a journal devoted to promoting the cause published by the Institute of Economic Research (Keizai Kenkyūjo) at Hitotsubashi University.[138] He lashed out at his fellow economists, writing that they had "long ago lost the courage to form hypotheses whose propositions could be proven true or false by exposure to the harsh light of reality." Though trained in the United States, he criticized what he saw as the slavish preoccupation among Japanese economists with interpreting theoretical developments from abroad. He exhorted his Japanese colleagues to engage in real testing and empirical analysis of circumstances in Japan.[139]

Tsuru's campaign for new applied and highly quantitative approaches to economic analysis was nowhere more evident than in his work on the extremely influential "First Report on Economic Conditions" (Dai ichiji keizai jissō hōkokusho). Released in 1947 by the Economic Stabilization Board, the report was the first of what famously came to be known as the government's annual "Economic White Papers" *(keizai hakusho)* and was inspired by a similar initiative undertaken by the British government to present a comprehensive analysis of current conditions and government policies. Tsuru's report was remarkable in its assertive deployment of statistical data (fragmentary as it was) to diagnose the macroeconomic sources of Japan's economic emergency. In essence, Tsuru was making a very public case for the potential of national income methodology. "Today," writes Kanamori Hisao,

> these [techniques] are the cornerstone of economic analysis. Any even fairly weak economist, following the framework of macroeconomics, can come up with some semblance of an analysis of a national economy by writing about what is happening with capital investment, what is the character and direction of investment and so on. But when the first White Paper came out, this was an entirely new approach. If it had been written according to the standards of the day, it would either have been a formulaic Marxist analysis or would have ended up as nothing more than descriptive economics that simply presented the facts about how much rice had been grown and how much iron had been produced.[140]

Based on his macroeconomic analysis, Tsuru disturbingly concluded that government, business, and households were all in debt and built a case for the emergency financial measures of the Katayama cabinet. While criticisms of the White Paper abounded, it struck many expert readers as a breathtaking effort. Even decades later, their vivid recollections of its publication commonly use phrases such as "fresh sensation" and "fresh breeze" to describe the impression it made.[141]

Tsuru's White Paper, however, caused such a stir in 1947 precisely because it represented an exception to the norm. Most of the government's economic analysis and planning in the early years after the war continued the microeconomic approaches of the wartime. Although plans such as the 1949 Economic Recovery Plan (Keizai fukkō keikaku) and the 1951 Economic Independence Plan (Keizai jiritsu keikaku) of the Economic Stabilization Board contained some estimation of national income, they were more on the order of materials mobilization plans rather than a Tsuruesque analysis of macroeconomic forces. Neither reflecting an "Olympian" desire to manipulate the aggregate forces of the national economy, nor aimed at economic growth in the way that national accounting practices would later become, early planning was driven by the more humble imperatives of a recovery of manufacturing output—specifically, the problems of physical plant, foreign reserves, and coal production.

Yet Tsuru's efforts did indicate that the conceptual terrain was beginning to change. Soon, the reformers of statistical institutions in the Statistics Commission, too, began to turn to national accounting approaches as an organizing theme. As they devised the "designated statistics" system and tried to coordinate the growing statistical machinery of the government, they found themselves groping for an overriding statistical framework by which to grasp in its entirety the economic muddle of the nation. They struggled, again, for a "system," only here the problem was not to create an institutional structure, but to identify an overarching paradigm of statistical analysis by which the economy as a unified whole might be rationally organized. By the late 1940s, it was becoming clear to the members of the Statistics Commission that national income might offer a solution. "The way things stood," recalls Kawai Saburō, a member of the secretariat of the commission, "we could have gone on saying, 'we need population stats, we need production stats, we need shipping stats,' but there would have been no end to it. So then we thought, 'the preparation of the statistics necessary for this thing "national income" would provide the statistical system required for us to set up a theoretical framework that is a bit more intelligent.' And this later slowly developed into national economic accounting."[142] This line of thinking led to the formation of a committee on national income within the Statistics Commission in September 1947. Just three months earlier, national income had been assigned, following SCAP suggestions, to the Economic Stabilization Board. It fell, then, to the commission to ensure the collection of the statistics appropriate for use in national income calculations by the ESB and its later incarnations. This it accomplished in large part through the new designated statistics system.[143]

The orientation of national statistical production around national income was reinforced well into the 1950s by the continuing interventions of foreign, overwhelmingly American, economists. This influence went beyond the training of young Japanese scholars in the United States and included study missions between the United States and Japan and direct reviews by American economists of Japanese national income practices. The Shoup Tax Mission, for example, criticized the national income figures for 1948 and 1949 compiled by the ESB as underestimating income by as much as one-third, and Richard Huber, an American scholar, provided GHQ with a detailed critique of ESB practices in 1950.[144] Members of the Rice Mission also continued to shape developments. Michael Sapir had continued after the end of the mission as an adviser in the Economic and Scientific Section of SCAP, and Rice himself returned with a new mission in 1951. In Rice's follow-up review of statistical systems in Japan, he continued to exhort Japanese officials to strengthen the research work of the ESB, "especially...the capability to carry out national income and related forms of analysis."[145] In response, the income unit of the ESB was further bolstered.

But it was not only bilateral exchange between the United States and Japan that shaped the development of national accounting in Japan. The spate of new institutions set up to manage postwar multilateral relations, particularly the United Nations, also played a role in promoting national income accounting in Japan and in nations the world over. Economists in the national income accounting unit at the UN quickly set out after the war to standardize statistical approaches. This was in part a response to a system in which member nations paid dues to the UN according to the size of their national income. Membership thus required some kind of formal accounting system, and UN experts conducted reviews of practices in member nations. In 1954, for example, the UN released a report by Harry Oshima of its Statistics Bureau critically evaluating the ESB's income calculation for 1951 and proposing changes to the methods used by the Japanese statisticians.[146]

The formulation of a standardized national income system also reflected postwar hopes that organizations such as the UN, the World Bank, and the IMF would work to stabilize the world economy and regularize its multilateral management. Soon these practices were also deployed more directly as a means of gauging and promoting the comparative development of national economies. By 1952 the UN, working with other institutions such as the Organization for Economic Cooperation and Development, completed a set of common national accounting conventions, known as the System of National Accounts (SNA), and it was expected that nations would work to conform to those standards. Japanese bureaucrats and scholars were in close contact with UN developments in national accounting and worked steadily through the 1950s to bring their practices more closely in line with these international standards.[147]

Japanese macroeconomic statisticians received further validation that their calculations formed a core element of the economic knowledge apparatus of the state when the now annualized national income accounting results for which they were responsible were elevated to official White Paper status ("White Paper on National Income," Kokumin shotoku hakusho) in 1954 and presented to the Diet as one of the touchstone statements by ruling governments of the state of the nation. When the Economic Planning Agency (EPA) replaced the short-lived successor to the ESB, moreover, national accounting activities found a home at the center of that new influential organization. The findings of the EPA's income White Papers, furthermore, increasingly informed the more famous and broadly portfo-lioed Economic White Papers for which the the agency is more commonly famous.

As with many nations, the national accounting systems and conventions created in Japan and institutionalized by 1955 at the EPA did not match the UN's System of National Accounts exactly, though they served as a suitably comparable system for many decades. The statistical guidelines codified by the United Nations, moreover, were themselves not fixed. The UN itself revamped the conventions in 1968 on the basis of continuing work spear-headed by British economist Richard Stone, who had been instrumental in the publication of the original standards in 1952, but also featuring the con-tributions to the evolving regime made by the scholarship of macrostatisti-cal researchers from around the world. EPA statisticians themselves would go on to reform the Japanese accounting conventions in 1978, touting these for the first time as now conforming, to an internationally lauded degree, to those of the UN.[148]

By the early 1950s, then, highly empirical, aggregative economic practices such as national accounting had increasingly come to form the concep-tual ether in which economists and bureaucrats operated. These modes of economic analysis lay at the heart of a new international institutional order that determined national income accounting standards, promoted their use throughout the world in a host of multilateral organizations, and employed them in an assertive program of economic developmentalism across the globe. At home, the dream of a comprehensive statistical struc-ture by which a true science of the economy might operate had necessi-tated the construction of a newly formalized national statistical machin-ery. Economic measures and modes of analysis that placed a premium on manipulation of aggregate flows and structures of the national economy, particularly as represented in the statistics of national income and GNP, grew from modest roles in early recovery plans increasingly to rule many of the chief analytical activities of this state statistical system. Regularized national income accounting by the government thus came to reflect the logic of the new institutional muscle of postwar technocracy. By the late 1950s the statistic of GNP would begin to assume an outsized place in offi-cial analysis, wider public discourse on the economy, and shared concep-tions of national purpose and power.

CHAPTER 3

New Economics and an Expanding Vision of Prosperity

A s analysts and reformers articulated a future vision of reconstruction in terms of humanistic technocracy, they simultaneously cast their critical gaze backward over the longer history of modern Japanese development. While not unitary in voice, their analysis, from an often surprising range of observers, amounted to a common diagnosis of Japanese capitalism that described Japan as uniquely inscribed by certain pathologies. Drawing connections between the particular path charted by the political economy of Japan and the disaster of the long war on the Chinese continent and against the Allied powers, many Japanese pinned their hopes for the new era on the chance to redress the failed history of modern Japan by setting the economy right.

Laying out the "the peculiarities of the Japanese economy," progressive intellectuals and planners adopted the prewar analysis of the Japanese state as a backward one in which the transformation to capitalism remained incomplete. Japanese society, they believed, was characterized by "feudalistic" socioeconomic structures: familialism and paternalism in the countryside as well as the small scale of agriculture and antiquated working conditions. The critics charged that capital accumulation in the relatively small industrial sector had been achieved on the backs of the vast numbers of farmers and those engaged in small business. This "abnormal" coexistence of feudalistic and capitalistic elements, coupled with what was generally lamented as Japan's "excess population," a problem now becoming more acute with the repatriation of demobilized soldiers and colonists from the former empire, conspired to depress wage levels, especially among the large agricultural class, critics reasoned. The "purchasing power" of the masses was limited, thus restricting domestic markets for Japanese manufactures. "Thus was the foundation built," the Special Survey Committee of the Foreign Ministry damningly concluded, "for Japan's progression toward becoming a militaristic and aggressive nation."[1] In its condemnation of Japan's "abnormal" capitalistic structure, the committee's report reflected the widely held view after the war that a successful economic reconstruction required new economic guarantees to promote the formation of a viable middle class.

The emphasis on the structural defects of the political economy in this retrospective analysis of the road to war drew heavily on Marxist debates dating from the 1920s on the so-called crisis of development of Japanese capitalism. Indeed, many of the vocal exponents of this diagnosis, economists such as Arisawa Hiromi and Ōuchi Hyōe, had been participants in those earlier debates, which had marked the first efflorescence of rigorous Marxist scholarship on the nature of Japanese capitalism (and many of them had been arrested in the late 1920s for the expression of their leftist ideas in those debates). Though sectarian differences existed, Marxists during those earlier years of debate had been united by a general belief that the structure of the Japanese economy was "backward," being characterized by great concentrations of wealth in a powerful industrial sector atop a vast "precapitalistic" agricultural and small-business sector operating on minute scales according to irrational, feudalistic practices. The seemingly intractable structural divide between the two sectors was believed to stand in contrast to the supposedly smooth trajectory of development in Western Europe and the United States, in which capital accumulation was seen as complete, and irrational elements universally replaced by the efficiencies of capitalist industry.

The tenor, if not the specific terms and conceptual categories, of the Marxist debates of the interwar period, in turn, shared much with a longer tradition of Japanese exceptionalism—a negative exceptionalism—dating from the Meiji period, in which what were seen as a "late-comer" status and general backwardness consistently colored views of national purpose and strategy.[2] In the context of crisis and the discrediting of earlier conservative orthodoxies after the war, the Marxist analysis enjoyed an enhanced status, and progressive intellectual opinion was largely united on the immediate postwar diagnosis. But it was not only on the pages of left-leaning journals like *Kaizō* and *Sekai* that such reformist attempts to address reconstruction and recovery appeared. The diagnostic vision, though differing in emphases and prescriptions, was acceptable in its general outline to a wide range of educated opinion. The vision soon found expression in the Ministry of Commerce and Industry, for example, when its Enterprise Bureau announced in 1949 that postwar industrial rationalization must be pursued through expansion of "consumption markets" at home and high wages.

Acknowledgment of the "unbalanced" nature of the productive sector was also a basic premise of industrial bureaucrats.[3] As refracted in such venues as the SSC report, the leftist critiques of the political economy of Japan were frequently formulated to steer clear of overtly ideological language, and they were also moderated by being couched in the language of the marketplace.

The diagnostic vision of the need for an unprecedented emphasis on welfare guarantees and the nurturing of a new middle class was reinforced by the confluence of two interrelated factors. First, the vision accorded with early Occupation views espoused by New Dealers and China experts such as the scholar Owen Lattimore, who took a more radical view than old Japan hands in regard to the task of rooting out the forces of militarism in Japanese society. American critics pointed to a conspiratorial triumvirate of the *zaibatsu* industrial combines, state bureaucrats, and military leaders who had highjacked popular liberal elements and whose lock on economic resources prevented the rise of a middle class that could act as the bearer of liberal values.

Second, the diagnostic vision had mutual affinities with an intense interest in Keynesianism gathering strength in Japan after the war. The rhetoric of full employment that accompanied the rising status of Keynes' ideas helped provide a formal economic voice to reformist arguments while providing theoretical support for new technocratic remedial approaches. It provided a bourgeois intellectual socket into which older Marxist impulses and categories might be plugged and thus made more palatable to conservatives in the bureaucratic and industrial elite.

"Keynes Fever"

The more explicit and persistent links between the ideal of planning and a range of welfare goals as they came to be articulated in diagnoses of Japanese capitalism after the war were not the products of a postwar flush of magnanimous humanism alone. Wider theoretical changes in economic thought and evolving beliefs about the basic workings of national economies played a role in reinforcing domestic prescriptions for rehabilitating the Japanese economy. In Japan, as elsewhere, Keynesianism, with its focus on macroeconomic intervention to boost aggregate demand and high levels of employment, began to exert considerable influence on economic thinking after the war. Although relatively few economics professionals, especially those in cabinet agencies and the bureaucracy, underwent a full conversion to some new Keynesian orthodoxy, proto-Keynesian and Keynesian approaches, broadly defined, did support new currents in domestic political-economic thought that raised troubling questions after the war about the inadequacy of the middle class. As Keynesian theory and national

accounting techniques of macroeconomic measurement and manipulation became part of mainstream economic analysis during the first postwar
decade, they worked together to imbue the questions of welfare guarantees
and employment policy with new urgency.

While the ideas contained in Keynes' classic *The General Theory of Employment, Interest and Money* did not become mainstream until after the war, Japanese economists had shown interest in Keynes' work from the 1920s, when
the British economist first began to make a mark in the profession through
his theoretical contributions to monetary economics and his efforts in the
realm of public policy. During the course of the following two and a half
decades, Keynes wrote treatises and advised governments on the pressing
economic questions of the age, including the gold standard, exchange rate
disequilibria, inflation and deflation, interest-rate policy, and unemployment. Staff members of the influential journal *Tōyō keizai shinpō* were aware
of Keynes' writings from these early years. One such writer, Ishibashi Tanzan, who later became the editor and an important postwar political figure, wrote a summary of Keynes' *The Economic Consequences of the Peace,* the
British economist's famous critique of what he considered the overly punitive nature of the Versailles Treaty, just three months after its 1919 release.
Ishibashi then formed a Keynes Research Association in the early 1920s.[4]
Interest in Japan continued to grow with the appearance of Keynes' *Tract
on Monetary Reform* in 1923, which appeared in Japanese translation the next
year, and *A Treatise on Money* in 1930. The latter was an attempt to theorize
the direct relation between interest rates and prices in the operation of
"credit cycles" (or, indirectly, increases and decreases in output), a topic
of immediate relevancy to economists trying to understand the previous
decade of difficulty in Japan in terms of the orthodoxy of classical economic
theory. While Marxist approaches and concerns had come to dominate Japanese economics departments of the time, some universities maintained
strong programs in the classical traditions. Tokyo Shōka Daigaku (Tokyo
Commercial University, the predecessor to Hitotsubashi University) taught
in the classical liberal tradition from its founding in the late nineteenth
century, as did Keiō University, the private university founded by entrepre-
neur and critic Fukuzawa Yukichi. Much of the work on Keynes in Japan was
done at these institutions. Kitō Nisaburō, professor of economics at Tokyo
Commercial University, for example, translated *A Treatise on Money* in five
volumes between 1932 and 1934, and in 1942 he released *The Dynamics of
Money and Interest (Kahei to rishi no dōtai),* a study that attempted to expand
on Keynesian theory.[5]

The release of Keynes' landmark *The General Theory on Employment, Interest and Money* (hereafter *General Theory*) in 1936 was eagerly awaited in Japan
by those familiar with his earlier work.[6] Keynes' introduction to *Treatise on
Money* had anticipated the new book, which seemed to promise fresh theo-

ries about the determinants of booms and depressions, and Keynes had also discussed his work on the forthcoming *General Theory* in his letters to Kitō while the Japanese economist was translating the *Treatise*.[7] Immediately upon the release of *General Theory*, Nakayama Ichirō, a leading professor of marginal utility economics at Tokyo Commercial University, used the British edition of the book as a text in an undergraduate seminar,[8] an act of pedagogical daring given the infamous difficulty of the work. The studies of *General Theory* that emerged from that seminar were edited by Nakayama and published in 1939 in an influential volume titled *A Commentary on Keynes' General Theory (Keinzu ippanriron kaisetsu)*.[9] Other students, professional economists, and journalists soon formed other *General Theory* study groups, and young staffers in the Ministry of Finance began their own study and translation circle.[10] The leading liberal journal of economics, *Tōyō keizai shinpō*, put on programs featuring Keynes' ideas, and staff members conducted nationwide lectures on the meaning of the British economist's latest theories.[11] In December 1941, a translation of *General Theory* appeared by economist Shionoya Tsukumo, who had graduated from Tokyo Commercial University and taught at Nagoya University. All seven thousand copies of the first printing of the translation quickly sold out, followed by an additional run of two thousand copies.[12]

Building on his earlier work on the relation of money to prices and business cycles, Keynes set out in *General Theory* to reconceive the causes of output fluctuations and the mechanisms of unemployment, the continuing scourge of the depression-plagued free-market economies of the mid-1930s. In the process, he worked to "throw over" many of the fundamental precepts that had prevailed in classical and neoclassical economic theory for the preceding century.[13] His point of departure was the classical theory of employment, which, he claimed, failed adequately to account for the intractable unemployment of the day, in which "the population generally [was] seldom doing as much work as it would like to do."[14] At the heart of the dilemma, Keynes maintained, was that fundamental principle of classical theory known as Say's Law, which held, according to the famous formulation, that all supply creates its own demand. That is, an increase in output would necessarily produce, through the incomes and wages derived from its production, the precise quantity of resources required for the consumption of that output.[15] In terms of employment, this translated into the notion that the price system in a free-competition economy tended automatically to produce full employment. Yet actual conditions provided prima facie evidence, Keynes said, that the theory of automatic adjustment was wrong. Say's Law was, according to J. S. Mill, "fundamental": "Any difference of opinion on it involves radically different conceptions of Political Economy." Without it, political economy had to explain, not only the laws of production and the laws of distribution, which it had been engaged in doing since the time of Ricardo, but also the problem of "how a market can be created for produce."[16] A disavowal of Say's Law raised the question of how a level of demand adequate to supply was to be secured, and it was precisely this question that Keynes proceeded to address in *General Theory*. He attempted to show that at fault in depressed economies and in the unemployment that accompanied them was not a glut of production—the long-accepted account of the problem—but insufficient demand.

In his attacks on orthodoxy, Keynes was not unique. He was participating in a broad current of dissatisfaction within the discipline of economics going back to the end of the Great War. Skeptical of "pure theory" and its failures to jibe with reality, many had turned to more descriptive economics. Setting in motion the so-called empirical revolution of the mid-twentieth century, institutionalists, especially scholars in the United States such as Mitchell and Veblen, had been producing a steady stream of economic and social data to show the ways in which orthodox theory failed to account for conditions in the real world, particularly in the unsettling cycles of booms and busts that had marked the history of capitalism. Nor was Keynes entirely alone in the sorts of theoretical solutions he sought to the classical dilemma. J. M. Clark, for example, had similarly pointed to a "chronic limitation of production owing to limitation of effective demand" as underlying the failure of economies to adjust automatically toward full employment. Yet it was only Keynes' attempt at a general theory that roused sufficient interest in the discipline to reexamine the classical assumptions from the ground up.[17]

Because interpretations of *General Theory* in Japan, no less than anywhere else, changed over time, there is some danger in providing a neat exegesis of the meaning of the book. All the same, two broad points may be made. First, Keynes seemed to explain the cause of what he called "involuntary unemployment," the possibility of which classical theory did not even admit.[18] Full employment conditions were not governed by some automatic adjustment of real wages, he said, but by aggregate demand (which itself was a function of the propensity to consume and the rate of investment). Second, Keynes offered a solution. The response to long-term unemployment should be, not to cut wages, which would only exacerbate the problem by decreasing aggregate demand, but to promote demand through a combination of lowered interest rates and government spending. Though *General Theory* dealt more with theory than practice, Keynes showed the possibility of new positive approaches to the disease of the era. By providing a theoretical basis for active governmental regulation of aggregate demand, he seemed to suggest that full employment might actually be achievable in the shaken economies of the capitalist world.[19]

Although receiving mild and unimpressed reviews at first, *General Theory* soon spawned an entire literature in which economists around the world debated, extended, and refined the theoretical innovations Keynes had essayed. It was eventually deemed a "revolutionary" achievement by most in the neoclassical tradition, perhaps most loudly so by Keynes' liberal votaries in the United States, who themselves would influence Keynesian studies in postwar Japan.[20] The research agenda and analytical approach that Keynes laid out formed the theoretical basis for much of what came to be known as macroeconomics and largely set the research program for that branch of economics until at least the beginning of the 1970s.

Keynes continued to be the subject of some interest in Japan as the war in China dragged on and the war with the United States began. For the scholars, students, and bureaucrats reading *General Theory*, however, the going was not easy. Given Keynes' departures from the standard postulates of political economy, it was a difficult work. What was more, even sympathetic readers pointed out, the exposition was often confusing, lines of argument were not fully explicated, the relation between the work and existing theory was poorly explained, and there were errors in analysis.[21] Keynes' early readers in Japan seemed united in recalling the Herculean labor required during their student days to comprehend *General Theory*. The influential postwar economist of the Ministry of Finance and the Development Bank (Kaihatsu Ginkō), Shimomura Osamu, recounts having to "wage a desperate fight" to digest the arguments of the book.[22]

As the strictures of militarism pressed in on free thinking during the 1930s and 1940s, there were fewer and fewer avenues by which to exchange ideas. The fate of Marxists as the years of "national emergency" wore on is well known. But it was not only Marxist economists who suffered under the boot of the "defense state," for liberal, non-Marxist economic thought, too, was often marginalized during the 1930s. In addition to discussions of Keynes, research did continue into such neoclassical fields as national income and the marginal utility economics of Jevons, Walrus, and Menges. And while many scholars of liberal economics larded their volumes with the obligatory nationalist cant of the day, the substance of their work usually remained at a remove from the issues of war and empire and unaffected by wartime orthodoxies.[23] Yet as ultranationalist views gained ascendancy in the academy, allegedly foreign ideas were greeted with rising suspicion. The distrust of both capitalism and communism that had animated earlier critics of liberal or Marxist economics from the turn of century now found new purchase as intellectuals sought to define indigenous approaches. Liberal economists were harassed by nationalist ideologues for their lack of concern with the state, as when Nakayama Ichirō's *Pure Economics (Junsui keizaigaku)* of 1933 became the subject of right-wing attacks.[24] Some liberal theorists such as Kawai Eijirō found themselves among the group otherwise comprised of left-wing Marxian economists dismissed from their academic posts in the infamous university purges of the late 1930s. Even without outright repression, the classical tradition of economic theory played a relatively marginal role in the national debates on Japanese political economy that rose to a crescendo during the renovationism of the "New Order" movement of the late 1930s and early 1940s. Those were the days, rather, of corporatist and national socialist ideas, of the controlled economy and five-year mobilization plans.

After the war, economists, students, and the educated elite in general hastened to familiarize themselves with wartime developments in the field of economics abroad. It was difficult to acquire foreign materials until around 1950, however, and the libraries at key institutions such as Tokyo University, which had a special reading room set up with entire runs of foreign journal back-issues from the years of the war, attracted eager readers. The American cultural center in Hibiya, Tokyo, and others like it located in large cities throughout the country also became important sources of information.[25]

This thirst for the latest foreign ideas was accompanied by an explosion in economics writing from myriad perspectives. Intellectuals in the various wings of Marxism resumed their analysis of Japanese capitalism with new vigor even as the problem of apostasy in leftist ranks during the war muddied the question of ideological purity. Neoclassical economists also came to the fore, jostling shoulder to shoulder with Marxist scholars. Analysts in the infant statistical field of econometrics scrambled for resources. Keynesianism now moved more and more to the center of focus. This welter of voices, welcomed after the repression of the war years yet nevertheless confusing, prompted vocal consideration by economics professionals of what new order might emerge in their field. Marxians, labor scholars of the Social-Policy School, neoclassical economists, statisticians, and others came together in the pages of prominent volumes such as *Keizaigaku no shōrai* (The future of economics) of 1946, and in the booming general-interest magazines, to examine how the discipline of economics might be reconstructed.[26]

A prominent participant in this scrutiny of the field was Sugimoto Eiichi, an econometrician at Tokyo Commercial University. In 1947, he proclaimed that a synthesis was possible between Marxist and what he termed *kindai riron keizaigaku* (modern theoretical economics), by which he generally meant all non-Marxist, liberal economics in the classical and neoclassical modes.[27] To scoff, as liberal economists did, that Marxism was not a science but a religious faith was unhelpful, he argued. Likewise, the refusal by Marxists to employ methods developed in bourgeois economics was, Sugimoto colorfully suggested, as foolish as refusing to use an American-made tractor on a Soviet-style collective farm.[28] Indeed, he went on to say, Marxist thought should not be categorized as separate from the rest, but ought rightfully to be seen as a member of the broad family of "modern economics."

Although Sugimoto's thesis sparked a robust debate, his proposal for a rapprochement met with a generally chilly response from members of the profession on both sides of the theoretical divide, who found it difficult to surmount their differences. These had existed during earlier years, of course, but seemed to grow more, not less, marked as the postwar period progressed and exciting new developments attracted attention in the respective camps. While predominantly academic in nature, the Sugimoto debate also reflected larger battles over the role various schools of thought would play in social and economic policy after the war. As debate over the "two economics" extended into the 1950s, it signaled a cooling of the hopeful cooperation that had reigned among economists and other experts of disparate persuasion during the initial days of postwar reconstruction. Generally tense relations between Marxists and liberal economists would continue to characterize the postwar decades well into the 1970s. Indeed, the Sugimoto debate was father to the term that rhetorically codified this divide: neoclassical economics became *kindai keizaigaku* (modern economics). Although Sugimoto had originally employed the term *kindai riron keizaigaku* (modern theoretical economics) to denote the non-Marxist tradition, the word "theoretical" was soon dropped by those participating in the debate in a sort of shorthand that tended to obscure some of the finer points of Sugimoto's argument and the theoretical work of Oscar Lange on which Sugimoto had drawn. This elision was reinforced by Sugimoto himself, who, in response to critics of his proposal, released a volume of essays in 1949 the title of which, *The Basic Character of Modern Economics (Kindai keizaigaku no kihon seikaku),* underscored the currency of the shortened phrase.[29] Although the phrase "modern economics" *(kindai keizaigaku)* was not unknown before the war, it had been used only sporadically. By the mid-1950s, writers had further abbreviated the phrase in Japanese to simply *kinkei,* and this had become a commonplace in the professional and public lexicons to distinguish non-Marxist from Marxist economics.[30]

As with all tidy labels, needless to say, this one in some ways described an artificial division. Neither Marxism nor "modern economics" was a unitary school of thought, and in practical application the boundaries between them could sometimes be messy. This seemed especially true in the crisis years after the war when it was difficult to apply easy labels to those shaping policy and public perceptions. Marxians who had earned their stripes in the debates of the 1920s, for example, many of whom, such as Arisawa Hiromi and Inaba Hidezō, had been arrested for their leftist sympathies, now promoted inflationary policies that were anathema to labor and played instrumental roles in determining the government's industrial development strategy. On the other side were liberal economists and economic bureaucrats who readily adopted the categories of Marxist analysis in their work after the war.

As scholars and journalists used the term *kinkei* with increasing frequency during the early postwar years to stake out the boundaries between Marxist and non-Marxist thought, Keynesianism quickly rose to occupy the center ground of *kinkei*, "modern economics," thought and research. Classical and neoclassical economists at Tokyo Commercial University (soon renamed Hitotsubashi University), Nagoya University, Osaka University—the last of which for the first time set up an economics department after the war independent from that of law and politics for the expressed purpose of pursuing *kinkei* studies—and others turned with enthusiasm to research into *General Theory* and Keynes' earlier work.[31] The years after the war saw an outpouring of publications on Keynesian theory and practice, both scholarly treatments and those intended for a wider educated audience. The thirst to understand Keynes' ideas prompted the release of primers such as the famous *Guide to Keynesian Economics (Keinzu keizaigaku kaisetsu)* of 1946 by Kito Nisaburō, translator of Keynes' *Treatise on Money*.[32] Introductory essays like the four-part series by *General Theory* translator Shionoya Tsukumo that appeared in the important economics journal *Ekonomisuto* (Economist) also proliferated, and exegeses, commentaries, and reviews of the structure and theory of *General Theory* itself soon filled the pages of scholarly and high-end general-interest periodicals.[33] Each of the subthemes of Keynes' thought—interest, employment, investment, savings, money volume, and national income among them—attracted the scrutiny of economic and public policy writers, as did the problem of locating Keynes in relation to classical theory. Yet another genre of essays examined Keynes the man and the scholar. Following the American Lawrence R. Klein's use of the phrase in his enormously successful 1947 book of the same title, Japanese intellectuals after the war, along with their counterparts in the United States, Britain, and Europe, were soon speaking of a "Keynesian revolution" *(Keinzu kakumei)* in economic thought.[34]

The "revolutionary" rise of Keynesianism within so-called *kinkei* thought was fed by several initial factors. The first was Finance Minister Ishibashi Tanzan's well-known inflationary policy speech (known as his *"Zaisei enzetsu"*) to the Lower House of the Imperial Diet on July 26, 1946. Ishibashi, who as a writer and editor of *Tōyō keizai shinpō* had followed Keynes' work from several decades before, was seeking political support for the Yoshida cabinet's attempt to spur industrial recovery through expansionary fiscal measures. Inflation was rising rapidly, however, and critics—SCAP among them—warned that Ishibashi's easy credit and spending policies were exacerbating the problem. Defending his strategy, Ishibashi noted that current economic thought supported expansionary policy as a means to jolt a slumping economy even if this meant creating a budget deficit, and he cited Keynes by name. The speech became emblematic of sharp divisions over inflation and, indeed, over larger strategies for economic recovery in general. Ishibashi's prominent use of Keynesian theory instantly placed the British economist at the center of the recovery debate, at least for the time being, and served to increase public awareness of his ideas.[35]

The first government white paper on the economy, released by the Economic Stabilization Board in 1947, though a more technical statement of Keynesian-influenced ideas than Ishibashi's speech, worked to similar effect. The author, Harvard-trained economist Tsuru Shigeto, made dramatic use of concepts suggested by Keynesian theory, as well as the aggregate techniques of Simon Kuznets and Colin Clark, prominently displaying the potential of these approaches in the public policy arena. The release in 1948 of *Foundations of Economic Analysis,* the groundbreaking textbook by Harvard economist Paul Samuelson, also supported the postwar vogue for Keynes. It was the first text to package Keynesian precepts for elementary-level students, presenting the case for a mixed economy in which government spending and taxation would play an important role in assuring economic health. It was available in photostat copies in Japan almost immediately upon its release, and it became the defining text for bourgeois economics education during the postwar period.[36] In addition, there was the fact that neoclassical marginalist economics was not yet so widely studied as it would later become in Japan and therefore presented less of an intellectual and institutional obstacle to the introduction of Keynesianism than might otherwise have been the case.[37]

Here, as the stature of the volumes by Klein and Samuelson suggest, the role of American economics was large. The broad new currents changing the face of economics—the empirical revolution, aggregate analysis, and the "new economics" in general—together with U.S. geopolitical hegemony after the war and the far-ranging cultural influence that followed in its train, increasingly positioned the United States as the metropole of theoretical production. As U.S. experts brought national accounting methods, econometrics, and new approaches for promoting prosperity in general to the task of reconstructing Europe and occupied territories after 1945, the importance of American economic knowledge and its practitioners grew in Japan. American economic thought, broadly defined, had not been without some effect in Japan in prior times. Taylor's theories of scientific management had sparked considerable excitement among factory managers during the teens and twenties, and the concepts and approaches of Taylorism later informed the insistent, if variously defined, industrial rationalization movement of the 1930s.[38] The literature on rationalized government administration and coordination with the private sector identified with Herbert Hoover had also exerted a shaping force on writers and would-be reformers of Japanese political economy during earlier decades, many of whom— improbable as it may sound in light of the dominant images of the United States and Japan during the post–World War II period—saw the United States as a model for cooperation between government and business.

Yet, for all of this early fascination with American fashions in management, the suddenly preponderant weight that American economics, now in the formal academic sense, held in postwar Japan represented a marked shift away from earlier European sources of inspiration. Many Japanese writers of political economy early in the modern period, in the 1870s, had taken Manchester School liberalism as a starting point. By the late nineteenth century, they often drew on ideas associated with economics in Germany such as Listian visions of "national economy" and the New Historical School. Various forms of socialism also gained strength by the century's start, and by the 1920s Marxism exercised formidable influence. As the Second World War receded into memory, however, the cream of Japanese students destined to become professional economists or economic bureaucrats were now sent to do their stints abroad at Harvard, Chicago, and other U.S. universities rather than those of Britain, Germany, or France. Beginning in the 1950s, the American Fulbright scholarship program funded overseas studies in the United States, with subsequent influence of considerable proportion on elite opinion.[39]

By the late 1940s, an almost febrile preoccupation with Keynesian economics had gripped economists, bureaucrats, and policy analysts.[40] Many, in fact, came to call the period from the end of the decade into the early part of the 1950s the "Golden Age" of Keynesian research in Japan. So strong was the surging Keynesian tide that publishers, assured of robust demand, scrambled to publish anything on Keynes they could put between covers. Works by the chief names in the field—Shionoya Tsukumo, Koizumi Akira, and Uchida Tadao—tumbled off the presses one after the other.

In addition to Klein's exegesis and Samuelson's textbook, other widely read U.S. works and their translations also helped spread the Keynesian word by the late 1940s: Dudley Dillard's *The Economics of John Maynard Keynes* (1948) and Seymour Harris' *The New Economics: Keynes' Influence on Theory and Public Policy* (1947) as well as his *Saving American Capitalism: A Liberal Economic Program* (1948). Official Japan took particular interest in Harris' *The New Economics*, which included essays by Harris himself, a Harvard economist and one of the key promoters of Keynesianism in the United States, as well as a Who's Who list of other economists and policy intellectuals.[41] Bank of Japan staff prepared a translation of the text, and it was released in three volumes between 1949 and 1950.[42] Harris and Alvin Hansen, another Harvard economist, were widely discussed along with Lawrence Klein in media and scholarly treatments in Japan of political economy during this period, both for their interpretations of Keynes himself and their own works based on Keynesian analysis.

One of the chief venues in which the ideas of these American Keynesians were introduced to the economics profession and bureaucratic circles was Tsuru Shigeto's *Keizai kenkyū* (The economic review), the new monthly publication of the Economic Research Institute of Hitotsubashi University. Inaugurated in 1950 at the height of the Keynes boom, the journal was intended from the first to promote the very sort of empirical and macroeconomic techniques for which Keynes provided such compelling theoretical support. In the first few issues, the journal reviewed Harris' *Saving American Capitalism,* a book by Hansen on monetary theory and fiscal policy, and another volume on employment and public policy published in Hansen's honor.[43] Understanding of Keynes among Japanese economics professionals was at least in part shaped by journals such as *Keizai kenkyū* as they presented these American boosters' arguments about the theoretical importance of Keynes, his revolutionary relation to classical tradition, and the far-reaching policy significance of his work.

By the turn of the decade, few in the academic profession and in the economic bureaucracy were unaware of the theoretical and policy implications of Keynes and the *General Theory.*[44] At the same time, only a minority were now pure Keynesians in a programmatic way. Economics training in the universities was still decidedly Marxian. Those who entered bureaucratic agencies, usually out of university faculties of law rather than economics, received economics training on the job, which was, to be sure, more and more colored by Keynesian and macroeconomics approaches. Even so, policy during these years of *General Theory* fever was not remade overnight according to a grand Keynesian blueprint. The particular problems that obtained to the tasks of reconstruction and recovery in Japan—reparations, wartime industry guarantees, deconcentration, *zaibatsu* dissolution, and so forth—had dominated the initial postwar years. Key government initiatives to restart the economy during the first half of the Occupation were based, not on pure Keynesian theories of interest and employment, but on old-style industrial policy in the mode of wartime mobilization. The strict retrenchments of the Dodge Line beginning in 1949, moreover, were anything but fiscally Keynesian, based as they were on orthodox beliefs in the primacy of budgeting balance and black ink.

All the same, Keynesian theories and the remedies they suggested spoke in practical ways to the range of anxieties that underlay the "diagnostic vision" of Japanese capitalism being articulated just as the romance with Keynesianism was beginning to sweep political-economic thought. Keynes' emphasis on the questions of aggregate demand and the mechanisms of employment dovetailed with the position that the postwar economy needed to ensure certain minimum levels of material well-being and to promote the formation of a middle class. If aggregate demand was now recognized as the engine of healthy economies, then it was only a short step to the argument that, in order to achieve recovery and return Japan to economic independence, policy makers should place new emphasis on improving national standards of living and on the welfare of a middle class with some measure of purchasing power. One could now theoretically show how old

nostrums about the welfare of the nation must go beyond the pious pronouncements of the past and be pursued as fundamental to economic performance. Keynesianism provided the theoretical tools to link the particular critiques of Japanese capitalism articulated by reformers after the war to
general economic laws. It seemed to validate postwar criticisms of Japan's
political-economic past and reformist visions, however hazily conceived,
of the future direction of reconstruction. The emergence of the loosely
related constellation of goals and ideals that raised the question of national
standards of living cannot be explained by the rise of Keynesianism alone.
The powerful domestic attacks on what were considered the historical
peculiarities of Japanese capitalism were already converging on a similar
set of values and approaches, on complementary social goals and remedies
to the problems of Japanese capitalism. Nonetheless, although direct lines
of affiliation are difficult to trace between the tenets of Keynesian theory,
their reception and deployment in Japan, and critics' prescriptions for
Japanese capitalism, it is clear that growing interest in Keynesian thought
reflected the shifting intellectual climate on the question of Japanese capitalism and at the same time supported the critical diagnoses. What's more,
Keynesianism seemed to offer hope to critics that the long-range goals of
the diagnostic vision might be placed within the practical grasp of analysts,
reformers, and decision makers.

The mutually supporting affinities between Keynesianism and the diagnostic vision were made especially apparent in the program of the American
interpreters of Keynes who were so widely read in Japan. Though assailed by
American conservatives and big business as anticapitalist, Keynesian theory
had been on the rise in the economics profession in the United States during the war years. While Keynes' policy recommendations varied, his generally consistent emphasis on promoting consumption to achieve economic
expansion merged with older strands of American thought that sought to
replace the concept of scarcity with that of the "surplus economy" and to
champion mass consumption as the road to social progress. Once the war
was over, Keynesian economists and their allies among the ranks of liberal
political advisers, social critics, and journalists set their sights on applying
the lessons of Keynes and the idea of the prosperity economy to postwar
America. The defining element of this political program was the slogan
of "full employment," which represented an expansive vision rejecting the
older ideal of production and price stability and embracing the goals of
growth, ever-increasing prosperity, and "continuous full employment, year
after year."[45] Only by ending "wasteful thrift," by expanding civilian consumption and getting money into people's hands so they could spend it on
the ever-multiplying wares of America's producers, these liberals believed,
could such a continuously prosperous economy be set in motion.[46]

Perhaps most important of those who took up the banner of the abundance economy were the Harvard economists Seymour Harris and Alvin Hansen, who were so central to the reception of Keynes in Japan. Harris' *Saving American Capitalism* of 1948 laid out the liberal postwar agenda in the boldest possible terms.[47] Hansen, surely the most powerful economist in Washington circles at the time, argued for full employment policies based on a high-consumption economic model.[48] This view was reinforced by an interpretative stance on the part of Hansen and compatriots such as Klein and Samuelson that saw in *The General Theory* an explication of national income rather than liquidity preference, which had dominated early interpretations. Keynesian-style approaches found formal, though circumscribed, expression in the U.S. Employment Act of 1946, which expressly acknowledged government responsibility for promoting the highest possible levels of employment, production, and purchasing power.

The Employment Act thus pointed up a significant element of the American liberal vision: the belief in government's responsibility for ensuring prosperity. American Keynesians believed that the Keynesian revolution had ushered in a new era in the economic functions of government. To the traditional notions of freedoms they added the freedom from abject want, which it was the duty of government to protect through manipulation of macroeconomic forces. This view was reflected in their confident push for planning to achieve greater consumption and full employment. Among other strategies, Seymour Harris emphasized fiscal measures, stating that the key to full employment was government spending. The so-called neoliberal view of active government expressed by American writers provided further intellectual legitimacy to Japanese demands for minimum guarantees of social well-being.[49] While the doctrine of fiscal interventionism found a greater number of adherents among Japanese economists in the academy than in government agencies, Keynesian theoretical support for official measures to regulate cycles held an attraction for those, whether inside or outside government, seeking technocratic guidance of the economy.

By the middle of the 1950s, Keynesianism had become a mainstay of the college curriculum, and non-Marxist departments focused considerable energies on Keynesian research through the 1950s and 1960s. Meanwhile, popularizers such as Itō Mitsuharu and Hayasaka Tadashi packaged Keynes' ideas for a wider public during these years of high growth. Yet Keynesianism and its research agenda did not by any means supplant other arenas of economic investigation. Marxist economics flourished in the academy during these same years, and the often considerable divide that widened between the two schools was captured in the early postwar debate about the relation between them: as one writer starkly phrased it in 1948, the problem was believed by many to come down to a choice, "Marx or Keynes?"[50] Neoclassical economics, with its stress on free markets and microeconomic forces, also rose to new prominence in Japan during these decades and constituted a significant portion of *kinkei* pursuits.

Many postwar academics reserved the right to draw on a range of traditions. Yet, while by no means a singular orthodoxy, the postulates of Keynesianism were rapidly becoming part of the common ground of economic thinking. The many prominent economists involved in shaping public perception and official opinion during these years provide a good example of how specialists increasingly turned to an eclectic toolbox of theoretical analysis that now included Keynesian principles and techniques. Nakayama Ichirō, the Tokyo Commercial University professor who had used *The General Theory* as an undergraduate text beginning in the 1930s, had already been known for his neoclassical work in general equilibrium economics and Schumpeterian cycle theory. In his postwar writings and his influential work on the Central Council on Labor (Chūō Rōdō Iinkai) and as the vice president of the Japan Productivity Center (Nihon Seisansei Honbu), for example, Nakayama made use of Keynesian concepts and aims while maintaining a neoclassical focus on microeconomic factors. (The coexistence of these two approaches in Nakayama's thinking reflected the largely amicable relations between neoclassical economics and Keynesianism until the 1970s, the two forming a so-called neoclassical synthesis in Japan like that of United States, Britain, and much of the rest of the world.) Similarly, Tsuru Shigeto, author of the first economic white paper, who has been mentioned here for his promotion of empirical aggregate economics and whose *Keizai kenkyū* did much to propagate Keynesian style research, all the while also embraced Marxist methods and critiques. Indeed, some of the most significant of the university-trained economists active in the postwar public arena (Arisawa Hiromi, Inaba Hidezō, Wada Hiroo) were able to draw on the Marxism in which they had been trained as well as neoclasssical and Keynesian concepts. This fact works against overly dramatizing the divide between Marxist and *kinkei* economics.

As Keynesianism was changing the discipline of economics, it also contributed to the postwar political environment. At a level different from the strict application of technical theory, Keynesian economics lent momentum to a complex of ideas for which it came symbolically to stand. It helped to create a perceptual context in which newly crafted remedial approaches to capitalism were gaining ascendancy. It gave new economic expression to the democratic and reformist political sentiments of the day,[51] in which calls for protections against the vicissitudes of the economy and for standard-of-living and employment guarantees were invested with greater urgency.

Full Employment, "Particularly for Japan"

As they increasingly explored the significance of Keynesian economics for their battered country, Japanese observers in the early postwar years seized upon the hope offered by the idea of full employment. Indeed, the principle of full employment was being touted by powerful leaders of opinion even before the Keynesian boom was in full swing. Not just the stuff of academic treatises, the ideal of full employment immediately found its way into the policy debates on recovery and reconstruction. Though conditions seemed to offer little encouragement to those seeking evidence in Japan of the "abundance economy" so heralded in the United States, labor and business groups, government ministries, leading economists, and politicians embraced the goal of full employment (*kanzen koyō, furu empuroimento,* or *kanzen kadō*) and placed it at the center of their recovery plans.

One of the most powerful figures in the campaign to promote this goal was Ishibashi Tanzan, who, in May 1946, became finance minister in the first cabinet of Prime Minister Yoshida Shigeru. He signaled this commitment to a full-employment strategy in his financial policy speech to the Diet of July 26, 1946. While, as noted earlier, the speech nominally centered around Ishibashi's tactical analysis of postwar inflation—an interpretation for which he credited Keynesian theory—full employment was its strategic organizing principle. Ishibashi explained that the economy was saddled with a ruinous combination of involuntary unemployment and idle productive capacity. Conditions were so desperate that over one-third of the current budget, he noted, was slated for unemployment relief of various kinds.[52] The government must solve these crippling problems as swiftly as possible: full employment (*kanzen kadō,* which Ishibashi also glossed with the Japanese transliteration of the English, *furu empuroimento*) should be, he maintained, the "paramount goal of economic policy."[53] The *kanzen kadō* phrase used by Ishibashi was an expansive one that referred to the full employment of all the various factors of production, including not only labor but capital and physical plant as well. Ishibashi's strategy was thus to link the problems of collapsed industrial production and acute unemployment in a comprehensive program to restart the economy.

Since assuming power in May 1946, the Yoshida cabinet had pursued an expansionary financial policy that sought to maintain a liberal flow of capital into the economy through a combination of easy credit and spending measures.[54] Over the sharp criticism of SCAP and domestic fiscal conservatives, the government doled out war guarantee payments, war contracts, and veteran pensions, and printed new currency even as prices charted precipitous rises and deficits mounted. Indeed, as Ishibashi himself catalogued in his presentation before the Diet, government budgets were awash in red ink in 1946, registering shortfalls of nearly 50 percent.[55] Consumer prices had risen by 295 percent between September 1945 and March 1946.[56] Even with a currency conversion in spring 1946, prices began shooting up again by the fall of that year. Yet Ishibashi remained unswayed. To achieve full employment of labor and factories, Ishibashi insisted, it was necessary that the liberal fiscal policies of the Yoshida cabinet be continued, even if this meant producing further red ink in government accounts. Fears of inflation and an unexamined clamor for balanced budgets were wrongheaded, Ishibashi claimed: "I don't believe that such a balanced-budget approach can be called sound financial policy *(kenzen zaisei)* as long as conditions prevail in which the numbers of unemployed are swelling and much of the productive elements of the economy are idle."[57] Indeed, contrary to the orthodoxies of the past, budget deficits and an increase in the volume of currency in circulation were, Ishibashi explained to the Diet, now recognized by "currrent economic theory" as indispensable measures for achieving full employment.[58]

Ishibashi had, in fact, proselytized for an expansionary fiscal policy and a full employment strategy even before he joined the cabinet ranks of the Yoshida administration. Launching an attack earlier that year against attempts by the Shidehara cabinet to control inflation through monetary controls (in the Emergency Financial Measures [Kin'yū kinkyū sochirei] of February 1946), Ishibashi downplayed the public hue and cry over "inflation, inflation." He argued that it was a mistake to assume that all price increases constituted inflation by definition. He insisted that a rise in prices could only be considered "bad inflation" if it rose faster than currency supply, and he urged critics to endure short-term deficits for the sake of an early recovery.[59] Ishibashi returned to this theme in his July 1946 speech to the legislature, noting that Keynes had said that "true inflation" occurred only under conditions of full employment. While such conditions had perhaps obtained during the war, now, in contrast, a situation of "underemployment" *(andā enpuroimento)* prevailed.[60] In his overall policy guidelines Ishibashi gave little indication of attempting to reverse economic stagnation by addressing the issue of aggregate demand per se. Nonetheless, his formulation of the problem of recovery owed much to the "full employment" ideal inspired by Keynesian economics, even when it did not necessarily make overt use of Keynesian technical accounts of economic slumps. Further, in the connections he saw between prices, deficits, and his full employment goal, Ishibashi sought to legitimate his expansionary strategy by explicitly pegging it to Keynesian principles that he portrayed as part of a new economic mainstream.

While posing what seemed to critics in the teetering economy after the war a newly acute danger, deficit financing as an object of contention was not a discovery of the postwar period. The inflated budgets of Finance Minister Takahashi Korekiyo during the middle years of the 1930s had caused considerable consternation among fiscal conservatives.[61] As a journalist at the time, Ishibashi too had offered a defense of the principle of government deficits that owed little to any technical principles of Keynes, on one occasion agreeing with Takahashi himself that, "as long as production follows along in equal measure," then "fiscal expansion up to a point should not be an impediment" to economic output. Ishibashi went on to liken the nation to a stock company, and thus deficit spending to the raising of corporate capital.[62] As finance minister himself, Ishibashi's postwar belief in the usefulness of government deficits was not necessarily dependent on the formal explications of Keynes' *General Theory*. His postwar use of Keynes does, however, underscore the powerful theoretical buttress the British economist provided to those like himself who were convinced of the efficacy of liberal fiscal strategies.

Ishibashi's advocacy of a full employment program reflected an intense international focus on employment as pivotal to the success of postwar economies. The debate over the Employment Act in the United States and its final passage in 1946 underscored a widespread shift in orientation away from the principle of business-cycle stability, which had long governed economic policy, and toward the maximization of output and employment. The hopes of Alvin Hansen and other assertive Keynesians notwithstanding, the U.S. Employment Act did not prescribe compensatory, counter-cyclical spending as the means by which to achieve these outcomes, nor did it endow the president with the executive authority and administrative structures to employ such fiscal devices. It did, however, require the government generally to promote the full-employment objectives spelled out in the law. Even where critics could not support institutionalization of fiscal intervention as a means to guarantee specific employment levels, there was widespread agreement in the United States that active measures had to be taken to avoid a predicted postwar downturn and the return of the moribund conditions of the 1930s.

As industrialized nations turned to constructing the economic foundations for peace, the emerging full-employment paradigm galvanized political rhetoric and action to varying degrees in other World War II belligerents as well. By 1944, in fact, the government of Great Britain had already declared, in its "White Paper on Employment Policy," its responsibility for maintaining a high level of employment after the war. The report used Keynesian aggregate demand analysis, although, as in the later U.S. Employment Act, it did not commit the government to Keynesian deficit financing.[63] The maximization of employment also became an organizing principle for postwar international institutions from their very inception. In a 1943 report on the transition from a war to a peace economy, the United Nations listed the complete elimination of all but frictional unem-

ployment as one of its top priorities, and the new international body continued actively to promote full employment through the postwar years.[64]
The representatives of the forty-four nations who met in Bretton Woods,
New Hampshire, in July 1944 to hammer out a new global financial system
similarly declared that a key goal of the postwar order would be promotion
of adequate employment in member nations, thus transforming employment from a domestic to an international problem. The worldwide focus
on employment was greatly shaped by a common acknowledgment of what
were understood as the failures of post–World War I arrangements adequately to promote healthy recovery. Anxiously mindful of the lessons for
war-ravaged countries provided by the World War I experience, Japanese
observers placed great emphasis on the reconstruction proposals of the victorious powers. There was scarcely a treatment of employment in Japan
immediately after the war that did not rehearse, and generally endorse, the
litany of employment declarations made in the United States and Britain,
at Bretton Woods and the United Nations.[65]

Against this international backdrop, economic specialists in Japan joined
their voices in a chorus asserting that a strong employment policy must play
a central role in recovery plans at home. As did the Central Committee
on Employment Policy (Chūō Shitsugyō Taisaku Iinkai), many declared
full employment "the key" to postwar recovery or, as more broadly stated
by others, even "decisive to the fate of postwar capitalism."[66] Their theoretical accounts of Keynesian full-employment economics and its application to Japan tended to lend a measure of analytical support to Ishibashi's
full-employment platform. The demobilization of what were estimated to
be over thirteen million Japanese (nearly fourteen million if women were
counted), the return of hundreds of thousands from the former empire,
and an accompanying surge in unemployment after the war only made the
need for a vigorous response seem more urgent.[67] In April 1946, the Labor
Ministry estimated that upwards of six million Japanese were less than fully
employed, and of this number, over one and a half million were believed
to be completely without work.[68] Economist Hijikata Seibi of Tokyo University, the critic of Marxism who had been a pioneer of national income
accounting during the 1920s and who had urged a reorganization of economic institutions along national socialist lines during the 1930s, was one
among many prominent economists after the war who turned his attention
to the theory and practice of full employment. As chief author of an extensive 1947 evaluation of Keynes' prescriptions and the courses charted thus
far in the Allied nations, Hijikata declared of special importance, "particularly for [Japan]," the attainment of high levels of employment given the
extraordinary challenges of Japanese recovery and the joblessness since the
end of the war. Although conditions in Japan differed from those in Great

Britain or the United States, and although the form that measures would take would certainly also differ, "nevertheless, the goal of full employment must," Hijikata dramatically pronounced, "no matter what, be achieved."[69]

The Politics of Employment

The sometimes indistinct nexus between the diagnostic vision of Japanese capitalism and its prescriptive expression in full-employment proposals proved capable of accommodating a variety of intellectual persuasions, even those with apparently quite different levels of commitment to the political cause of full employment. Communists and left-wing socialists, it is true, were frequently suspicious of Keynesian full-employment theory. They saw it, at best, as a postwar sop to the masses made restless by the privations of war and, at worst, as a potentially powerful means by which capitalism might further delay the eschatological implications of its own contradictions. "Up to now," wrote one Marxist economist several years later, summing up the perceived postwar challenge Keynes presented to basic Marxist beliefs, "we have not actually had any theory that required the overturning of Marx's assertion that capitalist economies would inevitably become socialist societies." This unswerving tenet of the Marxist faithful, however, was "by Keynes being threatened for the first time."[70] Simultaneously, communists declared that recovery should be based on full employment. The banner of full employment was more unproblematically attractive to less radical leftists and to progressive reformers in general because it offered correctives to the continuing problems of the capitalist system and to the specific difficulties of the Japanese economy. It presented a complementary macroeconomic dimension to the rise of an assertive unionism and to picket-line battles for enterprise-level democracy. The leftist economist Ōuchi Hyōe, for example, who spoke out prominently on the issue of wage and welfare protections for labor in the unsettled days after the war, endorsed the international movement spearheaded by the United States to ensure high employment even while acknowledging the element of economic self-interest that lay at the heart of this American strategy and remaining dubious of the ability of capitalism to overcome its internal problems on a permanent basis.[71]

The principle of full employment also found favor among scholars at such bastions of bourgeois economics as Hitotsubashi University precisely because it was remedial, not revolutionary, in its rhetoric. Balancing a neoclassical belief in the essential equity of free markets with a sense that new techniques were required to steer postwar capitalism successfully beyond the rocky shoals of past decades, such scholars as Nakayama Ichirō displayed in their support for full employment strategies a brand of practical Keynesianism. Nakayama, one of the most unstinting of Keynesian promoters after the war, produced a steady stream of writings on full-employment theory and policy. He marveled that full employment was so readily achieved during wartime but had thus far remained out of reach in peacetime economies: "Why is it that an economy that was able easily to achieve full employment when its purpose was destruction is now threatened by huge unemployment when its purpose is construction?" This was the question, Nakayama suggested, to which postwar humanity was bound to respond.[72] In the "new economics" he found appropriate tools to apply the lessons of planning to the employment problem while remaining true to capitalist principles.

"Full employment," like "democracy" and "peace," was the sort of watchword of the times for which all could register support with little political pain. Labor, of course, was prominent in calls for full employment as a postwar goal. Much of resurgent labor energy after the war was absorbed in the fight for workplace equity. Yet shop-floor battles for living wages and a worker voice in corporate management were also expressed as part of encompassing demands for assertive national employment guarantees. As new political parties jockeyed for power, many endorsed the full-employment agenda. Those drawing on the support of labor, of course, did so most vociferously. The Communist and Socialist parties declared full employment as part of their platforms directly after the war. So also did the centrist Japan Progressive Party, led by Machida Chūji. The Japan Liberal Party of Hatoyama Ichirō and Yoshida Shigeru favored unemployment protections of various kinds, but stopped short of an early commitment to full employment, believing that the operations of the free market would suffice.[73] With Ishibashi as finance minister and then head of the ESB, however, the Yoshida government was on record as supporting full employment as a long-term goal, though fundamental tensions remained between the party's laissez-faire philosophy and the activist, and in some ways interventionary, approaches pursued by "brain trust" advisers and leading economic policy makers such as Ishibashi and Arisawa. Organizations in the business world seeking active cooperation with the moderate wings of labor also embraced full employment. The Keizai Dōyūkai, for example, included an expressed commitment to employment as part of its democratizing campaign for "modified capitalism" *(shūsei shihonshugi)*. It declared that employers ought to place considerations of employment ahead of efficiency of capital but at the same time emphasized the responsibility of labor unions, acting through the management cooperation councils *(keiei kyōgikai)* at the heart of the entire Dōyūkai program, to do their part in the race to improve labor productivity.[74] Such support for the ideal of full employment likewise appeared in the pronouncements of Dōyūkai-affiliated organizations designed to achieve recovery through joint capital-labor initiatives. The Kokumin Keizai Kaigi, for example, a three hundred–member committee of representatives from business, labor, political parties, agriculture, forestry, engineering, and academia sponsored by the Dōyūkai-led Economic Recovery Council (Keizai

Fukkō Kaigi), declared its commitment to a recovery founded on the principle of full employment in 1948.[75]

The employment problem was also a key object of concern in the increasingly energetic planning activities of central authorities. Long-range planners in the Economic Stabilization Board, the dominant economic agency during most of the Occupation period, consistently declared their commitment to full employment. Zen Keinosuke, the first head of the ESB, announced soon after the formation of that organ that his aim was "to secure conditions of full employment,"[76] and this orientation was reflected in key ESB programs across the Yoshida and Katayama administrations. The famous priority production strategy for early industrial recovery, a brand of shock therapy that sought to funnel scarce resources into several strategic industries during 1947 and 1948, was seen by the ESB Coal Committee that devised the plan, as well as other official planning groups, as the best means to address unemployment over the long haul even as it promised to spark layoffs in the short term.[77] Full employment was even more expressly a target in the ESB's five-year Economic Recovery Plan of 1948, which had been several years in the drafting.[78]

The steady drumbeat on full employment notwithstanding, confidence was rarely high. While the full-employment vision was a common motive behind much of economic planning, postwar circumstances also prompted more sober evaluations of the possibility of achieving such a lofty goal in Japan. Keynes' theoretical formulations, analysts pointed out, assumed that poverty existed in the midst of abundance. Given that productive capacities in Japan were all but destroyed, they often cautioned, perhaps Keynesian understandings were based on "an economics not directly applicable to the current Japanese economy."[79] Indeed, the overall Keynesian concern with regulating—that is, promoting—consumption (aggregate demand) in order to foster higher employment often seemed inappropriate: "What we have to reform is not consumption, but in fact production," declared Arisawa Hiromi, a conclusion echoed in the identification by planners of "insufficient production" as the key characteristic of the postwar collapse.[80]

Other economists also publicly doubted Ishibashi's idea that since full employment did not exist, more capital could be thrown at business to achieve recovery even as prices rose. Surplus labor could not be absorbed, because "in the post-defeat economy of Japan today...other obstructions" of an elemental nature—lack of food and resources—prevented it.[81] Nakayama Ichirō himself believed that Japanese capitalism was not "mature"—was even "backward"—compared to that of the Western powers. It would thus be expected in some ways to correspond to a Pigouian model of full-employment self-adjustment rather than a Keynesian model of demand management.[82] Planners in the Economic Stabilization Board busy charting the Economic Recovery Plan (before it was shelved in the face of the Dodge Plan) and later Occupation-period plans continually pointed out that the fundamental recovery goals of raising labor productivity and pursuing full employment seemed to stand at cross-purposes with one another.[83]

Faced with these acknowledged theoretical and practical difficulties, planners such as Arisawa and Inaba in their work on the Recovery Plan Committee cast the issue in terms of long-run aims versus the near-term requirements for recovery. While never completely abandoning their commitment to full employment, they proceeded on the assumption that rapidly rising population and increasing foreign competition meant that the first stage on the road to economic independence was to boost labor productivity and promote the appropriate distribution of labor in the context of structural shifts in industry.[84]

These caveats about the applicability of full employment to Japan were the product of a blend of theoretical exegeses and accepted ideas about the special circumstances of Japan. A similar brew of analytical concerns also fed vitriolic debate over the best means to pursue the long-run ideal of full employment in the immediate context of the post-defeat crisis. Until the Dodge Plan at the close of the decade put an end to the question altogether, the Ishibashi-Yoshida line on expansionary fiscal and monetary policies to promote industrial recovery and "full employment" was the subject of bitter controversy. The left spoke out against them as anathema to the real interests of labor. They blamed loose financial policies for spurring galloping inflation. This hurt workers, for prices had risen far faster than wages. Ōuchi Hyōe, a strong voice for full employment, was also a leading critic of funneling capital to corporations by early postwar administrations and the deficit financing that supported it. Socialist and labor leaders believed that stabilization must be achieved immediately through an end to out-of-control currency expansion strategies.[85] Ishibashi, and such influential planners in the powerful ESB as Arisawa, thought that real stability would only be attained over time through the recovery of heavy industrial output.[86] General Courtney Whitney of SCAP's Government Section and Major General William Marquat of the Economic and Scientific Section tended to agree with advocates of currency stability and engaged in early battles with the Shidehara and Yoshida governments to win an end to wartime indemnity payoffs to corporations. Even after these payments ended in spring 1946, however, SCAP was forced to continue to pressure the Yoshida government to put the brakes on expansionary approaches to recovery until the issue was finally settled by Dodge's arrival in 1949.[87] Even as all agreed that stability and full employment were the end goal, sharply different notions persisted about how to achieve the necessary recovery to get there.

Doubts about the appropriateness of the goal, the tactical means to pursue it, and the appropriate timetable for achieving it aside, full employment remained an important animating ideal for those working for recovery. It linked the old nostrum that the productivity of the economy should "benefit the entire nation" to an attractive social program boasting theoretical legitimacy, international imprimatur, and specific economic yardsticks. By the immediate postwar years, older conceptions of unemployment as an industrial problem were being largely replaced by the recognition of it as a social problem. The question of full employment was increasingly understood as an indication of the "morals *(moraru)* of a national economy," observed one diverse group of important economists considering the postwar future of the discipline of economics. For them and others, the new prominence of the employment problem in economics revealed a sea change in the basic orientation of economics toward a common "humaneness" (variously *hūmaniti* or *ningenteki tachiba*), expressed in the rise of Keynesianism within "capitalist economics" and in the attempt to effect recovery on a world scale within "socialist economics."[88] Full employment was thus an early rallying cry that injected what were identified as the population and employment dilemmas of Japan into substantive debates on postwar recovery. It would remain the professed if sometimes hedged goal of long-range planners for the duration of the Occupation period and on into the 1950s.

Despite reservations about the strict applicability to Japan of full employment as theory and as practicable goal, such prescriptions for its pursuit as Ishibashi Tanzan's were part of a general, if uneven, movement in policy circles from the end of the war somehow to address the employment challenge in a concerted fashion. With the full-employment ideal as a conceptual backdrop, planners groped—within the constraints imposed by post-defeat economic circumstances and the uncertainties of Occupation policy—to formulate a programmatic response that was equal to the crisis. Running through official pronouncements and strategies during the initial years of the Occupation period, even where full employment was not the expressed aim, was an insistence on not merely ad hoc responses or general appeals to expansionary financial approaches but targeted "permanent measures" to alleviate unemployment.[89] Bureaucrats, cabinets, and their economist advisers moved in some measure to translate concern with unemployment into a brand of active policy that placed emphasis on maximizing employment levels.

Throughout his attacks on earlier administrations and his justifications of his own expansionary fiscal measures, Finance Minister Ishibashi Tanzan advocated just such an active employment policy as part of his "production first" line.[90] He called for a strong program to combat unemployment, not merely through a passive system of financial relief, but by means of an active campaign to put the able-bodied to work. While allowing that some might unavoidably lose their jobs due to rationalization of wartime industries and believing himself that there ought to be limits to the financial assistance

paid out to unemployed individuals, Ishibashi proclaimed that the government should play a significant role in the pursuit of full employment.[91] As
has been seen, he believed that this should be in part accomplished by
releasing adequate capital into the market for industrial recovery. On top
of this, he added, government should utilize its fiscal powers to fund vigorous work programs. Quite improbably in the postwar context, he cited
the example of post-1929 Nazi Germany as a model of a successful full-
employment program that relied on public works to achieve an impres-
sive economic recovery.[92] Nurturing a faith in the ability of government
to construct more assertive protections, Ishibashi envisioned an expanded
response to the old problem of employment, one that relied less on old-
style, reactive unemployment relief than on continuous efforts to ensure
work opportunities.

A desire to pursue such approaches was not confined to Ishibashi. Even
where their perspective was less overtly associated with Keynesian-style principles, officials began to move, even before Ishibashi's tenure as finance
minister, to erect public-works programs to employ the idle, alongside a
series of other employment security measures. The Ministry of Public
Welfare signaled the nature of the solutions that would be sought in the
coming years when in November 1945, citing unemployment as a "huge
obstacle in the path toward construction of a New Japan," it wrote cabinet
guidelines directing that civil works reconstruction projects be included as
a key element of unemployment policy.[93] The next month, the Shidehara
government created the Unemployment Policy Council to unite proposals
from all official quarters and, in the first attempt at a truly comprehensive
program, adopted guidelines by February the following year for emergency
employment measures that featured a commitment to expand public works
projects.[94] The Occupation issued a directive later that spring that underscored this emphasis on public works, insisting that all construction projects be planned with a view to employing as many out-of-work laborers as
possible.[95] The Occupation announced at the time that the government
should plan to put as many as 1–1.25 million people to work.[96] The focus
on employment programs that soon emerged among Japanese planners
was not prominent enough, in fact, for some New Dealers in SCAP. Norbert Bogdan, an economic adviser in the Economic and Scientific Section
of SCAP, had urged the Special Survey Committee to revise their report to
place more emphasis on active public works employment rather than passive relief measures alone.[97]

Although the government never met SCAP's ambitious goals for employing people in public works, considerable resources were committed to work
programs in the early postwar years. The amount spent on various public
works measures increased rapidly, more than doubling from 6.19 billion
yen in 1946 to 14.38 billion in 1947, and then more than tripling again to

48.17 billion in 1948. While these increases were logged in the context of rapid inflation, it is significant to note that spending on public works also charted steep rises when expressed as a percentage of the total general budget over these years, nearly doubling from 5.4 percent in 1946 to 10.4 percent in 1948.[98] It is estimated that 476,000 people per day were being put to work on all public works projects by 1947. This number rose to 533,000 in 1948, and jumped by almost another 100,000 the following year.[99]

In December 1948, SCAP announced its Nine-Point Economic Stabilization Program, signaling a shift to tight fiscal and monetary policies. Facing the prospect of sudden deflation, labor analysts anticipated a sharp increase in layoffs, euphemistically referred to by the Yoshida government as "personnel adjustments" (jin'in seiri), and moved to step up employment programs.[100] The month following the February 1949 arrival of Joseph Dodge, the Detroit banker charged with overseeing the newly conceived recovery program, the government formed a new Unemployment Policy Council (Shitsugyō Taisaku Shingikai). The council was headed by Arisawa Hiromi, the economist who before the war had been associated with the Rōnō faction of Marxist economists and who by 1949 had already, in his participation on the Special Survey Committee of the Foreign Ministry and the Coal Committee of the Economic Stabilization Board, assumed a primary role in determining recovery strategy. Business and labor representatives also served on the council, which reported to the prime minister and made periodic recommendations on the direction of employment policy. Despite the cuts in government expenditures that accompanied the Dodge Plan, the council promoted public works projects as an important response to rising unemployment.[101] In May 1949, an Emergency Unemployment Measures Law (Kinkyū Shitsugyō Taisaku Hō) was passed to "deal with the occurrence of large numbers of unemployed and absorb as great a number of the out-of-work as possible in unemployment measure works projects and public works projects...."[102] The law expanded the government's public works programs and formalized the use of new statistics to measure the effect of works projects on total unemployment levels. In addition, it directed the minister of labor to carry out ongoing research on employment conditions nationwide and to propose timely responses when unemployment threatened to rise.[103]

The creation of the Unemployment Council and the Emergency Law reflected a consensus on the need to move toward more regularized and responsive programs as a permanent feature of policy initiatives. As a gesture in this direction, a new division of responsibilities in regard to official employment programs was codified by the legislation. Previously, public works projects had been all classified as such, whether conceived specifically as make-work programs for the unemployed or more generally as projects for public construction, and they had been run by the Economic Stabilization Board. The new measure recognized what were now defined as "unemployment measure works projects" and "public works projects," the former falling now under the jurisdiction of the Ministry of Labor, the latter remaining under the Economic Stabilization Board. The requirement that the Ministry of Labor provide employment plans, for example, followed from this new arrangement, and the increased ability of the ministry to regulate employment measures was intended to improve the effectiveness of works projects to absorb those who had been laid off and to raise the flexibility of official responses to changing conditions. To facilitate these efforts, public agencies were now required to submit forecasts of labor needs to the ministry, and funding for unemployment works projects would now be dispensed separately.[104] Based on the Emergency Law, the amount spent on public works programs swelled by two-thirds to 100.78 billion yen between 1949 and 1950.[105] And the number of workers employed each day in the newly designated unemployment measure works projects specifically designed as targeted employment projects more than tripled from under 50,000 persons per day in 1949 to just under 150,000 in 1950.[106]

The public works approach was not the only element of the postwar response to unemployment. Programs moved along two fronts. The public works strategy carried forward by the Emergency Unemployment Measures Law of 1949 was designed to operate in coordination with the earlier Employment Stabilization Law (Shokugyō Antei Hō, 1947), which was written to create a progressive system of employment practice safeguards and counseling. It created public employment security offices that performed a variety of job placement activities and through which laborers on public works projects were to be placed. Another aspect of what may broadly be described as the postwar public relief system was the Subsistence Aid Law (Seikatsu Hogo Hō, 1946), which provided direct financial allowances for those in desperate need. Finally, an unemployment insurance system was created for the first time in 1947 (Shitsugyō Hoken Hō).[107]

The insurance system represented a great victory for postwar labor, the culmination of decades of legislative effort. Postwar public works relief, by contrast, had antecedents. Public employment security offices had been among the first official responses to the emerging social problem of unemployment beginning in 1911, and these were expanded in the 1920s.[108] The government introduced public works projects to employ the idle (known as unemployment aid work) as economic conditions deteriorated for many in the mid-1920s. This employment aid work system was expanded in the wake of the Depression in the beginning of the 1930s. Such public work aid steadily decreased, however, with the emergence of the military spending boom that followed the Manchurian Incident until it was rendered nugatory by the succession of labor draft ordinances of the labor mobilization system inaugurated in 1937.[109] Postwar public work programs drew on earlier "aid work" models, short-lived as they were, and the experience of wartime labor mobilization. By the time of the Emergency Unemployment Measures Law, however, they were conceived as a central element in a comparatively concerted and continuous effort to maximize employment.

By the postwar years, unemployment was a familiar problem. As in other industrialized economies, it had largely disappeared with wartime mobilization. In general, however, unemployment had been a continuing subject of economic debate and a menace to livelihood and health for many in a rapidly urbanizing Japan from at least the early years of the twentieth century. Similarly, few of the solutions sought during the Occupation years were previously untried. The controversial and short-lived expansionary financial approaches associated most closely with Ishibashi's tenure as finance minister had found earlier expression in Japan during Takahashi Korekiyo's leadership in that same post during the 1930s. While it is true that work programs were expanded and refined after the war, they too were based on older models.

Yet although the postwar responses to unemployment emerged out of a longer history, the intense anxiety that unemployment engendered after the war and widespread insistence on systemic remedies reflected a collective assumption that the new economy must swiftly address the threat. The belief was broadly held that prescriptions must go beyond the grudging workplace protections and industrial paternalism of past eras. This determination was highlighted in the liberalized climate for labor organization, for example, and in the extension of aid through the new unemployment insurance system. It was also reflected in the wide currency of the ideal of full employment directly after the war.

Not all of the full-employment language of the time should be taken at face value, of course. It was often used interchangeably with equally unassailable terms such as "stability" and "production recovery" as little more than a catch-all slogan. And for all the rhetoric, much of what was advertised as employment policy was only indirectly so. A great part of planning and policy amounted not so much to employment policy as industrial policy, related but not coterminous. As in the past, Occupation-period initiatives—both early recovery policy and those during the post-Dodge years—often remained as concerned with the problem of social administration as with the possibility of the elimination of unemployment.[110] Though inspired in general by Keynesian principles, the language of full employment rarely implied the macroeconomic attempt to regulate demand for labor. Although the loose Ishibashi-style tack taken by governments before the Dodge Plan operated through fiscal and monetary means, it betrayed a traditional supply-side approach that saw the problem of recovery in terms of large industry. Expressions of support for the goal of full employment by the ESB's Coal Committee were at the same time couched in the stark language of inputs and outputs, which again tended to subordinate the question of employment to the primary concern with industrial manufacturing.

Yet the desire for a more fully articulated employment policy after the war, while perhaps not translated into macroeconomic manipulation according to Keynesian theoretical precepts, did reveal a small but important shift in the orientation of national economic conceptions. The recurring problem of employment was assigned a stronger valence in the aftermath of defeat and collapse. The sense of what constituted an appropriate response was evolving, spurred by spreading interest in Keynesian analysis, the shining allure of ideas about the new age of prosperity economies, and a world focus on employment as an international question. An important role for government was now more generally accepted. As elsewhere, it was understood that the government should be responsible, if not for ensuring specific employment levels, then at least for safeguarding employment by more concerted initiatives to provide counterbalancing programs to the forces that threatened to fuel joblessness. Encompassing employment policies rather than reactive unemployment Band-Aids, it was broadly believed, should become a key attribute of state action.

The employment dilemma was argued as part and parcel of a host of welfare guarantees emerging out of the diagnostic critiques of Japanese political economy. It occupied central ground in intense postwar examination of the ways in which economic reconstruction might address what were identified as long-standing distortions within Japan's capitalist system. Although full employment was often less a concrete policy than a rhetorical device, the rhetoric itself took on new political weight, reworking basic assumptions about the economic directions of the nation.

Massive long-term unemployment was generally averted in the immediate postwar years despite the worst fears and unarguably desperate conditions. The Ministry of Welfare reported in the fall of 1947 that of the 400,000 people that it counted as completely out of work, only 230,000 expressed the desire to find a job. Employment offices during the first several years after the war also indicated that employers seeking job applicants consistently outnumbered registered job seekers.[111] Work programs helped to ameliorate the problem in the initial years. Returnees and those suddenly left without work when war industries closed also found employment directly after the war by returning to the countryside. Yet conditions tended to mask the problem of what analysts later labeled the "incompletely employed." Unemployment, moreover, began to rise after implementation of the Dodge Plan in 1949. In fact, the numbers of those with no work at all would increase, not decrease, into the 1950s, even as recovery gathered steam. The union setbacks suffered by labor beginning in the latter half of the Occupation period aside, the ongoing problem of semiunemployment, a rapid rise in total population and the size of the labor force into the 1950s, coupled with the language of full employment, would keep the employment issue at the forefront of reflections on the Japanese economy into the following decade and beyond. While long-range planners were dubious about the near-term possibility of full employment in Japan, it remained the professed goal of the central planning projects of the ESB and its later incarnations during the immediate postwar years and into the 1950s.

CHAPTER 4

Knowing Growth

K eynesian theoretical and political concerns continued to influence
the directions of modern economics research and analysis in Japan
beyond the Occupation years. With full employment and its attendant concerns as animating ideals, the research program of economics ramified in a multitude of technical directions, extending the aggregative
empirical techniques of macroanalysis that had begun to excite attention
in Japan in the context of postwar recovery. Japanese "modern economists"
in and out of government participated with their colleagues around the
world in pursuing such new subfields of statistical research as econometric
modeling, input-output analysis, business-cycle forecasting, and consumption demand analysis. These built on the macroeconomic concerns, the
quantifying agenda, and even the data of national income accounting, and
were intimately interconnected with the evolving practice of that statistical
branch of economic knowledge. For economics professionals, these statistical approaches promised to illuminate the relation between government
expenditures, capital investment, income, savings, and demand in the quest
for maximum employment and stable economic performance.

National income accounting itself continued to undergo refinements.
Analysts extended their uses of the procedure to get at the constituent
components of total income and the dynamic relation between them. They
applied national accounting as a method for determining the structure of
economic flows, the relationship between economic sectors, and the distribution of income. They saw it as an indispensable empirical tool for testing
their theories against the statistical pictures they were able to construct of
economic processes. Increases of national income, moreover, provided a
convenient yardstick to measure what was defined as the material progress of
economies. Taken together with the host of related statistical tools of the new
economics, national accounting offered technicians useful ways to define
the factors that determined this material increase. Thus, scholarly and official campaigns to extend and standardize national accounting and related

techniques, as well as to produce the comprehensive statistical data sets they required, contributed to a sharpening focus within the field on the question of the overall growth of national economies across time. These technocratic tools helped to define the parameters by which growth was known and, at the same time, served as the barometers by which it was monitored.

National accounting as pursued by the EPA, moreover, had assumed a more visible role in economic goal setting by the mid-1950s, and it increasingly shaped the vernacular language in which public discourse on the national economy was conducted. Beginning in 1954, the national income reports produced by the EPA assumed the status of white papers and were presented annually to the Diet. The findings of these reports figured prominently in the EPA's more famous annual Economic White Papers, which were best-sellers and extraordinarily influential in setting the growthist terms of national debate.

Within the professional field, economic growth became the object of intense theoretical definition and empirical documentation as never before in the decade roughly beginning with the end of the Occupation in 1952, and economics professionals in Japan, along with those from abroad, jumped to the task of applying the analytics of growth to Japanese experience. As the "miracle" of rapid recovery—and, soon enough, the "miracle" of post-recovery high-speed expansion—became a central theme of national self-images of the postwar years in Japan, fascination with theories of growth took on a particularly obsessive tenor there: economists pursued the latest ideas about the determinants of national income; technocrats publicly debated the technical assumptions separating competing predictions for GNP expansion; bureaucrats and industrial representatives traveled to the United States to divine the secrets of American prosperity; and official plans for growth at home replaced one another in quick succession.

The employment of new macroeconomic statistical procedures in the pursuit of growth supported the ideal of economic planning in Japan even as it changed the complexion of these plans. The increasing tendency to define the national economy as an abstraction in terms of its growth represented a refiguring of the economy as an object of study and control. Even as this process of growth was often understood in teleological terms that seemed to assume natural patterns of modern expansion, the task of ensuring its stable progress was increasingly cast as the rightful and necessary aim of state management. The very definition of economic policy was thus expanded during the decade to include the macroeconomic regulation of the national economy as an organic whole. In practical terms, this meant the wedding of the planning ideal to the goal of growth. Central authorities conceived of plans in terms of their long-run GNP forecasts, and their growthist vision of the economic future greatly contributed to the shared language in which national purpose by the end of the decade was articulated.

Growth as History, Growth as Future

Contributing to the rising prominence of GNP in public discourse and its elevation as the premier benchmark of economic expansion and national progress was an energetic burst of research on the long-run economic performance of nations. Conducted in the economics departments of universities the world over, these comparative studies sought to understand the factors that increased macroeconomic activity over time, and they were built upon historical series of national income and product statistics. Simon Kuznets, in fact, the economist most responsible for the national accounting rules and forms by which GNP was computed, led the way in accumulating historical income statistics and applying them to explorations of the dynamics of past economic increase. Kuznets was a pioneer of national income studies as a research member of the National Bureau of Economic Research in New York from the late 1920s, a position he held until 1961. The Social Science Research Council in the United States formed a Committee on Economic Growth, which Kuznets chaired for two decades after the war and which was a prime sponsor of growth research around the world. Such new organizations as the International Association for Research in Income and Wealth also helped direct the energy of the field into growth theory and empirical research. Growth studies programs and institutes sprang up in economics departments of major universities in the industrial nations. The question of national growth thus had become a central element of macroeconomic research the world over by the 1950s.

The ferment over the question of growth represented in some ways a return to older subjects in the history of political economics. As iconically represented in Adam Smith's *The Wealth of Nations,* formal economic thought during the classical period of the field, as it evolved into a distinctive discipline in Western countries, concerned itself with the laws of motion governing economic progress, a condition typically associated with expansion of material output. Several aspects set apart the revisiting of these concerns in the twentieth century, however. As has been well noted thus far, growth theory and the new economics in general were propelled by aggregative quantitative measurement on a scale unknown in earlier eras. The role of government, moreover, was now generally seen in a different light. Growth for Smith was a faceless force, and his treatise was an argument for state laissez-faire. Macroeconomics and growth theory, by contrast, on the whole accepted that government might have a significant role to play in assuring increases in national wealth.

The 1940 release of *Conditions of Economic Progress* by Colin Clark, an economist considered by many as the "coauthor" with Kuznets of the statistical revolution in national income beginning in the 1930s, was initial evidence of what would become an explosion of interest in the field in economic growth. A variety of approaches emerged over the course of the following decade. Kuznets played a leading role among scholars who sought to document common patterns in the historical experience of different countries. He claimed to identify long-run cycles of growth (Kuznets cycles), and his characterization of what he termed modern economic growth became a standard point of reference. W. W. Rostow, another significant theorist of historical growth, presented a stage theory revolving around the concept of what he called the "take-off into sustained modern growth," a process driven by "leading sectors" of national economies. Others, led by R. F. Harrod and E. D. Domar, extended Keynesian theoretical concern with the relations between investment, savings, and income to explore the principles by which to manage maximum growth. Whereas Keynes had focused on the short-period determinants of national income at a specific point, Harrod showed the dynamic processes governing the increase of income over the long period.

As researchers busied themselves identifying the morphology of growth and the conditions for "take-off," economists in Japan set out to apply the principles of growth analysis to the case of Japanese history. The Institute of Economic Research (Keizai Kenkyūjo) at Hitotsubashi University, part of the prestigious system of national universities, became center ground among Japanese academics pursuing the research agenda of growth theory. Underlying much of the work being pursued at the institute was the project to trace the historical trajectory of growth from the beginning of the Meiji period. The foundation of this research was the production of time-series data sets on all the various aspects of growth theory analysis—capital accumulation, investment and savings rates, consumption, national income, and so on. This required culling the documentary record and processing data to fit the questions and parameters of growth theory. The postwar work of the institute produced much of the empirical record utilized in growth analysis thereafter and remains key to conceptions today of the historical movements of the Japanese macroeconomy. Academicians associated with the institute were a dominant force in the literature and thinking on modern growth.

The Institute of Economic Research was founded in 1940 at Hitotsubashi, then Tokyo Commercial University, as the East Asian Economic Research Institute and was charged with conducting comprehensive research on the countries of the region on which Japan was staking its imperial future. With the end of the war, "East Asia" was dropped from the name, and the mandate of the institute was broadened to include "all the nations of the world." By 1948, the scholarly work of the institute had been broken down into disciplinary divisions that highlighted the centrality of the macroeconomic empirical studies with which it would be most closely identified. In addition to a division each for research on the United

States, Europe, the Soviet Union, China, and Japan, separate divisions were created for statistical research and "special issues," including national income studies.[1] In 1949, Tsuru Shigeto was elected the head of the institute. Under his leadership, it became the home of the boom in empirical research within "modern economics."[2] It was Tsuru who had experimented with macroeconomic methods in the first economic white paper of the Economic Stabilization Board in 1947 and who, the year after his selection for the top institute post, sounded a call in the pages of the institute's new organ, *Keizai kenkyū* (The economic review), for the inauguration of an era of hard-nosed factual analysis of actual economic conditions.

The economists in the national income and the individual country research units at the institute remained closely tied to theoretical and empirical research in growth theory around the world. Through *Keizai kenkyū*, the institute examined conceptual developments and accounting conventions and publicized the literature of the field to the economics profession in Japan through the 1950s and into the 1960s. Members of the institute established particularly close relations with leading lights of the field in the United States. Young scholars who had studied macroeconomic approaches in the States began returning in the early 1950s, some such as Shinohara Miyohei later to join the institute faculty. As chairman of the Committee on Economic Growth at the Social Science Research Council for two decades, Simon Kuznets maintained frequent contact with the institute; W. W. Rostow of MIT similarly worked with Tsuru during the Japanese economist's tenure there. These early connections with U.S. researchers led to ongoing collaboration into the next decade. Beginning in the 1960s, the Economic Growth Center at Yale University, which in 1962 became the home of the International Association for Research on Income and Wealth, cooperated with the Japan Economic Research Center to sponsor studies of Japanese modern development in which institute members were engaged. The Japan Economic Research Center was a private organization founded by Ōkita Saburō in 1964 of which Tsuru and Ōkawa Kazushi, another prominent member of the institute growth research team, served as directors.[3]

While the statistics and national income groups within the Institute of Economic Research worked on statistical and empirical developments in macroeconomics, it was Study Unit no. 1 on the Japanese economy that launched the massive project in 1951 to assemble the multitude of component data sets required to compute growth across the modern period. Other related endeavors were not unknown. In 1947 the Economic Stabilization Board (ESB) first attempted statistically to link the prewar and postwar periods by producing income figures for each year from 1930. Releasing the results in 1954, the Economic Deliberation Council (Keizai Shingichō), which was the diminished successor to the ESB, wrote that peaceful postwar recovery required such time-series income data to serve as a forecasting compass. It noted that the United Nations had lent support to such a claim when it recently announced that the 1938 income figure for each nation would serve as an analytical benchmark.[4] Several years later, the Economic Research Institute (Keizai Kenkyūjo) in the Economic Planning Agency continued these attempts by bureaucratic officials to construct a history of growth in Japan prior to the war, seeking to extend their findings at least back to the end of the First World War.[5] Hitotsubashi economist Yamada Yūzō's *Nihon kokumin shotoku suikei shiryō* (Sources on the estimation of the national income of Japan) of 1951, a pioneering effort that assembled and modified older income estimates covering the years between 1878 and 1942, was a more comprehensive precursor to the ambitions that Hitotsubashi's Institute of Economic Research had for historical data.[6]

But the monumental Hitotsubashi project, begun soon after the publication of Yamada's work, became the towering standard in the field.[7] This collaborative work occupied teams of economists, known informally as the "Hitotsubashi group" (although not all participants were members of the university), for the better part of thirty years. In fact the Japanese Economy Study Unit no. 1 at Hitotsubashi continued this earlier work through the end of the century, conducting empirical research on the prehistory and history of economic takeoff in the nineteenth century.[8] The final results of the initial statistical compilation, known as the Long-Term Economic Statistics (LTES), were issued in a series of fourteen volumes totaling upwards of four thousand pages beginning in the 1960s.[9]

From the statistical compendia of the LTES group sprang an entire generation of research projects on historical growth. Scholars sought to resolve their data into identifiable patterns and relate Japanese history to conceptual models of growth. Their findings appeared in a series of landmark monographs. After an interim report presented to the International Conference on Income and Wealth in 1953, institute member Ōkawa Kazushi and several colleagues released *The Growth Rate of the Japanese Economy (Nihon keizai no seichō ritsu)* in 1956.[10] This became the standard reference on the topic and paved the way for other works over the next two decades. Meanwhile, the staff at the institute expanded as the historical growth project progressed.[11] The institute also worked with other scholarly associations at home and abroad to mount conferences on growth. By the mid-1950s, publications by the institute on the charting of growth and related macroeconomic analysis had been awarded a "Cultural Advancement Prize" by the *Mainichi* newspaper, reflecting the significance with which the questions it addressed were invested by the intellectual elite of the time.[12] As the high-growth decade of the 1960s wore on, economists affiliated with Hitotsubashi and other institutions also turned to applying the techniques of growth theory and their accumulated statistical knowledge to explain change during the postwar years.[13]

Japan was a favorite object of comparative study among growth researchers outside of Japan as well. The initial report of the Hitotsubashi group appeared in English in 1953 as part of *Income and Wealth, Series III*, edited by Milton Gilbert. The Social Science Research Council in the United States, with Simon Kuznets as chairman of the Committee on Economic Growth, showed early and continued interest in the case of Japan.[14] Kuznets himself was a regular research visitor to Japan. He participated in both the conferences on Japanese growth sponsored by the Japan Economic Research Center (1966 and 1972) and was chairman of the publication committee responsible for a one-volume synopsis of the LTES series.[15] A conference on growth theory organized by the International Economics Association resulted in *The Economics of Take-Off into Sustained Growth*, a 1963 volume edited by Rostow that featured a piece by Tsuru Shigeto analyzing the applicability of the concept of "take-off" to Meiji Japan.[16] As the LTES group was getting under way at Hitotsubashi, Harry Oshima of the United Nations Statistical Office evaluated the various historical estimates of national product in Japan at the Conference on Economic Growth held in New York City in April 1952.[17] American scholarly and philanthropic institutions were avid supporters of growth research in Japan, frequently funding English translations of Japanese studies, for example. The Rockefeller Foundation partially supported the work of the LTES project, and the Ford Foundation helped sponsor studies such as *Japanese Economic Growth* by Ohkawa and Rosovsky.[18]

The interest of philanthropic foundations in the formalization of national income statistical series underscored the rising status of income and growth research during the 1950s and 1960s. It also showed the level of international interest in Japan as a developmental model by which to test new theoretical precepts on the wealth of nations. To be sure, many other nations were also the subjects of study. In fact, the idea of producing historical income data for as many nations of the world as possible was a basic thrust of the Kuznetsian program. But in the powerful success story of its emerging economic miracle, Japan seemed to be a particularly attractive object of scholarly enquiry. There was the appeal of the storybook plotline—from military defeat to economic victory, from vanquished fascist enemy to capitalist stronghold and ally. And there was also the easy assignment to Japan of the familiar role of earlier years, though now cast in economic terms stripped of the explicit geopolitical rivalries of the past, as the model of the successful non-Western modern nation. The national past of Japan during the modern, and even early modern, periods was now essentially retold as the story of the growth of GNP and its attendant macroeconomic measures. The unfolding story of the postwar years became only the latest and most dramatic chapter in the longer narrative of modern growth by which economists and historians had begun to recast the previous century of Japanese history. Indeed, the key to explaining what was by the mid-1950s already being dubbed the "miracle" of postwar recovery seemed precisely to lie in this historical record of past growth only now just discovered.

As academicians charted the historical record of growth, others in official arenas turned in the 1950s to the task of prognosticating its future course. Analysts in the Ministry of Finance and the Economic Planning Agency, in particular, prominently applied the concepts and methods of growth theory to their macroeconomic investigations, beginning an intense focus on the task of forecasting GNP growth rates. Shimomura Osamu, a Ph.D. in economics who had a strongly Keynesian orientation and worked in the Research Department of the Ministry of Finance, became the central figure from the early 1950s in a nearly continuous series of debates about competing growth-rate projections and the mechanisms of growth in the postwar economy. Beyond the disagreements over their respective growth predictions, critics also contended over what rate of economic expansion was most desirable and the appropriate policy mix to achieve it.

Shimomura first caught the attention of bureaucratic economists and policy makers when in 1954 he argued for loose macroeconomic policies even as trade balances dipped into the red during the Korean War boom. He criticized the government's attempt to slow down economic expansion through strict monetary measures in 1953 and 1954, insisting that the trade deficit was an unavoidable but passing result of rapid growth that would work itself out as rising investments increased exporting capacity. Bottlenecks were inevitable when production expanded quickly, he argued. This did not signal a need to apply the brakes. The government should maintain a financial environment that encouraged the rapid investment needed to ensure that production at home would keep pace with demand.[19] Although there was general concern at the end of the Korean War that the best days of the postwar economy might be over, Shimomura did not see the war boom as only a temporary fluke. He maintained an elemental optimism about the great "productive capacities" of the Japanese nation.[20]

Shimomura's iconoclastic views were controversial.[21] But after the strong recovery mid-decade, he became sought after as an interpreter of the movements of the economy. He continued to sound the basic themes of his growth doctrine—famously so in the so-called inventory debate (zaikō ronsō) of 1957–58, in which he again fought calls for monetary strictness, made this time by the author of the EPA's Economic White Paper of 1957.[22] Shimomura held that a rising trade deficit in the wake of the Jimmu economic boom of 1956–57 was not the result of economic expansion that had "gone too quickly," as the white paper had declared, but rather of increases in import inventories.[23] These skirmishes over macroeconomic policy culminated in an intense exchange over the growth potential of the economy, expressed in GNP, that became a keynote of public discourse on policy and national purpose well into the 1960s. The controversy was occasioned by the formulation of the EPA's New Long-Term Economic Plan, ratified by the cabinet in 1957. Shimomura took issue with what he considered to be an underestimation by Ōkita Saburō, by now the head of the planning bureau in the EPA, of the potential for growth. In place of Ōkita's 6.5 percent growth rate, Shimomura audaciously predicted 10 percent annual growth over the term of the plan:[24] "The growth capacity of the Japanese economy has been strengthening by great leaps over the last two or three years," he wrote in 1959. "Caught in old habits of thought from the end of the war, we have been held captive by the prejudiced view that the economy of 1956–57 [during the Jimmu boom] was one of excess investment and excess growth," he continued. Japanese must dispense with the timid view, he wrote, that "economic development should not come in rapid jumps."[25]

The debates over Shimomura's exuberant claims for the Japanese economy owed much to fashionable modes of analysis within the field of growth theory. The arguments were carried out largely in the technical terms of ongoing controversies in the field: capital-output ratios, investment multiplier and consumption accelerator functions, and so on. While making use of the shared theoretical innovations of the field, debaters also consciously set out to delineate the particular logic of Japanese growth, and their arguments were rigorously constructed on the empirical record of recent years in Japan. Indeed, Shimomura's doctrines, seen as so inventive and particularly tied to Japanese experience, were considered a brand of economic thought all their own—"Shimomura Theory," it was dubbed.[26]

At the same time, Shimomura's and Ōkita's debate was also a local instance of ongoing developments within the field of modern growth theory the world over. Growth theorists less interested in historical patterns and more in the instrumental means to secure current expansion had come, through the Keynesian dynamics of Harrod, to focus on capital investment as the key to growth. Every unit of investment was believed to result in a specific additional increment of national output according to a calculable and regular formula—the capital-output ratio. As analysts claimed to derive regular ratios from their statistical analysis, the capital-output concept was increasingly viewed as a determinant law of economic expansion. Growth economists soon employed the ratios as a tool for forecasting rates of growth under specific conditions. Those, such as W. W. Rostow, whose interest lay in locating historical patterns of growth also borrowed the concept of capital-output ratios from scholars of Keynesian dynamics to use as a tool in nailing down the slippery concept of "take-off."[27] It was on this concept of a determinant relation between investment and national product that much of the Shimomura debates hinged.[28]

The preoccupation by the late 1950s with divining the potential for future growth demonstrated the extent to which the concerns and techniques of growth theory had permeated official domains of economic practice. As employed in the research departments of the government's economic agencies, capital-output ratios were not an academic question: instrumental ends followed from theoretical concepts. The ratio one believed obtained for current conditions would determine the potential for GNP growth that one could expect; the potential for growth one believed to exist would determine one's position on whether current rates of growth were sound or unsound—that is, whether the economy was "healthy" or "overheated." This in turn would affect one's view of the need for remedial action and the forms in which it should come. Shimomura's insistence, for example, on a loose financial stance was driven by his beliefs about the close relation between capital investment and economic growth.

Growth as a concept also began by those years to permeate wider public discourses on national affairs. Public opinion surveys of the time do not yield direct information on the level of cognizance or understanding of GNP or "growth" at the time. But growth suddenly seemed in the air everywhere, cast in specific terms of the increases in "national income" more and more present in the news and as it appeared in the national media in the debates among public economists about its future prospects. Discussion of the "growth" potential of the Japanese economy filled articles in national newspapers, economics periodicals, and the interpretative guides to the annual economic white papers produced under the auspices of the Economic Planning Agency. Articles reflected with wonder on the facts of actual growth rates of late. But more reflexive publications also appeared that treated the very terminology of growth as a subject to be actively taught to a reading public. Such primers as *Our Work and Livelihoods: An Easy-to-Understand Chat about National Income (Watashitachi no hataraki to kurashi: Wakariyasui kokumin shotoku no hanashi)* or *The Japanese Economy in Five Years: A Discussion about the Five-Year Plan for Economic Independence That Anyone Can Understand (5-nengo no Nihon keizai: Dare mo wakaru keizai jiritsu 5-kanen keikaku no hanashi)*[29] were perhaps not best-sellers, but these efforts by the Economic Planning Agency and public economists in other settings surely contributed to a widening understanding of the vocabulary of growth and to its naturalization among nonspecialists within wider political and social discourses.

Planning "Frameworks for Growth"

The ideological attempt by wartime technocrats to redeem the ideal of planning after defeat was accompanied by a scramble to reassemble an institutional apparatus by which a course to recovery could be plotted. By early 1947, the powerful Economic Stabilization Board had assumed leadership over much of the economy, and bureaucrats there applied their wartime resource allocation experience to the quandary of recovery. Under the direction of the ESB, the Katayama and Ashida governments first pursued the priority production plan for revival of key industries. Over the course of the next two years, the same technocrats who had been responsible for priority production, first under the Katayama, then the Ashida and second Yoshida cabinets, went on to formulate the long-term Economic Recovery Plan in its various drafts.[30] Meanwhile, in contrast to the momentary policy

FIG. 1. The title of this comic strip is "Professor Slapdash." Sign in first frame: "The Slapdash Economic Research Institute." Quotation in final frame, Professor Slapdash to reporter: "This according to my own research: I declare that national income has increased quite considerably." While Professor Slapdash's method of listening for rattling coins while shaking the prayer-offerings coffer at his local Shintō shrine may not have represented the high point of economic research at the time, the lampooning here of the many pronouncements and debates of the 1950s on the level of national income and GNP reveals the degree to which the vocabulary of growth had begun to permeate public discourse. Sagawa Miyotarō, "Dehoraku sensei," *Nihon seisansei shinbun*, no. 25 (Jan. 1, 1957): 5. Used by permission of Kobayashi Minako. [Author's note: My thanks to Misako Matsubara for her help on the possible etymology of "deho" within Dehoraku sensei's name.]

void at the end of the war, officials churned out a profusion of smaller plans aimed at targeted sectors of the economy.

With the start of the Yoshida cabinet in 1949 and then the reorganization of the ESB and the diminution of its powers after the end of the Occupation, however, much of the impetus for comprehensive planning was lost. Although priority production continued for a time under Prime Minister Yoshida Shigeru's watch after its initial ratification by the Katayama cabinet, Yoshida and his Liberal Party had never been dedicated supporters of central planning, regardless of the form.[31] In May 1949, several months after Joseph Dodge arrived in Japan to oversee MacArthur's Nine-Point directive on fiscal balance, Yoshida finally scuttled the five-year Economic Recovery Plan devised by Inaba Hidezō and the Planning Commission for Economic Recovery, dismissing long-term planning as "meaningless."[32] This sudden end to the plan, in which had been invested the labors of upwards of two thousand participants over two years, prompted Inaba, who had thrown himself into the postwar mission to prove the true potential of planning, to resign his position with the Recovery Committee.[33]

The demise of the plan marked the beginning of a general turning away by political officials, led by Yoshida, from planning on the ambitious scale of the Economic Recovery Plan until the middle of the 1950s. The general disdain with which Yoshida regarded technocratic ideals of economic management eviscerated early postwar enthusiasm for planning within key economic agencies like the ESB. The government never officially adopted the recovery plan, and no similar global attempt to draft a comprehensive blueprint for official action was undertaken until the middle of the next decade. Some projects intended to grasp the overall movements of the national economy did continue, it is true, even after the Dodge-Yoshida turn toward conservative orthodoxies on planning and finance. The ESB recrafted earlier work after 1950 to make projections about when economic self-sufficiency might be achieved in light of an expected scaling back of U.S. aid. This self-sufficiency projection was quickly made obsolete by the windfalls of the Korean War procurements boom, but work continued, in the face of rapidly changing conditions, to project industrial output and import-export balance requirements. After the Occupation ended, the Economic Deliberation Council (Keizai Shingichō), the short-lived and less powerful successor to the ESB, also prepared several reports outlining a drive for exports and projecting economic output for strategic industries and the overall balance of payments. These were designed essentially as supporting materials for applications to the World Bank for development loans.[34]

Yet surprising as it may seem given common images of planned government management of the postwar economy in Japan, such was the situation in the later years of the Yoshida governments that to officials in international organs pressing for planned developmentalism across the world, Japan appeared woefully lacking in a comprehensive vision of the economy. In reaction to an ESB report making the case for Japan's need for loans, Robert Garner, vice president of the World Bank, noted at the end of 1953, "So far as I can see, the Japanese government appears to have neither an over-all plan of any sort nor a specific plan [for] channeling capital into the most important sectors of the economy." When confronted with such criticisms, Garner reported, Japanese government officials insisted that they were only adhering to the principles of a free-market economy.[35] The planning documents produced by the council during this period amounted to no more than semiofficial statements of that agency; none were adopted as official policy.

With the end of the Yoshida era in 1954 and the merging of the Liberal and Democratic parties in 1955, however, there was a renewed focus on the task of crafting comprehensive long-term plans after the manner of the early recovery blueprints prepared by the ESB. This shift was signaled in July 1955 by the immediate changing of the name of the Economic Deliberation Council to the Economic Planning Agency under the cabinet of Hatoyama. The formulation, promotion, and coordination of long-term plans were, needless to say, the raison d'être of the EPA, functions outlined in the 1955 law establishing the agency. These responsibilities were largely the same as those assigned the Deliberation Council before it, only now the EPA was charged with the more active promotion of the plans within the different ministries.[36] The New Long-Term Economic Plan of 1957 that prompted the most famous Shimomura debates with Ōkita Saburō on growth was only one of a new generation of umbrella plans shaping popular conceptions of the economy and serving as a shared reference point for both officials and private enterprise alike. Between 1955 and 1960, three different Liberal Democratic Party administrations (Hatoyama, Kishi, and Ikeda) officially adopted as government policy a succession of three long-term plans, each superseding the one before.

By the time Hatoyama Ichirō and his Democratic Party attained the prime ministership in 1954, bringing an end to the Yoshida era, Japanese widely believed that they had completed the task of immediate postwar "reconstruction." The end of the period of recovery, however, engendered a good deal more fretting anxiety than has commonly been remembered in historical accounts of that time. With the rapid expansion that reconstruction eventually had made possible and the windfall boom brought by the Korean conflict both now over, familiar doubts about the economic viability of the nation returned. In this context of uncertainty, Hatoyama, who lacked Yoshida's philosophical antipathy to an expanded government role in the economy, was quickly drawn to the ideal of coordinated pursuit of national economic goals. Upon assuming office, Hatoyama not only saw to it that the Economic Deliberation Council took on, in its new "Economic Planning Agency" designation, a more explicitly planning-forward name, but he also issued a call to the staff there to prepare an extensive plan setting guidelines for the remainder of the decade with the goal of achieving a stable economy independent of foreign aid. In 1955, Hatoyama's Liberal Democratic Party established its own internal Economic Planning Committee, which worked with the EPA from the end of that year on the implementation of the plan the prime minister had ordered written.[37]

Hatoyama's directive for an economic plan and the release of the resulting Five-Year Plan for Economic Independence (Keizai jiritsu gokanen keikaku) in December 1955 marked the beginning of the heyday of the EPA and the planning craft practiced there. After the suppression of a great deal of the planning impulse during the Yoshida years, the ramp-up once again within the planning agency sparked a surge of professional interest in planning theory and practice from the middle of the 1950s. A sudden profusion of planning research within the EPA and other government-related organizations was especially evident beginning in 1956 just as the cabinet was ratifying the five-year Hatoyama plan that the EPA had prepared. Academic and bureaucratic economists, and increasingly politicians within the ruling LDP as well, saw planning as one of the most important questions of contemporary economics: "The problem of planning," wrote the editors of a volume on the subject in 1960, "has become an indispensable factor in any analysis of the Japanese economy today."[38] Scholars and economic bureaucrats assiduously monitored innovations in the field worldwide and there found fresh indication that their immediate postwar faith in a coming age of planning would be borne out in the years to come: "The formulation of a vision or plan for the economic future," EPA technocrats explained, was "becoming a general requirement in every nation of the world."[39] A palpable new fervor took hold as researchers explored the plethora of new theoretical tools and quantified techniques being introduced as part of the unfolding revolution in macroeconomics.

As these macroeconomic modes of analysis gained popularity, the style of plans underwent a significant transformation. Materiel mobilization approaches of the wartime and the early postwar years of the ESB were increasingly replaced by macroeconomic models and input-output analysis. Planning within the EPA never completely lacked a concern with sectoral and industrial components—projections of capital and labor needs, for example, or fairly specific production targets—and these methods certainly continued within economic agencies with specific sectoral jurisdictions such as the Ministry of International Trade and Industry and the Ministry of Agriculture and Forestry. All the same, older ideas of resource allocation—the attempt by the state to assess and regulate the specific levels of materials and capital required by specific industries—gave ground within the EPA to an emphasis on regulating the macroeconomic environment in which private enterprise operated.

It was perhaps not incidental that such macroeconomic approaches should have most readily taken root within the EPA, for it was the agency with the clearest mandate to take a comprehensive view of the economy and without specific sectoral jurisdictions within the administrative structure of the government. The exponents of the reinvigorated vogue of planning as it was most conspicuously pursued within the EPA beginning in the 1950s maintained that planning in a capitalist system "did not mean the national management of industry," but rather "the regulation of economic cycles" based on a "foreknowledge of the trends of the private economy" and effected by manipulation of "trade, financial policy, nationalized enterprises and such similar sectors in which government can take direct action."[40] The changes taking place in planning went beyond methodological transformation, beyond expansions in the quantity of economic data, new computational techniques, or clever statistical tools. Rather, as new objects of inquiry were applied to questions of the rationalized study, prediction, and management of the larger processes of the economy, new purposes and instruments were added to the repertoire of the planning technocrat. Planning now implied a macroeconomic focus, and its overarching purpose was fundamentally seen as the pursuit of overall growth.

The intellectual ferment surrounding the problem of planning renewed the faith of economists and officials in its practical efficacy. As they drew more and more on macroeconomic techniques that seemed to offer increasingly sensitive explanations of the actual forces at work in the contemporary economy, economists believed that planning could now become truly scientific. In place of the rough-and-ready production blueprints of the past, plans could now be based on what were identified as the larger underlying laws of the economy. Economists increasingly formulated plans as forecasts of the regular and repeatable macroeconomic consequences that would follow from a sequence of given actions. The outcome toward which they increasingly directed planning, moreover, was now determinable rates of long-term growth. Economic history need be no longer punctuated by catastrophic failure. The economic statecraft of planning could now be imagined as a matter of technocratic manipulation, in the way a chemical reaction could in part be regulated with knowledge of the periodic table.

For the first generation of postwar public economists who had moved to redeem the ideal of planning after the war—such men as Arisawa Hiromi (b. 1896) and Inaba Hidezō (b. 1907)—the emergence of new planning modalities in the 1950s quickened their faith in the potential for planning to serve the needs of the nation and the pursuit of economic justice. These older hands continued on as the elder statesmen among economic technocrats. After leading the group in the ESB that devised the priority production recovery approach of the early postwar years, Arisawa Hiromi continued to play a prominent role in a host of planning activities and advisory councils while occupying a position in the economics department of Tokyo University. Inaba, following his official recovery efforts after the war as undersecretary of the ESB during the Katayama cabinet of 1947—a time during which he was known, along with Tsuru Shigeto and Yamamoto Takayuki, as one wing of the "three-winged bird of the ESB"—carried out long-range economic forecasting as the managing director of the Institute for Research on the National Economy, the organization he was instrumental in founding with support from the Ministries of Commerce and Industry (later International Trade and Industry), Agriculture and Forestry, and Education.

The planning sciences were now also being shaped by a slightly younger generation of technocrats who, though close to Inaba (b. 1907) in age, only first emerged as public figures in the immediate postwar years. Some, such as Ōkita Saburō (b. 1914) and Gotō Yonosuke (b. 1916), who have already appeared in this study in regard to their initial participation in the Special Survey Committee of the Foreign Ministry, Shimomura Osamu (b. 1910), the most vocal declaimer of the growth potential of the Japanese economy, and Hayashi Yūjirō (b. 1916) had graduated from university between the mid-1930s and early 1940s. This cohort had generally participated in the lower ranks of the mobilization technocracy during the war, and by the 1950s had risen to prominence on the strength of their official platforms in the postwar economic bureaucracy. They represented what might be seen as a bridge generation, playing an early role in efforts to revive the older planning ideal but also quick to embrace new developments in macroeconomics within the *kinkei*, "modern economics," line.

From his initial participation in the Special Survey Committee of the Foreign Ministry, Ōkita went on to occupy a central position in official economic research and planning, first as head of the Research Section of the Economic Stabilization Board and author of several early Economic White Papers, later as head of the planning bureaus of the Economic Deliberation Council and finally the Economic Planning Agency. In his official roles as chief planner and public proselytizer, Ōkita became perhaps the quintessential public economist of the era. Having also served on the Special Survey Committee of the Ministry of Foreign Affairs at the end of the war, Gotō Yonosuke, then only thirty-one years old, became a member of the ESB in 1947. Gotō's activities will be discussed at greater length in the following chapter, but here it will suffice to say that he became one of the most recognized figures of economic officialdom in the 1950s as the author of several of the influential Economic White Papers of that decade and as a golden-quilled publicist for growth planning and for the Keynesian-influenced image of the economics of prosperity that drew inspiration from the United States. Shimomura Osamu graduated with a degree in economics in 1934 and took a position with the Finance Ministry, eventually serving as the ministry's representative on the Policy Committee of the Bank of Japan. Based on his technical but seemingly extravagant predictions of high-speed growth, he achieved public stature during the 1950s remarkable for an economist and eventually became a member of the famous economic brain trust of Prime Minister Ikeda Hayato that was responsible for shaping the Income Doubling Plan of 1960. He remained a forceful, and controversial, advocate for planned promotion of the conditions for growth over the next several decades. Hayashi Yūjirō graduated in 1940 in the electrical and chemical sciences but, like Ōkita, found himself increasingly involved in economic planning activities. After first joining Inaba Hidezō's Institute for Research on the National Economy after the war, he entered the ESB in 1947 and there (and in its successor institutions) was occupied in official planning. He also taught macroeconomics at the university level and published widely on the theory and practice of planning in Japan.[41]

Bureaucratic economists who had graduated from university only after the war was over also began to play a role as planning advocates in the early postwar period. One of these was Kanamori Hisao (b. 1924), who entered the Ministry of Commerce and Industry after graduating in 1948 and joined the Economic Planning Agency in 1953. By mid-decade, he was participating in the Shimomura growth debates on the side of Ōkita and was sent off by the EPA on a study mission on planning and development to the United States. In the next decade, Kanamori became chief of domestic research for the EPA and as the author of several famous Economic White Papers became a leading proponent of planned growth. Other young economists outside official circles also began to assume leading positions in planning research and experimentation. Many of those writing on the subject were young *kinkei* economists at Hitotsubashi University, scholars such as Kurabayashi Yoshimasa, Shionotani Kazuo, and Imai Ken'ichi.[42] These specialists were all among the first generation of economists whose training fell almost entirely during the postwar years. Keynesianism, planning theory, and the entire range of macroeconomic fields that had energized the discipline since the end of the war thus formed common components of their intellectual background.

Along with elder predecessors such as Yamada Yūzō (b. 1902), many of these young Hitotsubashi economists were among the most prolific contributors to a flurry of texts on planning theory and practice that became a sign of the times within economics and bureaucratic arenas beginning in the latter half of the fifties decade. In those years and into the following decade, as the discipline of economics grew in prestige and as public attention was increasingly focused on questions of material prosperity and the growing economic prowess of the nation, multivolume series on contemporary economic approaches became a growth industry for major publishing houses, and these invariably contained a volume or two on the latest developments in planning technique.[43] The themes of these books and related reviews of the field by economics, statistics, and policy associations centered around technical explications of the statistical foundations of new planning.[44] They also employed the macroeconomics of planning to analyze contemporary conditions and the methods and aims of official government plans.

With Hitotsubashi University as the spiritual center of academic research on macroeconomic planning, the scholars of the field were confronted with an apparent contradiction between their espoused principles of free enterprise and the implied intermediations of planning. But wherever the *kinkei* economists of Hitotsubashi and elsewhere took up the question, they invariably proclaimed theirs a brand of planning compatible with a free-market system. Even in a capitalist economy some intervention is needed, Takahashi Chōtarō, a Hitotsubashi economist, explained in 1959:

> If the essence of capitalism lay in the "ungovernability of production,"
> *(seisan no museifusei)* or if production were the sole driving force behind
> all economic processes, then one would be forced to conclude that
> economic planning within a capitalist system was an almost entirely
> impossible endeavor. But provided it is deemed appropriate that
> various economic relationships—such as that between investment
> and production—should exist according to stable mathematical
> functions, this would then be an indication that stipulations about
> "ungovernability" or "unorderedness" do not necessarily obtain.

Drawing on standard Keynesian formulas, Takahashi noted that, under conditions of less than full employment, production (or supply) is not the only determining force. Effective demand plays a part, too, and this in turn is driven by consumption and investment functions. Thus, according to his argument, although the private realm of production may be considered sacrosanct, it becomes possible to talk about planning for the management of these other macro-factors. Assuming that it is the role of individuals to consume and enterprises to invest, Takahashi continued, the responsibility for such planning within a competitive capitalist system should rightfully be invested in the entity of government alone.[45] Another contributor to the volume in which Takahashi's discussion appeared described appropriate capitalist planning as "giving careful consideration to that which expands the creativity of private enterprise while at the same time attempting to shape the overall economy and to guide the direction and level of its development."[46]

Advocates were always quick to distinguish between the forms of macro-economic planning in Japan described by Takahashi and those practiced in socialist systems. In contrast to socialist planning, planning in Japan did "not possess powers of strong control," suggested Hitotsubashi economists Yamada Isamu and Yamada Yūzō, the latter of whom first made his mark earlier in the decade with his compilations of historical national income data. The practice of macroeconomic planning in Japan respected the free market, the two Yamadas maintained, while it simultaneously focused on "stabilizing the ground" on which free enterprise operated.[47] Scholarly defenders also revisited memories of the wartime control system, here again distancing latter-day planning practices from their earlier forms. In the process, old questions arose about whether the idea of a "new capitalism" based on planning was inevitably fascistic. Defenders drew on the writings of the likes of Schumpeter and Bruno Trentin to contrast what they perceived as the progressive potential of macroeconomic manipulation by technical managers with the coercive control of fascists.[48] Official publicists for planning, too, were adamant that Japan's was planning that respected the principles of the free market: EPA plans, unlike the strictly and minutely prosecuted plans of socialist societies, "do not imply a planned economy," declared an official handbook of the prime minister's office in 1960.[49]

Fundamental to the views of EPA planners and their scholarly backers by the latter half of the 1950s was the close connections they made between capitalist-style planning and the pursuit of growth. Official statements characterized the EPA plans of the late 1950s as "large frameworks for growth," contrasting them with the micromanagement styles of intervention into "every single area of the economy" implicitly imputed to socialist approaches.[50] Planning theorists, too, assumed a focus on stabilizing and regularizing growth as the defining characteristic of official blueprints. In the rationale given by economist Takahashi Chōtarō for the need for planned regulation of the relation between investment and output, the emphasis on capital-output ratios, discussed before in relation to the Shimomura growth debates, is once again evident. Despite his assurances that the potential purposes of contemporary planning vary, Takahashi's premise that the fundamental aim of recovery and development plans was the "long-term increase in national product" betrays an overriding focus on macroeconomic growth that characterized prevailing perceptions about what ends were appropriate to the planning endeavor.[51]

Needless to add, the same anxiety over distancing planning from socialism felt among bureaucratic and political officials, *kinkei* academicians, and industrial leaders was not shared by Marxist economists and those who belonged to the left-wing political parties. In one sense, less separated mainstream technocrats and Marxists on the issue of macroeconomics than might first be supposed: Marxist economists also pursued emerging

macroeconomic analytical techniques, as could be seen in the developments and controversies in communist countries that also attracted the
scrutiny of mainstream Japanese planners. Although the specific technical
standards often differed, an intense interest in national income accounting and growth theory existed in the Soviet bloc as well. That an overriding preoccupation with such technocratic orientations and methods
was not unique to either capitalist or communist systems was very much
a salient feature of the age. Yet for left-wing critics, of course, the official
view of macroeconomic planning was deficient in significant ways. Socialists would have preferred national control over industry, while communists
tended to dismiss the very possibility of planning in a capitalist society. Both
attempted to reveal how official plans worked to support state monopoly
capitalism.

The attacks on the prevailing cult of macroeconomics leveled by Ōuchi
Hyōe, the prominent Marxist economist of Tokyo University, were revealing
of the faults progressives found with official planning approaches. Ōuchi
himself had played an early role in reforms that laid the groundwork for the
boom in macroeconomic statistical research in Japan that lay at the heart
of the styles of planning at question here. As a visible leader of left-wing
economists, however, he was a consistent critic of official plans and reports,
helping to author, among other works, so-called people's white papers in
response to the EPA's documents. Ōuchi distrusted the preoccupation with
income accounting that increasingly governed conceptions of the national
economy. He disapproved of what he saw as the "reckless reasoning" that
often followed from the belief that quantitative material increase was inherently good, to the degree that any unit increase in wealth was as good as
any other: "To grasp every possible aspect of a country's economy through
numbers, and, what's more, to make the aim of such measurement to
gauge the quantitative progress of production, these are quintessentially
American endeavors," he wrote derisively. National accounting macroeconomic methods were not, he allowed, without any merit, particularly in
their power to provide a schematic representation of the entire economy.
Yet the fiscal economics or, in Ōuchi's term, the "state finance capitalism"
of Hansen and Gerhard Colm that followed from national income macroeconomics in the United States was, he insisted, "full of holes." He did
admit that American-style macroeconomic policies marked a progressive
improvement over prewar economic thinking in America and were more
"scientific" in their grasp of the broad cycles of the economy than, say, prewar German economics had been. Implicit in Ōuchi's view, however, was
regret over an emphasis on volume rather than value, on sheer material
increase rather than the problem of distribution. And he hinted at broader
Marxist categories by which left-wing detractors attempted to discredit offi-

cial methods when he suggested that American-style Keynesian macroeconomic policies were equivalent to a form of "imperialism."[52]

The surge in interest in planning and the pursuit of growth midway through the 1950s was partly reflected in research undertaken by the EPA and other agencies into the practical experiences of other countries. Even while they expended great efforts to pitch the planning endeavor in Japan as a legitimate means to guide capitalism gently, exponents at the same time paid close attention to the examples of the Soviet Union and other communist countries. The Research Bureau and other arms of the EPA pursued a program of translating Soviet and Chinese treatments of socialist planning techniques.[53] Scholars also examined the Soviet versions of debates over familiar questions about investment, for example, and other similar macroeconomic determinants of growth.[54] This desire to keep abreast of socialist planning harked back to an initial interwar period of excitement among Marxists and, later, conservative renovationists over the potential lessons of the early five-year plans of the Soviets.

Yet the view of growth planning as congruous with capitalist systems was particularly reinforced by what was perceived as the potent example of the United States. Technocrats believed the United States, the metropole of a host of planning innovations emerging within the context of the new economics, to be the home of a brand of planning appropriate to the Japanese political economy. This outlook was spurred by a new level of coordinated economic practice in the United States that was expressed through organizations and arrangements such as the Employment Act of 1946, the President's Council of Economic Advisors, the Joint Economic Report of Congress, and various regional development programs, some of which were new to postwar America, others of which had roots in Depression-era programs.

It was with such a vision of American economic practices that the Nihon Seisansei Honbu (Japan Productivity Center, hereafter JPC) dispatched a 1956 study mission to the United States that was representative of the dominant role the former American occupiers played in shaping Japanese conceptions of planning for capitalism. The JPC was a semiofficial organization funded in part by both the Japanese and U.S. governments, and it was the leading propagandist for a broad movement to increase economic productivity that began in the mid-1950s. This productivity campaign was the latest in a series of rationalization movements dating from the 1910s, only now an emphasis on the idea of a prosperity economy and a new consuming culture was a stronger keynote. One of the earliest of hundreds of so-called productivity missions sent abroad by the JPC was the one that visited the United States for two months in 1956 to investigate economic development policies. Ten management personnel from the research divisions of large industrial and financial concerns (Yawata Steel, Sumitomo Metals, Fuji Bank, etc.), backbone institutions of the Japanese financial system (the Bank of Japan, the Development Bank, etc.), as well as the EPA studied the role of the state in guiding development in its various aspects.[55] Through the lens of technocracy, the team hoped to understand the conditions behind American prosperity—or in the words of one mission member, "the secret of American economic development."[56]

Through conferences, lectures, and study tours, the mission was exposed to U.S. experiences with work programs; small business development; and local, state, and regional development projects such as the Tennessee Valley Authority and the interstate highway system. A central theme running throughout all the mission saw and heard was the importance of planning to development. Members of the mission concluded that, while in the United States "the nucleus of development was private initiative," efforts by all levels of government to assure the environment and the knowledge required to "assist the growth of private enterprise" were also key. Government in the United States engaged in "massive social investments, active research activities, and so on" and these were all, the mission concluded in its report, consciously "directed toward allowing private enterprise to naturally prosper."[57] The idea that the path to the "natural" prosperity of the free market was through the planned assistance of government was, on the face of it, perhaps not without some irony. Yet it showed just how deeply held was the conviction by this time, shared by even the industrial representatives on the mission, about the necessarily close relation of planning to postwar capitalism.[58]

The focus on ensuring the "growth of private enterprise" hinted at the macroeconomic aims that the mission concluded were most fundamental to development planning. In a portion of its report titled "The Theory of Economic Development," the mission defined "economic development" as the "continuous increase of real per capita income" and maintained that development was thus functionally no different from the concept of economic growth.[59] The lessons on macroeconomic planning with which the Japan Productivity Center mission members came away were of particular interest to the EPA. Among the youngest members of the mission was thirty-two-year-old Kanamori Hisao, a staff member in the Research Bureau who had joined the EPA from the Ministry of International Trade and Industry (formerly Commerce and Industry) just two years before, and who had already participated in the Shimomura growth debates on the side of Ōkita. Upon his return from the United States, Kanamori prepared a report on what the Japan Productivity Center mission had learned that zeroed in on the question of planning. This was released as an internal reference work within the EPA several months ahead of the official mission report put out by the JPC.[60] Kanamori's report traced the story of planning from the late nineteenth century, linking economic rationalization movements, city planning, and later Depression-era programs in an account that presented the United States as one of the historical homes of planning.[61] Based on what he learned during his two months in the States, moreover, Kanamori was left with a strong impression of the continuing development of planning practices there since the end of the war:

> While the American economy is based in principle on the activities
> of free capital, behind these processes exist effective plans that
> continuously work to regulate and promote those activities—the
> development of large rivers such as the Tennessee, the Columbia, and
> the Missouri; the expansion of highways; urban planning and housing
> developments; resource development and conservation; rationalization
> of industrial areas. All of these are ultimately linked, moreover, to the
> nationwide economic goals of maintaining full employment and stable
> economic growth.[62]

Surveying the latest advances in macroeconomic projection and the institutional framework in which goals were decided and coordinated, Kanamori focused in particular on the goals of employment and growth— as formally expressed in the Employment Act of 1946—that he concluded united the varieties of U.S. planning.[63] The mission had met Gerhard Colm, author of the influential *The American Economy in 1960* and the hottest name in economic forecasting techniques at the time, whose influential method of growth projections had just been put to use in the Hatoyama Plan. Kanamori went to considerable length laying out Colm's techniques, which were at heart based on computations of population and labor productivity, and particularly tried to impress on his EPA colleagues (a point the JPC report itself would soon emphasize) the startling accuracy with which Colm was able to estimate in 1952 the amount of the U.S. gross national product for 1955: his calculation was off by a mere 0.3 percent.[64]

The nature of planning as it was presented to and received by the mission members confirmed them in their view of planning as a critical element of successful capitalist systems. "American rationalism disavows the notion of 'expected equilibria' that says if you let the economy run free, it will run well naturally," Kanamori wrote, "and operates on the view that the economy must be led in proper directions according to plans."[65] Kanamori's report portrayed an idealized image of a highly coordinated system in the United States, in which a many-layered planning mechanism, distributed among different levels of government, employed a range of policy instruments all ultimately tied to the goal of growth at the highest levels of the federal government. Kanamori and the rest of the mission thus returned to Japan making strong declarations about the continuing lessons to be learned from such U.S. models.[66]

The reception of U.S. planning practices as the JPC mission perceived them and their employment in Japan in the mid-1950s were part of a longer postwar preoccupation with the macroeconomic revolution. Specific planning practices taken directly from U.S. practitioners, moreover, had already been employed even before the mission set out, for the five-year Hatoyama economic plan had been characterized by Colmian techniques of growth forecasting. But the JPC mission on development reflected the strong surge in planning research among technocrats in government, the academy, and industry beginning in the mid-1950s. The picture of the United States conveyed by the members of the mission certainly remained an ideal among many of these technocrats in the main economic agencies, particularly the EPA.

Businessmen, too, like those representatives on the mission from the heavy industrial concerns of Yawata Steel and Hitachi Manufacturing, supported the example that the United States provided of an effective but ultimately noninvasive form of planned capitalism. They welcomed the idea of a government content with manipulating macroeconomic levers, promoting the emerging message of growth and ensuring the systemic conditions it required. Besides, such planning at the national level seemed to reinforce the fad of enterprise planning (kigyō keikaku) that was flowering in corporate management circles at the same time. Here, too, the JPC had a significant hand. In the "Karuizawa Top Management Seminar" held by the JPC in 1959, the second in an annual series of seminars for corporate upper management on issues affecting the productivity movement, prominent public economists Ōkita Saburō and Nakayama Ichirō lectured attendees on national economic planning in Japan and the appropriate relationship between the directions being taken within the framework of the national economy and strategic corporate planning.[67] Managers attending the seminar were quick to acknowledge the potential benefits of long-term planning techniques honed in official macroeconomic policy making to the task of charting the future directions of their corporations. They believed that their corporate aims ought to be determined with an eye to the larger context of national economic growth and in alignment with official road maps for the economy. The enthusiasm of these reviewers of the seminar proceedings suggested the degree to which the ideal of long-range planning had become an organizing theme in the pursuit at all institutional levels of a technocratic rationalism that might overcome the pitfalls of the economic and social modern past and the particular weaknesses of the Japanese case.

The redemption of the planning ideal that had taken place immediately after the war did so in the context of a planning science that had to that time been largely governed by the methods and aims of materiel mobilization blueprints of the wartime: although grand in scope and ambition, plans were based on older principles of microeconomic resource allocation. During the mid-1950s, however, when the vogue of growth theory first began to take hold and the eyes of Japanese analysts turned to U.S. models of developmentalism, practitioners began to tie their hopes for planning to more explicitly macroeconomic analytical techniques and to the goal of rapid growth that those methods seemed to put in reach. For central planners and their scholarly compatriots, the task of forecasting growth became a predominant concern, and they stood at the forefront of efforts to marshal national opinion behind the growthist agenda. In Japan—as in the United States, Europe, and elsewhere—the faith in technocracy manifest in the evolving forms of postwar planning theory and practice became a crucial element in the rise of growthism as a conceptual paradigm.

CHAPTER 5

Structural Ills and Growth Cures

M any postwar advocates of the ideal of full employment in Japan had drawn, as we have seen, on mid-century Keynesian economic ideas. They were able to point to a new international consensus, expressed in postwar multilateral organizations and in the capitals of the victorious Allied powers, on the need to craft full-employment solutions in nations—winners and losers alike—across the world that were struggling to make the transition from war to a transformed peacetime system. In Japan, a sense of the importance of somehow crafting a new regime to address the employment question was intensified by the massive military demobilization that took place after surrender and by the hundreds of thousands of civilian returnees from the former empire who would come streaming back to Japan over the course of the first several postwar years.

There was yet one additional social factor in Japan, however, that underscored the case made by early proponents of the ideal of full employment: the soaring rate of natural increase in the population of the country. The perceived dilemma of "surplus population" had long vexed national leaders and ideologues during the modern period. But the swiftness and magnitude of its return in the straitened circumstances of the immediate postwar years seemed to portend a menace on a new scale to the well-being of the nation. The most calamitous fears of social collapse and mass starvation immediately after the war thankfully never came to pass. Yet even so, long after the worst of the early emergencies of immediate postwar recovery seemed to have been weathered, anxiety about population and employment returned once again a decade later, in the mid-1950s. Now, influential commentators redefined the old problem of population for the new post-recovery, post-Occupation age more explicitly, and with greater analytical rigor, in terms of the structural deficiencies that they believed distinguished Japanese capitalism from that of the leading economies of the West and held the nation in semi-backward status. By the second half of the 1950s, public economists dealt with their renewed fears about the "population problem" using assumptions and concepts taken from the new economics to argue, not in the rather more narrow language of full-employment policy that had governed discourse in the postwar 1940s, but rather in terms of a more expansive goal of rapid "economic growth" as the means at long last to achieve an internal reformation deferred by the errors of Japan's modern past.

Population Anxiety

Although the devastation that the war had wreaked upon the economy would increase the magnitude of the "population problem," anxiety over the number of people living in Japan had, in fact, been a perennial theme of the modern period. Official campaigns to encourage what were considered excessive numbers to move elsewhere began soon after the founding of the Meiji state, and efforts to promote emigration, especially from the countryside, were a continuing response of officials and reform groups in the decades that followed. The internal colonization of Hokkaidō involved the resettlement of ethnically Japanese immigrants from the southern home islands, so that by the end of the nineteenth century the indigenous Ainu people constituted less than a quarter of the population of that northern territory. After overseas emigration was legalized in 1884, Japanese were exhorted to relocate to Hawaii and the west coasts of the United States and Canada as well as to New Zealand, Australia, and South America. Official perception that there were more people than could be accommodated on the archipelago grew particularly strong as the hardships of the countryside in the 1910s and 1920s gave rise to potentially destabilizing political movements for tenants' rights. Emigration was increasingly frustrated, however, by racially motivated barriers to Japanese immigrants erected by destination countries.

The discourse on "surplus population" and the remedy of emigration were inextricably bound up with the pursuit of empire by the 1930s. The idea that the countryside could not support the numbers who sought to make their livings there created the perception of a land crisis for which empire was increasingly offered as the solution. With the rise of a form of imperial agrarianism, Louise Young demonstrates, empire was "rendered . . . as space," an outlet for surplus population, "lebensraum for Japan's overcrowded and socially conflicted villages." In 1936, the government instituted a Millions to Manchuria program. A vast migration machine comprised of national, prefectural, and community-level organizations eventually succeeded in persuading over three hundred thousand Japanese to seek better a lot in Manchuria.[1] Even so, relative to that of many European countries, the scale of emigration from Japan during the modern period was generally very small, averaging only 1 percent of the increase in population between 1850 and 1950.[2] While the numbers who actually left never matched the rhetoric exhorting them to seek lives elsewhere, the perception that exporting the problem of human surplus was a sound solution to domestic ills remained a constant for much of the period prior to the end of the Second World War.

After the war, empire as a captive outlet was no longer an option. Although some such as the Communist Party continued to advocate the voluntary resettlement of large numbers of Japanese, migration to other countries was for the most part a practical and political impossibility in the near term.[3] Cut off from external solutions, planners lamented the lack of a Japanese hinterland to receive the swelling numbers of the population in the way the American West had historically functioned in the United States. Without such an internal destination for perceived overflow, few options seemed available. Pronatalist strategies that had begun in the wartime 1940s to replace the push for emigration were now clearly untenable. At the same time, some postwar investigators were loath to endorse measures aimed at decreasing the population over time. Resorting to familiar formulas in the language of modern nationalism and race,[4] planners equated fewer people with regression and weakness; such reductions, they believed, were the beginning of racial decline. Progress, in contrast, meant forging national solutions to accommodate continually increasing numbers of people: "A progressive point of view emphasizes the search for the means to ensure survival for a growing population."[5]

The belief that the pressure of population posed a peculiar and chronic limitation on Japanese capitalism was a central component of the shared critical diagnosis given by so many post-defeat analysts. Commentators after the war almost invariably presented the issue of population as one of the most salient characteristics of the Japanese political-economic system. "The character of the Japanese economy," argued the ESB's Committee on Economic Recovery Planning in 1948, was determined by the fact that what would soon be eighty million people had somehow to be supported in a "small island country" with cultivable land "even smaller" in area. Japan was historically infamous for the density of its population, the committee reminded readers, and the ills suffered before the war due to a poverty of natural resources and what it deemed "overpopulation" (kajō jinkō) now only threatened to grow worse after the lands controlled by Japan had been reduced with the loss of empire. Rising population had historically been accommodated within the agricultural sector. This meant that agriculture was carried out on an extremely small scale in Japan and that the economy as a whole remained to a great degree agrarian in nature during the modern period. The problem for the present, the ESB's committee warned, was that agriculture now had "almost no room to absorb a greater number of people."[6]

The dire portrait of the population dilemma drawn by the nearly fifty members of the ESB's Committee on Economic Recovery Planning was repeated by analysts throughout government, academia, industry, and agriculture in the second half of the 1940s. The figure of eighty million persons, noted everywhere with foreboding, represented an ominous new watermark that starkly underscored the maddening number of handicaps an exhausted Japanese populace would face on the road to recovery. The prospect of so many people loomed as the unforgiving backdrop against which any recovery program had to be constructed. The problem of rising population was all the more pressing given the penurious state of the economy after the war. Indeed, in the somber calculations of available food calories per capita found in most reckonings of economic conditions in the first several years after the war, analysts spoke directly to the bare struggle for existence faced by so many.[7] It seemed a real possibility that the country might not be able to support all of the people who lived there.[8]

Nor did it seem likely that this was merely a short-term problem. Forecasts of future population growth were also troubling. Part of the scramble to restore statistical institutions after the war was an intensive effort thrown into census taking. In its demands for statistical data from the Japanese authorities, the Economic and Scientific Section of SCAP placed a priority on the collection of basic population data. Statisticians were eventually dispatched from the United States to Japan in 1948 to oversee extensive preparations for Japan's participation in the United Nations world economic census project of 1950, of which population was a key component.[9] Japanese planners had themselves already made some preliminary estimates of postwar population size and then conducted a more formal count in 1947. Data from this early research fed calculations by the Population Issues Research Institute of the Ministry of Health and Welfare used by ESB planners.[10] The institute measured the 1947 population at 78.6 million, up over 6 million since the end of the war. Most of this initial rise was due to returnees from the former empire, but natural increase was also becoming a serious factor. Due to rising birthrates and falling death rates during 1947, the population increased by 1.5 million persons that year, exceeding expectations and surpassing the previous high of 1941 by over four hundred thousand. Even allowing that this unprecedented jump was likely a one-time postwar phenomenon, researchers warned that the rate of natural increase nevertheless threatened to remain unusually high for some years to come: in 1948, the Population Issues Research Institute projected that within five years the number of Japanese would grow to almost 83 million.[11] What was more, the working population was expected to represent an increasing share of the total, a prospect that fueled the insistent calls by central strategists for a full-employment program.

Following the suggestion made by Harold Moulton at the Brookings Institution of the United States that Japan under the U.S. Occupation be allowed to achieve a standard of living equal to that of 1930—a date prior to the Manchurian Incident—recovery planners, first in the Foreign Ministry and then in the ESB, premised their recovery planning on the attainment of a standard of living equivalent to the average for the period between 1930 and 1934. The five-year Economic Recovery Plan of the ESB's Committee on Economic Recovery Planning was aimed at achieving this level of recovery by 1952.[12] This 1930–34 standard of living became a standard benchmark in economic thinking throughout the Japanese and Occupation establishments for the second half of the 1940s. The dilemma was that the average population during the 1930–34 period had only been 66 million people. The greater number of people after the war meant that to recover a standard of living equivalent to that of 1930–34 the economy would have to achieve a real national income by 1952 that was 125 percent of the level of that earlier period.[13]

Even as the government sought to craft an economic program to reach this ambitious goal, reformers attempted to address the population explosion in terms of social policy. The organization of the Birth Control Alliance (Sanji Seigen Dōmei) in November 1945 signaled the postwar reemergence of a movement for birth control and family planning that dated back to the 1920s. Amid debate about the "human flood" under which Japan appeared about to "sink," and despite the worst fears of some of racial decline, those responsible for social policy began to accept reforming calls for family-planning rights. The National Eugenics Law of 1940 was amended in 1948 to legalize abortion in cases of potentially severe mental handicaps or when the life of the mother was at risk. The right to abortion was then affirmed in 1949 for cases of economic hardship, and by 1952 the eugenics law was again revised essentially to allow for abortion on demand. By the beginning of the 1950s, an active movement made up of both official and private organizations sought, among other things, to ameliorate the population problem through the promotion of contraceptives. As contraceptive use and the number of legal abortions both rose during the 1950s, the rate of increase in birthrates began to drop.[14] Even so, the population continued to climb, and the postwar baby boom kept concern about managing the ballooning population an ever-present factor in conceptions of the economic future.

After "the Postwar Is Over": The "Weakest Link in the Chain"

Easily one of the most iconic events by which historians have charted Japanese history in the aftermath of World War II is the famous government declaration "the postwar is now over" *(mohaya sengo de wa nai)*, which appeared in the EPA's widely read Economic White Paper of 1956. Historians regularly cite this announcement as a turning point marking at least one of several possible ends to the postwar era, and where they do so, they almost without exception understand it as a celebration.[15] Based in part on its almost ubiquitous citation by historians, but also on contemporary reception of the evocative turn of phrase itself among Japanese of the 1950s, the declaration long ago passed into popular memory as an unproblematic collective sigh of relief that the darkest moment of Japanese modern experience had ended.

But closer examination of the influential report of 1956—and also of the general tenor of public discourse on the state of the nation and its prospects in those early "post-postwar" years—show that what has been generally understood to be a confident, trumpeting announcement of a new period of Japanese national strength was actually a far more somber portrayal of a post-reconstruction economy and society for whom the days ahead looked potentially more difficult, not less.

To be sure, the Korean War boom of the early 1950s had put a sudden end to initial fears about national survival and the ability to achieve the recovery goals of planners. Once the infusion of "special procurements" from the United States was over, however, the economy slumped and fear about the future returned. Even with the upturn in economic output in 1955 after the post–Korean War recession, many commentators believed that disconcertingly uncertain times lay ahead. It was true, allowed the EPA, that in 1955 exports had risen at the second fastest rate in the world, industrial output had increased, and national income had expanded at a 10 percent clip. Japanese economic performance was being compared favorably with that of Germany. "But is there good cause to allow ourselves to become drunk on these favorable reviews?" the EPA asked rhetorically.[16] The head of the agency, Takaki Tatsunosuke, himself concluded that there was "no excuse for optimism."[17] With the end of the Occupation, outside aid, and the war boom, economic expansion would have to come from internal impetus and would need to be based on more difficult modernizing transformations. Progress thus far only represented escape from the "deep trough" into which the economy had fallen by the time of defeat, the EPA warned in the Economic White Paper of 1956. The Japan Productivity Center, meanwhile, employed a different metaphor to make the same point about the true nature of the progress made so far, likening the postwar recovery to the rescuing of a patient by blood transfusion.[18]

Behind such guarded evaluations of national economic prospects always lay the question of population. Despite social efforts to curb population growth, the rate of increase fed perceptions of a lurking crisis that would not go away. True to the worst forecasts of earlier years, the number of people in Japan had risen to over 88 million by 1955 and was increasing by over 1 million each year.[19] Investigators placed the end of population growth

distressingly far into the future: not until the year 1995, projected one official research institute, would the population reach a plateau.[20] Of particular
concern in continuing watchfulness over population charts was the question of how productively to accommodate new workers: "surplus population" meant surplus labor. Eventual postwar recovery with the help of U.S.
aid and the inflow of capital during the Korean War, relatively aggressive
work and relief programs, and—despite worries that the countryside could
support few more—the at least temporary return of many to family agriculture had all combined to meet the immediate postwar unemployment
threat passingly well. With the end of the Korean War spurt, however, the
unemployment picture quickly deteriorated. In 1954, the number of jobless jumped to 590,000 people, an increase of 13 percent over the prior
year. This sudden upturn followed four years of either decreases or only
small increases in the number of unemployed and represented the highest percentage rise in the jobless numbers since the first year of the Dodge
pullback in 1949. Fears began to run high, and some reports had it that as
many as 840,000 people were out of work the following year.[21] Although not
as dire as these estimates, the 690,000 level recorded in 1955, another 10
percent increase over the previous year, nevertheless marked a new high.[22]
While the apparently enviable total unemployment rate in 1955 of 1.6 percent would seem to cast doubt on just how genuine the fears of potential
disaster of the time were, this figure reflected only those who were considered "completely unemployed." Those who worked for only a relatively
small portion of each month were not counted among these numbers.

The very question of how to define unemployment, in fact, emerged
significantly at this time to redirect the ongoing debate on population
and employment being played out with such intensity in the mid-1950s.
While official statistics showed a worsening situation, advisers to the government suggested that employment figures concealed the true magnitude of an even greater problem. This warning only increased the sense of
alarm among authorities and researchers as they watched the jobless rate
as currently measured rise. In 1949, the Council on Unemployment Measures (Shitsugyō Taisaku Shingikai) had been created as an advisory body
consisting of scholars and bureaucratic officials under the jurisdiction of
the Office of the Prime Minister. The council was led by the indefatigable
Arisawa Hiromi, whose industrial developmentalism tempered by old leftist roots and whose close connections in the top echelons of the political
world put him in line during the 1940s and 1950s to participate in or serve
as leader of a long list of official investigative and advisory organs, ranging
from the Statistics Commission to the Committee on Nuclear Power, the
Central Council on Wages, and the Employment Commission.[23] Conceived
in anticipation of the deleterious effects of the overbalance policies administered by Joseph Dodge, the more powerful Council on Unemployment

Measures superseded the Committee on Unemployment Measures that had begun operation at the end of 1946 largely under the direction of the Ministry of Health and Welfare.

In 1953, the Council on Unemployment Measures released a report arguing that large numbers of incompletely employed Japanese were not being accounted for in current computations. Below the surface numbers of those completely without work were many more who must be considered only partially employed. The majority of these were employed in family farming. Others worked in very small-scale, often family-owned enterprises. The wages of all were less than their counterparts in the more industrialized sectors of the economy. This "latent" or "hidden" unemployment *(senzai shitsugyō)* was estimated by the council to affect well over 7 million people.[24] The report on hidden unemployment shifted the conceptual terrain on population and employment, in great part setting the terms of debate for the next decade.[25] By citing the agrarian and small-business sectors of the economy as the locus of hidden semi-unemployment, the report and the analysis that followed in its wake implicitly tied these issues to what were long identified by critics as unfortunate characteristics of Japanese political economy. "Premodern" and "feudal" elements of the countryside labor market lamented from the time of the prewar Marxist critiques of capitalist development were now cast in the postwar language of full employment. The desire to promote a robust middle class and healthy domestic markets, always a part of immediate postwar diagnoses of the failures of Japanese capitalism, was now refracted through the lens of the prolonged postwar baby boom.

The report on latent unemployment became the first volley in the reshaped employment debate of the 1950s. To the anticipated coming of age of the postwar boom babies was added the problem now defined as semi-unemployment. By the middle of the decade, the explosive expansion of the labor force was a dominant preoccupation in public and official discourse on national political economy. The rate of natural increase—the difference between the birth and death rates per one thousand people—had fallen by half from highs of over twenty in the late 1940s yet still remained in double digits.[26] The former pyramidal shape of the population structure by age was now becoming "jar-shaped," with a bulge in the middle, warned the Council on Unemployment Measures in 1955.[27] Satirists found ample room to exploit the tension between unease and pride that the still growing Japanese population engendered. One cartoonist suggested with tongue in cheek that the rapid rate at which new babies were being born as the population passed the 90 million mark mid-decade—"every 18 seconds, another person"—constituted a special victory in the drive for increased economic "productivity" (see Figure 2).[28] And, as constantly noted, the size of the population comprised of people in their productive years (those fourteen years

荻 賢 の 生 産 性

人 口 九 千 万 ！
— お お ッ ！ 18 秒 に 1 人 —

FIG. 2. Top caption: "Ogiken's Productivity." Bottom caption: "A Population of 90 Million!: Wow! Every 18 seconds, another person." The cartoonist, Ogiwara Kenji (shortened here as Ogiken), plays on the idea of postwar drives to improve manufacturing productivity by portraying the high birthrate of the time as a hugely efficient conveyor-belt process of churning out new babies from factories, shipped complete with the tubs traditionally used to bathe infants. Ogiwara Kenji, "Ogiken no seisansei," *Nihon seisansei shinbun*, no. 9 (Sept. 10, 1956): 5. Used by permission of Iwai Shōko.

and over) was unprecedented. The size of the labor force was now growing faster than the population as whole, and the percentage of the total population it represented was rising across almost the entire decade, growing from 66.7 percent in 1950 to nearly 70 percent by 1956.[29] Projections indicated that the workplace would be faced with 750 thousand new workers each year into the foreseeable future.[30]

The EPA took a leading position in defining the problem from an overall perspective. In its white paper of 1956, made famous by its declaration "the postwar is now over" and so influential in shaping public opinion about the nature of post-recovery future, the EPA called the employment problem "the weakest link in the chain of the Japanese economy." Even so, the report worried, as long as the economy had been experiencing quick expansion, there was a tendency to avoid facing the issue. Now that the period of recovery had ended, it warned, employment threatened to explode into a "grave social problem" if positive measures were not taken to promote economic expansion. There were many ways to attack the problem through the boosting of aggregate demand, it suggested, including the raising up of segments of the economy that had been thus far left out of recovery: small and medium size businesses, local development, social security programs, and so on. Supporting these lagging elements, however, would place extra burdens on state finances. The only way to bear the heavier load would be for the financial base of the country to be broadened through the growth of total national income.[31]

The Surgeon's Scalpel of Growth

Technocrats at the EPA and other official bodies considering population and employment thus increasingly advanced the view that the menace could not be viewed in isolation but must be understood in terms of the larger structures of the economy. Official analysts and policy makers who expressed a brand of neoliberal reformism on this score certainly did not employ the same sort of class-based political analysis as the members of the communist and socialist parties and the growing number of Marxist economists in the academy, all of whom also saw deep structural inequalities at work within the recovery and post-recovery economies. Yet, taken together, the views of these disparate observers indicated that the critical postwar diagnosis of Japanese capitalist structures initially put forward to explain the war by the middle of the first post-Occupation decade had emerged as an organizing theme of economic thought for many across a broad political spectrum.

The population problem, an element of critical postwar diagnoses from the first, was now positioned as ever more pivotal to the current forms of old systemic conditions. Meeting the population challenge meant finally confronting the structural "distortions" (*yugami*) that the frantic years of recovery had left largely untouched. In the EPA view, the "various contradictions" nurtured in "late-developing sectors of the socio-economy," especially in agriculture and small business, would be eased over the long term only by long-term development of the economy as a whole, not piecemeal sectoral remedies. The recalcitrant unmodernized sectors of the economy were pools of semi-unemployment. Without modernizing these sectors while simultaneously expanding the size of the economy as a whole, the gap between the industrialized, modern elements and the traditional elements would remain. Productivity would suffer and growth would slow. Wages would not rise far enough for most Japanese. Domestic demand would lag. Industries would be more reliant on exports than ever, a danger given the propensity for foreign reserve shortages. Full employment, a healthy middle class, and the dream of more prosperous lifestyles all would remain out of reach.[32]

The comprehensive approach urged by the EPA was echoed in calls by the Council on Unemployment Measures for true employment programs that would go beyond the limited unemployment measures of the past. Aid and work relief programs should, of course, be continued, the council suggested, but the majority of energy should be thrown into promoting the expansion of the secondary economic sector of manufacturing. The council recommended measures to provide investment capital, the promotion of technology transfer and development, and the support of exporting industries in general.[33] Employment analysts increasingly distanced their proposals from the employment programs of the past, which, though more assertive after the war than before, were still directed only at alleviating joblessness during cyclical downturns. They remained reactive, critics charged, and treated joblessness as a temporary and unusual occurrence. One's theoretical position on the mechanisms of unemployment was beside the point, one imagines expert groups such as the council insisting, for the population problem in Japan was more than an ephemeral phenomenon. "Therefore," the council reported, "...a solution to the problem is impossible unless 'employment programs' go beyond...'unemployment programs' to enlarge employment both directly and indirectly through the expansion of production and the increase of national income."[34]

The advocacy of a macroeconomic attack on the problem by the EPA and the Council on Unemployment Measures increasingly became the keynote of debate on the issue in the second half of the 1950s. Targeted preferences for specific industrial sectors would play a part, according to this view. Yet there was now also a greater emphasis on the generalized goal of increasing the total size of the national income. As formulated by economist Kitami Toshirō, labor policy now would be determined as economic policy.[35] And more and more, economic policy meant macroeconomic manipulation—whether through government expenditures or monetary policy—to ensure the conditions of national income growth.

The connections drawn between the population quandary, what were cast as structural deficiencies, and national income growth were perhaps most fully articulated in any official setting by the EPA's white paper of 1957. This report, like the 1956 report before it, was written by Gotō Yonosuke, the skillful publicist for the growthist vision of national prosperity, EPA research bureau chief, and perhaps one of the least known today of the centrally important public economists of the early postwar period.

Gotō was born in 1916 and earned his degree in engineering from Tokyo Imperial University in 1941. Having received his undergraduate training outside the formal discipline of economics, Gotō reflected a common pattern within the bureaucratic elite of postwar Japan, one represented by other prominent figures such as Ōkita Saburō and Inaba Hidezō, who received degrees in electrical engineering and philosophy, respectively, but made their mark as economic analysts and opinion shapers in the 1950s and 1960s. Gotō entered the Electrical Energy Agency (Denkichō) after graduating and spent the war years there as a researcher. As the war ended, Gotō, then only twenty-eight years old, served on the secretariat of the Special Survey Committee of the Foreign Ministry, treated in Chapter 1 of this study and so important in setting the tone for immediate postwar conceptions of national purpose and the place of economics.

Based in part on the strength of his work with the Survey Committee, Gotō entered the growing ranks of the Economic Stabilization Board in 1947 just as that institution was assuming unprecedented powers over planning and resource allocation for postwar recovery. He continued on as an important analyst in the research departments of the Stabilization Board's successor agencies, the Economic Deliberation Council and the Economic Planning Agency, and he wrote all but one of the famous Economic White Papers of those institutions between the years 1952 and 1958. As the skilled author of the white papers of those critical years of the 1950s, Gotō became one of the most publicly recognized figures in economic officialdom of that decade, and through books, articles, interviews, and conference appearances, he acted as an ever present publicist for growth planning and for a U.S.-influenced image of a Japanese economics of prosperity. Unfortunately, Gotō died suddenly in 1960 in the prime of his career and thus did not live on to become one of the elder commentators on the boom economy of the 1960s, 1970s, and beyond as did such colleagues at the EPA as Ōkita Saburō. Certainly his early death contributed to his being relatively unknown in the historiography of the postwar period despite the prominent public stature he enjoyed during the years of transition from recovery to high growth.[36]

Gotō extended the analysis of the structural problems of the Japanese economy that he had begun in the white paper from the year before. His treatment now, however, applied a new name to the old perceived conundrum of structural peculiarity so central to the diagnostic vision of Japanese capitalism. The term Gotō used was the "dual structure" *(nijū kōzō)* of the economy, which had been coined in Japan just months before, in March 1957, by Arisawa Hiromi in a speech celebrating the second anniversary of the Japan Productivity Center.[37] The term referred to a fundamental division between a modern, industrial, capital-intensive sector and the traditional, labor-intensive sector, although it came to be applied, with differing emphases, to various aspects of this structural divide—wage and productivity differentials between industrial and small-scale enterprises, small-business exploitation by large combines, the small-scale irrationality of labor-intensive agricultural and small-business sectors. Gotō latched on to Arisawa's term as a pithy descriptor of the perceived structural weaknesses latent within the Japanese economy that he and the EPA had been working to define. Introduced to a wider audience by Gotō's popular white paper, the phrase "dual structure" to describe the socio-economy was in turn further promoted by Arisawa and Nakayama Ichirō. This was most prominently true in their use of the term in the publications of the Japan Productivity Center, as that organization found in the label a galvanizing bogey against which to promote its productivity agenda.[38] By the end of the summer of 1957, the term was fast becoming standard. Its simple evocation of a yawning structural chasm within the economy was a galvanizing force in national discussion of post-recovery purpose.

Expanding his discussion of the "weakest link" of employment from the year before, Gotō tied the concept of the dual economy in his 1957 white paper directly to the dangers of the surging working population and unemployment: in his view, the vast population of only semi-unemployed formed the substratum of the dual structure problem.[39] Because of the "backwardness" of agricultural and small-business segments, which were characterized by low wages and low productivity, Japanese could not be satisfied with rates of unemployment that apparently compared favorably with those of advanced industrial nations.[40] Applying the language of comparative growth and development theories to his diagnosis of the internal deficiencies of the domestic economy, Gotō strikingly maintained that these conditions amounted to a dual structure in which a "backward nation" *(kōshinkoku)* existed within an "advanced nation" *(senshinkoku)*.[41] Gotō presented this form of "backwardness" in Japan as "unique." Indeed, although exceptions existed, proponents of the concept frequently described the "dual structure" as a uniquely distinguishing feature of Japanese capitalism. Analysts and organizations that took this position invariably contrasted the Japanese case against what they posited as a model of Western economic development in which a "unitary structure with like characteristics" ensured that traditional and modernized elements rarely coexisted.[42] The notion of dual structure and its peculiarity to Japan became a given of economic analysis and, often stretched beyond its original meanings, continues to shape accounts of Japan today.

In the past, Gotō had chided in the white paper of the year before, Japan had avoided the hard work necessary to resolve its own internal distortions. The country had pursued, rather, an experiment in which, he argued, it "attempted to restructure the external world to fit domestic needs." This route, "in the end," Gotō lamented, had "led to militaristic expansion." With territorial expansion a failure and the postwar emergency over, now was the time, he urged, for an act of internal self-reformation *(mizukara o kaizō suru)* finally to resolve old maladies.[43] Gotō likened this task to performing a "surgical operation" *(shujutsu)*, and the surgeon's scalpel, the 1957 white paper implied, was to be economic growth *(keizai seichō)*.[44] Utilizing this instrument, the nation could once and for all excise the pathologies identified in the dual-economy diagnosis. The EPA thus offered what might be termed a postimperial growth solution to the problem of Japanese capitalism. Growth could rid the economy of the structural deficiencies that it was believed held Japan—uneasily balanced somewhere between backward and advanced status—in a limbo state among nations.[45] The internal processes of the capitalist economy could be harnessed, this view implicitly maintained, to eradicate essential contradictions. The pursuit of growth, moreover, would place Japan back into peaceful alignment with the family of nations, for growth was the proper expression of international rivalry in the postwar world. Ignoring the ways the Japanese economy was implicated in the Cold War strategies of the United States and had already benefited from the hot war of the Korea "disturbance," Gotō wrote that the weapons races of the past had been replaced by "peaceful coexistence" *(heiwateki kyōson)* over "the fight for economic growth" *(keizai seichōritsu no tatakai)*.[46]

Industrialists and others had advanced the idea before that the social challenges of a rapidly growing population in Japan could only be met by enlarging the size of the economic base.[47] Significantly, however, the proffered responses in the 1920s and 1930s had centered on emigration and empire as externalizing solutions to national socioeconomic dilemmas. More seldom were visions pursued that were directed toward what would later be called domestic economic growth as a means in itself to social or structural ends. Where industrial expansion was the goal, it was more and more characterized during that earlier era by the military and national security needs of empire rather than by ideas about domestic reformation or market development. Past failures truly to pursue the domestic expansionary idea were deeply embedded in the postwar argument for rapid growth as made by the EPA. The comeback after defeat seemed to put the war and the mistaken political choices of that time finally in the past. The end of recovery meant that the real possibility finally to get Japanese capitalism right now lay before the nation. As growth advocates implicitly, and in Gotō's case rather more explicitly, denounced the failures of the economic strategies of the past, they also challenged the critical view held by some in the present that their approach would only exacerbate the very social and economic divisions it was designed to close. The full-employment ideal and the Keynesian theoretical armature on which it hung strengthened the idea that growth could be technocratically managed in such a way that it brought new prosperity to all.

The EPA's vision as articulated by Gotō was instrumental in setting the national agenda for rapid growth in the second postwar decade. Both the EPA's Five Year Plan for Economic Independence of 1955 and its New Long-Term Economic Plan of 1957 forcefully announced national income growth as the means to full employment. By the time of the Ōkita-Shimomura growth debates on the 1957 plan, in fact, the quest for rapid growth was less the issue than the specific rate of expansion that the opposing sides deemed most beneficial. Both technocrats saw in economic growth the cure for what they believed ailed Japanese capitalism.

The various strands of the growthist vision of national reform and the technocratic practices that made it possible culminated in the Income Doubling Plan that formally inaugurated the high growthism of the 1960s and early 1970s. The ambitious motto of "income doubling" may have been inspired by a call in 1959 by Nakayama Ichirō, as head of the Central Council on Labor (Chūō Rōdō Iinkai) and promoter of the Japan Productivity Center's vision of the prosperity economy, for a drive for "wage doubling." As the strong performance of the economy was rapidly making the New Long-Term Economic Plan of 1957 obsolete, economists at the EPA and politicians began to devise a new statement of national goals. The plan became the chief plank in Prime Minister Ikeda Hayato's political program for the new decade. It was directly crafted by the EPA under the direction of Ōkita Saburō, with input from a Liberal Democratic Party committee created for the purpose. But the plan is most commonly associated with Shimomura Osamu, perhaps the most enthusiastic of growth champions and the key member of Ikeda's brain trust of economic advisers, who once again pressed for higher growth targets than Ōkita at the EPA was willing to accept. Although the concept of income doubling was first conceived in terms of individual wages, by the time the plan was adopted by the Ikeda administration in December 1960, it had come more generally to refer to a campaign conceived in national terms to raise total aggregate income.

The Income Doubling Plan followed the precedents of the two preceding plans organized according to the goal of growth but was far more ambitious. Planners and their political leaders were surprised and encouraged by the surpassing of prior projections: the targets of the growth plans of the late 1950s had been quickly overtaken by actual economic performance. While the Income Doubling Plan was drafted at the height of theoretical and statistical innovation in growth forecasting, the target rate of the plan, unlike its two predecessors, was not determined by calculation, but was fixed fairly arbitrarily as a pleasingly round figure—doubling in ten years: the goals of the plan were products of political sloganeering more than the formulae and modeling computations of growth theory. The ironies of such opportunistic mathematics notwithstanding, the plan was an indication of the depth of the national enchantment with the idea of growth and the new found power it commanded in the political arena. Even where economic targets were not derived through specialized analysis, however, the ability to imagine "income doubling" in those terms had been made possible by the statistical tools that had become so pervasive during the 1950s. (And, in fact, the drafters of the plan did employ such statistical procedures in order to set the parameters of component economic relationships that would have to have existed to be in accord with the preselected target rate for overall growth.)[48] Evidence of the influence of macroeconomic thought can also be found in the fact that the Income Doubling Plan was conceived on a newly long-term scale. Its ten-year duration doubled the five-year planning span customary in both overseas models and predecessor postwar plans at home. This again was a product of an iterative interplay between optimism fueled by recent economic gains, the long-run analysis of growth dynamics favored by those like Shimomura who were instrumental in devising the plan, and modes of forecasting within economics that seemed to enable the casting of accurate predictions ever further into the future.[49]

Although the basic conception of the plan stressed a broad view of national advancement in the aggregate, it also specifically declared the goal of doubling household income, thus creating the potential for a more consumerist domestic market than had existed in earlier periods of Japanese modern experience. It promised to address the dual economy and the weakness of the middle class by promoting a vision of prosperity defined by higher incomes and full employment on the one hand and a workforce with expanding consuming power on the other.

In truth, the Income Doubling Plan, like those before it, contained few operational details about how it was to be carried out. It did not lock in the specific measures to be taken within the various compartmentalized jurisdictions of the bureaucracy. There was also much wrangling between ministries over competing claims and approaches, both during the drafting of the plan and after. In addition, material changes on the ground had a way of upsetting the plans by which officials hoped to manage them. (The national economy did indeed double in total size during the period covered by the plan, but it did so, not in the ten-year period that planners had projected, but in a mere seven.) The plan assumed that the private sector would assume responsibility for driving investment for growth, but did address several areas in which government investment would be concentrated as a means to promote income doubling. Emphasis was placed on strengthening social overhead capital—the basic infrastructural and environmental frameworks of the economy, including roads, ports, forestry development, water control, public welfare facilities, and residential housing. The plan called for raising such investments by as much as 100 percent over earlier levels to nearly 8 percent of GNP. There was a sense of the responsibility of the government to ensure the conditions for growth through such investments in infrastructure. To a lesser extent, planners were cognizant that such capital infusions would have some ripple effect on aggregate domestic demand. Throughout, the plan stressed the importance of resisting excessive "consumption expenditures" to focus on spending rationally in ways that truly invested in the future productive stock of the economy.[50]

Due to Dodge-era statutory limitations on deficit financing, Keynesian fiscal strategies did not play a major role in growth management until the second half of the 1960s. Monetary policy was thus more significant in efforts to apply countercyclical pressure. Yet even here, the raising or lowering of interest rates, for example, was triggered less in response to demand or full-employment deficiencies than to recurring deficits in the foreign trade balance of payments. Beyond these approaches and considerable commitment in the plan to making social investments, the government also pursued growth through an array of "administrative guidance" industrial-policy strategies—preferential credit, grants, and subsidies; foreign exchange and licensing supports; government contracts, and so on—that continued a more microeconomic tradition of guidance that had already started to emerge beginning in the 1920s. In addition, the government encouraged private investment by imposing only a relatively light tax burden on corporations. Yet while often more classical methods than the Keynesian prevailed, the Income Doubling Plan did signal a new era in which a persistent macroeconomic orientation in economic management and political goal-setting ruled.[51]

Consumers and National Fortunes

At the same time that the dilemma of the "dual structure" became a commonplace in scholarly and media prognostications about the future of the nation, some simultaneously embarked on a public drive to open new opportunities for reconsidering the meaning of consumption for postwar society. In the face of economic collapse in the immediate aftermath of the Second World War, as Sheldon Garon has persuasively demonstrated, Japanese officials had proclaimed the "beautiful customs of diligence, thrift, and savings" the key to postwar recovery.[52] Yet although such appeals to a national ethic of frugality and financial restraint had animated campaigns to promote household savings from the early twentieth century—and indeed, Garon has extensively shown, continued to do so through the succeeding postwar decades as well—a sometimes competing language that explored the possibilities for new sorts of consumption also grew increasingly strong by the mid-1950s.[53]

The eventual rise of a more open rhetoric in the years after recovery that spoke of new understandings of personal spending and the role of consumption in the national economy sprang in some measure from increasing material prosperity itself. But it was also spurred by the belief, expressed in the diagnostic vision after the war, in the importance of raising standards of living and of promoting vital domestic markets based at least in some measure on middle-class consumers. Promoters who expressed newer, more optimistic views about the possibilities for consumption also drew on the essentially Keynesian idea, slowly becoming orthodoxy within the discipline of economics, that the demand side of the economic ledger was an important engine of a healthy economy. Taking the theoretical tenets of Keynesian thought as their starting point, some bureaucrats and economists beginning in the middle 1950s advertised to a popular audience the potentially positive relationship between productivity gains, high wages, economic growth, and personal consumption: thus, while many powerful institutions clearly continued to preach frugality, others at the same time began to legitimate new understandings of private spending that supported a broader faith in the possibility, even in Japan, of a rebuilt postwar economy eventually capable of producing the material prosperity on which new levels and types of mass consumption could be based.

As with the idea that a national mobilization for macroeconomic growth could serve as an internal postwar solution to the old national problems of population, employment, and "backwardness," the EPA's Gotō Yonosuke was one of the most outspoken of the believers in the possibilities for a

こ　と　し　も　豊　作

FIG. 3. Caption reads: "Another Abundant Crop This Year." By combining the culturally charged symbol of the bounty of the annual harvest of rice with the iconic objects of consumer desire of the second half of the 1950s, the washing machine and the television set, this cartoon provides a playful reflection on the emerging sense that abundance and prosperity in the new age would mean something significantly different than it had in simpler eras of the past. Ogiwara Kenji, "Ogiken no seisansei," *Nihon seisansei shinbun,* no. 7 (Aug. 27, 1956): 1. Used by permission of Iwai Shōko.

materially prosperous Japan and also one of the most influentially situated during the mid-1950s. Yet he was only one among a significant number of similarly prominent public economists, both those who were formally part of academia and those who were state bureaucrats, with a vision of post-recovery progress in which certain kinds of consumption were seen as newly important to the technocratic regulation of macroeconomic expansion. A formative influence in Gotō's thoughts on the increasingly fundamental importance of private mass consumption in postwar economies was a ten-month study mission he undertook to the United States from the end of 1954 to October 1955. Chosen by the newly instituted Eisenhower Exchange Fund as one of thirteen individuals from as many countries to study in America, Gotō traveled throughout the States interviewing prominent figures in economics and government administration. A book resulted from his investigations titled *Amerika keizai han'ei no kōzō* (The structure of American economic prosperity), released in 1956 just months prior to the famous 1956 white paper discussed earlier, and it provides an illuminating window onto the formation of the vision of postwar abundance that Gotō proposed in his prolific works and appearances during the second half of the decade.[54]

One of the long-standing themes of Gotō's analysis of the Japanese economy from after the war had been the need for improvements in the technological efficiency of industry. His earliest accounts near the beginning of the decade had spoken of the issue in terms of "industrial modernization," but with the release of *Amerika keizai han'ei no kōzō* and his subsequent mid-1950s EPA white papers, Gotō began writing principally in terms of an industrial "technology revolution."[55] The focus in this new elocution was less on shop-floor, machine-tool, or manufacturing technology per se, or raw materials extraction technology, though all of these were certainly important. Rather, the lesson he impressed upon his readers after his trip to the United States was that, in the postwar prosperity economy in its most idealized forms, what mattered would be the ways in which technology allowed consumer durables manufacturers to compete for mass consumer markets through a host of newly differentiated products and consumer conveniences. "Progress in technology," Gotō wrote in *Amerika keizai han'ei no kōzō*, "first and foremost works to stimulate consumer desire to buy." Such progress sets off a virtuous circle of expansionary impulses, whereby technology stimulates demand, Gotō explained, which in turn broadens markets for consumer goods, which then itself promotes business investment.[56]

Efforts by American manufacturers to incite demand for their new technologies and products seemed to be working, Gotō maintained. He was particularly impressed by the consumption boom logged by the U.S. economy beginning in 1954. Although the EPA economist did consider the danger that the American boom was too reliant on debt creation, Gotō argued that the American experience showed that material prosperity in this new era was largely driven by the motor of consumption, no longer to be understood in merely negative terms: "In America, the meaning of 'consumption' is changing. It now increasingly refers not to using a product until it is physically worn out, but rather to the act of replacing that item at some point with a new product." An analogous process also took place in the factory, where the pace of machine obsolescence was quickening. The rapidity with which equipment became outdated, however, only provided the opportunity for further expansion of technology investments.[57] Discussing in the conclusion of the book the lessons he had learned, Gotō exhorted Japanese to adopt an American-style optimism about the economic prospects of the nation and to abandon the defeatist negativism that he felt was too common among those considering the technology-centered economy of growth and consumer abundance inspired by U.S. models.[58]

Gotō's account of the mutually beneficial linkages between American growth, industrial production, the science of marketing, and private enrichment certainly represented one of the more ebullient expressions of the mechanics of postwar bounty and its possibilities for a Japan still far poorer than the United States. But in his attempt to work out what was different about postwar economic understanding, its applications to real-world conditions, and what about these might indeed be relevant to a Japanese society changing in directions not yet so clear, Gotō was not alone. Other prominent organizations with official sanction also proposed visons that made room for an expanded role for consumers in the post-recovery Japanese economy.

One of the most prominent of these organizations was the Japan Productivity Center (JPC), the semipublic agency already mentioned in the previous chapter as displaying great interest in the new growthist planning modalities of the postwar period. Some more detail here on the nature of the JPC and its origins will be important to understanding the particular significance of its attempts to articulate a postwar idea of consumption. Ministries such as International Trade and Industry had nurtured a growing interest from the early 1950s in the productivity movement in the United States, and after Japanese business leaders were approached by U.S. officials with an offer to sponsor a productivity program similar to those in place in Western Europe, a Japan Productivity Center was founded in 1955, jointly funded by the U.S. International Cooperation Administration, Japanese business associations, and the Japanese government.[59] The JPC thus represented a voice that relied in part on Japanese state support outside of Gotō's EPA, the bureaucracy arguably most influenced by the new economics of the mid-century period. The board of the JPC was also populated with business officials and economists who, in their participation on an assortment of government advisory panels and commissions, played key roles in shaping official policy.

Proclaiming the drive for higher productivity as Japan's "only road to prosperity," the JPC launched an active program to introduce Japanese business
to the newest management techniques and acted as the chief evangelist of
productivity ideology, coordinating education and research programs in
what amounted to a national mobilization for productivity gains.[60] As William Tsutsui convincingly demonstrates, this postwar productivity campaign
was heir to a string of rationalization movements dating from the 1910s
in Japan that shared much in common with those in other industrialized
economies in Europe and North America. It was based, like those that came
before it, on a pie theory of mutual interest between managers and labor:
by focusing on increasing the size of the economic pie rather than battles
over how it was divided, argued proponents, all would mutually benefit.

Yet to Tsutsui's important account of the JPC's place in the longer
twentieth-century history of similar movements it must also be added that
the JPC introduced a significant postwar dimension to older pushes for
economic rationalization: the celebration of certain forms of private consumption as fundamentally important to the drive for postwar economic
independence in Japan and, in particular, the consumption of a dazzling
new array of consumer durables—cameras, washing machines, electric
fans, vacuum cleaners, radios, and even televisions—in the manufacture
of which Japanese corporations were investing considerable effort as they
retooled for peace in the 1950s. Nakayama Ichirō, vice president of the JPC,
for example, proposed five elements necessary to national development in
the new economy; first on his list was the need for Japanese to accept into
their daily lives the new consumer products of the age.[61] Elsewhere the JPC
argued that to boost domestic consumption through high wages and agricultural price supports would foster domestic markets and decrease dependence on foreign trade.[62]

The JPC's formulations thereby reflected and supported the increasing assumption of responsibility by the state—announced in white papers
and planning reports by MITI and the Economic Planning Agency—to
promote overall aggregate demand through a variety of macroeconomic
means—infrastructure expenditures, tax credits, tax cuts, and the like. It
was increasingly accepted through the mid- to late 1950s that the state must
ensure the existence of an environment in which consumer goods makers
could continue to successfully sell new generations of wares to a domestic
market of laborer-consumers.

The JPC campaigns involved not only the relatively rarefied question
of macroeconomic demand, however, but the first concerted formulation by an officially sanctioned organization that cast Japanese citizens as
consumers. Such purposes were indeed very visibly signaled in the three
guiding principles of the JPC—always featured prominently in its publications—one of which declared that the gains of the productivity movement

洗たく機時代   荻 原 賢 次

一皆さん！むかしはこれを
　　タライでやつたものでございます一

FIG. 4. The name of the performer on the platform is "Circus San'e." Bottom caption: "The Age of the Washing Machine." "Ladies and gentlemen, in the past, he used to perform this acrobatic trick with a simple washing tub!" Here the JPC attempts to have some fun with the way in which national attention—that of manufacturers, consumers, economic planners, and the media—seemed galvanized by the new consumer durable goods of the age and the new levels of ease they appeared to promise for the daily lives of most Japanese (excepting perhaps circus performers). Ogiwara Kenji, "Ogiken no seisansei," *Nihon seisansei shinbun,* no. 3 (July 30, 1956): 1. Used by permission of Iwai Shōko.

would be "fairly shared among managers, workers, and consumers."[63] To the old rationalization movement dyad of management and labor was now added this third element: the end-consumer of the ever-multiplying goods of domestic manufacture.[64]

This formulation conforms, of course, to the rather familiar Fordist vision of worker-consumers that had played an increasingly significant role in American conceptions of the mass production economy for decades. Yet in Japan such high-wage, high-consumption ideas had been largely rejected in the 1910s and 1920s: the capitalization of Japanese manufacturers was low in relative terms, so they could not afford the high wages required in a consumption-oriented economy; plus such a strategy would risk Japan's comparative advantage of cheap labor in relation to international markets. With increasing insistence during the 1950s, in contrast, some organizations and agencies such as the JPC cast Japanese not only as laborers but, more than in early decades, as consumers too, portraying them in word and image as an integral part of the new economy of the postwar period and as rightful beneficiaries of the drive for productivity.

More striking, however, was that the JPC not only promoted an emphasis on domestic markets and proselytized about the benefits to consumers of the high-productivity economy, but that it also seemed, in some places, to be actively working to create demand among consumers for the new products of the age. In *Assembled in Japan,* Simon Partner shows how corporations such as Matsushita helped produce demand for electrical goods during the 1950s where none might have been expected to exist in Japan's still relatively impoverished economy.[65] Partner's fascinating account specifically reveals the ways in which corporations took entrepreneurially long views of the potential in Japan of consumer markets and the techniques they used to promote products to a conservative consumer base.

That corporations played active roles in promoting the purchases of their products is in itself perhaps not immediately surprising. In the JPC, however, we significantly see an organization in part established with financial and administrative support from the government engaging in a similar program to encourage new kinds of consumption by educating potential buyers about the conveniences of the new generations of electrical products. In the pages of its many publications aimed at wide public audiences, the JPC explained that the term "productivity" referred, not only to improvements in production technology, but indeed also to the indispensability of these products to the household and to the productivity gains that they could bring to daily life. These messages were most prominently and consistently displayed in the JPC's weekly *Nihon seisansei shinbun* (Japan productivity news), which began publication in 1956 and was intended for distribution to businesses, work sites, and labor and consumer unions, and which has not been the subject of historical examination in the important accounts thus far of the JPC's postwar activities (see Figure 5). The *Nihon seisansei shinbun* reveals that JPC boosterism from the middle years of the 1950s attempted to legitimate a new excitement about postwar consuming options, encouraging the desire for new amenities through testimonials on how much easier life was after purchasing a washer, for example, and breezy pieces on such new neighborhood phenomena as "electric washing machine rental stores," now otherwise known as laundromats (or, in Japan, "coin laundries").[66] Feature stories routinely attempted to demonstrate the long-run economic efficiency of investing in large convenience products— in one instance, by revealing how many calories one expended in traditional methods of housework and suggesting the lower energy output the housewife would have to expend once she had acquired an electric vacuum cleaner or washing machine.[67] The newspaper also frequently touted the efforts of the JPC to support an emerging consumer protection movement and followed the meetings and factory inspection tours of new consumer organizations with women in leadership roles.[68]

While working hard to create the impression of a groundswell of longing for electrical durables, the JPC's publications at the same time revealed the strongly perceived need to overcome consumer skepticism about the value of expensive new products. Into this space between longing and skepticism

FIG. 5. The top half of the front page of the inaugural edition of the *Nihon seisansei shinbun* (Japan productivity news), July 16, 1956. The *Japan Productivity News* was an institutional organ aimed at the discussion of contemporary economic affairs, drawing at times on quite technical analysis and theoretical concepts. Yet the editors also put considerable energy into making the issues the paper covered relevant to the everyday work and consuming lives of readers, and into explaining for a lay public the links between the individual experiences of Japanese and the prospects for the economic future of Japan. The editorial staff also attempted to promote their views of the postwar economy by making the paper visually appealing and peppering it with regular cartoons that injected lighthearted and often satirical commentary on national issues. At the left of the nameplate at the top of the front page can be seen listed the three principles of the JPC, number three being that the productivity gains of the new economy would be "fairly shared among managers, workers, and consumers." As can be seen in the smaller subtitle headline on the right side of the page, this first edition featured debate about, among other things, the "problem of employment." *Nihon seisansei shinbun*, no. 1 (July 16, 1956): 1. Used by permission of the Shakai Keizai Seisansei Honbu.

stepped organizations such as the JPC, on the front line of the drive for a new kind of economy of prosperity, eager to train potential consumers of these products to fulfill their appointed role in what was becoming known as the "electrical lifestyle."[69]

The *Nihon seisansei shinbun,* it is true, always couched its coverage of the new age of consumer products of convenience and entertainment in language that made it clear that consumption must itself be rationally managed. Japanese could simply not yet afford indiscriminate purchases of relatively expensive items. Common sense and the important ethic of personal and household restraint, moreover, militated against impulsive outlays. The JPC therefore emphasized the importance of savings and ran instructional pieces invoking older discourses on the prudent management of household financial management. All the same, the act of saving today might not necessarily mean a refusal to spend altogether, but merely temporary deferral of spending: present saving could make later, larger-scale consumption possible, and such were often the arguments made by the JPC about household finances.

A *Nihon seisansei shinbun* fall 1957 series on "Household Productivity" *(katei no seisansei)* in the "Study Hall" column of the paper reveals the strategies that the JPC suggested for rationally marshaling household financial resources in order to make appropriate purchases that would improve the productivity of the home. Saving up to buy such appropriate new technologies as washing machines was perfectly rational. By doing so, past "time-worn habits" of home care and management, requiring long, tedious hours of work from women, could be discarded without endangering the financial health of the household. Productivity gains were thus not only a phenomenon of the national economy as a whole, but could be experienced at home as well and were, indeed, one of "the secrets to improving household harmony" in the new age.

Women were prominently portrayed here as the both the recipients and the managers of such improvements in productivity through consumer durables. In one story, the *Nihon seisansei shinbun* featured a housewife who had just purchased her washing machine for the home and recounted that her husband had been adamant in his opposition to the idea of spending money on the appliance: "That's a waste of money!" he had said before they had bought the machine. But once the couple had purchased the washer, even the husband had to agree that it was "a plus" for their "finances and lifestyle." One of the installments of the "Study Hall: Household Productivity" series declared that "Wives Are Company Presidents" who, like the leader of any sound company, had to maintain adequate resources to cover expenses and emergencies but also needed at times to spend, that is, to invest in ways that added over the long term to the well-being of the institution.[70]

The efforts of the JPC were part of a larger process that included manu-facturers themselves, advertisers, the introduction of new marketing tech-niques, and reform movements that championed the "bright life" of leisure and comfort based on highly idealized images of U.S. affluence. It must be added, however, that the belief remained strong that limits on overall national consumption were required by the domestic need for investment capital and the continuous threat that imports would outweigh exports. Moreover, no one among those exploring what the new mid-century eco-nomics seemed to imply about the role of consumption ever advocated a wholesale adoption of postwar American modes and levels of consumerism, however those might be defined, either as a matter of state policy or family lifestyle. Even while the EPA, for example, played a significant role during the 1950s in explaining the importance of aggregate demand to postwar economies and promoting technical approaches to its measure and man-agement, the agency's long-term plans at the same time warned of the need for prudent economizing on the part of individual consumers.[71]

But long-standing dubiousness about the proper role in Japanese society of private consumption increasingly existed in tension with the conviction that mass consumption would play a larger role in the growth economy of the future. Analysts, even those most interested in the new field of mac-roeconomics and its focus on the consumption side of the production-consumption ledger, never defined consumption solely in terms of end-consumer purchases of, say, washing machines or radios. New technical and political focus on the importance of consumption always referred to the idea of "aggregate demand," the total demand for buying things and services throughout an entire economy. This broader concept thus consisted not only of end-consumer spending, but also of the consumption, or spending, of government and business. Yet, even though household consumption itself was never presented as the whole story, many economists in important positions in Japan did increasingly articulate rationales for a careful kind of individual consumerism that would account for special Japanese circum-stances while supporting the new demands of postwar growthism and their most idealistic visions of middle-class prosperity.

While Japanese across the postwar decades of growth were famously high savers, they also began spending on a new scale to buy succeeding genera-tions of durable consumer products of domestic manufacture. Despite the continued strength of Japanese cultural values of thrift and long experi-ence talking about the importance of saving, campaigns that helped to give shape to new levels of acceptance of mass consumer culture in Japan func-tioned alongside more recognized efforts to promote industry and produc-tivity as part of the postwar history of high growth. That some attempted to legitimate new patterns of private consumption while others simultaneously

redoubled their efforts to exhort Japanese to save speaks to the political and
cultural anxieties that the prospect of mass consumer culture has repeatedly
prompted in societies around the world.[72]

It is difficult to assess the direct effect of the JPC's consumption education campaigns. Yet the significance of its propaganda at least in part lies
in the fact that it was an expression of the desire of at least some among
economic goal-setters—in this case an organization sponsored in part by
the Japanese government—to legitimate domestic consumption as part of
the rapid growth economy. Even where policies did not explicitly follow
Keynesian orthodoxies,[73] the more open celebration of consumption—
albeit "rationalized" consumption that took into account the relative limits
of the Japanese economy and its consumers—as publicized in places like
the JPC and in the writings of growthists like Shimomura Osamu and Gotō
Yonosuke, became one of the bedrock conceptions of economic growth. In
the process, the idea gained new acceptance that eventually consumption
would both reflect and help fuel new levels of material prosperity for all.

The descriptive devices of backwardness and deformity, expressed in a variety of ways, had a venerable history in Japan extending back to the begin-
nings of modern social scientific thought in the nineteenth century. These
conceptual categories proved resilient. After the interregnum of the Second
World War, when such talk of national deficiencies was less possible, analysts of a variety of persuasions quickly breathed new life into, to paraphrase
Andrew Barshay, the "tradition" of "backwardness."[74] First revived in the
context of recovery and reconstruction, postwar negative exceptionalism
by the 1950s, chiefly expressed now in terms of the new label of the "dual
structure" of the economy, was taken up by state economic organs in more
formalized ways to champion an active, if fragmented, program to promote
rapid growth. The concept of backwardness had moved beyond the 1920s
academic treatises of the Kōza faction of Marxists from which it was perhaps
most directly derived. Devoid now of the radical impulses that had informed
Kōza formulations and rearticulated in the "modern economics" language
of the central bureaucracy, it operated as an animating orthodoxy within
official and public discourse. The postwar response to the premise of backwardness was the replacement of an earlier territorialist logic of national
power by one founded on a domestic notion of material expansion. Thus
the loss of empire formed the seldom articulated backdrop to the mobilization for growth as it took place in postwar Japan. The descriptive regime
that found in the Japanese economy a uniquely dualistic split between large-
enterprise, high-wage, high-productivity sectors and small-scale, low-wage,
low-efficiency sectors continued to operate, in fact, in a variety of forms at
the center of socioeconomic thought in Japan for decades beyond 1960

and the formative years of the growth idea, even as quantitative economists and world-systems theory scholars showed, each from their own angles, that unevenness in development, both between national economies and within them, was not by itself a particularly distinguishing feature anywhere, but one of the common hallmarks of the rise of modern capitalism.[75]

The idea of growth as an internal solution to the national problem of perceived "backwardness" was at the same time bolstered by a vision of progress in which the consumer would play a new role in ensuring national economic welfare. Through their use of new Keynesian-inspired suppositions about the mechanics of healthy economies, prominent organizations and public economists tried to demonstrate links between the goal of full employment, rising levels of consumption—even at the level of household spending—and national fortunes in ways that were certainly new to that era. Cautious moves to celebrate prudently the possibility for mass consumption that the mass production of new consumer conveniences enabled (and seemed to require) represented a specifically postwar inflection on national campaigns for economic development. The dawning of an era of private consumption on a new scale, however, invited the anxieties about its moral and financial consequences that have proved common everywhere the emergence of a high-consumption culture has taken place. Boosters sought, therefore, to help Japanese supplement their perceptions of the positive values of saving and thrift—values with unquestionably deep roots in the history of cultural self-definition—to allow for an expanded view of the possibility of a material prosperity that at the same time would play a role in keeping the economy running smoothly. Thus, the rise of "electrical lifestyles" of material convenience was accompanied by elaborate attempts on the part of idealistic planners and the corporations who made the products to legitimate private consumption by showing how it improved household economy and by linking it at the same time to national fortunes. In so doing they lent credibility to hopes for an economy of prosperity that exponents like Gotō Yonosuke explicitly tied to the growthist ideal.

Conclusion

Economic Knowledge and the Naturalization of the Growth Ideal

In the 1961 series of *Asahi* newspaper essays quoted in the introductin to this study, the well-known economic writer Ryū Shintarō wondered aloud at the sudden ubiquity of the word "growth" *(seichō)* on the public stage. His observation was a reflection of the novelty of the national preoccupation with rapid macroeconomic growth. Although it arose out of longer streams of economic thought and practice stretching back as far as the eighteenth century, growth as the prescriptive ideal and abiding obsession of modern societies was a distinguishing hallmark of the years following the end of World War II.

Indeed, the very word "growth," as Ryū and others pointed out, seemed new.[1] The concept of growth, borrowed from the biological sciences, had operated in political-economic thought from its classical period. Yet it was the words "progress" and "advancement" that had more often than not been used during earlier times to convey the idea of an increase in material wealth. In Japan, too, *seichō* appeared only infrequently in public writings on the economy before the end of World War II. The expansion or strengthening of economic output had instead been described by a variety of words like *kōgyō* (promotion of industry), *hatten* (development), *kakuchō* (increase), and *kakudai* (expansion). Yet by the turn of the 1960s, as Ryū tells us, the term *keizai seichō* (economic growth) had become the dominant description of material increase and positive economic performance.

This transformation in the language of the economy represented more than a rhetorical replacement of one word for others. It was in part by these shifting terms and what Ryū called metaphors that the economy was framed, understood, and managed. The newer term *seichō* was bound up with a set of technical and ideological developments that provided the conditions under which "growth" could be naturalized as the overriding definition of national purpose. The very real power of the concept of growth to set the parameters of national and social expectation depended on the exquisite coupling of a new, highly successful numerical scientism within economics and an inherent optimism at the heart of a future-oriented heuristics of social change and possibility, one attractively packaged for national publics. Researchers and policy makers pitched the potentially dry statistical claims and prognostications of postwar economic analysis in terms of compelling national quests for progress and accomplishment. At the same time, they leveraged these new forms of macroeconomic knowledge to support enticing visions of personal prosperity for individual citizens. The successful wedding of such technocratic analysis to nationalist image making in Japan and elsewhere secured the place of growthism as one of the defining ideologies of the second half of the twentieth century.

Growth in Japan thus had attained a new valence during the 1950s that went beyond the less rigorously defined and often more sectorally delimited conceptions of material increase of earlier eras. Because it became the object of intense theoretical and empirical scrutiny within the ascendant discipline of economics at the same time that it was cast in political terms as the path to a better future, "growth" came to bear a heavy burden of meaning. By 1960, it represented an encompassing vision of national purpose and peacetime redemption.

This study has examined the history of growth in terms of its postwar deployment as a policy solution to what were commonly perceived as the ills of Japanese capitalism and also its technical foundations within social science. The far-reaching changes in economic knowledge in the mid-twentieth century—the simultaneous moves toward arithmetical measurement and new theoretical concerns with aggregative macroeconomic abstractions—acted as an "enabling technical revolution" to the rise of growthist ways of seeing the national economy. In truth, however, there was no single revolution in economic thought, but the opening up of a series of interrelated research agendas that helped to remap the discipline of economics and position the question of total economic output at the center of public concern around the world as perhaps never before. Without these developments in the modes and objects of economic knowledge, the specifically growthist forms of the economism of the postwar period could not have taken the shape that they did.

The influence of these developments was by no means confined to a field of economics the boundaries of which were coterminus with those of academia; it also reshaped conceptions at the center of the economic apparatus of the state. Much has been made in Japan of the postwar divide between *keizaigakusha* (professional academic economists) and *kanchō ekonomisuto* (economic bureaucrats), since bureaucrats with jurisdiction over economic matters were rarely professionally trained economists. Comparatively few received undergraduate preparation in economics, and far fewer held higher degrees. The majority were educated as undergraduates in faculties of law. After passing an entrance examination, they were admitted to the lowest rungs of the bureaucratic ladder, where they received general training that included instruction in economics. The career-track conditions under which candidates were employed and rose in the bureaucracy meant that there was very little moving in and out of formal positions within bureaucratic agencies by academic economists. Yet a rich network of institutional arrangements—advisory councils, study committees, and the like—ensured increasingly close interconnections between professional economists and their bureaucratic counterparts during the postwar period.

Despite the institutional divide, these relations provided one important avenue for the interchange of ideas between the academy and the state. The activities of many of the economists who figure prominently in this study offer ample evidence of the varieties of close connections that existed between academic economic knowledge and its official uses after the war. The controversial first Economic White Paper in 1947 reflected Tsuru Shigeto's interest in the emerging forms of macroeconomic analysis that he first explored while a student and researcher at Harvard and continued to promote during his tenure at the Institute of Economic Research at Hitotsubashi University. Ishibashi Tanzan's long interest in Keynes, beginning when Ishibashi was still a writer at the journal *Tōyō keizai shinpō,* certainly later influenced his full-employment rhetoric as finance minister. The Hitotsubashi group's empirical documentation of the history of growth fueled research into growth forecasting at the Economic Planning Agency. University of Tokyo economist Arisawa Hiromi's couching of the flaws of Japanese capitalism in terms of a "dual structure" informed the battle cry by the EPA's Gotō Yonosuke to address Japan's "backward nation within an advanced nation" through a drive toward growth.

Nor were official practitioners merely passive adopters of the economic concepts and techniques introduced by academicians; they took active roles themselves in developing the approaches of the growthist era. As I show in my discussions of the Economic Planning Agency, state organs took the lead in refining and employing such statistical tools of the new economics as national accounting. Of the major economic agencies of government, the EPA was by inclination perhaps the most oriented toward developments in economic knowledge within the scholarly world. From its creation, the agency boasted a comparatively high number of members with some measure of education in economics, and its researchers and analysts actively kept abreast of the latest developments in the discipline, attending conferences and, particularly through its Economic Research Institute, engaging in cooperative research with scholars on growth.

What is more, the technical and methodological revolutions in economics affected wider public discourse on the economy and the course of the nation. Here again a class of what I suggest be called public economists, many of whom were bureaucratic economists and some not, performed a major role. As economics assumed an ever larger place in public life in the decades after the war, figures like Arisawa, Ōkita, Gotō, and Shimo-mura rose to prominence and actively broadened economic discussion for national publics, concerned in the words of Ōkita soon after the war that the specialized knowledge of their field be made intelligible to a concerned reading public so that "the cooperation of Japan's eighty million citizens be gained through their willing assent" to the policies and directions the public economists proposed.² It is true that they infrequently sought direct feedback from the general public in any idealized democratic sense. In this regard, public economists conducted their activities as experts in the classi-cally technocratic forms so common to the mid-twentieth century period.³ Nevertheless, through the introduction of frequent reports, white papers, and plans that were a signature of the era, as well as through more popular publicizing activities including primers on economic concepts, education campaigns, and frequent appearances in the mass media, they did help to introduce a shared vocabulary of growth and to elevate national aspirations expressed in terms of GNP and of broadly related ideas about new possibili-ties for social prosperity that helped set the postwar period in Japan apart from the conceptions and experiences of earlier eras.

The fervor for planning in all of the guises that gripped policy elites in industrial and so-called developing economies alike in the 1950s and 1960s has largely come to an end. In Japan, the slowdown of go-go growth in the 1970s and failures by economic forecasters to anticipate major shifts together served to take much of the wind out of the sails of the postwar boom in long-term planning. The Heisei-era economic slump further dis-credited economic intervention in Japan in its various forms and eroded faith in what was once celebrated as a world-beating "economic system" that had pundits and political leaders in the United States calling for adoption of Japanese methods of economic guidance. The hardships with which the countries of Eastern Europe themselves had to struggle during the 1990s showed the command economies of the Soviet era to have been debacles. Nearly everywhere, liberalization, the free market, and so-called Anglo-American models seemed to be the watchwords of the day at the end of the century.

Despite the general demise of the ideal of planning and the only indi-rect credit it can provably be given for the material record of high growth, postwar planning and macroeconomic forecasting did matter in that they represented the apogee of a faith in technocratic ideals that characterized much of the twentieth century as a whole. The practice of planning and the growthism it helped support—with their emphasis on efficiency, the spe-cialized knowledge of technical experts, formalized empirical techniques, a more interventionist state, and universal prescriptive programs—reflected widely shared beliefs in the possibility for rationalized regulation of the social and material world that had been taking shape for decades. But post–Second World War growthism and its attendant practices also extended earlier technocratic ambitions in several ways. The primacy of economics in setting national agendas and solving political problems that had begun to emerge following the First World War reached new heights after 1945. It was then, especially, that economists took their place as high priests of technocracy alongside earlier standard bearers in the fields of urban planning and civil engineering, and also in forestry and other forms of modernist management schemes to "tame nature" cast as national or imperial resource.[4] The views of Arisawa, Inaba, Shimomura, and the rest fit into a wider postwar pattern whose general developmentalism and specific focus on aggregate growth included the Marshall Plan, the reconstruction projects of Jean Monnet in France, and the U.S. Council of Economic Advisors. As statistical modeling and national income analysis broke new ground, economists began to make more assertive claims about the scientific authority of their field. Despite their limitations, plans moved beyond the "manifestos," as Paul Rabinow describes them, of the past.[5] They were now based on more refined theoretical knowledge that employed higher levels of statistical objectification and seemed to boast greater power to explain the real economy and thus make predictions about its future course. Economic planning was also large-scale with pretensions to a macro-level comprehensiveness. And a new muscularity marked the specialized institutions, many of them part of the state, that were responsible for producing economic knowledge and acting on it.

The status of these developments as heirs, certainly, to older modernist ideals but now in more complex, specifically postwar forms speaks to the overlapping chronologies of technocracy in the nineteenth and twentieth centuries. The history of the technocratic faiths as these took shape around the world in the modern period, and of the modes by which its practitioners attempted to reshape societies, was not over by the beginning of the twentieth century. All manner of utopian experimentation and of deep-rooted beliefs in the powers of science, rationality, and the predictability of the outcomes of planned reformations of society have a continuing history that flows powerfully out of early forms of modernism in the eighteenth and nineteenth centuries and right through the middle of the twentieth. This fact has been perhaps most richly explored in relation to the history of urban planning and intense desires around the world for bringing new modern forms to the city, whether that of the imperial center or the colonial outpost. But only in comparatively recent years has scholarship begun to make serious efforts to account for the rise of twentieth-century economics from a historical perspective, and to insert into this history of modernism new forms of economic knowledge, the practices these made possible, and the new institutional settings, both national and international, in which these both appeared.

The Growth Fetish

As with any coherent ideology, growthism could not have flourished if its descriptive and prescriptive claims had not borne convincing relationships to real developments. In this respect growth, at least for a time, did a credible job. In contrast to the clear disconnect that had occurred between economic understanding and the calamitous conditions in much of the world of the rich nations after 1929, growth thought just some three decades later seemed to have demonstrated the ability to explain the comparatively positive dynamics of the postwar years reasonably well. The apparent verisimilitude of its theoretical foundations and predictive capacities contributed powerfully to the allure of growthist modes of understanding.

Two decades out from of the end of the Second World War, however, the concept of growth began to be transmuted from an idealistic means by which to rebuild shattered economies, overcome scarcity, and redress social inequalities in a new age of abundance to an overdetermined goal in itself, one that came to govern the identities of both metropole and postcolonial nations at the height of Cold War contention. While in the case of Japan high growth was presented as the means to achieve certain structural ends and a new economy of domestic possibility, in many ways it became an end in itself there during the 1960s. Elsewhere as well, economic discourses and national self-conceptions were governed more and more by a sort of thralldom of growth. At the same time that income doubling became the highest expression of national goals in Japan, John F. Kennedy in the United States was declaring 5 percent annual growth, the most concerted use of growth targets there thus far, the pillar of both his domestic platform and his Cold War strategy. As the United Nations declared its first Development Decade in 1961, it elevated global GNP goals above all others, thus appearing to draw the member states together as, in the phrase of one accountant, "One Statistical World" for a common progressive purpose.[6]

But internationalist cooperation was not all that was at work in global pushes for growth. Cold War rivalries, superpower competition by proxy through client states, of which Japan became a premier example, and the forced and fitful retreat of colonial empires all contributed to a postwar "growthmanship" in which the drive to create monster economies dominated national agendas and intruded into a deeply competitive order of international relations.[7] In Japan, however, wartime defeat, the end of empire, and a mortgaged postwar sovereignty eventually turned growth into a particularly powerful obsession that soon enough came to inform nationalist representations of a Japan that had lost the war but won the peace.

Indeed, by the later years of the second postwar decade, the abstract goal of growth might be said to have taken on the forms and functions of a true fetish.[8] The sense of "fetish" as extravagant trust placed in an object believed to be imbued with supernatural curative or protective powers is instructively homologous to the almost totemic meaning that came to be attached to the statistic of GNP by that time. Moreover, while human agency could help midwife its birth in places in which growth had not yet begun, its technical and political votaries often reified GNP growth as a self-regulating process that, once certain conditions were in place, unfolded autonomously. Indeed, imbedded in the very word "growth" itself, used to signify an increase in overall economic production, was the implication of an assumed telos, an unfolding of the natural life of an economy like a tree from a sprout.[9]

By and large, theorists and practitioners understood this fetishized process of growth as operating at the level of the nation. They posited the possibilities for growth, measured it and promoted it almost always within the perceived unit of the national economy, as if these systems were discrete from external forces and unified in their internal structures. This highly abstracted schema did not account well for material and social unevenness between national economies or within them, for structural discontinuities that could only be seen at the level of the region or the global system as a whole, or for the entropy and unintended consequences that occurred within self-regulating systems such as those which national economies were supposed to represent. Yet experts and the publics to whom they spoke, in wealthy nations and in poor around the world, came to see the vision of rapid macroeconomic growth as imbued with universal application and promise.

The last quarter of the twentieth century thus came to be characterized by an oddly unwavering continuity in the fables of never-ending growth as these had taken shape in the early decades after the war on which this book has particularly focused. Such fables held almost unchallenged sway in even the richest of countries, those that had attained levels of material abundance fantastically impossible to imagine in decades past. They often depended, moreover, on a near amnesia for end purposes of social betterment and for normative concerns about meaning and individual happiness. By the beginning of the 1970s progressive and internationally prominent economist Tsuru Shigeto lamented that too many had for too long set store by a sort of overweening "growthmanship" alone, thus betraying a terrible "lack of conviction" in any grander vision of social purposes.[10] The new orthodoxy that emerged out of the developments of the early postwar decades seemed to hold that as long as growth continued apace, in the words of another prominent international critic, E. F. Schumacher, no one ought to inquire "after its final shape."[11]

Nowhere did this fetish for growth come to have stronger resonance, it seems, than in the case of Japan. First coherently articulated during the middle of the post-Occupation 1950s, the growth vision was aimed at ambitious but definable goals related to the recovery of the economic levels of prewar times and seen as a remedy for what analysts at the time described as a troubling "dualism" between wealthy and poor sectors of the economy. By the 1960s, however, growth had become one of the significant raisons d'être of the state and in especially intense ways determined the lineaments of national agenda setting for Japanese society as a whole for the remainder of the century. The claim here is not that growthist institutions and modes of knowing supplanted all other instrumental goals and approaches to national policy setting, but that they contributed significant postwar layers to older techniques of industrial policy making for promoting economic power and wealth as these had slowly evolved during the modern period. Even after unprecedented year-on-year gains for the better part of two decades, after many postwar goals had been met and Japan had become the third largest economy in the world after the United States and the Soviet Union,[12] growthism tenaciously defined baseline assumptions about the course of the Japanese nation.

The continued afterlife of this prepossessing faith in the national project of macroeconomic growth can be seen, for example, in Tanaka Kakuei's famous plan of the early 1970s to "Remodel the Japanese Archipelago." Even as he hoped to address the urban overcrowding and pollution that he saw as the result of growthist success, Tanaka still unabashedly assumed that the modal purpose of national life continued to be macro-expansion of the GNP. The unresolved tension between his lament, on the one hand, for the cherry trees wilting under excesses of industrial waste and his drive, on the other, for more bridges and highways to smooth the course of economic increase remains a fitting symbol of the unchallenged place that growth had come to hold in the national imagination.[13] During the 1980s and 1990s, the demands of growthist expectation, even where growth itself was not always present, continued to define Japanese purpose, though only rarely were earlier issues of structural imbalance (except where it now had to do with trade rivalries and current account surpluses) or social deprivation ever at the forefront of national growth conceptions.

The fetishistic life of growthist expectation permeated the very language that, by the closing decades of the twentieth century, had habitually come to communicate the narratives of the national subject of Japan. This was true both in terms of domestic self-conceptions and in the ways in which foreign powers and a postwar class of experts on Japan in the academy in the United States and Europe made their assessments, whether praising or damning, of that East Asian power. As can be seen in the hidden assumptions lurking within the language of 1990s "loss," the growthist fetish has worked in the case of Japan more strongly than perhaps anywhere else to set up implied oppositional binaries at the discursive level that functioned to make normative prescriptions about what it was that the Japanese nation, above all else, was supposed to do. If the opposite of "growth" as the definition of "success" or "gain" was "no growth" as "failure" or "loss," then a string of other binary possibilities for gauging national progress necessarily follows as multiple ulterior meanings, synonymous with one another, along this success–loss axis: increase in size of GDP versus no increase in size of GDP; expansion in material and financial accumulation versus stagnation in the rate of accumulation; progress versus lost time.

This fetishistic dualism conditions our readings of the recent Japanese past in particular troubling ways. A double exchange or substitution seems regulary to take place in our storytelling about Japan, in which a lexicon of "success" (and "loss") is laid over an underlying syntax of growth, which is thus continually disguised, hidden from view as the truly governing narrative. Most critically, this grammar of growth itself tends to foreclose other potential narratives of the national subject, and thus possible alternative conceptions of success.

Box Canyons and Beyond

In the forms that it assumed in the 1950s and 1960s, growthism remains with Japan even today and with the rest of us as well. Although diminished in rhetorical intensity and less often pursued with the overwrought programmatic urgency of earlier times, it continues to govern our most basic views of national economies. Growth remains the essential measure of national economic success, and this assumption underlies the notions of globalization that animate today's economic discourse. Although refinements have been made, the basic conceptual framework of growth remains unchanged: growth means growth in GDP. And governments continue to assume responsibility for managing macroeconomic tools to achieve conditions favorable to growth. While it is true that large-scale planning as such is generally defunct, significant and unceasing tinkering for growth on the part of economists and governments, their fiscal and monetary adjustments of national macroeconomies, remains today as a contemporary legacy of postwar technocracy.

Yet, whether through applying leverage with budgets and interest rates or through larger structural reforms, no one seemed to know the secret to achieving growth in Japan during much of the last decade of the twentieth century. The economic malaise that lingered for much of the 1990s and even into the new century represented the longest recessionary period in

Japan since the end of the Second World War. In more recent years, at the end of the second Heisei-era decade, a more satisfactory growth performance seems perhaps to have returned to a Japan now in part benefiting from the dramatic economic rise of China. The ways in which contemporary economic conditions have been interpreted in both of these periods and the approaches prescribed, however, indicate the continuing power of the concept of growth as the most important yardstick of economic performance and the perceived shaper of national destinies: even when relatively little growth exists compared to earlier postwar decades, growthism remains. Nervously watching every quarterly tick up or down of GNP growth, Japanese governments during the 1990s repeatedly attempted to jump-start the economy through massive infusions of government spending. Indeed, Heisei-era pump-priming represented the most patently fiscally Keynesian orientation to direct economic management in Japan of the entire postwar period. U.S. reactions to the state of the Japanese economy during the final years of the century only underscored the continuing currency of basic tenets of growthist orthodoxy. In its role as watchman over the health of the global economy, the United States insistently chided Japanese for their failures in growth management. Japan was not consuming enough, said U.S. leaders and economic analysts, and they goaded Japanese officials on to ever-larger spending packages designed to promote domestic demand and thereby macro-growth. Current anxiety over low birthrates in Japan similarly stems in part from the belief that (leaving aside the matter of per capita income) Japan's power will "wane" as the total size of the GNP grows smaller as a result of a shrinking population.

At times, the "poetics" of historicization can seem to pitch the historian into a sort of default mode of critique, one that risks appearing facile or smug. Although the history of the growth ideal I have presented has been informed throughout by an underlying concern with the structures of thought and practice that seem to have trapped us, perhaps unnecessarily, in a rather unrelenting fixation on economic increase, my intent here is not simplistically to vilify the social scientists and public practitioners who, in their dedication to the postwar social science of economics and the pursuit of their apparently laudable goals, played such important roles in the narrative of this book. Growth, it goes without saying, has indeed served useful purposes, and in the gory history of the twentieth century it was without doubt one of the most beneficent of the mass faiths to which nations subscribed. It addressed well the problems of adequate production and, in regard to the basic requirements for a comfortable life, largely removed the threat of wholesale scarcity in the growth centers of the global economy. Growth has raised living standards, lengthened lives, and broadened education. The pursuit of growth was also comparatively peaceful. Although it did benefit when war occurred, it nevertheless remained a more desirable expression of national rivalries than the destructive alternatives that characterized the twentieth century.

In the case of Japan economic growth did indeed seem to help address the structural dilemmas that planners had seen at every turn as they attempted to determine the directions of the postwar nation. It led there, much as elsewhere, to a democratization of wealth, though disparities do remain. It certainly eradicated early postwar fears about socially disruptive levels of unemployment, putting Japanese to work in numbers that were impressively high in comparative terms for many decades, and doing so during the 1950s and 1960s, when the population of Japan was rapidly increasing. So successful was the growth economy at putting increasing numbers of Japanese to work that the perception of dire labor surpluses was supplanted in the early 1960s by the opposite fear that companies would not find enough employees to meet business demand. Furthermore, it helped bring a material prosperity to the countryside unimaginable in earlier times. Formerly the site of recurring material hardships, by the end of the twentieth century rural Japan enjoyed standards of material affluence higher in some ways than those of its urban counterpart.

The worst sort of inequalities to which analysts applied the dual structure concept, setting aside the persistent claims of the postwar years that such socioeconomic unevenness was in itself a unique feature of the Japanese case, also seemed to be eased across the years of high growth. As apparent labor surpluses in the postwar 1940s and the 1950s changed to relative labor shortages during the high-growth 1960s, the wages of unskilled labor increased, and wage differentials between unskilled and skilled labor and between small and large enterprises, though persisting to a degree late into the century, were also eased. The share of income in nonagricultural industries garnered by labor in those industries was higher compared to prewar times, rising from an average of 57.2 percent in 1930, for example, to 67.1 percent in 1960, and reversing a long-term decline dating back to the turn of the twentieth century. Indeed, the share of national income earned by labor as a whole rose during the postwar period.[14] It is true that no one believed after the war that the American-style materialist ideals from which Japanese certainly drew energy, both inspirational and technical, ever could be or ought to be directly replicated in Japan. Still, the growthist vision in the 1950s and 1960s of the potential, even in Japan, for a new order of relative prosperity clearly was quite spectacularly achieved.

Yet although the ideal of prosperity has been amply realized in Japan and the other rich nations of the world, the unflagging pursuit of economic growth does seem to be drawing us ever deeper into box canyons, where a host of unintended consequences of rapacious economism, environmental and social, seems at every turn to block our way to sustainable arrangements that adequately provide for the material needs of all while preserving the very conditions that make such goals possible at all. On the one hand, when economies cease to grow, as in Japan during the 1990s, we hasten to bring a return to material prosperity by applying the concepts and techniques of growth management forged and put in place in the mid-twentieth century. On the other hand, we are increasingly forced to confront the logical impossibility and ecological folly of continued pursuit of unending economic growth. The failures on both scores, when they come, make it clear, as Ulrich Beck and others have suggested, that only the certainty of uncertainty has so far replaced earlier faith in the technocratic "controllability" of side effects and in the possibility of discovering final remedies to social and economic maladies.[15]

In truth, it seems difficult to think realistically about economies—how they ought to perform and ought to be managed—in any terms other than growth. This prison house, of sorts, of prevailing economic conceptions places limits on definitions of national prosperity and power and on collective choices about the means to the good life. Within the discipline of economics, competing ideas have existed. As is often pointed out, many of the classical political economists believed in the inevitability of a "stationary state" when material expansion would cease, a welcome condition that, free of the ugly clamor of economic competition, in Mill's formulation, would allow the higher faculties of the human being to unfold more fully. Keynes himself also held that a future "quasi-stationary community" could be achieved where only tastes, institutional arrangements, and population would continue to be subject to change.[16] Such ideas about the desirability of a steady state that some in the early twentieth century saw around the corner were quite thoroughly dethroned by the 1950s and replaced by a more glittering vision of ever-growing affluence.

Not that celebration alone prevailed during the high years of growthism. Many leftists were convinced that growth would only succeed in making the rich richer. The standard literature on Japan always emphasizes the rise of a vigorous antipollution movement, one of whose slogans, *Kutabare GNP!* (To Hell with GNP!), neatly encapsulated the power of the day's statistical rhetoric and the depth of outrage over the unwanted effects of growthism.[17] But critics also pursued other lines of attack, at the forefront of which Japanese thinkers often stood. Shinohara Miyohei, for a time during the early 1970s head of the Research Bureau of the EPA, was a leader in the development of such concepts as Net National Welfare (NNW), for example, by which economists tried to achieve a better understanding of the level of total social prosperity than measurements like GNP alone made possible.[18] Ōkita Saburō, who played such a central role in articulating the growth goals of postwar Japan, was also active in the international Club of Rome group of researchers responsible in the early 1970s for the first significant effort to employ empirical modeling techniques to demonstrate, as the famous title of the group's report put it, the "Limits to Growth." More recently, the sustainable development movement among economists and activists worldwide has attempted to define approaches that allow for the necessity of material progress while respecting the limits the planet imposes.[19] Whether these efforts will suggest new conceptions able to supplant, or only supplement, those founded on a faith in growth is yet unclear, but understanding the historicity of growthist thought can help us to imagine at least the possibility of persuasive and durable alternatives.

Notes

Introduction: The Growth Idea and Early Postwar History

1. For examples of notions of a "lost decade" and a "miracle" ended, see Harada Yutaka, *Nihon no ushinawareta jūnen: shippai no honshitsu, fukkatsu e no senryaku* (Nihon Keizai Shinbunsha, 1999); Toshida Seiichi, *Nihon keizai no shukudai: "ushinatta jūnen" o koete* (Daiyamondosha, 2001); Ōtake Fumio, Yanagawa Noriyuji, Noguchi Yukio, *Kenshō: ushinawareta jūnen, Heisei fukyō no ronten* (Tōyō Keizai Shinbunsha, 2004); Tokyo Daigaku Shakai Kagaku Kenkyūjo, *Ushinawareta 10-nen o koete* (Tokyo Daigaku Shuppankai, 2005–6); Hiroshi Yoshikawa, *Japan's Lost Decade*, trans. Charles H. Stewart. LTCB International Library Selection, no. 11 (LTCB International Library Trust/International House of Japan, 2001); Gary R. Saxonhouse and Robert M. Stern, eds., *Japan's Lost Decade: Origins, Consequences and Prospects for Recovery* (Malden, MA: Blackwell Publishing, 2004); Tim Callen and Jonathan D. Ostray, eds., *Japan's Lost Decade: Policies for Economic Revival* (International Monetary Fund, 2003); Richard Katz, *Japan, the System That Soured: The Rise and Fall of the Japanese Economic Miracle* (Armonk, NY: M. E. Sharpe, 1998); Edward W. Desmond, "The Failed Miracle," *Time,* April 22, 1996.

2. There were a number of interrelated trends, to be sure, on the Japanese national scene in the last years of the twentieth century that did by conventional measures seem rightful causes for worry. Several posed a particularly tough set of interlinked challenges to Japanese social and economic policy makers and began to exert a certain amount of constraining influence on personal experience and life trajectories: the aging of the population, an increase in government and corporate red ink, a rising tide of bad debt held by the financial industry, and a slowing of the total annual increase in national economic production of goods and services. Invocations of these factors became a constant refrain in Heisei-era Japan, but it was perhaps the last of these that was most broadly lamented.

3. Ryū Shintarō, "Hanamizake no keizai," in *Ryū Shintarō Zenshū,* vol. 3: *Seichō keizai no yukue* (Asahi Shinbunsha, 1968), 116. This *Asahi* series was collected with others to form the basis of Ryū's well-known volume *Hanamizake no keizai,* published by Asahi Shinbunsha in 1962.

4. Ryū, "Hanamizake no keizai," 116. In daily parlance, *keiki* implied a general sense of "good economic times" and "business" being "up." In more technical senses, the term stood in close relation to study of business cycles that had so dominated certain branches of neoclassical economics from the end of the nineteenth century into the early decades of the twentieth.

5. Mizutani Michikazu, *Sengo Nihon keizaishi: sangyō, ryūtsū, shōhi kōzō no henka* (Dōbun Kanshutsu, 1991), 68, tables 3–5.

6. Timothy Mitchell, *Rule of Experts: Egypt, Techno-Politics, Modernity* (Berkeley: University of California Press, 2002), 82.

7. On the expansion of credit and marketing, see Andrew Gordon, "From Singer to Shinpan: Consumer Credit in Modern Japan," in Sheldon Garon and Patricia L. Maclachlan, eds., *Ambivalent Consumer: Questioning Consumption in East Asia and the West* (Ithaca, NY: Cornell University Press, 2006), 137–62; Lendol Calder, *Financing the American Dream: A Cultural History of Consumer Credit* (Princeton, NJ: Princeton University Press, 1999), and Simon Partner, *Assembled in Japan: Electrical Goods and the Making of the Japanese Consumer* (Berkeley: University of California Press, 1999), 168–71.

8. Sheldon Garon has elegantly and persuasively illustrated the continued force in the second half of the twentieth century of campaigns by some to control consumption and promote savings. His research has traced the ways in which these movements invoked both culturalist and political-economic rationales for their goals. For Sheldon Garon's work in these regards, see *Molding Japanese Minds: The State in Everyday Life* (Princeton, NJ: Princeton University Press, 1997), 153–57; "Japan's Post-war 'Consumer Revolution,' or Striking a Balance between Consumption and Saving," in John Brewer and Frank Trentmann, eds., *Consuming Cultures, Global Perspectives: Historical Trajectories, Transnational Exchanges* (New York: Berg, 2006), 189–217; "The Transnational Promotion of Saving in Asia: 'Asian Values' or the 'Japanese Model'?" in Garon and Maclachlan, eds., *The Ambivalent Consumer,* 163–87. In my own research, I have also found that those pushing for a reconsideration of consumption as not necessarily antithetical to happy economic outcomes always did so in a manner that also emphasized the importance that it be sober and rational.

9. The tension between ideals of frugality and simplicity on one hand and the consuming impulse on the other has been important throughout early modern and modern Japanese history. It turns out, however, that such tensions have played important roles everywhere one looks. A great deal of interesting scholarship exists demonstrating that consumption had to be ideologically validated over time even in Western societies, and that it was championed by a whole variety of popularizers and promoters in the commercial, academic, and political realms. See William Leach, *Land of Desire: Merchants, Power and the Rise of a New American Culture* (New York: Random House, 1993); Gary Cross, *An All-Consuming Century: Why Commercialism Won in Modern America* (New York: Columbia University Press, 2002); Jackson Lears, *Fables of Abundance: A Cultural History of Advertising in America* (New York: Basic Books, 1994); Lizabeth Cohen, *A Consumers' Republic: The Politics of Mass Consumption in Postwar America* (New York: Knopf, 2003); Calder, *Financing the American Dream;* Daniel Horowitz, *The Morality of Spending: Attitudes toward the Consumer Society in*

America, 1875–1940 (Baltimore and London: Johns Hopkins University Press, 1985); Alan Brinkley, *The End of Reform: New Deal Liberalism in Recession and War* (New York: Vintage Books, 1996).

10. Sada Kaiseki, "Saibai keizairon" (1878), in Meiji Bunka Kenkyūkai, ed., *Meiji bunka zenshū*, vol. 15: *Shisō hen* (Nihon Hyōronsha, 1955–74), 307–411.

11. The most prominent among these postwar figures have become the focus of increasing interest in Japan through histories, memoirs, interview collections, and roundtables. A group of scholars in the United States have also turned their attention to such influential economists and bureaucrats in recent years. For historical treatments in Japan, see, for example, Kanamori Hisao, *Watashi no sengo keizaishi: ekonomisuto no 50-nen* (Tōyō Keizai Shinpōsha, 1995); Asai Yoshio, "Keizai antei honbu chōsaka to Ōkita Saburō," Seijō Daigaku keizai kenkyūjo kenkyū hōkoku, no. 11 (March 1997); Sugita Hiroaki, *Shōwa no ekonomisuto* (Chūō Keizaisha, 1989). In the United States, see the following important works of Bai Gao: "Arisawa Hiromi and His Theory for a Managed Economy," *Journal of Japanese Studies* 20, no. 1 (Winter 1994): 115–53, and *Economic Ideology and Japanese Industrial Policy: Developmentalism from 1931 to 1965* (Cambridge: Cambridge University Press, 1997). On economists and new forms of statistical knowledge and practice, see Scott P. O'Bryan, "Economic Knowledge and the Science of National Income in Twentieth-Century Japan," *Japan Studies Review* 6 (2002): 1–19. Laura Hein has also been a leading scholar on economic discourse in Japan. For discussion of postwar concepts of reconstruction, see her *Fueling Growth: The Energy Revolution and Economic Policy in Postwar Japan* (Cambridge, MA: Council on East Asian Studies, Harvard University, 1990), 107–28, and for economists as political intellectuals, see her *Reasonable Men, Powerful Words: Political Culture and Expertise in Twentieth-Century Japan* (Berkeley: University of California Press, 2005) and "Statistics for Democracy: Economics as Politics in Occupied Japan," *Positions* 11, no. 3 (Winter 2003): 765–78.

12. Today, in fact, the Economic Planning Agency no longer exists as a separate agency at all. In 2001, the Central Government Reform initiative merged the functions of the old EPA into several research institutes and policy councils within a new Cabinet Office, all part of an overall attempt to streamline the organization of the national government and to strengthen the cabinet and the office of prime minister.

13. Yet, in this regard, I am thankful to remember Keith Tribe's somewhat tongue-in-cheek warning that, in order to avoid the "illusion" that economic discourse is wholly unproblematic, it is best if the historian's knowledge of it not be so completely thorough. Keith Tribe, *Genealogies of Capitalism* (New York: Macmillan, 1981), 126.

14. Tribe, *Genealogies of Capitalism;* see also his *Strategies of Economic Order* (Cambridge: Cambridge University Press, 1995); Philip Mirowski, *More Heat Than Light: Economics as Social Physics; Physics as Nature's Economics* (Cambridge: Cambridge University Press, 1989); and Deirdre N. McCloskey, *If You're So Smart: The Narrative of Economic Expertise* (Chicago: University of Chicago Press, 1990). For the place of emerging economic knowledge in political practice during the twentieth century, Mary O. Furner and Barry Supple, eds., *The State and Economic Knowledge: The American and British Experiences* (Cambridge: Woodrow Wilson International Center for

Scholars and Cambridge University Press, 1990), and Peter A. Hall, ed., *The Political Power of Economic Ideas: Keynesianism across Nations* (Princeton, NJ: Princeton University Press, 1989), have also both proved useful to me.

15. Ian Hacking, *The Taming of Chance* (Cambridge: Cambridge University Press, 1990); Martin J. Wiener, *English Culture and the Decline of the Industrial Spirit, 1850–1980* (Cambridge: Cambridge University Press, 1981); Leach, *Land of Desire*.

16. Silvana Patriarca, *Numbers and Nationhood: Writing Statistics in Nineteenth-Century Italy* (Cambridge: Cambridge University Press, 1996), 11–12.

17. Mary Poovey, *A History of the Modern Fact: Problems of Knowledge in the Sciences of Wealth and Society* (Chicago: University of Chicago Press, 1998); Patriarca, *Numbers and Nationhood*. Other books insightful on these scores include Judy L. Klein and Mary S. Morgan, eds., *The Age of Economic Measurement,* supplement to vol. 33 of *History of Political Economy* (Durham, NC: Duke University Press, 2001), and Daniel Breslau, *In Search of the Unequivocal: The Political Economy of Measurement in U.S. Labor Market Policy* (Westport, CT: Praeger, 1998).

18. Such interest in the way newly invented numerical measures defined the aspirations of peoples and nations across the globe during the twentieth century has gathered speed from a variety of angles, particularly among scholars of international relations who are showing that, even in the apparently lowly case of the statistic of the calorie, for example, "numerical indicators prepared the way," in Nick Cullather's words, for transnational "doctrines of development"; Nick Cullather, "The Foreign Policy of the Calorie," *American Historical Review* 112, no. 2 (April 2007): 337–64. See also David C. Engerman, "Bernath Lecture: American Knowledge and Global Power," *Diplomatic History* 31, no. 4 (Sept. 2007): 599–622.

19. The "strong state" versus "weak state" formulation of the terrain of the debates is Watanabe Osamu's; see his "The Weakness of the Contemporary Japanese State," in Banno Junji, ed., *The Political Economy of Japanese Society,* vol. 1: *The State or the Market?* (Oxford: Oxford University Press, 1997), 109–11. Watanabe usefully lists the U.S. Commerce Department as one of the early articulators of the strong state interpretation, cast in that case in terms of the phrase "Japan Inc.," thus inaugurating a concept that would go on to have a long afterlife in Japanese studies. The classical scholarly texts of the strong state interpretation are Chalmers Johnson, *MITI and the Japanese Miracle: The Growth of Industrial Policy, 1925–1975* (Stanford, CA: Stanford University Press, 1982), and Ezra Vogel, *Japan as Number One: Lessons for America* (Cambridge, MA: Harvard University Press, 1979). James Fallows and Karl van Wolferen were the most prominent of the weak state proponents of the 1980s and early 1990s, though this "weakness" in their view, because no governing central authority controlled the Japanese "system" and its rising economic power, only made Japan a greater potential threat to the position and power of the United States, one that required "containment" from the outside. ("Containment" was Fallows' phrase. On Fallows and van Wolferen, see Osamu Watanabe, "The Weakness of the Contemporary Japanese State," 111.) Such later works as Daniel Okimoto's responded specifically to Chalmers Johnson's strong industrial policy treatise by arguing that a variety of political and market forces were more involved in economic outcomes than what "cooperative-functional" theories of bureaucratic power seemed to allow. Scott Callon, in turn, maintained that whatever cooperative coherence there may have been in industrial policy in early postwar decades, such con-

sensus between state actors and business had come apart by the 1970s. See Daniel I. Okimoto, *Between MITI and the Market: Japanese Industrial Policy for High Technology* (Stanford, CA: Stanford University Press, 1989), and Scott Callon, *Divided Sun: MITI and the Breakdown of Japanese High-Tech Industrial Policy, 1975–1993* (Stanford, CA: Stanford University Press, 1995). "Cooperative-functional" is Callon's phrase (1).

20. Representative works include Noguchi Yukio, *1940 Nen taisei: saraba senji keizai* (Tōyō Keizai Shinpōsha, 1995); Hara Akira, *Nihon no senji keizai: keikaku to shijō* (Tokyo Daigaku Shuppankai, 1995); and Tetsuji Okazaki and Masahiro Okuno-Fujiwara, eds., *The Japanese Economic System and Its Historical Origins* (Oxford: Oxford University Press, 1999).

Chapter 1. A New Mobilization

1. See State–War–Navy Coordinating Committee, "U.S. Initial Post-Surrender Policy for Japan," *Department of State Bulletin* 13, no. 326 (Sept. 23, 1945): 423–27, which declared: "The plight of Japan is the direct outcome of its own behavior, and the Allies will not undertake the burden of repairing the damage." See also Jerome B. Cohen, *Japan's Economy in War and Reconstruction* (Minneapolis: University of Minnesota Press, 1949), 418–19, for a discussion of U.S. policy planning for postwar Japan.

2. Supreme Commander for the Allied Powers, *Heavy Industry,* monograph no. 47 of *History of Nonmilitary Activities of the Occupation of Japan, 1945–1951* (Washington, DC: National Archives, 1951), 1.

3. Official planning centered on so-called emergency mobilization plans, which by the end of the war had largely devolved into desperate attempts to provision the home islands with such basic foodstuffs as soybeans and salt before the Allies cut all shipping lanes.

4. Quoted in Nihon Ginkō, Hyakunenshi Hensan Iinkai, *Nihon ginkō hyakunenshi,* vol. 5 (Nihon Ginkō, 1985), 9.

5. James W. Morley, "The First Seven Weeks," *Japan Interpreter* 6 (Feb. 1970): 155. A case in point was the Bank of Japan, which in the spring of 1945 had begun limited studies of post–World War I inflation policy in Germany and the new Bretton Woods system, but which only initiated a comprehensive study of reconstruction once the war was over. See Nihon Ginkō, Hyakunenshi Hensan Iinkai, *Nihon ginkō hyakunenshi,* vol. 5 (Nihon Ginkō, 1985), 9.

6. Arisawa Hiromi, *Arisawa Hiromi sengo keizai o kataru: Shōwashi e no shōgen* (Tokyo Daigaku Shuppankai, 1989), 3; Special Survey Committee, Ministry of Foreign Affairs, *Postwar Reconstruction of the Japanese Economy,* 1946, comp. Ōkita Saburō (University of Tokyo Press, 1992), 65. This report of 1946 (about which more in this chapter), the earliest comprehensive survey of postwar conditions, went on to lament that "definite ideas are lacking both in government and private circles as to the direction and means by which the postwar economy should be reconstructed, with the result that various measures tend to have a makeshift or 'patched together' character and do not provide a firm basis for the promotion of production" (Special Survey Committee, *Postwar Reconstruction,* 66).

7. For calls to settle the reparations issue once and for all so that government and business in Japan might set to work on recovery, see Jerome B. Cohen, "Japan: Reform vs. Recovery," *Far Eastern Review* 17 (Dec. 1948): 137–38.

8. Special Survey Committee, *Postwar Reconstruction*, 65.

9. Inaba Hidezō, *Gekidō 30 nen no Nihon keizai* (Jitsugyō no Nihonsha, 1965), 138.

10. Elizabeth Tsunoda, "Rationalizing Japan's Political Economy: The Business Initiative, 1920–1955" (Ph.D. diss., Columbia University, 1993), 535–36.

11. See, for example, Inaba, *Gekidō 30 nen*, 130.

12. See David R. Ambaras, "Social Knowledge, Cultural Capital, and the New Middle Class in Japan, 1895–1912," *Journal of Japanese Studies* 24 (Winter 1998): 1–33; Kenneth Pyle, "Advantages of Followership: German Economics and Japanese Bureaucrats, 1890–1925," *Journal of Japanese Studies* 1 (Autumn 1974): 127–64.

13. A later English translation of this report is titled *Postwar Reconstruction of the Japanese Economy* (see note 22 for bibliographic details). Laura Hein was, to my knowledge, the first English-language scholar to discuss this significant report. See chapter 5, "Government Economic Planning and the Debate over State Control of the Coal Mines, 1946–1948," in her *Fueling Growth: The Energy Revolution and Economic Policy in Postwar Japan* (Cambridge, MA: Council on East Asian Studies, Harvard University, 1990), especially 111–16.

14. For discussion of the Shōwa Juku, see Saburō Ōkita, *Japan's Challenging Years: Reflections on My Lifetime*, trans. Graeme Bruce (Boston: George Allen and Unwin, 1985), 14–15.

15. Tokuko Ōmori, Introduction 2, in Special Survey Committee, *Postwar Reconstruction*, xv.

16. Ōkita, *Japan's Challenging Years*, 29.

17. Ōmori, Introduction 2, in Special Survey Committee, *Postwar Reconstruction*, xv. See also the preface of the report itself for a list of members.

18. The secretariat consisted of four members: Ōkita, who was thirty years old; Namiki Masayoshi, twenty-nine; Gotō Yonosuke, twenty-eight; and Oda Hiroshi, whose age is unknown, though it is assumed by Ōkita's comment about all four being of a similarly young age that Oda, too, was roughly thirty years old (Ōkita, *Japan's Challenging Years*, 28). Ōkita and Gotō would go on to be important members of the Economic Planning Agency (and its earlier incarnations) during the late 1940s and 1950s and were responsible during many of those years for the EPA's famous Economic White Papers. Namiki would become an influential economic bureaucrat in the General Research Office of the Ministry of Agriculture and Forestry.

19. Arisawa Hiromi, "Fukahiteki na mono: Nihon keizai gendankai no tenbō," *Sekai*, no. 3 (March 1946): 32. Optimism was not exclusive to planners associated with the political left, however. Though perhaps in a different spirit than that evinced by Arisawa, captains of industry also found initial cause for hope as the war ended, believing that the end of militarist control and occupation by capitalist America would usher in—in the oft-quoted phrase—"the age of the industrialists" (quoted in William M. Tsutsui, *Manufacturing Ideology: Scientific Management in Twentieth Century Japan* [Princeton, NJ: Princeton University Press, 1998], 122; see also Michael Schaller, *The American Occupation of Japan: The Origins of the Cold War in Asia* [New York: Oxford University Press, 1985], 4). It goes without saying that the harsh reality of reform at the hands of Occupation "New Dealers" would soon temper such unguarded optimism.

20. Ōkita, *Japan's Challenging Years*, 33. Ōkita later noted by use of a proverb that the coming together on the committee of such a diverse group of planners

appeared in retrospect as a case of "enemies in the same boat" (*goetsu dōshu mitai na kan ga aru;* Arisawa, *Sengo keizai o kataru,* 6).

21. Ōuchi Hyōe, *Keizaigaku gojūnen,* 2 vols. (Tokyo Daigaku Shuppankai, 1959), 2:329.

22. Although completed after the original had been reviewed by Norbert Bogdan of the Occupation's Economic and Scientific Section, the revised version of the report hewed closely to the view and retained the name of the former edition. I have consulted two versions of this second edition of the report in the writing of this study. The first is a reprint of the original Japanese-language version in Nakamura Takafusa and Ōmori Tokuko, eds., *Nihon keizai saiken no kihon mondai,* vol. 1 of *Shiryō: sengo Nihon no keizai seisaku kōsō,* edited by Arisawa Hiromi (Tokyo Daigaku Shuppankai, 1990), 143–263. The second version of the report I have used is a published English translation: Special Survey Committee, Ministry of Foreign Affairs, *Postwar Reconstruction of the Japanese Economy,* 1946, compiled by Ōkita Saburō (University of Tokyo Press, 1992). Most direct quotations are taken from the translation of the report, though I have slightly altered the wording in places. Where changes have been made in the English translation, I indicate the page numbers of the reprinted Japanese original in brackets after the page number of the translated version. The report was not available for sale to the public when it was released in 1946, but was distributed widely throughout the Diet and the bureaucracy (Tokuko Omori, Introduction 2, Special Survey Committee, *Postwar Reconstruction,* xxi). For the number of copies distributed, see Ōkita, *Japan's Challenging Years,* 34.

23. Ōmori, "Introduction 2," Special Survey Committee, *Postwar Reconstruction,* xvi.

24. Hein, *Fueling Growth,* 111 and 116.

25. Arisawa, *Sengo keizai o kataru,* 15–16. The SSC report had a more practical role in the formation of priority production policy as well. Prime Minister Yoshida Shigeru had heard about the SSC's work, probably from Agriculture Minister Wada Hiroo, who had read one of the early reports by the committee. Around the beginning of 1946, Yoshida called Ōkita in to see him about the committee's work, and from this initial meeting were born the famous lunchtime meetings of Yoshida's so-called economic brain trust *(keizai burēin).* The issue of priority production, Ōkita notes, was first raised in the course of these meetings during 1946. See Arisawa, *Sengo keizai o kataru,* 17–18.

26. Takafusa Nakamori, "Introduction 1," Special Survey Committee, *Postwar Reconstruction,* ix; Ōmori, "Introduction 2," Special Survey Committee, *Postwar Reconstruction,* xxviii.

27. Special Survey Committee, *Postwar Reconstruction,* 9.

28. Special Survey Committee, *Postwar Reconstruction,* 9.

29. For the history of gold standard politics and policies in the case of Japan, the definitive monographic work is Mark Metzler, *Lever of Empire: The International Gold Standard and the Crisis of Liberalism in Prewar Japan* (Berkeley: University of California Press, 2006).

30. Kazami had been a friend of Ōkita's father, and Ōkita had visited Kazami's home during Ōkita's time at the Shōwa Juku (Ōkita, *Japan's Challenging Years,* 20). Konoe had only recently resigned as P.M. (October 1941) in a dispute with War Minister Tōjō Hideki over the army's insistence on continuing the conflicts in China.

31. Kazami quoted in Ōkita, *Japan's Challenging Years,* 20–21.
32. Inaba Hidezō, *Gekidō 30 nen,* 66–67.
33. Special Survey Committee, *Postwar Reconstruction,* 9–10. Such notions that the modern nation-state system would soon give way in the interests of world peace in a nuclear age were a part of common discourse taking place around the world at the time. This hope was not exclusive to Japanese as citizens of the only nation to have experienced the atomic bomb. For widespread American calls for the creation of a world government in the early years after the dropping of the bombs on Hiroshima and Nagasaki, see Paul Boyer, *By the Bomb's Early Light: American Thought and Culture at the Dawn of the Atomic Age* (New York: Pantheon, 1985), chap. 3.
34. Special Survey Committee, *Postwar Reconstruction,* 10.
35. Special Survey Committee, *Postwar Reconstruction,* 10–11.
36. Special Survey Committee, *Postwar Reconstruction,* 12–13.
37. Uno Kōzō, "Shihonshugi no shoshikika to minshushugi," *Sekai,* no. 5 (May 1946): 16–28.
38. See also Special Survey Committee, *Postwar Reconstruction,* 97, 131, and 186, for the use of "systematize" and "systematization"; Gaimushō, Chōsakyoku, Kongo no kokunai keizai shisaku ni kan suru hitokōsatsu" (Sept. 18, 1945), in Nakamura Takafusa and Ōmori Tokuko, eds., *Nihon keizai saiken kihon mondai,* 56, for the idea of "systematization" of the economy in an early SSC working paper; Sugihara Shirō et al. eds., *Nihon no keizai shisō no yonhyaku nen* (Nihon Keizai Hyōronsha, 1990), 378–79, for use of *soshiki* as "organization" or "system" in Arisawa Hiromi's explanation of the priority production industrial recovery plan he authored. Sugihara et al. excerpt, Arisawa Hiromi, "Nihon keizai no hakyoku o sukū mono" (Dec. 10, 1946), in *Infureshon to shakaika* (Nihon Hyōronsha, 1948): 68–69.
39. Wakimura Yoshitarō, "Sengo sekai keizai no tenbō: tenkan no shomondai," *Sekai,* no. 6 (June 1946): 48 and 50.
40. Special Survey Committee, *Postwar Reconstruction,* 12–13.
41. Special Survey Committee, *Postwar Reconstruction,* 12.
42. In effect, a dual process of projection has occurred whereby the shadow of *fukoku kyōhei,* on one end, has been cast forward onto the intervening decades leading up to the 1930s, and the shadow of mobilization planning during the war years of the 1930s and 1940s has been cast backward, each coloring the period from the 1880s with shades of planning.
43. Tetsuo Najita, *Japan: The Intellectual Foundations of Modern Japanese Politics* (Chicago: University of Chicago Press, 1974), 2–6 and chapter 2; Chalmers Johnson, *MITI and the Japanese Miracle: The Growth of Industrial Policy, 1925–1975* (Stanford, CA: Stanford University Press, 1982), 35–40. Revisionist treatments that reject the theory that the bureaucracy wielded autonomous policy-making power have emerged. See, for example, J. Mark Ramseyer and Frances M. Rosenbluth, *The Politics of Oligarchy: Institutional Choice in Imperial Japan* (Cambridge: Cambridge University Press, 1995).
44. Thomas C. Smith, *Political Change and Industrial Development in Japan: Government Enterprise, 1868–1880* (Stanford, CA: Stanford University Press, 1955), 36–41. In addition to providing data revealing the relatively low levels of banking capital in Japan, Smith also refers to contemporary accounts of the dearth of investment capital, writing that "there was scarcely an official document proposing the estab-

lishment of a new government enterprise that did not argue that private capital was too weak for the undertaking" (Smith, *Political Change,* 37). For treatments of liberal economic thought in Meiji period Japan, see Sugihara Shirō, ed., *Kindai Nihon no keizai shisō* (Mineruva Shobō, 1971); Sugihara Shirō, *Seiō keizaigaku to kindai Nihon* (Miraisha, 1972), 3–16 and 124–43.

45. Tetsuji Okazaki and Masahiro Okuno-Fujiwara, eds., *The Japanese Economic System and Its Historical Origins* (Oxford: Oxford University Press, 1999).

46. Johnson, *MITI,* 88.

47. It has been pointed out by economic historians that the Japanese economy actually grew at a considerable clip across the decade of the 1920s. Important to remember, however, is that this fact was only known retrospectively, applying knowledge and techniques largely unavailable at the time. The perception of crisis and lingering economic malaise, especially in regard to the hardship of the countryside, the unfavorable balance of payments, and falling corporate profits, was almost the constant tenor of the times. These began to be seen as intractable problems.

48. Business initiative on this score was not unique to Japan, but a common feature of industrial capitalism at the time in France, the United States, and elsewhere.

49. Tsunoda, "Rationalizing Japan's Political Economy," 6–8, 268–72. *Kontsuerun* was a term borrowed from the German *Konzerne.* Closely resembling an American holding company, a *kontsuerun* was a diversified business conglomerate in which there was a division between centralized planning, carried out in the *honsha,* and decentralized operational management, carried out in separate business units. Most *zaibatsu*—the vast, family-held business organizations that rose to dominate the economy early in the twentieth century—were organized into *kontsuerun* structures in the 1920s, but not all *kontsuerun* were *zaibatsu.*

50. Nakahashi quoted in Tsunoda, "Rationalizing Japan's Political Economy," 329. Several years later, Nakahashi continued in a similar vein: "It is an evil for government to intervene, and it is not appropriate. Moreover, our commerce and industry have the ability to develop beautifully without waiting on government leadership and intervention" (see Tsunoda, "Rationalizing Japan's Political Economy," 329n29).

51. For a useful discussion of the system of wartime plans, see Tetsuji Okazaki and Masahiro Okuno-Fujiwara, "Japan's Present-Day Economic System and Its Historical Origins," in Okazaki and Okuno-Fujiwara, *The Japanese Economic System,* 17–21.

52. See Tsunoda, "Rationalizing Japan's Political Economy," chap. 9, for the Cabinet Planning Board Incident and its significance. Mark Peattie notes that the "conflicting pressures from business and military leadership" meant that the economy during the war "remained partly free and partly controlled." Moreover, it "could hardly be called totalitarian" (Mark Peattie, *Ishiwara Kanji and Japan's Confrontation with the West* [Princeton, NJ: Princeton University Press, 1975], 219; quoted in Johnson, *MITI,* 154). The Munitions Ministry was created through a merger of the Ministry of Commerce and Industry and the Cabinet Planning Board, with Tōjō Hideki as its head. For a comparison to centralized mobilization structures in the Allied nations, see Richard Rice, "Economic Mobilization in Wartime Japan," *Journal of Asian Studies* 38, no. 4 (1979): 691n10.

53. See, for example, Yukio Noguchi, *1940 Nen taisei: saraba senji keizai* (Tōyō Keizai Shinpōsha, 1995), and Okazaki and Okuno-Fujiwara, *The Japanese Economic System*.

54. John W. Dower, "The Useful War," in John W. Dower, *Japan in War and Peace: Selected Essays* (New York: New Press, 1993), 22.

55. Special Survey Committee, *Postwar Reconstruction*, 12.

56. Special Survey Committee, *Postwar Reconstruction*, 12, 73 [188].

57. Special Survey Committee, *Postwar Reconstruction*, 13.

58. Arisawa, "Fukahiteki na mono," *Sekai*, no. 3 (March 1946): 32.

59. Special Survey Committee, *Postwar Reconstruction*, 65–66, 72–73, and 94.

60. See John W. Dower, *Embracing Defeat: Japan in the Wake of World War II* (W. W. Norton and Company and The New Press, 1999), 533.

61. Wada Hiroo, "Keizai kinkyū taisaku ni kansuru dai ikkai kokka enzetsu" (July 1, 1947), in Arisawa Hiromi and Inaba Hidezō, eds., *Keizai*, vol. 2 of *Shiryō: sengo nijūnenshi*, edited by Tsuji Kiyoaki et al. (Nihon Hyōronsha, 1966), 56.

62. Special Survey Committee, *Postwar Reconstruction*, 84 and 94.

63. Special Survey Committee, *Postwar Reconstruction*, 84–85.

64. Special Survey Committee, *Postwar Reconstruction*, 94.

65. Shūsen Renraku Jimukyoku Keizaibu, "Bogudan shi no 'Nihon keizai saiken no kihon mondai' sono hoka ni kan suru dan" (June 5, 1946), in Nakamura and Ōmori, eds., *Nihon keizai saiken no kihon mondai*, vol. 1 of *Shiryō: sengo Nihon no keizai seisaku kōsō*, edited by Arisawa Hiromi (Tokyo Daigaku Shuppankai, 1990), 115 and 117.

66. For the quotation and the argument about the desire of the Occupation to create a rationalized and efficient bureaucracy, see T. J. Pempel, "The Tar Baby Target," in Robert E. Ward, ed., *Democratizing Japan: The Allied Occupation* (Honolulu: University of Hawai'i Press, 1987), 164–73.

67. Harry Emerson Wildes, *Typhoon in Tokyo: The Occupation and Its Aftermath* (New York: Macmillan Co., 1954), 91–92. Where cuts were made in the name of scientific management, they came only during the Dodge years and were used, T. J. Pempel argues, as weapons against blue-collar government workers. The reductions were primarily directed at the National Railways Corporation, the Ministry of Postal Services, and the Ministry of Telecommunications, all of which had been centers of union strength (Pempel, "The Tar Baby Target," 172–73). Wildes notes that the total number of national government employees was cut to 1.4 million in 1952 (Wildes, *Typhoon*, 92).

68. Leon Hollerman, "International Economic Controls in Occupied Japan," *Journal of Asian Studies* 38, no. 4 (1979): 708. Here again is evidence of the disinclination of Japanese bureaucrats to involve themselves in the operating details of the economy. They left these functions to the private sector for the most part, and during the mobilization campaigns of the war, had "preferred to deal with a small group of powerful private or 'designated' agents, who in turn mastered the network of details" (Hollerman, "International Economic Controls in Occupied Japan," 709).

69. Hollerman, "International Economic Controls," 708n6.

70. For details of Economic Stabilization Board strengthening, see Keizai Kikakuchō, Sengo Keizaishi Hensanshitsu, *Sengo keizaishi*, vol. 7: *Keizai antei honbushi* (Ōkurashō Insatsukyoku, 1964), 47–49.

71. Theodore Cohen, *Remaking Japan: The American Occupation of Japan as New Deal* (New York: New Press, 1987), 328.

72. Yamanaka Shirō, "Keizai antei honbu no unyō ni kansuru shiken" (March 17, 1946), in Nihon Tōkei Kenkyūjo, *Nihon tōkei seido saikenshi: tōkei iinkai shikō, shiryō hen 1* (Nihon Tōkei Kenkyūjo, 1962), 3; Special Survey Committee, *Postwar Reconstruction*, 95, 112, 182.

73. Special Survey Committee, *Postwar Reconstruction*, 95, 186.

74. This survey of the scientific management movement is drawn from Tsutsui, *Manufacturing Ideology*, 14–121.

75. For "visible hand," see Tsutsui, *Manufacturing Ideology*, 64.

76. Tsutsui, *Manufacturing Ideology*, 90–121.

77. Special Survey Committee, *Postwar Reconstruction*, 72 [188].

78. Zen Keinosuke, Speech before the 90th session of the Diet, quoted in *Asahi nenkan* (Asahi Shinbunsha, 1947), 167.

79. For accounts of the mismanagement of war mobilization, see Jerome B. Cohen, *Japan's Economy in War and Reconstruction*, especially chapter 2, and 271 and 274–75; Nakamura Takafusa, *Nihon no keizai tōsei* (Nihon Keizai Shinbunsha, 1974). The best English-language treatment of the political failures of the wartime controlled economy is Tsunoda, "Rationalizing Japan's Political Economy," especially chap. 9, "The Controlled Economy and Ir-rationalization of Economic Governance." Richard Rice, "Economic Mobilization," 689–706, is also valuable on the organizational and political battles. See also Johnson, *MITI*, 140–43, 157–72.

80. Johnson, *MITI*, 169.

81. Richard Rice, "Economic Mobilization," 689.

82. Inaba, *Gekidō 30 Nen*, 23.

83. Zen Keinosuke, Speech before the 90th session of the Diet, quoted in *Asahi nenkan*, 167.

84. Special Survey Committee, *Postwar Reconstruction*, 72 [188].

85. Inaba Hidezō, Review of *Kokka sōdōin*, vol. 1: *Keizai*, in *Ekonomisuto*, May 12, 1970. Cited in Ueno Masaji, "Keizaishigaku," in Miyazawa Toshiyoshi and Okōchi Kazuo, series eds., *Kindai Nihon shisōshi taikei*, vol. 6: *Kindai Nihon keizai shisōshi*, edited by Chō Yukio and Sumiya Kazuhiko, part 2 (Yūhikaku, 1971), 209.

86. Ōtsuka Hisao, "The Formation of a Modern Man: The Popular Base of Democratization," translated by Patricia Murray (1946), *Japan Interpreter* 6, no. 1 (1970): 3.

87. Andrew E. Barshay, "Toward a History of the Social Sciences in Japan," *Positions* 4, no. 2 (1996): 236–37. Barshay cites Yanaihara Tadao, "Kanrika no Nihon" (Oct. 1948), in *Yanaihara Tadao zenshū*, vol. 19, 405–16.

88. Ōuchi Hyōe, "Raisu hakasei ikkō kangei no kotoba" (Jan. 17, 1947), in Nihon Tōkei Kenkyūjo, *Nihon tōkei seido saikenshi*, shiryō hen 2, 81. Ōuchi went on to muse that if only Japanese "had learned much more from America about what science is" when Admiral Perry arrived on Japan's shores in 1853, "we in Japan might have been able to avoid great crimes such as the ones we have recently committed" (Ōuchi, "Raisu hakasei ikkō," 82).

89. Kimura Kihachirō, "Keizai saihen no zentei," *Asahi hyōron* 2, no. 11 (1947): 12.

90. For a typical example of this argument as voiced by postwar policy advisers and planners, see Chūō Shitsugyō Taisaku Iinkai, "Kengi: shitsugyō taisaku to shite

kyūsoku sochi subeki jikō ni kansuru iken" (Feb. 9, 1946), in Ōkouchi Kazuo, ed., *Rōdō*, vol. 4 of *Shiryō: sengo nijūnenshi*, edited by Tsuji Kiyoaki et al. (Nihon Hyōron-sha, 1966), 3.

91. Dower, *Embracing Defeat*, 290.

92. Zen, speech before the 90th session of the Diet, quoted in *Asahi nenkan*, 167.

93. Zen, speech before the 90th session of the Diet, quoted in *Asahi nenkan*, 167.

94. Inaba Hidezō, "Kanshūsha no kotoba," in Inaba Hidezō, ed., *Nihon keizai no shōrai* (Chūō Rōdō Gakuen, 1948), preface 1.

95. Wada Hiroo, "Keizai kinkyū taisaku ni kansuru dai ikkai kokka enzetsu" (July 1, 1947), in Arisawa Hiromi and Inaba Hidezō, eds., *Keizai*, 55–56.

96. Special Survey Committee, *Postwar Reconstruction*, 85–86.

97. "Kanryō o dō suru," *Chūō Kōron* 62, no. 8 (Aug. 1947): 3, slightly altered from the Chalmers Johnson quotation in *MITI*, 44. See also the Special Survey Committee, *Postwar Reconstruction*, 85–86, for a similar admonition that the planning and controls necessary for democratization not be allowed to devolve into a "resurgence of the past bureaucracy."

98. Nakayama Ichirō, "Keizai minshuka no kihon mondai," *Chūō Kōron* 61, no. 1 (Jan. 1946): 20.

99. Ōuchi, "Raisu hakasei ikkō," 81–82.

100. Special Survey Committee, *Postwar Reconstruction*, 97 [203].

101. On the Cooperation and Harmony Society as a conservative reform organization intended to help keep in check a surging labor movement, see W. Dean Kinzley, *Industrial Harmony in Modern Japan: The Invention of a Tradition* (New York: Routledge, 1991), entire.

102. Inaba, *Gekidō 30 nen*, 61–68 and 70–72.

103. Inaba, *Gekidō 30 nen*, 68, 73–89, and 118–21.

104. Inaba, *Gekidō 30 nen*, 68–69.

105. Ōkita, *Japan's Challenging Years*, 33.

106. Ōkita, *Japan's Challenging Years*, 33.

107. Inaba, *Gekidō 30 nen*, 128–29.

108. Inaba, *Gekidō 30 nen*, 129–30 and 135.

109. Inaba, *Gekidō 30 nen*, 135–41 and 172–80.

110. Inaba Hidezō, "Kanshūsha no kotoba," in Inaba Hidezō, ed., *Nihon keizai no shōrai* (Chūō Rōdō Gakuen, 1948), preface 1.

111. Special Survey Committee, *Postwar Reconstruction*, 72 [188] and 73 [188].

Chapter 2. The Measures That Rule

1. While Japanese interest in national statistical comparison was certainly fueled by national and geopolitical considerations, the eagerness with which scholars imported these texts also reflected a sophisticated culture of quantification, which itself had a rich publishing history of encyclopedia and statistical compendia *(mei-sūki)*. Speaking both to the newer interest in international comparison and this older Japanese culture of quantification, translations of international statistical works in particular—featuring Japanese titles such as *Bankoku seihyō* and *Bankoku meisūki*—experienced a publishing explosion. See Yabuuchi Takeshi, *Nihon tōkei hat-*

tatsushi kenkyū, Gifu keizai daigaku kenkyū sōsho, no. 7 (Kyoto: Hōritsu Bunkasha, 1995), 266–69; Nihon Tōkei Kenkyūjo, ed., *Nihon tōkei hattatsushi* (Tokyo Daigaku Shuppankai, 1960), 5. See Kojima Katsuji, *Nihon tōkei bunkashi josetsu* (Tokyo: Miraisha, 1972), 154–205, for the culture of quantification in urban areas during the Tokugawa period.

2. Paul Studenski, *The Income of Nations: Theory, Measurement, and Analysis, Past and Present* (New York: New York University Press, 1958), 159.

3. See Yabuuchi, *Nihon tōkei hattatsushi,* main text 2; Nihon Tōkei Kenkyūjo, ed., *Nihon tōkei hattatsushi,* 4–5; and Okuno Sadatori, "Nihon no tōkei jijō," in Nihon Seisansei Honbu, *Seisainsei no riron to jissai,* vol. 10 (Nihon Seisansei Honbu, 1959), 56, for a brief treatment of early institutions and the formalization of what came to be known as *tōkeigaku* (statistics).

4. The term "national wealth" is used here in a nontechnical sense to refer generally to calculations intended to indicate the overall prosperity and economic power of the nation. As shown below, a statistic specifically called "national wealth" was to become, when such calculations were carried out at all, one benchmark of national prosperity in the first half of the twentieth century.

5. Okuno, "Nihon no tōkei jijō," 56.

6. Nihon Tōkei Kenkyūjo, *Nihon tōkei hattatsushi,* 12.

7. The Nihon Tōkei Kenkyūjo points out that, while statistical collection by the government was in part motivated by the drive to promote industrial expansion, the issue of tax collection was also important. Nihon Tōkei Kenkyūjo, *Nihon tōkei hattatsushi,* 12.

8. Studenski, *Income of Nations,* 129–41 and 159. For representations of civilization and increasing use of statistical expression, see Silvana Patriarca, *Numbers and Nationhood: Writing Statistics in Nineteenth-Century Italy* (Cambridge: Cambridge University Press, 1996), 137–38.

9. Keizai Kikakuchō, Chōsabu, Kokumin Shotokuka, *Kokumin shotoku to kokumin keizai keisan,* Kokumin shotoku kaisetsu, shiryō dai 2 go (Keizai Kikakuchō, 1953), 223.

10. Keizai Kikakuchō, Keizai Kenkyūjo, *Keizai kenkyū nijūnen* (Keizai Kikakuchō, 1978), 327.

11. Prominent among those pushing for change was Sugi Kōji, earlier a member of the Meirokusha (Meiji Six Society) and the government's chief statistician during much of the Meiji period. See Nihon Tōkei Kenkyūjo, *Nihon tōkei hattatsushi,* 7–8 and 23–24.

12. This point is well remarked on in survey histories of economic thought. Even so, little detailed work has been done on the history of the statistical transformation in economic theory and practice in the twentieth century and its effects in postwar political-economic discourse. For a survey of representative changes in economics, especially the rise of quantification, statistical methodologies, and mathematical models, during the postwar half-century in the United States (in many ways the center of economic research during that period), see the articles by Robert M. Solow, David M. Kreps, and William J. Barber in the *Daedalus* issue titled "American Academic Culture in Transformation: Fifty Years, Four Disciplines" (126, no. 1 [1997]). For an extremely detailed treatment of the rise of the modern statistical state in Germany, see J. Adam Tooze, *Statistics and the German State, 1900–1945:*

The Making of Modern Economic Knowledge (Cambridge: Cambridge University Press, 2001).

13. John Kenneth Galbraith, *Economics in Perspective: A Critical History* (Boston: Houghton Mifflin, 1987), 245. Eric Roll similarly writes: "Much of the statistical work of the century preceding the second world war was carried on virtually in isolation from Economics..."; Eric Roll, *A History of Economic Thought*, 4th ed. (London: Faber and Faber, 1979), 500. Joseph A. Schumpeter also notes that "the alliance between statistics and theoretical economics was not complete until the emergence of modern Econometrics"; Joseph A. Schumpeter, *History of Economic Analysis*, edited by Elizabeth Boody Schumpeter (New York: Oxford University Press, 1954), 1141.

14. Daniel Bell, "Models and Reality in Economic Discourse," in Daniel Bell and Irving Kristol, eds., *The Crisis in Economic Theory* (New York: Basic Books, 1981), 58. A more contemporary yet still retrospective critique along the same lines was made by Paul A. Samuelson, one of the dominant figures in postwar economic thought, who wrote of the "unmistakable signs of decadence which were clearly present in economic thought prior to 1930" (quoted in Roll, *Economic Thought*, 521).

15. Tamanoi Yoshirō, *Nihon no keizaigaku*, Chūkō Shinsho no. 267 (Chūō Kōronsha, 1971), 224–25.

16. Okuno, "Nihon no tōkei jijō," 56.

17. Kazushi Ohkawa, *The Growth Rate of the Japanese Economy since 1878*, Hitotsubashi University, Institute of Economic Research, Economic Research Series, no. 1 (Kinokuniya Bookstore, 1957), 136.

18. Hijikata Seibi, *Kokumin shotoku no kōsei* (Nihon Hyōronsha, 1933), 5; see also Nihon Tōkei Kenkyūjo, *Hattatsushi*, 107–8.

19. Okuno, "Nihon no tōkei jijō," 56.

20. The materials from the 1935 research were largely destroyed during the war. Keizai Kikakuchō, Chōsabu, Kokumin Shotokuka, *Kokumin shotoku to kokumin keizai keisan*, 225.

21. Hijikata was a Tokyo University economist perhaps best known as a critic of Marxist economics, especially in regard to the labor theory of value, and for his influential formulations in the 1930s of a corporatist reordering of the Japanese political-economic system. Though his conception of an economic general headquarters was never fully implemented, his ideas spurred calls by nationalist intellectuals during the war for a brand of national socialism appropriate to Japanese circumstances. For a brief discussion, see Tessa Morris-Suzuki, *A History of Japanese Economic Thought* (New York: Routledge and Nissan Institute for Japanese Studies, Oxford University, 1990), 99–100. (To avoid confusion, it should be noted that Morris-Suzuki renders Hijikata's given name as "Narumi.")

22. Ōkawa Kazushi et al., *Kokumin shotoku*, Kazushi Ōkawa, Miyōhei Shinohara, and Mataji Umemura, series eds., *Chōki keizai tōkei: suikei to bunseki*, vol. 1 (Tōyō Keizai Shinpōsha, 1974), introduction 1.

23. Hijikata also attempted to calculate income for the years 1900–1918, although he arrived at his estimates for that period by extending backward his calculations of average index levels for the 1919–30 period.

24. Hijikata, *Kokumin shotoku*, preface 1 and main text 1–2.

25. For the most comprehensive and insightful treatment of Takahashi Korekiyo's fiscal policies, see Richard Smethurst, *From Foot Soldier to Finance Minister:*

Takahashi Korekiyo, Japan's Keynes (Cambridge, MA: Harvard University Asia Center, 2007), chaps. 12 and 13 and conclusion.

26. Keizai Kikakuchō, *Keizai kenkyū nijūnen*, 327–28, including table 2; Keizai Kikakuchō, Chōsabu, Kokumin Shotokuka, *Kokumin shotoku to kokumin keizai keisan*, 224; Mitsubishi Economic Research Bureau, *Japanese Trade and Industry: Present and Future* (London: Macmillan, 1936), 9 and 82; Studenski, *Income of Nations*, 497–98.

27. For the new link of statistical and theoretical work to policy considerations see Roll, *Economic Thought*, 502 and 504. Policy considerations had of course played a part in earlier concern with statistical calculation but, as Roll notes, "these examples remain isolated" (*Economic Thought*, 500). The argument here is that, beginning with the Great Depression and then into the World War II, the degree to which socioeconomic conditions were quantified and those calculations linked to public decisions about the allocation of resources was amplified so greatly as to represent a qualitative change.

28. Studenski, *Income of Nations*, 153.

29. Galbraith, *Economics in Perspective*, 246.

30. Ōuchi Hyōe, *Keizaigaku gojūnen*, vol. 2 (Tokyo Daigaku Shuppankai, 1959), 331.

31. See, for example, Isoshi Asahi, *The Economic Strength of Japan* (Hokuseido, 1939), especially chapter 4, "Growth of National Income."

32. Not all such examinations of Japan's fighting ability, however, came to equally sanguine conclusions. See, for example, Isoshi Asahi's rebuke of the foreign press for concluding that it was " 'doubtful that [Japan] could continue [fighting] longer than one year without obtaining large foreign loans on credit' "; Asahi, *Economic Strength of Japan*, 1. Asahi quotes the English Union of Democratic Control, *Far Eastern Menace: The Story of Japanese Imperialism* (London, 1936), 19.

33. Asahi, *Economic Strength of Japan*, chap. 3, "Increased Capacity to Bear Tax Burden," especially 14–19.

34. Keizai Kikakuchō, *Keizai kenkyū nijūnen*, 329.

35. Studenski, *Income of Nations*, 497.

36. National economic power *(keizai kokuryoku)* is Ōuchi Hyōe's term (Ōuchi, *Keizaigaku gojūnen*, vol. 2, 330). For creation of Kokka Shiryoku Kenkyūjo, see Ōuchi, *Keizaigaku gojūnen*, vol. 2, 330–31; Nihon Tōkei Kenkyūjo, *Nihon tōkei seido saikenshi: tōkei iinkai shikō*, kijutsu hen (Nihon Tōkei Kenkyūjo, 1962), 3; Keizai Kikakuchō, *Keizai kenkyū nijūnen*, 329–30.

37. Okuno, "Nihon no tōkei jijō," 56. Ōuchi Hyōe concurs: "The Japanese government didn't produce statistics during the war, and even when they did, they didn't save them" (Ōuchi, *Keizaigaku gojūnen*, vol. 2, 333); see also Nihon Tōkei Kenkyūjo, *Nihon tōkei seido saikenshi*, kijutsu hen, 1.

38. Nihon Tōkei Kenkyūjo, *Hattatsushi*, 32.

39. Nihon Tōkei Iinkai, Sōrifu Tōkeikyoku, *Nihon tōkei nenkan*, vol. 1 (Nihon Tōkei Kyōkai, 1949), preface 3–4. The *Yearbook* resumed publication only in 1949 with the volume cited here.

40. Studenski, *Income of Nations*, 497.

41. The English government's first national accounts white paper was titled *An Analysis of the Sources of War Finance and an Estimate of National Income and Expenditure in 1938 and 1940* (1941), indicating how important the question of wartime

revenues was in the minds of the Whitehall authorities engaged in calculating the national accounts.

42. Roll, *Economic Thought*, 505.

43. For quotation, see Galbraith, *Economics in Perspective*, 247; for general discussion of wartime ramifications of national accounting innovations, see 245–47, and John Kenneth Galbraith, *A Journey through Economic Time: A Firsthand View* (Boston: Houghton Mifflin, 1994), 115.

44. Mitsuharu Itō, "Munitions Unlimited: The Controlled Economy," *Japan Interpreter* 7, nos. 3–4 (1972): 362.

45. The prior eight were England, France, the United States, Russia, Austria, Germany, Australia, and Norway. Estimates for only thirteen countries had been made before the end of World War I. Studenski, *Income of Nations*, table 10.15, 156–57.

46. With no good idea of how resources were being employed, civilian consumption and the use of labor power in civilian goods production remained comparatively high in Germany throughout the war; see Galbraith, *Economics in Perspective*, 247. National income estimates were not unknown in Germany, but newer innovations probably were. The practical knowledge of the value of these techniques for forecasting in the context of total war was not yet a self-evident truth. See also Adam Tooze, *Statistics and the German State*, 105–30 and 247–69, for Weimar-era experimentation and the later incoherence of wartime statistical systems in Germany.

47. Studenski, *Income of Nations*, 151–52.

48. Annual national account reports were instituted in 1947. For this, the campaign to implement official national income calculations in England, and the citation of R. F. Harrod, *The Life of John Maynard Keynes* (London: Macmillan, 1951), see Studenski, *Income of Nations*, 152–53.

49. None of these caveats meant to warn us from reading this account of national accounting history in horse-race terms should, of course, obscure historical facts: namely, that the national accounting methods that became de facto standard procedure through much of the world during the postwar period were first devised in the United States and England, and that many of these were introduced to Japanese experts under the auspices of personnel participating in a military occupation.

50. This posed an awkward problem for analysts such as Asahi Isoshi, who found himself evaluating Japanese national income in 1939 using data from 1930—this despite his warning that conditions were changing so fast in Japan that books on the economy written even just after the 1931 "Manchurian Affair" were already "mere records of the past" (Asahi, *Economic Strength of Japan*, vii and 23).

51. Hijikata, *Kokumin shotoku*, 2.

52. Yano Tsuneta, *Nihon kokusei zue* (Nihon Hyōronsha, 1929), 31–32; also Asahi, *Economic Strength of Japan*, 25–32.

53. Yano, *Nihon kokusei zue*, 31–32.

54. Hijikata, *Kokumin shotoku*, 5. "Objective methods" referred to the supposedly more direct determination of income by measuring output, in contrast to ascertaining income by what was called the "subjective method" of using tax receipt data.

55. Elizabeth Tsunoda, "Rationalizing Japan's Political Economy: The Business Initiative, 1920–1955" (Ph.D. diss., Columbia University, 1993), 274. The quoted source is "Sangyō gōrika zadankai," *Kagaku kōgyō jihō* 3, no. 1 (1930): 12 and 19.

56. Tsunoda, "Rationalizing Japan's Political Economy," 274. Quoted source is "Hūbā to sangyō gōrika," *Daiyamondo,* March 1, 1930, 16. Returning to a by now common theme, it bears noting that this sense of an empirical gap, so to speak, between available knowledge and newly held visions of the way economies ought to be managed was not unique to Japan. John Kenneth Galbraith notes, for example, that in the United States at the time "even on urgent matters there were serious statistical gaps." He writes that "until well into the depression years, the United States had no useful figures on the level or distribution of unemployment" (Galbraith, *Economics in Perspective,* 245).

57. Quoted in Itō, "Munitions Unlimited," 361–62.

58. Ōuchi, *Keizaigaku gojūnen,* vol. 2, 330–31.

59. Ōuchi, *Keizaigaku gojūnen,* vol. 2, 330–31. Japan had ended its participation, for example, in groups such as the International Statistics Association; see Zen Keinosuke, "Beikoku tōkei shisetsudan shōen ni okeru sōri daijin dairi Zen kokumu daijin aisatsu" (Jan. 17, 1947), in Nihon Tōkei Kenkyūjo, *Nihon tōkei seido saikenshi,* shiryō hen 2, 80. Even before the war, Japanese researchers had little contact with the explosion of empirical research taking place from the late 1920s at institutions such as Harvard's Economic Research Committee and the National Bureau of Economic Research. Tamanoi Yoshirō argues that knowledge of this American work was little known in the prewar period (Tamanoi, *Nihon no keizaigaku,* 223).

60. See, for example, Hara Akira, *Nihon no senji keizai: keikaku to shijō* (Tokyo Daigaku Shuppankai, 1995).

61. Mobilization in the United States as well was accompanied by considerable wrangling between representatives of big business, small companies, conservative politicians, and interventionist bureaucrats over the appropriate relation between government and capital. For the politics of wartime planning in the United States, see Alan Brinkley, *The End of Reform: New Deal Liberalism in Recession and War* (New York: Vintage Books, 1996).

62. Itō Mitsuharu concurs, although his teleological "stages" mode of describing the state of affairs is regrettable: "There were no analytical tools at all for planning. The so-called modern economics of that period was still at a primitive stage in Japan and the theories of the reform bureaucrats were abstract.... The technical tools of planning did not even exist at the time" (Itō, "Munitions Unlimited," 362). Paul Rabinow echoes this point in regard to French discourses on urban planning at the same time: "During the 1930s there was a good deal of discussion about planning.... However, as the technical tools and statistical data required for modern planning were largely unavailable, most of the self-proclaimed plans of the interwar period were little more than manifestos." Paul Rabinow, *The French Modern: Norms and Forms of the Social Environment* (Cambridge, MA: MIT Press, 1989), 322.

63. Nihon Tōkei Kenkyūjo, *Hattatsushi,* 2–3 and 34–37.

64. The revision of neoclassical economic thought set in motion by national accounting and Keynesian analysis prompted the creation of a neologism by which the theoretical object of this new science might be described: the "macroeconomy." The study of "macroeconomics" is concerned with the behavior of a national economy as an aggregated whole, including issues of employment, demand, output, inflation, the balance of payments, and growth. Put another way, macroeconomics,

writes Paul Samuelson, is the "study of the aggregate performance of the whole of GNP and the general price level" (cited in Roll, *Economic Thought*, 522). The term was applied over against what only then came to be known as "microeconomics": the behavior of individuals, firms, and prices under specific, generally ideal conditions. This invention of "macroeconomics" in effect renamed the "microeconomic" fields of enquiry that had formerly dominated neoclassical economic thought.

65. Brinkley, *The End of Reform*, 7.

66. See Nihon Tōkei Kenkyūjo, *Hattatsushi*, 30–31 for discussion of the *Rinji kokusei chōsa*.

67. Ōuchi, *Keizaigaku gojūnen*, vol. 2, 331.

68. Nonomura Kazuo, "Nihon no 'kiki' keizai no shoriron," in Osaka Shiritsu Daigaku, Keizai Kenkyūjo, *Sengo shakai kagaku bunken kaisetsu* (May 1947–Dec. 1947). Reprinted in *Keizaigaku bunken shūmoku*, 4th ser. *Shakai kagaku bunken kaisetsu, 1945–1947*, 2 vols. in 1 (Bunshō Shoin, 1984), 22, of reproduced original.

69. Saburō Ōkita, *Japan's Challenging Years: Reflections on My Lifetime;* adapted from the Japanese by Graeme Bruce (Boston: George Allen and Unwin, 1985), 43.

70. Nonomura, "Nihon no 'kiki' keizai," 22–23 of reproduced original. The Nihon Tōkei Kenkyūjo later used similar language, lamenting that there remained a "blank gap" in knowledge of social and economic conditions in Japan during the war (Nihon Tōkei Kenkyūjo, *Hattatsushi*, 33).

71. Ōuchi, *Keizaigaku gojūnen*, vol. 2, 333.

72. Nihon Tōkei Kenkyūjo, *Nihon tōkei seido saikenshi*, kijutsu hen, 1.

73. Ōuchi, *Keizaigaku gojūnen*, vol. 2, 331.

74. Arisawa Hiromi, *Arisawa Hiromi sengo keizai o kataru: Shōwa shi e no shōgen* (Tokyo Daigaku Shuppankai, 1989), 53–54.

75. Ōuchi Hyōe, "Sengo tōkei kotohajime," in *Tōkei jōhō* (August 1957), reprinted in Ōuchi Hyōe, *Chosakushū*, vol. 12 (Iwanami Shoten, 1975), 261; Ōuchi, *Keizaigaku gojūnen*, vol. 2, 333.

76. Nihon Tōkei Kenkyūjo, *Nihon tōkei seido saikenshi*, kijutsu hen, 1.

77. "Tōkeihō no rippō no shui" (Feb. 12, 1947), in Nihon Tōkei Kenkyūjo, *Nihon tōkei seido saikenshi*, shiryō hen 2, 55.

78. Special Survey Committee, Ministry of Foreign Affairs, *Postwar Reconstruction of the Japanese Economy*, compiled by Ōkita Saburō (1946; University of Tokyo Press, 1992), 96. See also the original Japanese-language version as reprinted in Nakamura Takafusa and Ōmori Tokuko, eds., *Nihon keizai saiken no kihonmondai*, in Arisawa Hiromi, ed., *Shiryō: sengo Nihon no keizai seisaku kōsō*, vol. 1 (Tokyo Daigaku Shuppankai, 1990), 143–263.

79. Kawashima Takahiko, "Waga kuni tōkei seido kaikaku no shushi" (July 1946), in Nihon Tōkei Kenkyūjo, *Nihon tōkei seido saikenshi*, shiryō hen 1, 121.

80. Yamanaka Shirō, "Keizai antei honbu no unyō ni kansuru shiken" (March 17, 1946), in Nihon Tōkei Kenkyūjo, *Nihon tōkei seido saikenshi*, shiryō hen 1, 1–3.

81. Tsūshō Sangyōshō, "Kigyō gyōsei no shintenkai ni tsuite" (Aug. 1, 1949), in Tsūshō Sangyōshō, Kigyōkyoku, *Sangyō gōrika, ge*, vol. 10 of *Shōkō seisakushi* (Shōkō Seisakushi Kankōkai, 1972), 38.

82. Special Survey Committee, *Postwar Reconstruction*, 128.

83. William M. Tsutsui, "W. Edwards Deming and the Origins of Quality Control in Japan," *Journal of Japanese Studies* 22, no. 2 (1996): 301–7.

84. Quotations are from Tsutsui, "W. Edwards Deming," 306 and 311.
85. "Tōkeihō no rippō no shui" (Feb. 12, 1947), in Nihon Tōkei Kenkyūjo, *Nihon tōkei seido saikenshi*, shiryō hen 2, 54.
86. "Tōkei hōan teian riyū setsumei (honkaigi yō)" (date unclear) and "Tōkeihō no rippō no shui" (Feb. 12, 1947), in Nihon Tōkei Kenkyūjo, *Nihon tōkei seido saikenshi*, shiryō hen 2, 52 and 54–55.
87. Ōuchi Hyōe, "Raisu hakasei ikkō kangei no kotoba" (Jan. 17, 1947), in Nihon Tōkei Kenkyūjo, *Nihon tōkei seido saikenshi*, shiryō hen 2, 82.
88. "Tōkei hōan teian riyū setsumei (honkaigi yō)" (date unclear) and "Tōkeihō no rippō no shui" (Feb. 12, 1947), in Nihon Tōkei Kenkyūjo, *Nihon tōkei seido saikenshi*, shiryō hen 2, 51–52 and 54–55.
89. Kimura Kihachirō, "Keizai saihen no zentei," *Asahi hyōron* 2, no. 11 (1947): 12.
90. "Tōkei seido kaizen ni kansuru iinkai no tōshin," in Nihon Tōkei Kenkyūjo, *Nihon tōkei seido saikenshi*, shiryō hen 1, 257.
91. Ōuchi, *Keizaigaku gojūnen*, vol. 2, 331–33. In addition to Ōuchi, well-known names in the Tōkei Kenkyūjo included Arisawa Hiromi, Nakayama Ichirō, Takahashi Masao, Morita Yūzō, and Kondō Michio.
92. Arisawa Hiromi guesses that GHQ complaints about the data problem may have been voiced directly to Prime Minister Shidehara himself (Arisawa, *Sengo keizai o kataru*, 54.)
93. For a briefer discussion of the Statistics Commission and of the Stuart Rice Statistical Mission to Japan, to be discussed in this chapter shortly, see Scott P. O'Bryan, "Economic Knowledge and the Science of National Income in Twentieth-Century Japan," *Japan Studies Review* 6 (2002): 1–19. Also Laura Hein, "Statistics for Democracy: Economics as Politics in Occupied Japan," *Positions* 11, no. 3 (Winter 2003): 765–78.
94. "Tōkei iinkai kansei" (Dec. 28, 1946), Nihon Tōkei Kenkyūjo, *Nihon tōkei seido saikenshi*, shiryō hen 1, 262–63; Nihon Tōkei Kenkyūjo, *Nihon tōkei seido saikenshi*, kijutsu hen, 1–5; Ōuchi Hyōe, *Chosakushū*, vol. 12, 262–63; Ōuchi, *Keizaigaku gojūnen*, vol. 2, 334. Including the prime minister as president of the committee and the head of the Economic Stabilization Board as vice president, the Statistics Commission began its work with twelve sitting members and three special members.
95. In addition to both Rice and Deming, four other members of the Statistical Mission to Japan were also from the Division of Statistical Standards within the U.S. Bureau of the Budget: Peyton Stapp, who normally served under Rice as assistant chief of the Division of Statistical Standards and who served as deputy chief of the mission; Edward T. Crowder, who was an expert in finance and banking statistics and formerly taught at Rutgers University; Michael Sapir, whose specialty was national income accounting and who was working with the United Nations on determining the share of UN costs to be levied on each member nation based on such income statistics; and Ernest Tupper, a former faculty member at the Wharton School of the University of Pennsylvania and a specialist on industrial production. The final member of the mission was Jerome Cornfield, a member of the U.S. Bureau of Labor Statistics. For details on the membership and creation of the Statistical Mission, see Stuart A. Rice, "Preliminary Report on Japanese Statistical Organization" (n.d.), 1–2, in National Archives, College Park, Military Records, Record Group 331 (Allied Operational and Occupation Headquarters, World War II), Box 7975

(2); Stuart A. Rice et al., "Modernization of Japanese Statistics: Summary Report of the Statistical Mission to Japan" (April 1947), cover page, in National Archives, College Park, Military Records, Record Group 331 (Allied Operational and Occupation Headquarters, World War II), Box 8352; "Origin and Purpose of the Mission" (n.d.), in National Archives, College Park, Military Records, Record Group 331 (Allied Operational and Occupation Headquarters, World War II), Box 8348 (17). See also the section on the origin of the Rice Mission in the later Japanese translation: Stuart A. Rice et al., "Nihon tōkei soshiki no kindaika no hitsuyō" (Nihon Tōkei Kenkyūjo trans. of original) (April 1947), in Nihon Tōkei Kenkyūjo, *Nihon tōkei seido saikenshi*, shiryō hen 2, 83. This Japanese translation is most likely, given the date and other close textual correlations, a translation of the Stuart A. Rice et al. "Modernization of Japanese Statistics: Summary Report of the Statistical Mission to Japan" of the same month and year, though the Japanese title, with its extra phrase, *"no hitsuyō"* (the necessity of), offers room for lack of complete certainty that the two reports are precisely the same documents. Given the many reports and memoranda produced by the mission, in both draft and official form, and the often scattered and incomplete nature of the archival record of the original documents in the Occupation files, where appropriate in my subsequent notes, I will also cite the translated document, which I used at an early stage of this research prior to location of the Occupation sources. It is hoped that the Japanese translation will provide corroborating evidence of the themes struck by the Rice Mission. On Deming, see Tsutsui, "W. Edwards Deming, 295–325.

96. S. A. Rice et al., "Modernization of Japanese Statistics, entire; S. A. Rice, "Preliminary Report on Japanese Statistical Organization," entire.

97. Zen Keinosuke, "Beikoku tōkei shisetsudan shōen ni okeru sōri daijin dairi Zen kokumu daijin aisatsu" (Jan. 17, 1947), in Nihon Tōkei Kenkyūjo, *Nihon tōkei seido saikenshi*, shiryō hen 2, 80.

98. S. A. Rice et al., "Modernization of Japanese Statistics," 2–3, 7–9, 12. Here Rice and the others may be referring to wartime organizations such as the *tōseikai* (control associations), joint public-private corporations that functionally resembled government-authorized cartels.

99. The report is S. A. Rice et al., "Modernization of Japanese Statistics" (n. 95 above). For the link between statistical reform and democratization, see p. 1. Members of the mission also wrote many preliminary reports and memoranda. For an example of another comprehensive statement by the mission of its views and goals at a preliminary stage, see S. A. Rice, "Preliminary Report on Japanese Statistical Organization," entire. Also S. A. Rice, "Nihon no tōkei soshiki no kindaika no hitsuyō", 83–119.

100. S. A. Rice, "Preliminary Report on Japanese Statistical Organization," 7–8; S. A. Rice et al., "Modernization of Japanese Statistics," 5. See also S. A. Rice, "Nihon no tōkei soshiki no kindaika," 83–119, especially 88–89, for portrayals of the United States and Japan.

101. For quotations in this and the prior paragraph and discussion of the need for statistical training and education, see S. A. Rice, "Preliminary Report on Japanese Statistical Organization," 8–24. See also Rice, "Nihon tōkei soshiki no kindaika," 83–119, especially 88–89 and 109–10.

102. Nihon Tōkei Kenkyūjo, *Nihon tōkei seido saikenshi*, kijutsu hen, 17–18.

103. Ōuchi, "Raisu hakasei ikkō kangei no kotoba" (Jan. 17, 1947), in Nihon Tōkei Kenkyūjo, *Nihon tōkei seido saikenshi*, shiryō hen 2, 81.

104. Rice himself returned to Japan with two others four years later, in March 1951, for a follow-up mission visit. See, for example, "Outline of Second Rice Mission Report on Japanese Statistics, Draft" (n.d.), in National Archives, College Park, Military Records, Record Group 331 (Allied Operational and Occupation Headquarters, World War II), Box 7688 (22).

105. The law was not, however, completely without opposition. In an address before the House of Peers, then Viscount Ōkouchi Masatoshi derided the Tōkei Law as fascistic because in his view it concentrated too much of the government's responsibilities for statistics in one agency. See Arisawa, *Sengo keizai o kataru*, 75, for a brief account.

106. Keizai Tōkei Kenkyūjo, *Hattatsushi*, 2–3, 6–7; Special Survey Committee, *Postwar Reconstruction*, 97; Nihon Tōkei Kenkyūjo, *Nihon tōkei seido saikenshi*, kijutsu hen, 30.

107. An amendment to the Statistics Law added by the Diet committed the government to the expansion of *chihō tōkei kikō*. Auxillary policy guidelines ("Chihō tōkei kikō seibi yōkō") that detailed the implementation of the reform then were passed by the cabinet in July 1947.

108. *Tōkei hō*, Law no. 18 (March 26, 1947), in Nihon Tōkei Kenkyūjo, *Nihon tōkei seido saikenshi*, shiryō hen 2, 67–71; on the *todokede* (reporting) system, see also Nihon Tōkei Kenkyūjo, *Nihon tōkei seido saikenshi*, kijutsu hen, 27.

109. Tōkei Iinkai, "Chihō tōkei kikō seibi yōkō" and Tōkei Iinkai, "Chihō tōkei kikō seibi yōkō ni tsuite no hōkoku," in Nihon Tōkei Kenkyūjo, *Nihon tōkei seido saikenshi*, shiryō hen 2, 209–18; Nihon Tōkei Kenkyūjo, *Nihon tōkei seido saikenshi*, kijutsu hen, 7 and 22–23.

110. See Nihon Tōkei Kenkyūjo, *Nihon tōkei seido saikenshi*, kijutsu hen, 22–24, for increases in local staff. Prefectural-level increases included personnel provided for by the Tōkei Law as well as a crew of 1,564 people provided for by the Ministry of Commerce and Industry to conduct production surveys. It is unknown how many statistics personnel were in place at the city, town, and village levels before the reforms of 1947. A report by the Hiroshima Prefecture government to Occupation officials reported that four years after the inauguration of the 1947 law three times as many statistical officials were working at the prefectural level as before the law was enacted, and that 5 city and 338 town and village offices now had officials responsible for statistical collection. "Report on the Statistical Activities of Hiroshima Prefecture," 2, in National Archives, College Park, Military Records, Record Group 331 (Allied Operational and Occupation Headquarters, World War II), Box 8348 (12).

111. Special Survey Committee, *Postwar Reconstruction*, 97 and 187.

112. *Tōkei hō*, Law no. 18 (March 26, 1947), art. 10 and *Tōkei hō shikōrei*. Imperial Ordinance no. 164 (April 30, 1947), art. 8, in Nihon Tōkei Kenkyūjo, *Nihon tōkei seido saikenshi*, shiryō hen 2, 69 and 71–72.

113. Nihon Tōkei Kenkyūjo, *Nihon tōkei seido saikenshi*, kijutsu hen, 64–65.

114. Sōrifu, "Tōkei iinkai tōkei kōshūkai junsoku," Sōrifu Kokuji, no. 8 (May 23, 1947), in Nihon Tōkei Kenkyūjo, *Nihon tōkei seido saikenshi*, shiryō hen 3, 160–61.

115. See "Tōkei tanki daigaku setchi yōkō (an)" (July 18, 1950), in Nihon Tōkei Kenkyūjo, *Nihon tōkei seido saikenshi,* shiryō hen 3, 160–63; Nihon Tōkei Kenkyūjo, *Nihon tōkei seido saikenshi,* kijutsu hen, 66–67.

116. "Report on Statistical Association of Hiroshima Prefecture," 1–2.

117. Nihon Tōkei Kenkyūjo, *Nihon tōkei seido saikenshi,* kijutsu hen, 49–50.

118. Okita, *Japan's Challenging Years,* 44–45.

119. Arisawa, *Sengo keizai o kataru,* 63.

120. Nihon Tōkei Kenkyūjo, *Nihon tōkei seido saikenshi,* kijutsu hen, 51. As indication of the business opportunity Japan seemed to represent to American corporations in the years of reconstruction, the purchases of these machines by Japanese organizations, and of successive rounds of them, occasioned considerable competitive elbowing among the corporations themselves, which sought assurances from the SCAP authorities that earlier sales contracts would be upheld and that "discontinued tabulating equipment" manufactured by competitors and already in Japan would not be "dumped" on the Japanese market by being passed around to Japanese agencies hoping to receive the used machines instead of having to purchase new ones. See Letter from J. H. Jacobsen, Far Eastern Manager, Export Tabulating Machines Division, Remington Rand, Inc., to General W. F. Marquat, Chief of the Economic and Scientific Section, SCAP, June 20, 1951, and also "Contract Awards" documents of SCAP. In National Archives, College Park, Military Records, Record Group 331 (Allied Operational and Occupation Headquarters, World War II), Box 8352 (24).

121. Kawashima had written a proposal in the days before the creation of the Statistics Commission that had argued for strict centralization. Arisawa, too, had pushed for such an arrangement. Ōuchi later complained about the lingering inefficiences of the postwar statistical system. He argued that "sectionalism" within the government had prevented a more rational centralization in the Statistics Bureau of the Office of the Prime Minister (Ōuchi, *Keizaigaku gojūnen,* vol. 2, 337).

122. See Nihon Tōkei Kenkyūjo, *Nihon tōkei seido saikenshi,* kijutsu hen, 19, on the placement of experienced statisticians, often chosen from the ranks of the Statistics Commission itself, in ministry statistics bureaus.

123. This term was a central theme of the Statistic Commission's planning and of the Statistics Law itself. See, for example, "Tōkeihō no rippō no shui" (Feb. 12, 1947), in Nihon Tōkei Kenkyūjo, *Nihon tōkei seido saikenshi,* shiryō hen 2, 54 and 56.

124. Arisawa Hiromi has characterized the Statistics Commission as wielding a "considerable amount of power" and controlling a significant budget for its operations (Arisawa, *Sengo keizai o kataru,* 79).

125. Keizai Kikakuchō, Sengo Keizaishi Hensanshitsu, *Sengo keizaishi,* vol. 6: *Kokumin shotoku* (Ōkurashō Insatsukyoku, 1963), 5; Studenski, *Income of Nations,* 497.

126. Arisawa, *Sengo keizai o kataru,* 94.

127. Nihon Tōkei Kenkyūjo, *Nihon tōkei seido saikenshi,* kijutsu hen, 2; Arisawa, *Sengo keizai o kataru,* 58 and 94.

128. Arisawa, *Sengo keizai o kataru,* 95.

129. Studenski, *Income of Nations,* 151. It is instructive to note that Simon Kuznets and Richard Stone, the American and British pioneers, respectively, of early national income research, both were to become Nobel Laureates for their work. Analytical

objects such as GNP, so common to today's conception of economics, were considered revolutionary introductions to the field at the time.

130. A woman, given name unclear.

131. For C. Patrick's recommendations and their effects, see Keizai Kikakuchō, Sengo Keizaishi Hensanshitsu, *Sengo keizaishi,* vol. 6: *Kokumin shotoku,* 5 and 15–16. It is worth noting that the emphasis here on personal income reflected both the need to deal with the inflation that so threatened to swamp any effort at economic stabilization and the generally New Deal–like orientation of Occupation policy at this early stage concerning issues of employment, income, and standards of living. These are themes that resonated with the concerns of a significant portion of Japanese analysts at the time.

132. Michael Sapir, "Nihon no kokumin shotoku tōkei (keikaku to hyōka)" (Keizai Kikakuchō trans. of original), in Keizai Kikakuchō, Sengo Keizaishi Hensanshitsu, *Sengo keizaishi,* vol. 6: *Kokumin shotoku,* 231 and 234. On the critical importance of gross national product and income estimates, see also S. A. Rice, "Preliminary Report on Japanese Statistical Organization," 1; and Stuart A. Rice, "Statistical Mission: Summary Report" (n.d.), National Income Needs and Japan's Statistical System section, 1–3. In U.S. National Archives, Military Records, Record Group 331 (Allied Operational and Occupation Headquarters, World War II), Box 8348 (17). The cover sheet found accompanying this last lists a report titled "Japanese National Income Statistics—Appraisal and . . ." by Michael Sapir, the Rice Mission's expert on national income accounting, but a copy of this report could not be found in the U.S. Occupation archives. It seems fair to surmise that the translated document cited first in this note corresponds to this missing report in the English original.

133. Sapir, "Nihon no kokumin shotoku tōkei", 231–70; S. A. Rice et al., "Modernization of Japanese Statistics," table of contents and 12–15. Also S. A. Rice, "Nihon tōkei soshiki no kindaika," 113–14. National income appeared immediately after industrial production statistics in general in Rice's report. Although the date of Sapir's report on national income is unclear, sources indicate that it was released early in 1947, at least before June when national accounting work moved to the ESB. See notes on the text of the Sapir report, Keizai Kikakuchō, Sengo Keizaishi Hensanshitsu, *Sengo keizaishi,* vol. 6: *Kokumin shotoku,* 231.

134. Rice et al., "Modernization of Japanese Statistics," 12–15; Rice, "Nihon tōkei soshiki no kindaika," 113–14.

135. The forty-two staff members included only those responsible for computing national income statistics in the Economic Stabilization Board from the basic data provided to them by many others in relevant ministries and agencies throughout the government. Keizai Kikakuchō, Sengo Keizaishi Hensanshitsu, *Sengo keizaishi,* vol. 6: *Kokumin shotoku,* 16–18.

136. Chalmers Johnson, *MITI and the Japanese Miracle: The Growth of Industrial Policy, 1925–1975.* (Stanford, CA: Stanford University Press, 1982), 183.

137. The dominance of U.S. economic knowledge after the war in Japan represented a significant shift away from earlier sources of inspiration. During prior years, Japanese scholars had more often drawn on ideas produced in Germany as well as Britain and France.

138. The title chosen was significant in its purposeful avoidance of the *"keizaigaku kenkyū"* alternative. The journal thus announced its intention to quantitatively study

actual economic phenomena rather than "theory" per se or the history of economic thought. The portrayal of Tsuru here in no way represents a comprehensive characterization, for his work spanned a broad range of concerns, and like so many of the prominent public economists of his age in Japan, he defied facile categorization.

139. Tsuru Shigeto, "Sōkan no kotoba," in *Keizai kenkyū* 1, no. 1 (Jan. 1950): 2; see also Keizaigakushi Gakkai, *Nihon no keizaigaku: Nihonjin no keizaiteki shii no kiseki* (Tōyō Keizai Shinpōsha, 1984), 180–81.

140. Kanamori Hisao, *Watashi no sengo keizaishi: ekonomisuto no 50-nen* (Tokyo Keizai Shinpōsha, 1995), 35.

141. See Tamanoi, *Nihon no keizaigaku,* 220, and Kanamori, *Watashi no sengo keizaishi,* 36. Tsuru was just thirty-five at the time he wrote the white paper.

142. Arisawa, *Sengo keizai o kataru,* 95.

143. The statistics used in computing national accounting were not collected solely for that purpose or by the group responsible for the computation in the Economic Planning Agency and its earlier incarnations.

144. Keizai Kikakuchō, Sengo Keizaishi Hensanshitsu, *Sengo keizaishi,* vol. 6: *Kokumin shotoku,* 10–11.

145. Stuart A. Rice, "Nihon no tōkei kikō no arikata" (trans. of original; 1951), in Keizai Kikakuchō, Sengo Keizaishi Hensanshitsu, *Sengo keizaishi,* vol. 6: *Kokumin shotoku,* 19.

146. See the synopsis of Oshima's report in Keizai Kikakuchō, Sengo Keizaishi Hensanshitsu, *Sengo keizaishi,* vol. 6: *Kokumin shotoku,* 400–416.

147. The OECD required entering member nations to submit formal income calculations beginning in 1953.

148. Yoshimasa Kurabayashi and Hiroshi Matsura, "Progress of Japanese National Accounts in an International Perspective of the SNA Review," in Ryuzo Sato and Takashi Negishi, eds., *Developments in Japanese Economics* (Tokyo: Academic Press, Harcourt Brace Jovanovich, 1989), 99–100.

Chapter 3. New Economics and an Expanding Vision of Prosperity

1. Special Survey Committee, *Postwar Reconstruction,* 28.

2. Andrew Barshay discusses this obsession with the "special character" of Japanese socioeconomic structures by showing how the analytical "gaze" of such Marxists of the Kōza (Lectures) faction as Yamada Moritarō created an inseparable link between the "particularism" of the case of Japan and the notion of "backwardness"; Andrew Barshay, *The Social Sciences in Modern Japan: The Marxian and Modernist Traditions* (Berkeley: University of California Press, 2004), chap. 3. I have chosen to use the term "exceptionalism" in that it evokes the affective orientation that often surrounded even such exceptionalisms with a negative valence as I am examining here, an emotional and intellectual obverse to the negative evaluations that left open the possibility of their use in more assertively positive claims about uniqueness, ones that at times underwrote, not critiques of the nation or national development, but nationalist celebrations of special Japanese ways or models.

3. Tsūshō Sangyōshō, "Kigyō gyōsei no shintenkai ni tsuite," in *Sangyō gōrika,* part 2, sengo hen, vol. 10 of *Shōkō gyōseishi* (Shōkō Seisakushi Kankōkai, 1972), 36–37.

4. Sharon H. Nolte, *Liberalism in Modern Japan: Ishibashi Tanzan and His Teachers, 1905–1960* (Berkeley: University of California Press, 1987), 224 and 233.

5. Kitō Nisaburō, *Kahei to rishi no dōtai* (Tokyo: Iwanami Shoten, 1942). See Takahashi Yasuzō, preface, in *Gendai kyōyō bunko*, no. 80, Kitō Nisaburō, *Keinzu keizaigaku kaisetsu* (Shakai Shisōsha, 1953), 1.

6. As an indication of the level of interest in Keynes' work exhibited by economists in Japan, Keynes was once heard to remark that as soon as one of his books was announced he received five or six letters from Japan asking for the translation rights. "This happens only in Japan," Keynes quipped (Koichi Hamada, "The Impact of the General Theory in Japan," *Eastern Economic Journal* 12, no. 4 [1986]: 451n6).

7. Kitō Nisaburō, *Keinzu keizaigaku kaisetsu*, Tōyō keizai kōza sōsho dai 10 kan (Tōyō Keizai Shinpō, 1946), 3; see also interview with Tatsumi Kazuhiro in Hayasaka Tadashi, ed., *Keinzu no deai: Keinzu keizaigaku no dō'nyūshi* (Nihon Keizai Hyōronsha, 1993), 27; Hayasaka Tadashi and Masamura Kimihiro, *Sengo Nihon no keizaigaku: hito to gakusetsu ni miru ayumi*, Nikkei shinsho, no. 207 (Nihon Nikkei Shinbunsha, 1974), 20–21.

8. Interview with Tatsumi Kazuhiro in Hayasaka, *Keinzu no deai*, 5–7; Hamada, "Impact of the General Theory," 451.

9. Interview with Tatsumi Kazuhiro in Hayasaka, *Keinzu no deai*, 8–9, on the writing of the *Kaisetsu*. Though, like many neoclassical economists, Nakayama found ample grounds for criticism of *General Theory*, he would, as shall be discussed below, expound employment policies after the war that owed much to Keynes' theoretical innovations.

10. Ekonomisuto Henshūbu, *Shōgen: Kōdo seichōki no Nihon*, vol. 1 (Mainichi Shinbunsha, 1984), 12.

11. Nolte, *Liberalism in Modern Japan*, 234.

12. Hayasaka and Masamura, *Sengo Nihon no keizaigaku*, 21; Hamada, "Impact of the General Theory," 451. A translation produced by the Finance Ministry was also published around this time (interview with Asai Yoshio, Seikyō University, Tokyo, May 11, 1997).

13. For Keynes' use of "throw over," see *General Theory*, 16–17. Keynes uses the single term "classical economics" to denote the strands of economic thought now commonly described as "classical" and "neoclassical." Though "neoclassical" had been coined prior to Keynes' *General Theory*, the term first came into general usage after the so-called Keynesian revolution, particularly with Samuelson's use of the term the "neoclassical synthesis."

14. Keynes, *General Theory*, 7.

15. In his *Principles of Political Economy*, J. S. Mill explains the principle behind Say's Law, and it is from this classical description of the dynamic involved that Keynes himself quotes in *General Theory*: "Each person's means of paying for the productions of other people consists of those which he himself possesses.... Could we suddenly double the productive powers of the country, we should double the supply of commodities in every market; but we should, by the same stroke, double the purchasing power. Everybody would bring a double demand as well as supply; everybody would be able to buy twice as much, because every one would have twice as much to offer in exchange." J. S. Mill, *Principles*, Book III, chap. xiv (see *General Theory*, 18).

16. This argument on the fundamental place of Say's Law in classical economics follows a line borrowed from Alvin H. Hansen, *A Guide to Keynes* (New York: McGraw-Hill, 1953), 12–13, who quotes these passages from Mill.

17. Hansen, *Guide to Keynes*, 7–11, for Clark's investigations of the problem. Quotation is from J. M. Clark, "Productive Capacity and Effective Demand," in *Report of the Columbia University Commission on Economic Reconstruction* (New York: Columbia University Press, 1934), 105. The writings from the 1920s of the more popular American writers William Trufant Foster and Waddill Catchings sounded the similar theme that the propensity to thrift had to be overcome in the new economy by government measures to boost consumption. See Foster and Catchings, *The Road to Plenty* (Boston: Houghton Mifflin, 1928).

18. Classical economics had allowed that unemployment could appear only where certain temporary "frictions" existed and that, over the long term, these would be overcome by the self-adjusting nature of the price system.

19. Again in this regard, Keynes was not altogether alone in the policies he favored. From the 1920s there had been those who had advocated fiscal measures—public works projects and the like—to meet the challenge of stagnated economies. This was certainly true in Japan, where Finance Minister Takahashi Korekiyo's famous inflationary policies are credited with the country's comparatively rapid turnaround from the effects of the depression that began in 1929. Yet everywhere unbalanced budgets and massive government works projects caused anxiety in the minds of officials and experts alike, for they seemed to fly in the face of prudence and the long-held doctrines of economic science. Once again, Keynes' important contribution was to provide the theoretical structure by which such policies might be legitimated. At the same time, Keynes' efforts were not limited to theory. He was an indefatigable public promoter of using government fiscal policy as a stimulus to the economy, not only in the Britain, but in the United States as well.

20. For Keynes as "revolutionary," see Lawrence R. Klein, *The Keynesian Revolution* (1947; New York: Macmillan, 1966).

21. For an extended catalogue of faults by one of the work's foremost interpreters, see Paul A. Samuelson, "*The General Theory* (3)," in Seymour Harris, ed., *The New Economics: Keynes' Influence on Theory and Public Policy* (New York: Alfred A. Knopf, 1947), 148–49; see also Seymour Harris' foreword to Hansen, *Guide to Keynes*, ix–x.

22. Ekonomisuto Henshūbu, *Kōdō seichōki no Nihon*, vol. 1, 11. Also see Hayasaka, *Keinzu no deai*, 6–7, for early student experiences with Keynes. Japanese students of Keynes were not alone in their struggle with *General Theory*. Paul Samuelson, one of the brilliant students of economics at Harvard during the 1930s and a future Nobel laureate who later played a leading role in formalizing the synthesis between neoclassical and Keynesian thought, wrote of his first encounter with *General Theory:* "My rebellion against its pretensions would have been complete, except for an uneasy realization that I did not at all understand what it was about. And I think I am giving away no secrets when I solemnly aver—upon the basis of vivid personal recollection—that no one else in Cambridge, Massachusetts really knew what it was about for some twelve to eighteen months after its publication" (Samuelson, "The *General Theory* [3]," 146).

23. Keizaigakushi Gakkai, *Nihon no keizaigaku: Nihonjin no keizaiteki shii no kiseki* (Tōyō Keizai Shinpōsha, 1984), 145.

24. See the interview with Nakayama Ichirō in Hayasaka, *Keinzu no deai*, 234. Nakayama Ichirō further notes that "the climate in which we [liberal economists] operated was hardly different from that in the Marxists' case" (p. 234).

25. Hamada, "Impact of the *General Theory*," 452; Hayasaka and Masamura, *Sengo Nihon no keizaigaku*, 28–29.

26. Tokyo Keizaigaku Kenkyūjo, *Keizaigaku no shōrai* (Hirobumisha, 1946).

27. See Sugimoto Eiichi, "Kindai riron keizaigaku to Marukusu keizaigaku," *Kikan riron*, no. 1 (May 1947): 28–45.

28. Miyazawa Giichi, "Sugimoto Eiichi," *Asahi jinbutsu jiten: gendai Nihon* (Asahi Shinbunsha, 1990), 860.

29. The essays had originally appeared in the journal *Keizai hyōron*.

30. For discussion of the transformation of the phrase and the books that helped cement it in the professional and popular lexicons, see Hayasaka and Masamura, *Sengo Nihon no keizaigaku*, 17–19.

31. Eleanor Hadley, "The Diffusion of Keynesian Ideas in Japan," in Peter A. Hall, ed., *The Political Power of Economic Ideas: Keynesianism across Nations* (Princeton, NJ: Princeton University Press, 1989), 299–300.

32. Kitō Nisaburō, *Keinzu keizaigaku kaisetsu*, Tōyō keizai kōza sōsho dai 10 kan (Tōyō Keizai Shinpō, 1946). Kitō's somewhat breezy book was the product of a series of three lectures he gave on Keynes apparently under the auspices of the journal *Tōyō keizai shinpō*, though it is unclear when these lectures were given. The popular success of the book was reflected in its 1953 re-release, slightly edited, as volume 80 of Shakai Shisōsha's *Gendai kyōyō bunko* (Contemporary Education Library) series.

33. Shionoya Tsukumo, "Keinzu keizaigaku," 1–4, *Ekonomisuto* 31, no. 21 (1953): 47–49; 31, no. 22 (1953): 46–49; 31, no. 23 (1953): 49–51; 31, no. 24 (1953): 44–47. Other examples of general primer texts include Chigusa Yoshisodo, "Keinzu keizaigaku 2," *Zaisei* 19, no. 5 (1954): 98–104; Okamoto Yoshihiro, "'Keinzushugi' no kisoteki shomondai," *Keizai kagaku* 1, no. 2 (Oct. 1951): 91–104; and Horiya Bunkichirō, "Keinzu tebikisō," *Tsukue* 4, no. 11 (Dec. 1953): 4–5. For representative articles on *General Theory*, see Nakayama Ichirō, "Keinzu no kasetsu: *Ippan riron* no kihon mondai," *Keizai* 3, no. 1 (1949): 4–11; and Matsumura Toshi, "Keinzu *Kōyō, rishi oyobi kahei ippan riron* no chūshin kadai," *Shisō to kagaku* 3 (Nov. 1948): 66–75.

34. For journal essays on Klein's book and for use of the term *kakumei* (revolution), see Koizumi Akira, "Kurain *Keinzu kakumei*," *Keizaigaku* 1 (April 1949); Koizumi Akira, "Kurain *Keinzu kakumei* no hitokōsatsu: kindai riron to marukusu riron no kōshō," *Riron* 6 (Sept. 1948): 63–70; Watabe Fukutarō, "'Keinzu kakumei' ni kansuru kōsatsu," *Shōgaku ronshū* 19, no. 1 (1950): 81–101; Nakamura Seiichi, "L. R. Kurain *Keinzu kakumei* no konponteki tachiba ni tsuite," *Seiji keizai ronsō* 2, no. 1 (1951): 94–98; Hara Yūzō, "Keinzu kakumei to wa: hyakuman nin no keizaigaku 19," *Keizai shinshi* 7, no. 3 (1952): 29–30; and Sobashima Shōzō, "'Keinzu kakumei' wa nani yue ni kakumeiteki de aru ka," *Bankingu*, no. 80 (Dec. 1954): 10–19. Though influential in the original English, Klein's book was translated into Japanese by Shinohara Miyohei in 1952. The book did very well in Japan, and lectures

Klein delivered at Osaka, Hitotsubashi, and Nagoya universities in 1963 inspired the issuing of a second edition of the volume, which included new material taken partly from those addresses in Japan. See the preface to Lawrence R. Klein, *The Keynesian Revolution*, 2nd ed. (New York: Macmillan, 1966), vii.

35. Ishibashi Tanzan, "Shōwa nijūichi nendo shūgiin zaisei enzetsu" (July 26, 1946); reprinted in Itō Mitsuharu and Chō Yukio, eds., *Keizai no shisō*, vol. 8 of *Sengo Nihon shisō taikei* (Chikuma Shobō, 1971), 42–45.

36. See Nihon Keizaigakushi Gakkai, *Nihon no keizaigaku*, 178, on photostat reprint copies in Japan of Samuelson's *Foundations of Economic Analysis* immediately after the book came out in 1948.

37. Hamada, "Impact of the *General Theory*," 452.

38. The definitive study of the Japanese reception and uses of Taylorism is William Tsutsui, *Manufacturing Ideology: Scientific Management in Twentieth-Century Japan* (Princeton, NJ: Princeton University Press, 1998).

39. Eleanor Hadley points out a marked increase in the diffusion of Keynesian ideas in Japan after those with Fulbrights and other fellowships returned from their studies in the 1950s (Hadley, "The Diffusion of Keynesian Ideas," 299).

40. The phrase "Keynes fever" became a common epithet to describe the phenomenon.

41. It included Paul Samuelson and Wassily Leontief, both future Nobel laureates, Joseph Schumpeter, R. F. Harrod, Arthur Bloomfield, chief of the reports and analysis division of the Federal Reserve Bank in New York, and Gerhard Colm, economist on the U.S. Council of Economic Advisers.

42. Nihon Ginkō, Chōsakyoku, "Yakusha jo," in Seymour Harris, ed., *Atarashii keizaigaku: riron to seisaku ni tai suru Keinzu no eikyō*, vol. 1, trans. Nihon Ginkō, Chōsakyoku (Tōyō Keizai Shinpōsha, 1949), 9.

43. Ohara Keiji, "Amerika shihonshugi o sukū michi," *Keizai kenkyū* 1, no. 1 (1950): 61–65; Ohara Keiji, "Review of Alvin Hansen, *Monetary and Fiscal Policy*," *Keizai kenkyū* 1, no. 2 (1950): 146–51; Shinohara Miyohei, "Review of *Income, Employment and Public Policy: Essays in Honor of Alvin Hansen*," *Keizai kenkyū* 2, no. 1 (1951): 72–77. In addition, the journal published many feature articles on Keynesian theory and policy, including Abe Osamu, "Kanzen koyō to keizai keikaku: saikin no ei-bei keizaigaku seisakuteki kiyo" (*Keizai kenkyū* 1, no. 1 [1950]: 18–31), and Miyazawa Ken'ichi, "Keinzu no keizai junkan ron" (*Keizai kenkyū* 2, no. 4 [1951]: 312–17).

44. See Hayasaka, *Keinzu no deai*, 26, for this point regarding the bureaucracy.

45. The quotation is from liberal journalist George Soule, in Alan Brinkley, *The End of Reform: New Deal Liberalism in Recession and War* (New York: Vintage Books, 1996), 229.

46. "Wasteful thrift," quoted in Brinkley, *End of Reform*, 76. Harris argued that "the individual who seeks security through saving may well be behaving in an antisocial manner, in that he contributes to declining demand and depression" (Seymour E. Harris, "Introduction," Part Five: "Stabilization of Demand," in Seymour E. Harris, ed., *Saving American Capitalism: A Liberal Economic Program* (New York: Knopf, 1948), 212. For the development of the liberal consumptionist program of "full employment," see Robert M. Collins, "The Emergence of Economic Growthmanship in the United States: Federal Policy and Economic Knowledge in the Truman Years," in Mary O. Furner and Barry Supple, eds., *The State and Economic Knowledge:*

The American and British Experiences (New York: Woodrow Wilson International Center for Scholars and Cambridge University Press, 1990), 138–45; Brinkley, *End of Reform*, chaps. 4 and 10.

47. Harris, *Saving American Capitalism*, especially Chester Bowles, "Blueprints for a Second New Deal"; A. A. Berle, Jr., "A Liberal Program and Its Philosophy"; Leon H. Keyserling, "Deficiencies of Past Programs and Nature of New Needs"; Charles E. Merriam, "The Place of Planning"; Alvin H. Hansen, "Needed: A Cycle Policy"; and Lorie Tarshis, "Why Demand Must Be Kept High."

48. William J. Barber, "Government as Laboratory for Economic Learning in the Years of the Democratic Roosevelt," in Furner and Supple, *The State and Economic Knowledge*, 120 and 134; Robert M. Collins, "The Emergence of Economic Growthmanship in the United States: Federal Policy and Economic Knowledge in the Truman Years," in Furner and Supple, *The State and Economic Knowledge*, 144 and 146; Brinkley, *End of Reform*, 233.

49. See Abe, "Kanzen koyō to keizai keikaku," 18–31, for an example of Japanese consideration of these issues as they were being treated in the United States and Britain.

50. Takahashi Taizō, "Marukusu ka, Keinzu ka," *Seikei jichō* 5, no. 3 (March 1950): 5–6. Also Koizumi Akira, "Kurain 'Keinzu kakumei' no ichi kōsatsu: kindai riron to Marukusu riron no kōshō," *Riron* 6 (Sept. 1948): 63–70; and Shionoya Tsukumo, "Marukusu ni taiketsu suru mono to shite no Keinzu," *Yomiuri hyōron* 2, no. 3 (1950): 13–17.

51. For the idea of Keynes as an "economic expression" of political movements for reform, see Pierre Rosanvallon, "The Development of Keynesianism in France," in Hall, *The Political Power of Economic Ideas*.

52. Ishibashi, "Zaisei enzetsu," 40–41.

53. Ishibashi, "Zaisei enzetsu," 41.

54. Mark Metzler, "Ishibashi Tanzan and the 'Positive Policy' in Economics," paper delivered at the Annual Meeting of the Association for Asian Studies, March 29, 2003, is extremely insightful on Ishibashi's approaches during this period.

55. Ishibashi, "Zaisei enzetsu," 39–40.

56. Jerome B. Cohen, *Japan's Postwar Economy* (Bloomington: Indiana University Press, 1958), 84.

57. Ishibashi, "Zaisei enzetsu," 42 and 44.

58. Ishibashi, "Zaisei enzetsu," 44.

59. Ishibashi Tanzan, "Kinshuku seisaku ka, bōchō seisaku ka," *Tōyō keizai shinpō* (Feb. 2, 1946): 7–9 and 13.

60. Ishibashi, "Zaisei enzetsu," 42–43.

61. Richard Smethurst, *From Foot Soldier to Finance Minister: Takahashi Korekiyo, Japan's Keynes* (Cambridge, MA: Harvard University Asia Center, 2007), chaps. 12 and 13 and Conclusion.

62. Ishibashi Tanzan in interview of Takahashi Korekiyo, "Keizai seidan," in Takahashi Korekiyo, *Zuisōroku* (Senzō Shobō, 1936), 403. See also Tsunoda, "Rationalizing Japan's Political Economy," 270.

63. George C. Peden, "Old Dogs and New Tricks: The British Treasury and Keynesian Economics in the 1940s and 1950s," in Furner and Supple, *The State and Economic Knowledge*, 221.

64. As in its report titled *National and International Measures for Full Employment* of 1949. See Kenneth K. Kurihara, "The United Nations and Full Employment," *Journal of Political Economy* 58, no. 4 (1950): 353–58, for analysis of this report. "Frictional unemployment" referred to the relatively small level of joblessness seen as an unavoidable outcome of short-term delays in the ability of market mechanisms to achieve employment equilibria.

65. For example, see Ōuchi Hyōe, "Sekai shintsūka seido no kenkyū" (1946), reprinted in *Ōuchi Hyōe Chosakushū* vol. 6 (Iwanami Shoten, 1975), 5 and 131–32; Hijikata Seibi, Chō Shuzen, and Iwano Chūjirō, *Kanzen koyō no riron to jissai* (Daiyamondosha, 1947), 67–186; Nakayama Ichirō, "Kanzen koyō no riron," *Keizai hyōron* 1, no. 5 (Aug. 1946): 4, the text of which reappeared as a chapter bearing the same title in Nakayama's book, *Sengo keizai no tenbō* (Hakunichi Shoin, 1947); Yasui Inomata, "Koyō riron to tenbō," *Keizai hyōron* 1, no. 8 (1946): 16–29; Iso Rankuji, "Jiyū shakai ni okeru kanzen koyō: koyō seisaku hakusho to Bīvuarijji hōkoku no komentarī," *Keizai hyōron* 2, no. 1 (1947): 9–20.

66. Chūō Shitsugyō Taisaku Iinkai, "Kengi: shitsugyō taisaku to shite kyūsoku sochi subeki jikō ni kansuru iken" (Feb. 9, 1946), in Ōkouchi Kazuo, ed., *Rōdō*, vol. 4 of *Shiryō: sengo nijūnenshi,* edited by Tsuji Kiyoaki et al. (Nihon Hyōronsha, 1966), 2; Nakayama Ichirō, "Kanzen koyō no riron," 7. See also Hijikata, Chō, and Iwano, *Kanzen koyō no riron to jissai,* preface 2.

67. Eisei Daijin, "Eisei daijin kakugi yōbō jikō: fukuin oyobi shitsugyōsha no suitei ni kansuru chū" (Dec. 16, 1945), in Ōkouchi, *Rōdō*, 1.

68. Rōdōshō, *Shitsugyō taisaku nenkan* (1951), 3; cited in Ōkouchi, *Rōdō*, 1.

69. Hijikata, Chō, and Iwano, *Kanzen koyō no riron to jissai,* preface 2.

70. Chigusa Yoshisodo, *Shihonshugi no shōrai* (Kōbundo, 1951), 114.

71. Ōuchi, "Sekai shintsūka seido," 132–34. Ōuchi remained dubious of the liberationist aspects of Keynesian thought. He somewhat later dismissed the stature that Keynes had achieved in the United States, noting that this was the same "country, after all, that had crowned [Charlie] Chaplin as a king," Ōuchi, *Keizaigaku gojūnen*, vol. 2, 467.

72. Nakayama Ichirō, "Keizai minshuka no kihon mondai," *Chūō kōron* 6, no. 1 (1946): 24; Nakayama, "Kanzen koyō no riron," 20.

73. For treatment of the economic platforms of the political parties directly after the war, see Yamamoto Kiyoshi, "'Sangyō saiken' to shoseiji shutai," in Tokyo Daigaku Shakai Kagaku Kenkyūjo, ed., *Rōdō kaikaku*, vol. 5 of *Sengo kaikaku* (Tokyo Daigaku Shuppankai, 1974), 181–88.

74. Keizai Doyūkai, *Keizai Dōyūkai 10 nen shi* (Keizai Dōyūkai, 1956), 40–44.

75. Hayakawa Shōichirō and Yoshida Kenji, "Keizai fukkō kaigi no soshiki to undō," installment 2, *Kenkyū shiryō geppō,* no. 284 (March 1982): 34–40, especially "Dai ikkai kokumin keizai kaigi gian taikō, dai ichigo: kezai saiken chōki keikaku," 37. For the Keizai Fukkō Kaigi in general, see Hayakawa Shōichirō and Yoshida Kenji, "Keizai fukkō kaigi no soshiki to undō," installment 1, *Kenkyū shiryō geppō,* no. 283 (Feb. 1982): 1–34.

76. Zen Keinosuke, "Nihon keizai no saiken," *Nihon keizai shinbun* (Dec. 9, 1946); reprinted in Yoshino Kōichi, ed., *Zen Keinosuke tsuisōroku* (Nihon Dantai Seimei Hoken Kabushiki Kaisha, 1959), 168.

77. Gaimushō, Chōsakyoku, Daisanka, "Shitsugyō taisaku ni kanren suru yū'nyū shinsei no ken" (Aug. 12, 1946), and Keizai Antei Honbu, "Sangyō fukkō shitsugyō taisaku ni kanren suru yū'nyū shinsei no ken" (Sept. 4, 1946), in Nakamura Takafusa and Miyazaki Masayasu, eds., *Keisha seisan hōshiki to sekitan shōiinkai*, vol. 2 of *Shiryō: sengo Nihon no keizai seisaku kōsō*, ed. Arisawa Hiromi (Tokyo Daigaku Shuppankai, 1990), 41 and 46.

78. Keizai Antei Honbu, "Keizai fukkō keikaku dai ichiji shian no gaiyō" (May 17, 1948), and Keizai Fukkō Keikaku Iinkai, "Keizai fukkō keikaku iinkai hōkokusho" (May 30, 1949), in Nakamura Takafusa and Hara Akira, eds., *Keizai fukkō keikaku*, vol. 3 of *Shiryō: Sengo Nihon no keizai seisaku kōsō*, edited by Arisawa Hiromi (Tokyo Daigaku Shuppankai, 1990), 19, 35–38, and 197. The early drafts of the plan called for unemployment rates no higher than the 2.4% of the total population logged during the period between 1930 and 1934 (Keizai Antei Honbu, "Keizai fukkō keikaku dai ichiji shian no gaiyō," 37).

79. Nihon Ginkō, Chōsakyoku, "Yakusha jo," in Seymour Harris, ed., *Atarashii keizaigaku*, 8.

80. Arisawa Hiromi, "Nihon keizai no hakyoku o sukū mono: genjitsu katei no bunseki," *Hyōron* (Jan. 1947), excerpted in Makino Noboru, *Kuronikaru Nihon keizai jiten, 1945–1994* (Tōyō Keizai Shinpōsha, 1996), 24; Keizai Antei Honbu, "Keizai fukkō keikaku dai ichiji shian," in Nakamura Takafusa and Hara Akira, eds., *Keizai fukkō keikaku*, vol. 3 of *Shiryō: sengo Nihon no keizai seisaku kōsō*, edited by Arisawa Hiromi (Tokyo Daigaku Shuppankai, 1990), 50.

81. Takahashi Kamekichi et al., "Kiki zaisei to keizai antei honbu: Ishibashi zaisei no hihan to tōsei keizai seikaku kentō," *Kaizō* 27, no. 8 (Aug. 1946): 39. The quoted speaker is economist Takahashi Kamekichi.

82. In the end, Nakayama held that Keynesian public expenditures to achieve full employment must also be pursued in Japan, but that they should be seen as necessary not because savings is too high, as in the model case of a mature British capitalism, but because it is too low. Government expenditures must be employed to build up adequate stocks of capital accumulation. (Economist A. C. Pigou was often used by Keynesian promoters everywhere to represent the "self-adjusting" theory of economies.) Nakayama, "Kanzen koyō no riron," 16–20.

83. See, for example, Keizai Antei Honbu, "Keizai fukkō keikaku dai ichiji shian no gaiyō," 35–36; Inaba Hidezō, ed., *Nihon keizai no shōrai: keizai fukkō keikaku no zenbō to hihan* (Chūō Rōdō Gakuen, 1948), 220, a volume produced by the Keizai Fukkō Keikaku Iinkai within the ESB.

84. Keizai Fukkō Keikaku Iinkai, "Keizai fukkō keikaku iinkai hokokusho," 197.

85. In a radio address in February 1946, Ōuchi famously denounced the expansionary policy of the finance minister of the Shidehara cabinet, Shibusawa Keizō. For the criticisms of prominent socialist voices in this regard, see for example Ōuchi Hyōe et al., "Keizai hakusho no igi," *Sekai* 21 (Sept. 1947): 2–3; Uno Kōzō, "Keizai antei no gainen," *Hyōron* 7 (Sept.–Oct. 1946): 2–10; Kimura Kihachirō, "Keizai saiken no zentei," *Asahi hyōron* 2 (Nov. 1947): 15–16.

86. For Arisawa's later comment that to have implemented inflation-fighting measures before production had recovered would have risked making the same mistake the Germans had after World War I when they had successfully "killed inflation

in one quick stroke" but as a result also caused devastatingly steep drops in economic activity and employment, see Keizai Kikakuchō, *Sengo keizai fukkō to keizai antei honbu* (Keizai Kikakuchō, 1988), 76–77.

87. Chalmers Johnson, *MITI and the Japanese Miracle: The Growth of Industrial Policy, 1925–1975* (Stanford, CA: Stanford University Press, 1982), 178–79.

88. Tokyo Keizaigaku Kenkyūjo, *Keizaigaku no shōrai*, 274–80. The economists contributing to this volume, which features something of a *taidan* round-table and interview format, included the ubiquitous Arisawa Hiromi, as well as Tsuchiya Takao, Ōkouchi Kazuo, Nakayama Ichirō, and Yamada Yūzō; see also Nakayama, "Kanzen koyō no riron," 10–11.

89. See, for example, Chūō Shitsugyō Taisaku Iinkai, "Kengi: shitsugyō taisaku to shite kyūsoku sochi subeki jikō ni kansuru iken" (Feb. 9, 1946), in Ōkouchi, *Rōdō*, 1–2.

90. The term is one Ishibashi quoted from Shibusawa Keizō, finance minister in the Shidehara government, deciding that it corresponded to his own ideas. See Ishibashi Tanzan, "Kinshuku seisaku ka, bōchō seisaku ka: mokka no infure mondai no kaibō," *Tōyō keizai shinpō* (Feb. 2, 1946), 7.

91. Ishibashi, "Zaisei enzetsu," 49–50.

92. Ishibashi was quick to add that, while the lessons of Nazi Germany were instructive, Japanese had to learn how to accomplish similar outcomes within a democratic system. Ishibashi, "Kinshuku seisaku ka," 13.

93. Eisei Daijin, "Shitsugyō taisaku ni kansuru kakugi yōbō" (Nov. 16, 1945), in Ōkouchi, *Rōdō*, 1. The ministry with jurisdiction here was that of Public Welfare. The Ministry of Labor was not created until 1947.

94. Shibuya Naozō, *Sengo Nihon no koyō shitsugyō to sono taisaku* (Rōdō Hōrei Kyōkai, 1957), 124; "Kakugi kettei: kinkyū shūgyō taisaku yōkō" (Feb. 15, 1946). For discussion and original text of the cabinet guidelines, see Shibuya, *Sengo Nihon no koyō shitsugyō*, 134–38; partial text also in Ōkouchi, *Rōdō*, 3.

95. "GHQ meirei: Nihon kōkyō jigyō keikaku gensoku" [Japanese trans. of original] (May 22, 1946), as attachment to "Kinkyū shitsugyō taisaku hōan teian riyū setsumei" (April 23, 1949); in Ōkouchi, *Rōdō*, 125.

96. Murakami Shigetoshi, *Nihon no shitsugyō to sono taisaku* (Kawade Shobō, 1955), 116–17.

97. Shūsen Renraku Jimukyoku Keizaibu, "Bogudan shi no 'Nihon keizai saiken no kihon mondai' sono hoka ni kan suru dan" (June 5, 1946), in Nakamura Takafusa and Ōmori Tokuko, eds., *Nihon keizai saiken no kihon mondai*, vol. 1 of *Shiryō: Nihon no keizai seisaku kōsō*, ed. Arisawa Hiromi (Tokyo Daigaku Shuppankai, 1990), 117.

98. Rōdōshō Shokugyō Anteikyoku Shitsugyō Taisakubu, *Shitsugyō taisaku jigyō nijūnenshi* (Rōdō Hōrei Kyōkai, 1970), 139, table 1–3.

99. Rōdōshō Shokugyō Anteikyoku Shitsugyō Taisakubu, *Shitsugyō taisaku*, 142, table 1–7.

100. "Kakugi kettei: genka no shitsugyō jisei ni taisho subeki shitsugyō taisaku" (March 4, 1949), in Ōkouchi, *Rōdō*, 124.

101. Shibuya Naozō, *Sengo Nihon no koyō shitsugyō*, 593–600; for original text of Shingikai reports and opinions, see 691–98.

102. Kinkyū Shitsugyō Taisaku Hō (May 20, 1949), Law no. 89, article 1, reprinted in Murakami, *Nihon no shitsugyō,* 169.

103. Kinkyū Shitsugyō Taisaku Hō (May 20, 1949), Law no. 89, articles 6, 12, and 13, reprinted in Murakami, *Nihon no shitsugyō,* 171–72.

104. Kinkyū Shitsugyō Taisaku Hō (May 20, 1949), Law no. 89, article 2, reprinted in Murakami, *Nihon no shitsugyō,* 169–70; "Kinkyū shitsugyō taisaku hōan teian riyū setsumei" (April 23, 1949), in Ōkouchi, *Rōdō,* 124–25; "Kakugi kettei: genka no shitsugyō jisei ni taisho subeki shitsugyō taisaku" (March 4, 1949), in Ōkouchi, *Rōdō,* 124.

105. Murakami, *Nihon no shitsugyō,* 119, table 44.

106. Murakami, *Nihon no shitsugyō,* 126, graph 28. This does not include the numbers routinely employed in public works now categorized independently from works projects specifically designed as unemployment programs. The two categories had been split apart by the Shitsugyō Taisaku Hō of 1949.

107. See "Kyū Seikatsu Hogo Hō," Law no. 17 (Sept. 9, 1946), and "Shitsugyō hoken seido yōkō" (Oct. 1945), in Ōkouchi, *Rōdō,* 33 and 69–70. On the overall welfare system that eventually took shape in postwar Japan, see Gregory J. Kasza, *One World of Welfare: Japan in Comparative Perspective* (Ithaca, NY: Cornell University Press, 2006).

108. The prewar version of the postwar employment security offices *(kōkyō shokugyō anteijo)* were called employment placement offices *(shokugyō shōkaijo).* See Murakami, *Nihon no shitsugyō,* 71–75.

109. See Kase Kazutoshi, *Senzen Nihon no shitsugyō taisaku: kyūsaigata kōkyō doboku jigyō no shiteki bunseki* (Nihon Keizai Hyōronsha, 1998), 25–41; Murakami, *Nihon no shitsugyō,* 78–89.

110. For this idea of social administration, see José Harris, *Unemployment and Politics: A Study in English Social Policy, 1886–1914* (Oxford: Clarendon Press, 1972), 6. Quoted in Donald Winch, "Economic Knowledge and Government in Britain: Some Historical and Comparative Reflections," Furner and Supple, *The State and Economic Knowledge,* 63n81.

111. Keizai Antei Honbu, *Keizai jissō hōkokusho* (1947); reprinted in *Keizai hakusho zenbun* (Sakagaki Shoten, 1949), 75. See also Keizai Antei Honbu, "Keizai fukkō keikaku dai ichiji shian no gaiyō," 37, for a 1948 assessment of the problem of unemployment after the war as "not emerging as acutely" to that point as it had in the years before the war.

Chapter 4. Knowing Growth

1. Hitotsubashi Daigaku Keizai Kenkyūjo, *Keizai kenkyūjo yōran* (Hitotsubashi Daigaku Keizai Kenkyūjo, 1998), 1–4.

2. Tsuru replaced Nakayama Ichirō, then president of the university who was serving concurrently as chief of the institute (Keizai Kenkyūjo, *Keizai kenkyūjo yōran,* 3–4).

3. For the Yale Economic Growth Center and the Japan Economic Research Center, see Lawrence Klein and Kazushi Ohkawa, eds., *Economic Growth: The Japanese Experience since the Meiji Era* (Homewood, IL: Richard D. Irwin, 1968), v and vii.

4. Keizai Shingichō, *Nihon keizai to kokumin shotoku: Shōwa 5-nen–27-nen Kokumin shotoku to kokumin keizai keisan* (Gakuyō Shobō, 1954), jo no. 2, 3.

5. See Keizai Kikakuchō, Keizai Kenkyūjo, *Kokumin sōseisan no chōki suikei: dai ichiji shian, Shōwa gannen–32-nen.* Kenkyū shiryō (Keizai Kikakuchō, 1959), 1.

6. Yamada Yūzō, *Nihon kokumin shotoku suikei shiryō* (Tōyō Keizai Shinpōsha, 1951). Among the works Yamada built on was Hijikata Seibi's estimates from the 1930s. Yamada had also released an earlier book titled *Kokumin shotoku no kenkyū* (1948).

7. The Hitotsubashi group received inspiration from Yamada, himself a Hitotsubashi economist. Although they took his estimates as starting points, they also made revisions (Prof. Minami Ryōshin, interview with the author, Institute of Economic Research Hitotsubashi University, Kunitachi, Tokyo, Jan. 13, 1997; see also Kazushi Ohkawa, *The Growth Rate of the Japanese Economy since 1878* [Kinokuniya Bookstore, 1957], iv–v).

8. Hitotsubashi Daigaku Keizai Kenkyūjo, *Keizai kenkyūjo yōran*, 254.

9. Volume 1 covered national income *(kokumin shotoku)*. Ōkawa Kazushi, Shinohara Miyohei, and Umemura Mataji, eds., *Chōki keizai tōkei: suikei to bunseki*, 14 vols. (Tōyō Keizai Shinpōsha, 1965–79).

10. Ōkawa Kazushi, ed., *Nihon keizai no seichō ritsu: 1878–1942 nen ni kansuru jisshōteki kenkyū* (Iwanami Shoten, 1956). The updated English-language version of this was Ohkawa, *Growth Rate of the Japanese Economy.*

11. Ōkawa Kazushi et al., eds., *Shihon sutokku*, vol. 3 of *Chōki keizai tōkei: suikei to bunseki* (Tōyō Keizai Shinpōsha, 1966), iii.

12. Ohkawa, *Growth Rate of the Japanese Economy*, i.

13. See, for example, Ryūtaro Komiya, ed., *Postwar Economic Growth in Japan,* Selected Papers of the First Conference of the Tokyo Economic Research Center, trans. Robert S. Ozaki (Berkeley: University of California Press, 1966); and Shinohara Miyohei, *Nihon keizai no seichō to junkan* (Sōbunsha, 1961), as well as Miyohei Shinohara, *Structural Changes in Japan's Economic Development,* Hitotsubashi University, Institute of Economic Research, Economic Research Series, no. 11 (Kinokuniya Bookstore, 1970). Such studies as Kazushi Ohkawa and Henry Rosovsky, *Japanese Economic Growth: Trend Acceleration in the Twentieth Century,* Studies in Economic Growth in Industrialized Countries (Stanford, CA: Stanford University Press, 1973), followed during the 1970s. Although only completed in 1973, the Ohkawa and Rosovsky project was begun in 1961 (Ohkawa and Rosovsky, *Japanese Economic Growth*, vii).

14. See, for example, Simon Kuznets, Wilbert Moore, and Joseph Spengler, eds., *Economic Growth: Brazil, India, and Japan* (Durham, NC: Duke University Press, 1955), which was the product of an SSRC conference held in 1952. Later works were also supported by the SSRC, including Ohkawa and Rosovsky, *Japanese Economic Growth,* which was published as part of the council's series titled Studies of Economic Growth in Industrialized Countries, edited by Kuznets.

15. Kazushi Ohkawa and Miyohei Shinohara, eds., *Patterns of Japanese Economic Development: A Quantitative Appraisal* (New Haven, CT: Yale University Press, 1979).

16. (Macmillan and St. Martin's Press, 1963). Tsuru's is chapter 3 ("The Take Off in Japan, 1868–1900"), 139–50.

17. The conference was sponsored by the Social Science Research Council. Oshima's "Survey of Various Long-term Estimates of Japanese National Income" was published in Japan in *Keizai kenkyū* 4, no. 3 (July 1953): 248–56. Oshima has

previously been mentioned in regard to his UN critiques of the national income computations of the Economic Stabilization Board. He later took part in scholarly investigations into growth as a professor at the University of Hawai'i. See the participant list for the first International Conference on Economic Growth of the Japan Economic Research Center, in Lawrence Klein and Kazushi Ohkawa, *Economic Growth*, xiii.

18. On support for LTES, see Ōkawa Kazushi and Takamatsu Nobukiyo, eds., *Kokumin shotoku*, vol. 1 of *Chōki keizai tōkei: suikei to bunseki* (Tōyō Keizai Shinpōsha, 1974), vi; on support for the Ohkawa and Rosovsky volume, see Ohkawa and Rosovsky, *Japanese Economic Growth*, vii. Rosovsky was an economist at Harvard University.

19. Shimomura Osamu, "Kin'yū hikishime seisaku: sono tadashii rikai no tame ni," in Tamura Toshio, ed., *Keizai seichō jitsugen no tame ni: keizaigaku hakase Shimomura Osamu ronbun shū* (Kōchikai, 1958), 42–70.

20. See Shimomura Osamu, *Nihon keizai seichō ron* (Kin'yū Zaisei Jijō Kenkyūkai, 1962), maegaki, 2–3, for celebration of the productive capacities of the Japanese nation.

21. His financial policy proposals drew heated responses from many quarters. See Tamura, *Keizai seichō jitsugen*, 83–122.

22. Shimomura had publicly sparred during this period with Gotō Yonosuke and Kanamori Hisao, both economists in the EPA. See Shimomura Osamu, "Tōmen no keizai kyokumen o tsuranuku kihon dōkō: keizai no bōchō wa hatashite genkaiten ni kita ka," and Gotō Yonosuke, "Keiki dōkō to junkan kyokumen no rikai no tame: Shimomura shi shoron no gimonten o tsuku," in Tamura, *Keizai seichō jitsugen*, 227–68; Kanamori Hisao, *Watashi no sengo keizaishi: ekonomisuto no 50-nen* (Tōyō Keizai Shinpōsha, 1995), 175–76. This phase of the 1950s growth debates was often known as the Shimomura-Gotō debate, Gotō Yonosuke being head of the EPA's Research Bureau and the author of the 1957 white paper. (For more on Gotō, see Chapter 5 of this study.) Shimomura himself was a bureaucratic economist, but also a public economist in the sense I have used the term, appearing constantly in the national economic press of the day. For a representative piece, see "Taidan: watashi wa keizai no kichō o kō kangaeru," *Tōyō keizai shinpō*, no. 2792 (Aug. 24, 1957): 38–43.

23. The Economic White Paper of that year was famously subtitled, "Hayasugita kakudai to sono hansei" (Excessively rapid expansion and a reconsideration of approaches). For discussion of what was deemed a "tempo" of economic expansion that had "gone too quickly," see Keizai Kikakuchō, *Keizai hakusho: hayasugita kakudai to sono hansei* Shōwa 32-nendo (Shiseidō, 1957), 2–10.

24. The New Long-Term Economic Plan's 6.5% growth per year, needless to say, was a pace that itself would be considered blistering today. In 1960, Shimomura was saying that growth as high as 11% per year and over for the first half of the 1960s was within the capacity of the economy; Shimomura Osamu, "Seichō seisaku no kihon mondai," *Kin'yū zaisei jijō*, no. 518 (Nov. 7, 1960), reprinted in Shimomura Osamu, *Nihon keizai seichō ron*, 13. For an entry in Ōkita's ongoing response to Shimomura's attacks, see Ōkita Saburō, "Nihon keizai no seichōryoku to 'Shin chōki keizai keikaku': Shimomura Osamu shi 'Kadai seichō ron hihan' no kentō," *Kin'yū zaisei jijō* 10, no. 12 (1959); reprinted in Kin'yū Zaisei Jijō Kenkyūkai, ed., *Nihon keizai no seichōryoku: "Shimomura riron" to sono hihan* (Kin'yū Zaisei Jijō Kenkyūkai, 1959), 31–47.

25. Shimomura Osamu, "Nihon keizai kichō to sono seichōryoku: kadai seichō ron hihan to seichōryoku no ginmi," *Kin'yū zaisei jijō* 10, no. 9 (1959); reprinted in Kin'yū Zaisei Jijō Kenkyūkai, ed., *Nihon keizai no seichōryoku*, 29.

26. See, for example, Kushida Mitsuo, "Henjo," in Kin'yu Zaisei Jijō Kenkyūkai, ed., *Nihon keizai no seichōryoku*, 2.

27. W. W. Rostow, *The Stages of Economic Growth: A Non-Communist Manifesto* (Cambridge: Cambridge University Press, 1960), 37–39 and 41.

28. Shimomura calculated a capital-output ratio between 1951 and 1955 for the Japanese economy of 1:1.1. His startling contention was, then, that in the Japanese case, each unit of capital investment in one year could be expected to produce an equal unit of output increase in the following year. This output per unit of investment was far higher than what was considered the norm in other countries. For figuring future growth potential, Shimomura conservatively dropped this ratio down to 1:0.9. Shimomura Osamu, "Seichō seisaku no kihon mondai," 8–9, especially table 1.

29. Keizai Kikakuchō, *Watashitachi no hataraki to kurashi: Wakariyasui kokumin shotoku no hanashi* (Tōyō Keizai Shinpōsha, 1955). Keizai Kikakuchō, *5-nengo no Nihon keizai: Dare mo wakaru keizai jiritsu 5-kanen keikaku no hanashi* (Daiyamondosha, 1956).

30. For the story of the formation and a list of the almost fifty members of the Committee on Economic Recovery Planning responsible for the plan, see Keizai Fukkō Keikaku Iinkai, "Keizai fukkō keikaku iinkai hōkokusho," in Nakamura Takafusa and Hara Akira, eds., *Keizai fukkō keikaku*, vol. 3 of *Shiryō: sengo Nihon no keizai seisaku kōsō*, edited by Arisawa Hiromi (Tokyo Daigaku Shuppankai, 1990), 256–57 and 276–78.

31. Yamada Yūzō, "Nihon no keizai keikaku ni kansuru mondai ten," in Yamada Yūzō and Hisatake Motohiko, eds., *Nihon no keizai keikaku*, Keizai bunseki shimupojiumu, vol. 8 (Nihon Hyōron Shinsha, 1957), 1; Asai Yoshio, "Kaidai," in Sōgō Kenkyū Kaihatsu Kikō, Sengo Keizai Seisaku Shiryō Kenkyūkai, ed., *Sengo keizai keikaku shiryō: Keizai Antei Honbu sengo keizai seisaku shiryō*, vol. 1 (Nihon Keizai Hyōronsha, 1997), v.

32. Quoted in Shigeto Tsuru, "Economic Planning and Programming in Japan," in *Essays on Economic Development*, The Institute of Economic Research, Hitotsubashi University, Economic Research Series, no. 9 (Kinokuniya Bookstore, 1968), 184.

33. Hara Akira, "Kaidai," in Nakamura Takafusa and Hara Akira, eds., *Keizai fukkō keikaku*, vol. 3 of *Shiryō: sengo Nihon no keizai seisaku kōsō*, edited by Arisawa Hiromi (Tokyo Daigaku Shuppankai, 1990), 13.

34. Asai Yoshio, interview with the author, Seikyō University, Tokyo, May 11, 1997.

35. Hayashi Yūjirō, ed., *Nihon no keizai keikaku: Sengo no rekishi to mondaiten* (Tōyō Keizai Shinpōsha, 1957), 144–45. Garner's quotation appears in Hayashi's book in Japanese translation. The version of the quotation used here is taken from Tsuru, "Economic Planning and Programming in Japan," 192.

36. Sōrifu, *Sōrifu V*, vol. 5 of *Kanchō benran* (Ōkurashō Insatsukyoku, 1960), 7 and 10.

37. On Hatoyama, see Shigeto Tsuru, *Japan's Capitalism: Creative Defeat and Beyond* (Cambridge: Cambridge University Press, 1993), 94; on the LDP's new com-

mittee, see Haruhiro Fukui, "Economic Planning in Postwar Japan: A Case Study in Policy Making," *Asian Survey* 12, no. 4 (1972): 339.

38. Yamada Yūzō and Yamada Isamu, eds., *Keizai keikaku*, vol. 12 of *Nihon keizai no bunseki* (Shunjūsha, 1960), hashigaki 1.

39. Keizai Kikakuchō, *Shinchōki keizai keikaku* (Dec. 17, 1957) (Ōkurashō Insatsukyoku, 1957), 1.

40. Suzuki Kyōichi, *Nihon keizai to keizai keikaku* (Senbundō, 1959), jobun 1.

41. See Hayashi, *Nihon no keizai keikaku*. For his activities at the center of official planning, see the chosha ryakureki and iii–v of this volume.

42. As an example, these economists were contributing authors to Yamada Yūzō and Hisatake Motohiko, eds., *Nihon no keizai keikaku*, vol. 8 of *Keizai bunseki shinpojiumu* (Nihon Hyōron Shinsha, 1957). Imai was on staff at the Electrical Power Central Research Institute (Denryoku Chūō Kenkyūjo) when this book was published, but he would join Hitotsubashi in 1964.

43. For example, see Nihon Hyōronsha's *Keizai keikaku to yosoku* and *Nihon no keizai keikaku*, vols. 7 and 8 respectively of its *Keizai bunseki shimupojiumu* series (1957), and Shunjūsha's *Keizai keikaku*, vol. 12 of its *Nihon keizai no bunseki* series (1960). A somewhat later example during the height of the high-growth 1960s is Kawade Shobō's *Keizai no keikakuka: seichō o meguru hoshu to kakushin*, vol. 9 of its *Gendai no keizai* series (1965).

44. For an example of the works of scholarly associations, see Nihon Keizai Seisaku Gakkai's *Keizai keikaku no sho keitai*, Nihon keizai seisaku gakkai nenpō, no. 7 (Keisō Shobō, 1959).

45. Takahashi Chōtarō, "Keizai keikaku no tame no mokei kōsei," in *Keizai keikaku no sho keitai*, Nihon keizai seisaku gakkai nenpō, no. 7 (Keisō Shobō, 1959), 25.

46. Mezaki Kenji, "Ronsetsu: jiyū to tōsei no jintēze no keizai keikaku," in *Keizai keikaku no sho keitai*, Nihon keizai seisaku gakkai nenpō, no. 7, 1.

47. Yamada Yūzō and Yamada Isamu, eds., *Keizai keikaku*, hashigaki 1.

48. Takefuji Mitsuaki, "'Keikaku to jiyū' no mondai no keizai rinriteki sokumen," in *Keizai keikaku no sho keitai*, Nihon keizai seisaku gakkai nenpō, no. 7, 15–16; Yamada and Yamada, *Keizai keikaku*, hashigaki, 1. Also, along the same lines although later, see Chikaraishi Sadakazu, *Keizai no keikakuka*, vol. 9 of *Gendai no keizai* (Kawade Shobō, 1965), 60–62.

49. Sōrifu, *Sōrifu V*, 11.

50. Sōrifu, *Sōrifu V*, 11–12.

51. Takahashi Chōtarō, "Keizai keikaku," 25–28.

52. Ōuchi Hyōe, *Keizaigaku gojūnen*, vol. 2, 469–71.

53. Keizai Kikakuchō, Chōsabu, *Jinmin minshushugi shokoku ni okeru kokumin keizai keikaku no soshiki to hōhō*, Keikichō shō 31 dai 7 go (Keizai Kikakuchō, 1956); Keizai Kikakuchō, Kaihatsubu, *Kokumin keizai keikaku sakusei no hōhōronjō no shomondai: Soren*, Zenkoku sōgō kaihatsu keikaku sankōshi 13 (Keizai Kikakuchō, 1956).

54. Katō Kan, "Keizai seichō to keizai keikaku no ikkei: Sovieto genka shōkyaku ronsō o megutte," in *Keizai keikaku no sho keitai*, Nihon keizai seisaku gakkai nenpō, no. 7 (Keisō Shobō, 1959), 46–57.

55. June to August 1956, financed by the U.S. and Japanese governments. Nihon Seisansei Honbu, *Keizai kaihatsu no shomondai: Keizai Kaihatsu Kōshūkai Sankadan hōkokusho* Productivity Report No. 20 (Nihon Seisansei Honbu, 1957), 1–5.

56. Nihon Seisansei Honbu, *Keizai kaihatsu kōshūkai*, 63–66; Keizai Kikakuchō, Chōsabu, *Amerika no keizai keikaku ni manabu*, Keikichōgai shō 32 dai 2 go (Keizai Kikakuchō, 1957), hashigaki (unnumbered).

57. Nihon Seisansei Honbu, *Keizai kaihatsu kōshūkai*, 67.

58. The prominent presence of members of the U.S. Operations Mission and the International Cooperation Agency of the U.S. State Department in a four-week conference on development in which the JPC mission members participated lent credence to the JPC mission's perceptions of a significant commitment to planning by U.S. officials. For participants in the conference held at Vanderbilt University, see Nihon Seisansei Honbu, *Keizai kaihatsu kōshūkai*, 13.

59. Nihon Seisansei Honbu, *Keizai kaihatsu kōshūkai*, 15.

60. Kanamori's report, like many internal documents, was handwritten, and it was dated January 24, 1957. Kanamori may have had a hand in drafting the JPC report: some of the text of his report appears nearly verbatim in the JPC report, which was released four months afterward. The exact relation between the two texts, however, is unclear.

61. Keizai Kikakuchō, Chōsabu, *Amerika no keizai keikaku*, 2–5. Here Kanamori and the JPC's Economic Development Mission were in good company, for the impression of a long history of planning in the United States was reinforced by many who wrote on the topic. See Mezaki, "Ronsetsu: jiyū to tōsei no jintēze no keizai keikaku," 3; Suzuki, *Nihon keizai to keizai keikaku*, 3–5.

62. Keizai Kikakuchō, Chōsabu, *Amerika no keizai keikaku*, hashigaki (unnumbered).

63. Keizai Kikakuchō, Chōsabu, *Amerika no keizai keikaku*, yōyaku and main text 7–12 and 30–42.

64. For the meeting with Colm, see Nihon Seisansei Honbu, *Keizai kaihatsu kōshūkai*, 63; for Kanamori on Colm, see Keizai Kikakuchō, Chōsabu, *Amerika no keizai keikaku*, yōyaku and main text 27–30 (misnumbered) and 44–47.

65. Keizai Kikakuchō, Chōsabu, *Amerika no keizai keikaku*, hashigaki (unnumbered).

66. Nihon Seisansei Honbu, *Keizai kaihatsu kōshūkai*, 86.

67. For a summary of the 1959 seminar on "Long Term Planning," see Nihon Seisansei Honbu, *Karuizawa toppu seminā o kaerimiru: arata na hatten o motomete* (Nihon Seisansei Honbu, 1985), 7–10. This volume was released in celebration of the thirtieth anniversary of the so-called Top Management Seminars of the JPC.

Chapter 5. Structural Ills and Growth Cures

1. Louise Young, *Japan's Total Empire: Manchuria and the Culture of Wartime Imperialism* (Berkeley: University of California Press, 1998), 334. Much of the discussion here on emigration is based on chapter 7 of this work, "Reinventing Agrarianism: Rural Crisis and the Wedding of Agriculture to Empire," 307–51.

2. D. Eleanor Westney, "Emigration," in *Kodansha Encyclopedia of Japan*, vol. 2 (Kodansha, 1983), 200.

3. For the Communist Party plank on resettlement, see Martin Bronfenbrenner, "Four Positions on Japanese Finance," *The Journal of Political Economy* 58, no. 4 (1950): 288.

4. By the early 1940s, visions of racial and imperial expansion fueled pronatalist policies that seemed to contradict campaigns to promote emigration. In 1941, it became an official goal, represented in the slogan "give birth and multiply" *(umeyo fuyaseyo)*, to increase the Japanese population to 100 million in twenty years. On pronatalist ideology beginning in the Meiji period, see Yasuko Tama, "The Logic of Abortion: Japanese Debates on the Legitimacy of Abortion as Seen in Post–World War II Newspapers," trans. Scott O'Bryan, *U.S.-Japan Women's Journal,* English Supplement, no. 7 (1994): 6–8 and 10.

5. Special Survey Committee, *Postwar Reconstruction,* 25 and 189. See also Nakayama Ichirō, "Nihon keizai no kao," *Hyōron,* no. 38 (Dec. 1949): 1–9, for a positive assessment of rapid population increase in Japan as reflecting rises in productivity and other progressive economic developments. Cited in Aiko Ikeo, "Economic Development and Economic Thought after World War II: Non-Marxian Economists on Development, Trade and Industry," in Shiro Sugihara and Toshihiro Tanaka, eds., *Economic Thought and Modernization in Japan* (Northhampton, MA: Edward Elgar, 1998), 138–39.

6. Keizai Antei Honbu, "Keizai fukkō keikaku dai ichiji shian," 50–51. On the inability of the agrarian sector to support more people, see also Ōuchi Hyōe, "Nihon wa kongo dore hodo no jinkō o yashinaieru ka" (1946), in *Ōuchi Hyōe chosaku shū,* vol. 6 (Iwanami Shoten, 1975), 305–7. For use of the term "overpopulation" or "surplus population," see also Special Survey Committee, *Postwar Reconstruction,* 23 and 33.

7. Keizai Antei Honbu, "Keizai fukkō keikaku dai'ichiji shian no gaiyō" (1948), 20, 26–29; Keizai Antei Honbu, "Keizai fukkō keikaku dai ichiji shian" (1948), 47 and 58, table 13.

8. On the problem of food, see, for example, Ōuchi Hyōe, "Nihon wa kongo dore hodo no jinkō o yashinaieru ka," 313.

9. Nihon Tōkei Kenkyūjo, *Nihon tōkei seido saikenshi: tōkei iinkai shikō,* kijutsu hen (Nihon Tōkei Kenkyūjo, 1962), 28–33 and 67–72; Nihon Tōkei Kenkyūjo, *Nihon tōkei seido saikenshi,* shiryō hen 3, 25–81; Arisawa Hiromi, *Arisawa Hiromi sengo keizai o kataru: Shōwa shi e no shōgen* (Tokyo Daigaku Shuppankai, 1989), 78–91.

10. For an example of use by ESB planners, see Keizai Antei Honbu, "Keizai fukkō keikaku dai ichiji shian," 56; for discussion of the 1947 count as the beginning of reliable census taking in the postwar period, see Nihon Tōkei Gakkai, *Nihon no tōkeigaku 50 nen* (Tokyo Daigaku Shuppankai, 1983), 48. The first postwar attempts at a population count were made by the Cabinet Statistics Office in April 1946.

11. Keizai Antei Honbu, "Keizai fukkō keikaku dai ichiji shian," 56.

12. Keizai Antei Honbu, "Keizai fukkō keikaku dai ichiji shian no gaiyō," 19; Keizai Antei Honbu, "Keizai fukkō keikaku dai ichiji shian," 44–45.

13. Keizai Antei Honbu, "Keizai fukkō keikaku dai ichiji shian," 44–45.

14. The treatment of social policy approaches and the quotations in this paragraph are drawn from Yasuko Tama, "Logic of Abortion," 10–17. See also Tiana Norgren, *Abortion before Birth Control: The Politics of Reproduction in Postwar Japan* (Princeton, NJ: Princeton University Press, 2001), chaps. 5 and 6.

15. For examples of glosses of the phrase as apparent celebration and positive turning point, see Nakamura Takafusa, *Shōwa shi,* vol. 2 (Tōyō Keizai Shinpōsha, 1993), chap. 6; and Carol Gluck's reference to it in "The Past in the Present," in Andrew Gordon, ed., *Postwar Japan as History* (Berkeley: University of California

Press, 1993), 72, though she herself is doing so, it must be noted, with specific reference to the ways others have deployed the phrase in what she usefully labels the "establishment history" of postwar success.

16. Keizai Kikakuchō, *Keizai hakusho: Nihon keizai no seichō to kindaika*, Shōwa 31-nendo (Shiseidō, 1956), 1.

17. Takaki Tatsunosuke, "Keizai hakusho happyō ni sai shite no keizai kikakuchō chōkan seimei," in Keizai Kikakuchō, *Keizai hakusho*, Shōwa 31-nendo (unnumbered).

18. Keizai Kikakuchō, *Keizai hakusho*, Shōwa 31 nendo, 42; Japan Productivity Center, *Guide Book for Productivity Drive* [*sic*] (Japan Productivity Center, 1957), 10.

19. Shibuya Naozō, *Sengo Nihon no koyō shitsugyō to sono taisaku* (Rōdō Hōrei Kyōkai, 1957), 34, table 16.

20. Shitsugyō Taisaku Shingikai, *Koyō oyobi shitsugyō ni kansuru chōsa hōkokusho* (April 1955) (Shitsugyō Taisaku Shingikai, 1955), 3. The Shingikai was quoting the Population Issues Research Institute of the Ministry of Health and Welfare.

21. Minami Ryōzaburō, "Sengo jūnen no rōdō seisaku," in *Sengo jūnen no Nihon keizai seisaku no hensen: kaiko to hansei*, Nihon keizai seisaku gakkai nenpō, no. 4 (Keisō Shobō, 1956), 45.

22. Shibuya, *Sengo Nihon no koyō shitsugyō*, 35, table 18-1.

23. Tōkei Shingikai, Genshiryoku Shingikai, Chūō Chingin Shingikai, and Koyō Shingikai, respectively.

24. The report was titled "Senzai shitsugyō ni kan suru chōsa hōkokusho." For the text of the report, see Shitsugyō Taisaku Shingikai, *Koyō oyobi shitsugyō*, fuzoku shiryō, 319–44. There were estimated to be roughly 7 million semi-unemployed and a half million or so completely unemployed. Though somewhat more than the total of these two numbers, the figure of 8 million in terms of hidden unemployment was commonly quoted in discussions of the problem. See Arisawa, *Sengo keizai o kataru*, 123–24 and 133.

25. See, for example, the treatment of the issue in the EPA's Economic White Paper of 1957, Keizai Kikakuchō, *Keizai hakusho*, Shōwa 32-nendo, 34–35.

26. Shibuya, *Sengo Nihon no koyō shitsugyō*, 36, table 18-1.

27. Shitsugyō Taisaku Shingikai, *Koyō oyobi shitsugyō*, 4.

28. Ogiwara Kenji, "Ogiken no Seisansei," *Nihon seisansei shinbun*, no. 9 (Sept. 10, 1956): 6.

29. Shitsugyō Taisaku Shingikai, *Koyō oyobi shitsugyō*, 3–4; Shibuya, *Sengo Nihon no koyō shitsugyō*, 36, table 18-1.

30. Shitsugyō Taisaku Shingikai, *Koyō, shitsugyō ni kan suru tōshinsho* (April 5, 1955), reprinted in Murakami Shigetoshi, *Nihon no shitsugyō: sono keikō to taisaku* (Kawade Shobō, 1955), 160.

31. Keizai kikakuchō, *Keizai hakusho*, Shōwa 31-nendo, 37–38.

32. Keizai kikakuchō, *Keizai hakusho*, Shōwa 31-nendo, 22–42. For slower growth, see also Japan Productivity Center, *Guidebook*, 10.

33. Shitsugyō Taisaku Shingikai, *Koyō, shitsugyō ni kan suru tōshinsho*, 160–64.

34. Shitsugyō Taisaku Shingikai, *Koyō, shitsugyō ni kan suru tōshinsho*, 160.

35. Minami Ryōzaburō, "Sengo jūnen no rōdō seisaku," 46, question no. 2 by Kitami Toshirō.

36. Gotō has appeared more frequently in Japanese accounts, particularly those that address the important place of the EPA in the 1950s and Gotō's influence on the Economic White Papers of the era. See, for example, Masamura Kimihiro, "'Seichō to kindaika' no seisaku shisō: gijutsu kakushin shita no Nihongata Keinzushugi," in Chō Yukio and Sumiya Kazuhiko, eds., *Kindai Nihon keizai shisōshi,* part 2, vol. 6 of Miyazawa Toshiyoshi and Ōkouchi Kazuo, eds., *Kindai Nihon shisōshi taikei* (Yūhikaku, 1971), 399–404; Kanamori Hisao, *Watashi no sengo keizaishi: ekonomisuto no 50-nen* (Tōyō Keizai Shinpōsha, 1995), 247–50.

37. On Arisawa's coining of the term, see Keizai Gakushi Gakkai, *Nihon no keizaigaku: Nihonjin no keizaiteki shii no kiseki,* 185. The Economic White Papers were released each year in July.

38. For an early example, see the *teidankai* round-table discussion among Arisawa, Wakimura Yoshitarō, and Takahashi Masao, as covered and analyzed by the JPC in "Keizai kōzō no nijūsei o daha suru ni wa, seisan kōjō to kanren shite," in *Nihon seisansei shinbun* 56 (Aug. 5, 1957), 1.

39. Keizai Kikakuchō, *Keizai hakusho,* Shōwa 32-nendo, 33–38.

40. Keizai Kikakuchō, *Keizai hakusho,* Shōwa 32-nendo, 34.

41. Keizai Kikakuchō, *Keizai hakusho,* Shōwa 32-nendo, 36.

42. Nihon Seisansei Honbu, Seisansei Kenkyūjo, Koyō Mondai Iinkai, *Nihon no keizai kōzō to koyō mondai,* Koyō mondai iinkai Shōwa 31-nendo hōkokusho (Nihon Seisansei Honbu, 1957), 14. The Uno Kōzō school of Marxists was an example of those who rejected the idea of the divided structural characteristics of Japanese capitalism as unique, seeing it instead as a common condition among late-developing countries. This view owed much to the Rōnō faction of Marxists from the 1920s, who similarly resisted the "special" *(tokushu)* view of Japanese capitalist development held by the rival Kōza Marxist faction.

43. Keizai Kikakuchō, *Keizai hakusho,* Shōwa 31-nendo, 43.

44. Keizai Kikakuchō, *Keizai hakusho,* Shōwa 31-nendo, 43; Keizai Kikakuchō, *Keizai hakusho,* Shōwa 32 nen do, 36–37 and 44.

45. For the idea of Japan as having middling status *(chūshinkoku),* see Keizai Kikakuchō, *Keizai hakusho,* Shōwa 32-nendo, 36.

46. Keizai Kikakuchō, *Keizai hakusho,* Shōwa 31-nendo, 43.

47. Tsunoda, "Rationalizing Japan's Political Economy," 295–98.

48. Tsuru, "Economic Planning and Programming in Japan," 199–202.

49. For Shimomura's focus on growth dynamics, see Masamura Kimihiro, "'Seichō to kindaika' no seisaku shisō: gijutsu kakushin shita no Nihonkei Keinzushugi," in Chō Yukio and Sumiya Kazuhiko, eds., *Kindai Nihon keizai shisōshi,* part 2, vol. 6 of Miyazawa Toshiyoshi and Ōkouchi Kazuo, eds., *Kindai Nihon shisōshi taikei* (Yūhikaku, 1971), 405–7; Kanamori, *Watashi no sengo keizaishi,* 148–50.

50. Keizai Kikakuchō, Sōgō Keikakukyoku, *Zusetsu shotoku baizō keikaku: Nihon keizai no seichō* (Shiseidō, 1960), 14–15.

51. For a useful treatment of the forms of postwar macroeconomic regulation, see Yutaka Kosai, "The Politics of Economic Management," in Kozo Yamamura and Yasukichi Yasuba, eds., *The Domestic Transformation,* vol. 1 of *The Political Economy of Japan,* edited by Yasusuke Murakami and Hugh T. Patrick (Stanford, CA: Stanford University Press, 1987), 562–75.

52. Sheldon Garon, *Molding Japanese Minds: The State in Everyday Life* (Princeton, NJ: Princeton University Press, 1997), 155. See also his persuasive work on official savings campaigns and on questions of saving and consumption in "Fashioning a Culture of Diligence and Thrift: Savings and Frugality Campaigns in Japan 1900–1931," in Sharon Minichiello, ed., *Japan's Competing Modernities: Issues in Culture and Democracy, 1900–1930* (Honolulu: University of Hawai'i Press, 1998), 312–34; "Japan's Post-war 'Consumer Revolution,' or Striking a Balance between Consumption and Saving," in John Brewer and Frank Trentmann, eds., *Consuming Cultures, Global Perspectives: Historical Trajectories, Transnational Exchanges* (New York: Berg, 2006), 189–217; "The Transnational Promotion of Saving in Asia: 'Asian Values' or the 'Japanese Model'?" in Sheldon Garon and Patricia L. Maclachlan, eds., *The Ambivalent Consumer: Questioning Consumption in East Asia and the West* (Ithaca, NY: Cornell University Press, 2006), 163–87. See also Nihon Ginkō, Kin'yū Kenkyūjo, *Nihon kin'yūshi shiryō*, vol. 20, Shōwa zokuhen (Ōkurashō Insatsukyoku, 1990), 830–42.

53. For the ways in which institutions such as the Bank of Japan and the Finance Ministry, as well as women's groups acting through National Salvation Savings Campaigns, invoked cultural norms of frugality and restraint during the postwar period, see Garon, "Japan's Post-war 'Consumer Revolution,' " 194–210.

54. Gotō Yonosuke, *Amerika keizai han'ei no kōzō* (Chūō Kōronsha, 1956).

55. Gotō Yonosuke, "Nihon no keizairyoku," in Keizai Saiken Kenkyūkai, ed., *Pōrē kara Daresu e: senryō seisaku no keizaiteki kiketsu* (Daiyamondosha, 1952), 178; Keizai Kikakuchō, *Keizai hakusho*, Shōwa 31-nendo.

56. Gotō, *Amerika keizai han'ei no kōzō*, 246.

57. Gotō, *Amerika keizai han'ei no kōzō*, 122, 231, 246.

58. Gotō, *Amerika keizai han'ei no kōzō*, 253.

59. Nihon Seisansei Honbu, *Seisansei 30 nen shi* (Nihon Seisansei Honbu, 1985), 94–115. The JPC continued in existence through the postwar decades and was then reorganized in 1994 as the Japan Productivity Center for Socioeconomic Development (Shakai Keizai Seisansei Honbu), the form in which it remains today as an economic policy research center. William Tsutsui was the first English-language author that I am aware of to do any work on the original JPC. His highly instructive *Manufacturing Ideology: Scientific Management in Twentieth-Century Japan* (Princeton, NJ: Princeton University Press, 1998) discusses the organization in regard specifically to the connections between the postwar idea of productivity and prewar rationalization drives in manufacturing and the economy as a whole.

60. Gōshi Kōhei, "Warera han'ei e no yuiitsu no michi," *Nihon seisansei shinbun*, no. 1 (July 16, 1956): 1.

61. Nakayama Ichirō, "Han'ei e no michi," *Seisansei no riron to jissai*, vol. 3 (Nihon Seisansei Honbu, 1956), 57.

62. Japan Productivity Center, *Guidebook*, 13.

63. See the "Three Principles of the Productivity Movement" to the left of the nameplate at the top of the front page of the *Nihon seisansei shinbun*.

64. The focus on the benefits to consumers in the new economy was trumpeted throughout JPC publications. See, for example, "Nissan jidōsha no baai: shōhisha ni wa rieki o, rōdōsha ni wa kōfuku o, kigyō ni wa han'ei o," *Nihon seisansei shinbun*, no. 9 (Sept. 10, 1956): 3.

65. Simon Partner, *Assembled in Japan: Electrical Goods and the Making of the Japanese Consumer* (Berkeley: University of California Press, 1999), 149–71.

66. "Kari sentakuki ya: onajimi mo fueta," *Nihon seisansei shinbun,* no. 3 (July 30, 1956): 4.

67. "Sentakuki wa yakudatsuka," *Nihon seisansei shinbun,* no. 3 (July 30, 1956): 4. See Partner, *Assembled in Japan,* 157–58, for a similar use by the Matsushita corporation of comparative statistical analyses of caloric expenditures.

68. On the politics of the postwar consumer protection movement, see Patricia L. Maclachlan, *Consumer Politics in Postwar Japan: The Institutional Boundaries of Citizen Activism* (New York: Columbia University Press, 2002), 85–110.

69. For some specific examples of the JPC's attempts to overcome consumer skepticism, see the following series from the first year of the JPC's weekly newspaper: "Waga ie no seisansei," and Noda Nobuo, "Seisansei tekisuto," *Nihon seisansei shinbun* (1956).

70. "Benkyōshitsu: katei no seisansei—Okusama wa shachō no kan," *Nihon seisansei shinbun,* no. 67 (Oct. 21, 1957): 6.

71. See, for example, Keizai Kikakuchō, *Keizai jiritsu 5-kanen keikaku* (Shōwa 30-12-23) (Keizai Kikakuchō, 1955), 31; Keizai Kikakuchō, Keizai Kenkyūjo, *Kokumin sōseisan no chōki suikei: Dai ichiji shian Shōwa gannen–32-nen.* Kenkyū shiryō (Keizai Kikakuchō, 1959), especially 2–4; Keizai Kikakuchō, Chōseikyoku, *Shōhi juyō yosoku chōsa kekka no bunseki* (Keizai Kikakuchō, 1958); Economic Planning Agency, Economic Research Institute, *Consumption and Its Degree of Dependence on Imports in Postwar Japan,* Economic Bulletin No. 3 (Economic Planning Agency, 1959).

72. For analogous expression of cultural anxiety about materialist ideals and new patterns of private consumption in other national settings, see, for example, William Leach, *Land of Desire: Merchants, Power, and the Rise of a New American Culture* (New York: Random House, 1993); Martin Wiener, *English Culture and the Decline of the Industrial Spirit, 1850–1980* (Cambridge: Cambridge University Press, 1981); Kristin Ross, *Fast Cars, Clean Bodies: Decolonization and the Reordering of French Culture* (Cambridge, MA: MIT Press, 1995).

73. Indeed, the extent to which policy did in any of the industrialized countries during the same period is a matter of considerable debate.

74. Andrew E. Barshay, "'Doubly Cruel': Marxism and the Presence of the Past in Japanese Capitalism," in Stephen Vlastos, ed., *Mirror of Modernity: Invented Traditions of Modern Japan* (Berkeley and Los Angeles: University of California Press, 1998), 243.

75. See, for example, Sugiyama Mitsunobu's treatment of economic historian and theorist Iwata Hiroshi's analysis of capitalism in "The World Conception of Japanese Social Science: The Kōza Faction, the Ōtsuka School, and the Uno School of Economics," in Tani E. Barlow, ed., *New Asian Marxisms,* trans. Scott O'Bryan (Durham, NC: Duke University Press, 2002), 235. Sugiyama explains Iwata's argument that uneven development and the "imperialism" that resulted did not just take place between national economies; it also occurred within them: "Even within advanced capitalist countries, all sectors of the economy did not achieve a complete capitalist transformation. Rather, the capitalist organizations within the few advanced industrial sectors of the domestic economy achieved monopolistic control over both slower developing industrial sectors and the agricultural sector" (235).

Conclusion

1. For a popular introduction to the word *seichō*, see Keizai Kikakuchō, Sōgō Keikakukyoku, *Zusetsu shotoku baizō keikaku*, 2.

2. Ōkita was speaking in 1947 on the "necessity of economic whitepapers" that would be publicly disseminated. Quoted in Asai Yoshio, "Keizai antei honbu chōsaka to Ōkita Saburō," Seijō Daigaku keizai kenkyūjo kenkyū hōkoku, no. 11 (March 1997): 29.

3. Kristin Ross, *Fast Cars, Clean Bodies: Decolonization and the Reordering of French Culture* (Cambridge, MA: MIT Press, 1995), 176–78.

4. See James C. Scott, *Seeing Like a State: How Certain Schemes to Improve the Human Condition Have Failed* (New Haven, CT: Yale University Press, 1998), part 1, for an introductory discussion of high-modernist, technocratic "projects of legibility and simplification" and also chapter 8 for "taming nature."

5. Paul Rabinow, *The French Modern: Norms and Forms of the Social Environment* (Cambridge, MA: MIT Press, 1989), 322.

6. David C. Engerman, "Bernath Lecture: American Knowledge and Global Power," *Diplomatic History* 31, no. 4 (Sept. 2007): 620.

7. Richard Nixon first coined the word "growthmanship" when he was vice president (echoing, or perhaps anticipating, the better-known Cold War word, "brinkmanship"). In the words of Colin Clark, "growthmanship" referred to "an excessive preoccupation with economic growth, advocacy of unduly simple proposals for obtaining it, and the careful choice of statistics to prove that countries with a political and economic system which you favour have made exceptionally good economic growth, and that countries administered by your political opponents have made exceptionally poor economic growth." Colin Clark, "Growthmanship: A Study in the Mythology of Investment," Institute for Economic Affairs, Hobart Paper, no. 10 (London: Barrie and Rockliff, 1961), 12.

8. At roughly the same time as I was settling on the term to describe the global life of the growth idea after its early formative years, at least one other author, I later discovered, also fixed on the notion of growth as a late-century "fetish"; see Clive Hamilton, *Growth Fetish* (London: Allen and Unwin, 2003). Driven by contemporary frustration with global economic approaches, Hamilton's is not a work of history per se, but the intelligent cri de coeur of a professional economist. Reflecting the current climate of increasing political and environmental suspicions about growthist views of the world, it is a book with which I certainly find myself in great sympathy.

9. In one of the foundational texts of international growth theory, W. W. Rostow speaks of stages of growth in national economies in terms of "preconditions" for growth and a "drive to maturity," elocutions that underscore what he describes as his "essentially biological" view of growth. Rostow even more explicitly casts growth as self-organizing telos where he writes about examining sectoral structures of economies "as they transformed themselves for growth, and grew." W. W. Rostow, *The Stages of Economic Growth: A Non-Communist Manifesto* (Cambridge: Cambridge University Press, 1960), 4–10, 16, 36.

10. Shigeto Tsuru, "In Place of Gross National Product," xxi–xxii, in Asahi Shinbun Keizaibu, ed., *Kutabare GNP: Kōdo keizai seichō no uchimaku* (Asahi Shinbunsha, 1971).

11. E. F. Schumacher, *Good Work* (New York: Harper and Row, 1979), 30.

12. A fact known precisely through the statistical measures yielded by GNP accounting.

13. Kakuei Tanaka, *Building a New Japan: A Plan for Remodeling the Japanese Archipelago,* English ed., trans. Simul International (Simul Press, 1973), 37–39, 58–63, 114–58.

14. For numerical data on labor's relative share of nonprimary industry income, see Ryōshin Minami, *The Economic Development of Japan: A Quantitative Study* (New York: St. Martin's Press, 1986), 321. Support for my other statements in this discussion concerning structural change in employment and labor sectors may be found in Minami's comprehensive anaysis in chapter 9, "Labour Structure and Dual Economy," of that study, especially 294–321.

15. Ulrich Beck, "Self-Dissolution and Self-Endangerment of Industrial Society: What Does This Mean?" in Ulrich Beck, Anthony Giddons, and Scott Lash, *Reflexive Modernization: Politics, Tradition, and Aesthetics in the Modern Social World* (Stanford, CA: Stanford University Press, 1994), 178–83.

16. In *The General Theory of Employment, Interest and Money* (New York: Harcourt, Brace and Co., 1936), quoted in Martin J. Wiener, *English Culture and the Decline of the Industrial Spirit: 1850–1980* (Cambridge: Cambridge University Press, 1981), 92.

17. For a representative collection of essays, see Asahi Shinbun Keizaibu, ed., *Kutabare GNP: Kōdo keizai seichō no uchimaku* (Asahi Shinbunsha, 1971).

18. Net National Welfare Committee, Economic Council of Japan, *Measuring the Net National Welfare of Japan: Report of the Net National Welfare Measurement Committee* (Printing Bureau, Ministry of Finance, 1974); Kanamori Hisao, *Watashi no sengo keizaishi,* 252–53. See also Shigeto Tsuru, *Japan's Capitalism: Creative Defeat and Beyond* (Cambridge: Cambridge University Press, 1993), 146, for comment on the general feeling among many professional economists by the end of the 1960s that other means of measuring social goods needed to be defined.

19. The literature on sustainable economics is now quite large. Two important examples that have contributed to my thinking on these issues are Herman E. Daly, *Beyond Growth: The Economics of Sustainable Development* (Boston: Beacon Press, 1996), and Herman E. Daly and John B. Cobb Jr., *For the Common Good: Redirecting the Economy toward Community, the Environment, and a Sustainable Future* (Boston: Beacon Press, 1994).

Bibliography

Unless otherwise indicated, the city of publication for all Japanese titles is Tokyo.

Abe Osamu. "Kanzen koyō to keizai keikaku: saikin no ei-bei keizaigaku seisakuteki kiyo." *Keizai kenkyū* 1, no. 1 (Jan. 1950): 18–31.

Akuto Hiroshi. *Shōhi bunka ron: atarashii raifusutairu kara no hassō.* Chūō Keizaisha, 1985.

Ambaras, David R. "Social Knowledge, Cultural Capital, and the New Middle Class in Japan, 1895–1912." *Journal of Japanese Studies* 24 (Winter 1998): 1–33.

Arisawa Hiromi, ed. *Shiryō: sengo Nihon no keizai seisaku kōsō.* 3 vols. Tokyo Daigaku Shuppankai, 1990.

———. *Arisawa Hiromi sengo keizai o kataru: Shōwa shi e no shōgen.* Tokyo Daigaku Shuppankai, 1989.

———. "Fukahiteki na mono: Nihon keizai gendankai no tenbō." *Sekai,* no. 3 (March 1946): 31–48.

———. "Nihon keizai no hakyoku o sukū mono: genjitsu katei no bunseki." *Hyōron,* no. 9 (Jan. 1947): 2–11.

Arisawa Hiromi and Inaba Hidezō, eds. *Keizai.* Vol. 2 of *Shiryō: sengo nijūnenshi,* edited by Tsuji Kiyoaki et al. Nihon Hyōronsha, 1966.

Asahi, Isoshi. *The Economic Strength of Japan.* Hokuseido, 1939.

Asahi jinbutsu jiten: gendai Nihon. Asahi Shinbunsha, 1990.

Asahi nenkan. Asahi Shinbunsha, 1947.

Asahi Shinbun Keizaibu, ed. *Kutabare GNP: Kōdo keizai seichō no uchimaku.* Asahi Shinbunsha, 1971.

Asai Yoshio. "'Shinchōki keizai keikaku' to kōdo seichō shoki no keizai, sangyō seisaku." Seijō Daigaku keizai kenkyūjo kenkyū hōkoku, no. 25 (March 2000).

———. Interview with the author, Seikyō University, Tokyo, May 11, 1997.

———. "Kaidai." In *Sengo keizai keikaku shiryō: Keizai Antei Honbu sengo keizai seisaku shiryō,* edited by Sōgō Kenkyū Kaihatsu Kikō, Sengo Keizai Seisaku Shiryō Kenkyūkai, iii–xvi. Nihon Keizai Hyōronsha, 1997.

——. "Keizai antei honbu chōsaka to Ōkita Saburō." Seijō Daigaku keizai ken-kyūjo kenkyū hōkoku, no. 11 (March 1997).

Banno, Junji, ed. *The Political Economy of Japanese Society.* Vol. 1, *The State or the Market?* Oxford: Oxford University Press, 1997.

Barber, William J. "Reconfigurations in American Academic Economics: A General Practitioner's Perspective." *Daedalus* 126, no. 1 (1997): 87–103.

Barnhart, Michael A. *Japan Prepares for Total War: The Search for Economic Security, 1919–41.* Cornell Studies in Security Affairs. Ithaca, NY: Cornell University Press, 1987.

Barshay, Andrew E. *The Social Sciences in Modern Japan: The Marxian and Modernist Traditions.* Berkeley and Los Angeles: University of California Press, 2004.

——. " 'Doubly Cruel': Marxism and the Presence of the Past in Japanese Capitalism." In *Mirror of Modernity: Invented Traditions of Modern Japan,* edited by Stephen Vlastos, 243–61. Berkeley and Los Angeles: University of California Press, 1998.

——. "Toward a History of the Social Sciences in Japan," *Positions* 4, no. 2 (1996): 217–51.

Bartholomew, James R. *The Formation of Science in Japan: Building a Research Tradition.* New Haven, CT: Yale University Press, 1989.

Beck, Ulrich, "Self-Dissolution and Self-Endangerment of Industrial Society: What Does This Mean?" In *Reflexive Modernization: Politics, Tradition, and Aesthetics in the Modern Social World,* Ulrich Beck, Anthony Giddons, and Scott Lash, 174–83. Stanford, CA: Stanford University Press, 1994.

Bell, Daniel. "Models and Reality in Economic Discourse." In *The Crisis in Economic Theory,* edited by Daniel Bell and Irving Kristol. New York: Basic Books, 1981.

Bell, J. F. "Origins of Japanese Academic Economics." *Monumenta Nipponica* 16, nos. 3–4 (1960–61): 42–68.

Bodkin, Ronald G., Lawrence R. Klein, and Kanta Marwah, eds. *A History of Macroeconometric Model-Building.* Aldershot, Hants, and Brookfield, VT: Edward Elgar, 1991.

Breslau, Daniel. *In Search of the Unequivocal: The Political Economy of Measurement in U.S. Labor Market Policy.* Westport, CT: Praeger, 1998.

Brinkley, Alan. *The End of Reform: New Deal Liberalism in Recession and War.* New York: Vintage Books, 1996.

Bronfenbrenner, Martin. "Four Positions on Japanese Finance." *Journal of Political Economy* 58, no. 4 (Aug. 1950): 281–88.

Calder, Lendol. *Financing the American Dream: A Cultural History of Consumer Credit.* Princeton, NJ: Princeton University Press, 1999.

Callen, Tim, and Jonathan D. Ostray, eds. *Japan's Lost Decade: Policies for Economic Revival.* International Monetary Fund, 2003.

Callon, Scott. *Divided Sun: MITI and the Breakdown of Japanese High-Tech Industrial Policy, 1975–1993.* Stanford, CA: Stanford University Press, 1995.

Cassidy, John. "The Decline of Economics." *The New Yorker,* Dec. 2, 1996, 50–60.

Chigusa Yoshisodo. "Keinzu keizaigaku 2." *Zaisei* 19, no. 5 (1954): 98–104.

——. *Shihonshugi no shōrai.* Kōbundo, 1951.

Chikaraishi Sadakazu. *Keizai no keikakuka.* Vol. 9 of *Gendai no keizai.* Kawade Shobō, 1965.

Chō Yukio and Sumiya Kazuhiko, eds. *Kindai Nihon keizai shisōshi.* Vols. 5–6 of *Kindai Nihon shisōshi taikei,* edited by Miyazawa Toshiyoshi and Ōkouchi Kazuo. Yūhikaku, 1969–71.

Chūō Shitsugyō Taisaku Iinkai. "Kengi: shitsugyō taisaku to shite kyūsoku sochi subeki jikō ni kansuru iken" (Feb. 9, 1946). In Ōkouchi Kazuo, ed., *Rōdō,* 1–3. Vol. 4 of *Shiryō: sengo nijūnenshi,* edited by Tsuji Kiyoaki et al. Nihon Hyōronsha, 1966.

Clark, Colin. "Growthmanship: A Study in the Mythology of Investment." Institute for Economic Affairs, Hobart Paper, no. 10. London: Barrie and Rockliff, 1961.

Cohen, Jerome B. *Japan's Postwar Economy.* Bloomington: Indiana University Press, 1958.

———. *Japan's Economy in War and Reconstruction.* Minneapolis: University of Minnesota Press, 1949.

———. "Japan: Reform vs. Recovery." *Far Eastern Review* 17 (Dec. 1948): 137–42.

Cohen, Lizabeth. *A Consumers' Republic: The Politics of Mass Consumption in Postwar America.* New York: Knopf, 2003.

Cohen, Theodore. *Remaking Japan: The American Occupation of Japan as New Deal.* New York: New Press, 1987.

Collins, Robert M. *More: The Politics of Economic Growth in Postwar America.* Oxford: Oxford University Press, 2000.

Cross, Gary. *An All-Consuming Century: Why Commercialism Won in Modern America.* New York: Columbia University Press, 2000.

Crowley, James B. "Intellectuals as Visionaries of the New Asian Order." In *Dilemmas of Growth in Prewar Japan,* edited by William James Morley. Princeton, NJ: Princeton University Press, 1971.

Cullather, Nick. "The Foreign Policy of the Calorie." *American Historical Review* 112, no. 2 (April 2007): 337–64.

———. "Miracles of Modernization: The Green Revolution and the Apotheosis of Technology." *Diplomatic History* 28, no. 2 (April 2004): 227–54.

Daly, Herman E. *Beyond Growth: The Economics of Sustainable Development.* Boston: Beacon Press, 1996.

Daly, Herman E., and John B. Cobb Jr. *For the Common Good: Redirecting the Economy toward Community, the Environment, and a Sustainable Future.* Boston: Beacon Press, 1994.

De Grazia, Victoria, with Ellen Furlough, eds. *The Sex of Things: Gender and Consumption in Historical Perspective.* Berkeley and Los Angeles: University of California Press, 1996.

de Marchi, Neil. *Non-Natural Social Science: Reflecting on the Enterprise of More Heat Than Light.* Annual Supplement to Vol. 25, *History of Political Economy.* Durham, NC: Duke University Press, 1993.

Desmond, Edward W. "The Failed Miracle," *Time,* April 22, 1996.

Dower, John W. *Embracing Defeat: Japan in the Wake of World War II.* W. W. Norton and Company and The New Press, 1999.

———. "The Useful War." In John W. Dower, *Japan in War and Peace: Selected Essays,* 9–32. New York: New Press, 1993.

Economic Planning Agency, Economic Research Institute. *Consumption and Its Degree of Dependence on Imports in Postwar Japan.* Economic Bulletin No. 3. Economic Planning Agency, 1959.

Eisei Daijin. "Eisei daijin kakugi yōbō jikō: fukuin oyobi shitsugyōsha no suitei ni kansuru chū" (Dec. 16, 1945). In Ōkouchi Kazuo, ed., *Rōdō*, 1. Vol. 4 of *Shiryō: sengo nijūnenshi*, edited by Tsuji Kiyoaki et al. Nihon Hyōronsha, 1966.

———. "Shitsugyō taisaku ni kansuru kakugi yōbō" (Nov. 16, 1945). In Ōkouchi Kazuo, ed., *Rōdō*, 1. Vol. 4 of *Shiryō: sengo nijūnenshi*, edited by Tsuji Kiyoaki et al. Nihon Hyōronsha, 1966.

Ekonomisuto Henshūbu. *Shōgen: kōdō seichōki no Nihon*. 2 vols. Mainichi Shinbunsha, 1984.

Engerman, David C. "Bernath Lecture: American Knowledge and Global Power." *Diplomatic History* 31, no. 4 (Sept. 2007): 599–622.

Foster, William Trufant, and Waddill Catchings. *The Road to Plenty*. Boston: Houghton Mifflin, 1928.

Fukui, Haruhiro. "Economic Planning in Postwar Japan: A Case Study in Policy Making." *Asian Survey* 12, no. 4 (1972): 327–48.

Furner, Mary O., and Barry Supple, eds. *The State and Economic Knowledge: The American and British Experiences*. New York: Woodrow Wilson International Center for Scholars and Cambridge University Press, 1990.

Gaimushō, Chōsakyoku, "Kongo no kokunai keizai shisaku ni kan suru hitokōsatsu" (Sept. 18, 1945). In *Nihon keizai saiken no kihon mondai*, edited by Nakamura Takafusa and Ōmori Tokuko, 54–59. Vol. 1 of *Shiryō: sengo Nihon no keizai seisaku kōsō*, edited by Arisawa Hiromi. Tokyo Daigaku Shuppankai, 1990.

Gaimushō, Chōsakyoku, Daisanka. "Shitsugyō taisaku ni kanren suru yū'nyū shinsei no ken" (Aug. 12, 1946). In *Keisha seisan hōshiki to sekitan shōiinkai*, edited by Nakamura Takafusa and Miyazaki Masayasu. Vol. 2 of *Shiryō: sengo Nihon no keizai seisaku kōsō*, edited by Arisawa Hiromi, 41–43. Tokyo Daigaku Shuppankai, 1990.

Galbraith, John Kenneth. *A Journey through Economic Time: A Firsthand View*. Boston: Houghton Mifflin, 1994.

———. *Economics in Perspective: A Critical History*. Boston: Houghton Mifflin, 1987.

Gao, Bai. *Economic Ideology and Japanese Industrial Policy: Developmentalism from 1931 to 1965*. Cambridge: Cambridge University Press, 1997.

———. "Arisawa Hiromi and His Theory for a Managed Economy." *Journal of Japanese Studies* 20, no. 1 (Winter 1994): 115–53.

Garon, Sheldon. "Japan's Post-war 'Consumer Revolution,' or Striking a Balance between Consumption and Saving." In *Consuming Cultures, Global Perspectives: Historical Trajectories, Transnational Exchanges*, edited by John Brewer and Frank Trentmann, 189–217. New York: Berg, 2006.

———. "The Transnational Promotion of Saving in Asia: 'Asian Values' or the 'Japanese Model'?" In *The Ambivalent Consumer: Questioning Consumption in East Asia and the West*, edited by Sheldon Garon and Patricia L. Maclachlan, 163–87. Ithaca, NY: Cornell University Press, 2006.

———. "Fashioning a Culture of Diligence and Thrift: Savings and Frugality Campaigns in Japan 1900–1931." In *Japan's Competing Modernities: Issues in Culture and Democracy, 1900–1930*, edited by Sharon Minichiello, 312–34. Honolulu: University of Hawai'i Press, 1998.

————. *Molding Japanese Minds: The State in Everyday Life.* Princeton, NJ: Princeton University Press, 1997.

George, Timothy S. *Minamata: Pollution and the Struggle for Democracy in Postwar Japan.* Cambridge, MA: Harvard University Asia Center, 2001.

Go Seikō. *Gendai shōhisha keizai ron.* Seibundō, 1979.

Gordon, Andrew. "From Singer to Shinpan: Consumer Credit in Modern Japan." In *The Ambivalent Consumer: Questioning Consumption in East Asia and the West,* edited by Sheldon Garon and Patricia Maclachlan, 137–62. Ithaca, NY: Cornell University Press, 2006.

————. *The Wages of Affluence: Labor and Management in Postwar Japan.* Cambridge, MA: Harvard University Press, 1998.

————. *Labor and Imperial Democracy in Prewar Japan.* Berkeley: University of California Press, 1991.

Gotō Yonosuke. "Keiki dōkō to junkan kyokumen no rikai no tame: Shimomura shi shoron no gimonten o tsuku." In *Keizai seichō jitsugen no tame ni: Shimomura Osamu ronbun shū,* edited by Tamura Toshio, 251–68. Kōchikai, 1958.

————. *Amerika keizai han'ei no kōzō.* Chūō Kōronsha, 1956.

————. *Nihon keizai no mondaiten: Kyō to ashita.* Shiseidō, 1954.

————. "Nihon no keizairyoku." In *Pōrē kara Daresu e: senryō seisaku no keizaiteki kiketsu,* edited by Keizai Saiken Kenkyūkai, 161–80. Daiyamondosha, 1952.

Hacking, Ian. *The Taming of Chance.* Cambridge: Cambridge University Press, 1990.

Hadley, Eleanor. "The Diffusion of Keynesian Ideas in Japan." In *The Political Power of Economic Ideas: Keynesianism across Nations,* edited by Peter A. Hall. Princeton, NJ: Princeton University Press, 1989.

Hall, Peter A., ed. *The Political Power of Economic Ideas: Keynesianism across Nations.* Princeton, NJ: Princeton University Press, 1989.

Hamada, Koichi. "The Impact of the *General Theory* in Japan." *Eastern Economic Journal* 12, no. 4 (1986): 451–66.

Hamilton, Clive. *Growth Fetish.* London: Allen and Unwin, 2003.

Hansen, Alvin H. *A Guide to Keynes.* New York: McGraw-Hill, 1953.

Hara Akira. *Nihon no senji keizai: keikaku to shijō.* Tokyo Daigaku Shuppankai, 1995.

————. "Kaidai." In *Keizai fukkō keikaku,* edited by Nakamura Takafusa, 3–15. Vol. 3 of *Shiryō: sengo Nihon no keizai seisaku kōsō,* edited by Arisawa Hiromi. Tokyo Daigaku Shuppankai, 1990.

Hara Yūzō. "Keinzu kakumei to wa: hyakuman nin no keizaigaku." *Keizai shinshi* 7, no. 3 (March 1952): 29–30.

Harada Yutaka. *Nihon no ushinawareta jūnen: shippai no honshitsu, fukkatsu e no senryaku.* Nihon Keizai Shinbunsha, 1999.

Harris, José. *Unemployment and Politics: A Study in English Social Policy, 1886–1914.* Oxford: Clarendon Press, 1972.

Harris, Seymour, ed. *Atarashii keizaigaku: riron to seisaku ni taisuru Keinzu no eikyō.* Vol. 1. Translated by Nihon Ginkō, Chōsakyoku. Tōyō Keizai Shinpōsha, 1949.

————, ed. *Saving American Capitalism: A Liberal Economic Program.* New York: Knopf, 1948.

————, ed. *The New Economics: Keynes' Influence on Theory and Public Policy.* New York: Knopf, 1947.

Harrod, Roy Forbes. *The Life of John Maynard Keynes*. London: Macmillan, 1951.

Hayakawa Shōichirō and Yoshida Kenji. "Keizai fukkō kaigi no soshiki to undō." Parts 1–3: *Kenkyū shiryō geppō*, no. 283 (February 1982): 1–34; no. 284 (March 1982): 1–57; no. 292 (Dec. 1982): 1–22.

Hayasaka Tadashi, ed. *Keinzu no deai: Keinzu keizaigaku no dō'nyūshi*. Nihon Keizai Hyōronsha, 1993.

Hayasaka Tadashi and Masamura Kimihiro. *Sengo Nihon no keizaigaku: hito to gakusetsu ni miru ayumi*. Nikkei Shinsho no. 207. Nihon Nikkei Shinbunsha, 1974.

Hayashi Yūjirō, ed. *Nihon no keizai keikaku: sengo no rekishi to mondaiten*. Tōyō Keizai Shinpōsha, 1957.

Hazama Hiroshi. *Keizai taikoku o tsukuriageta shisō: Kōdo keizai seichōki no rōdō ētosu*. Bunshindō, 1996.

Hein, Laura. *Reasonable Men, Powerful Words: Political Culture and Expertise in Twentieth-Century Japan*. Berkeley: University of California Press, 2005.

———. "Statistics for Democracy: Economics as Politics in Occupied Japan." *Positions* 11, no. 3 (Winter 2003): 765–78.

———. *Fueling Growth: The Energy Revolution and Economic Policy in Postwar Japan*. Cambridge, MA: Council on East Asian Studies, Harvard University, 1990.

Hijikata Seibi. *Kokumin shotoku no kōsei*. Nihon Hyōronsha, 1933.

Hijikata Seibi, Chō Shuzen, and Iwano Chūjirō. *Kanzen koyō no riron to jissai*. Daiyamondosha, 1947.

Hitotsubashi Daigaku Keizai Kenkyūjo. *Keizai kenkyūjo yōran*. Hitotsubashi Daigaku Keizai Kenkyūjo, 1998.

Hollerman, Leon. "International Economic Controls in Occupied Japan." *Journal of Asian Studies* 38, no. 4 (1979): 707–19.

Honda Yasuhara. *Nihon no neo kanryōron*. 2 vols. Kōdansha, 1974.

Horiya Bunkichirō. "Keinzu tebikisō." *Tsukue* 4, no. 11 (Dec. 1953): 4–5.

Horowitz, Daniel. *The Morality of Spending: Attitudes toward the Consumer Society in America, 1875–1940*. Baltimore and London: Johns Hopkins University Press, 1985.

Hoston, Germaine A. *Marxism and the Crisis of Development in Prewar Japan*. Princeton, NJ: Princeton University Press, 1986.

Ikema, Makoto, Yoshio Inoue, Tamotsu Nishizawa, and Susume Yamauchi, eds. *Hitotsubashi University, 1875–2000: A Hundred and Twenty-Five Years of Higher Education in Japan*. London: Macmillan Press, 2000.

Ikeo, Aiko. "Economic Development and Economic Thought after World War II: Non-Marxian Economists on Development, Trade and Industry." In *Economic Thought and Modernization in Japan*, edited by Shiro Sugihara and Toshihiro Tanaka. Northhampton, MA: Edward Elgar, 1998.

Inaba Hidezō. *Gekidō 30 nen no Nihon keizai*. Jitsugyō no Nihonsha, 1965.

———, ed. *Nihon keizai no shōrai: keizai fukkō keikaku no zenbō to hihan*. Chūō Rōdō Gakuen, 1948.

Ishibashi Tanzan. "Shōwa nijūichi nendo shūgiin zaisei enzetsu" (July 26, 1946). Reprinted in *Keizai no shisō*, edited by Itō Mitsuharu and Chō Yukio, 39–52. Vol. 8 of *Sengo Nihon shisō taikei*. Chikuma Shobō, 1971.

———. "Kinshuku seisaku ka, bōchō seisaku ka: mokka no infure mondai no kaibō." *Tōyō keizai shinpō*, no. 2207 (Feb. 2, 1946): 7–14.

Iso Rankuji. "Jiyū shakai ni okeru kanzen koyō: koyō seisaku hakusho to Bīvuarijji hōkoku no komentarī." *Keizai Hyōron* 2, no. 1 (March–April 1947): 9–20.

Itō, Mitsuharu. Interview with the author, Tokyo, May 7, 1997.

———. "Munitions Unlimited: The Controlled Economy." *Japan Interpreter* 7, no. 3–4 (Summer–Autumn 1972): 353–63.

Itō Mitsuharu and Chō Yukio, eds. *Keizai no shisō.* Vol. 8 of *Sengo Nihon shisō taikei.* Chikuma Shobō, 1971.

———. *Tairyō shōhi jidai: shōhi kakumei, ryūtsū kakumei, sangyō kōzō.* Vol. 7 of *Gendai no keizai.* Kawade Shobō, 1964.

Japan Productivity Center. *Guide Book for Productivity Drive.* Japan Productivity Center, 1957.

Johnson, Chalmers. *MITI and the Japanese Miracle: The Growth of Industrial Policy, 1925–1975.* Stanford, CA: Stanford University Press, 1982.

"Kakugi kettei: genka no shitsugyō jisei ni taisho subeki shitsugyō taisaku" (March 4, 1949). In Ōkouchi Kazuo, ed., *Rōdō,* 124. Vol. 4 of *Shiryō: sengo nijūnenshi* edited by Tsuji Kiyoaki et al. Nihon Hyōronsha, 1966.

"Kakugi kettei: kinkyū shūgyō taisaku yōkō" (Feb. 15, 1946). In Shibuya Naozō, *Sengo Nihon no koyō shitsugyō to sono taisaku,* 134–38. Rōdō Hōrei Kyōkai, 1957.

Kanamori Hisao. *Watashi no sengo keizaishi: Ekonomisuto no 50-nen.* Tōyō Keizai Shinpōsha, 1995.

"Kanryō o dō suru." *Chūō Kōron* 62, no. 8 (Aug. 1947): 3–5.

Kase Kazutoshi. *Senzen Nihon no shitsugyō taisaku: kyūsaigata kōkyō doboku jigyō no shiteki bunseki.* Nihon Keizai Hyōronsha, 1998.

Kasza, Gregory J. *One World of Welfare: Japan in Comparative Perspective.* Ithaca, NY: Cornell University Press, 2006.

Katō Kan. "Keizai seichō to keizai keikaku no ikkei: Sovieto genka shōkyaku ronsō o megutte." In Nihon Keizai Seisaku Gakkai, *Keizai keikaku no sho keitai,* Nihon keizai seisaku gakkai nenpō, no. 7. Keisō Shobō, 1959.

Katz, Richard. *Japan, the System That Soured: The Rise and Fall of the Japanese Economic Miracle.* Armonk, NY: M. E. Sharpe, 1998.

Kawashima Takahiko. "Waga kuni tōkei seido kaikaku no shushi" (July 1946). In Nihon Tōkei Kenkyūjo, *Nihon tōkei seido saikenshi: tōkei iinkai shikō,* shiryō hen 1, 121–23. Nihon Tōkei Kenkyūjo, 1962.

Keizai Antei Honbu. "Keizai fukkō keikaku dai ichiji shian" (1948). In *Keizai fukkō keikaku,* edited by Nakamura Takafusa and Hara Akira, 41–186. Vol. 3 of *Shiryō: sengo Nihon no keizai seisaku kōsō,* edited by Arisawa Hiromi. Tokyo Daigaku Shuppankai, 1990.

———. "Keizai fukkō keikaku dai'ichiji shian no gaiyō" (1948). In *Keizai fukkō keikaku,* edited by Nakamura Takafusa and Hara Akira, 17–39. Vol. 3 of *Shiryō: sengo Nihon no keizai seisaku kōsō,* edited by Arisawa Hiromi. Tokyo Daigaku Shuppankai, 1990.

———. *Keizai jissō hōkokusho* (1947). Reprinted in *Keizai hakusho zenbun.* Sakagaki Shoten, 1949.

———. "Sangyō fukkō shitsugyō taisaku ni kanren suru yū'nyū shinsei no ken" (Sept. 4, 1946). In *Keisha seisan hōshiki to sekitan shōiinkai,* edited by Nakamura Takafusa and Miyazaki Masayasu, 46–52. Vol. 2 of *Shiryō: sengo Nihon no keizai seisaku kōsō,* edited by Arisawa Hiromi. Tokyo Daigaku Shuppankai, 1990.

Keizai Dōyūkai. *Keizai Dōyūkai 10 nen shi.* Keizai Dōyūkai, 1956.

Keizai Fukkō Keikaku Iinkai. "Keizai fukkō keikaku iinkai hōkokusho." In *Keizai fukkō keikaku,* edited by Nakamura Takafusa and Hara Akira, 187–253. Vol. 3 of *Shiryō: sengo Nihon no keizai seisaku kōsō,* edited by Arisawa Hiromi. Tokyo Daigaku Shuppankai, 1990.

Keizai Kikakuchō. *Sengo keizai fukkō to keizai antei honbu.* Keizai Kikakuchō, 1988.

―――. *Keizai antei honbushi.* Vol. 7 of *Sengo keizaishi.* Keizai Kikakuchō, 1968.

―――. *Keizai hakusho: hayasugita kakudai to sono hansei,* Shōwa 32-nendo. Shiseidō, 1957.

―――. *Shinchōki keizai keikaku.* Ōkurashō Insatsukyoku, 1957.

―――. *5-nengo no Nihon keizai: Dare mo wakaru keizai jiritsu 5-kanen keikaku no hanashi.* Daiyamondosha, 1956.

―――. *Keizai hakusho: Nihon keizai no seichō to kindaika,* Shōwa 31-nendo. Shiseidō, 1956.

―――. *Keizai jiritsu 5-kanen keikaku* (Shōwa 31.12.23) Keizai Kikakuchō, 1955.

―――. *Watashitachi no hataraki to kurashi: Wakariyasui kokumin shotoku no hanashi.* Tōyō Keizai Shinpōsha, 1955.

Keizai Kikakuchō, Chōsabu. *Amerika no keizai keikaku ni manabu.* Keikichōgai shō 32 dai 2 go. Keizai Kikakuchō, 1957.

―――. *Jinmin minshushugi shokoku ni okeru kokumin keizai keikaku no soshiki to hōhō.* Keikichō shō 31 dai 7 go. Keizai Kikakuchō, 1956.

Keizai Kikakuchō, Chōsabu, Kokumin Shotokuka. *Kokumin shotoku to kokumin keizai keisan.* Kokumin shotoku kaisetsu, shiryō dai 2 go. Keizai Kikakuchō, 1953.

Keizai Kikakuchō, Chōsabu, Tōkeika. *Keizai hendō bunseki no tame no chōsa to shōhisha kin'yū chōsa.* Keiki kansoku shiryō dai 3 go. Keizai Kikakuchō, 1956.

Keizai Kikakuchō, Chōseikyoku. *Shōhi juyō yosoku chōsa kekka no bunseki.* Keizai Kikakuchō, 1958.

Keizai Kikakuchō, Kaihatsubu. *Kokumin keizai keikaku sakusei no hōhōronjō no shomon-dai: Soren.* Zenkoku sōgō kaihatsu keikaku sankōshi, no. 13. Keizai Kikakuchō, 1956.

Keizai Kikakuchō, Keizai Kenkyūjo. *Keizai kenkyū nijūnen.* Keizai Kikakuchō, 1978.

―――. *Kokumin sōseisan no chōki suikei: dai ichiji shian Shōwa gannen-32-nen.* Kenkyū shiryō. Keizai Kikakuchō, 1959.

Keizai Kikakuchō, Sengo Keizaishi Hensanshitsu. *Sengo keizaishi.* 7 vols. Ōkurashō Insatsukyoku, 1957–64.

Keizai Kikakuchō, Sōgō Keikakukyoku. *Zusetsu shotoku baizō keikaku: Nihon keizai no seichō.* Shiseidō, 1960.

Keizaigakushi Gakkai. *Nihon no keizaigaku: Nihonjin no keizaiteki shii no kiseki.* Tōyō Keizai Shinpōsha, 1984.

Keizai Shingichō. *Nihon keizai to kokumin shotoku: Shōwa 5-nen–27-nen kokumin shotoku to kokumin keizai keisan.* Gakuyō Shobō, 1954.

Keynes, John Maynard. *The General Theory of Employment, Interest and Money.* New York: Harcourt, Brace and Co., 1936.

Kimura Kihachirō. "Keizai saihen no zentei." *Asahi hyōron* 2, no. 11 (1947): 12–20.

Kinkyū Shitsugyō Taisaku Hō. Law no. 89 (May 20, 1949). *Nihon no shitsugyō to sono taisaku,* edited by Murakami Shigetoshi, 169–75. Kawade Shobō, 1955.

"Kinkyū shitsugyō taisaku hōan teian riyū setsumei" (April 23, 1949). In Ōkouchi Kazuo, ed., *Rōdō*, 124–25. Vol. 4 of *Shiryō: sengo nijūnenshi*, edited by Tsuji Hiroaki et al. Nihon Hyōronsha, 1966.

Kin'yū Zaisei Jijō Kenkyūkai, ed. *Nihon no seichōryoku: Shimomura riron to sono hihan*. Kin'yū Zaisei Jijō Kenkyūkai, 1959.

Kitō Nisaburō. *Keinzu keizaigaku kaisetsu*. Gendai kyōyō bunko, no. 80. Shakai Shisō-sha, 1953.

————. *Keinzu keizaigaku kaisetsu*. Tōyō keizai kōza sōsho, no. 10. Tōyō Keizai Shinpō, 1946.

————. *Kahei to rishi no dōtai*. Tokyo: Iwanami Shoten, 1942.

Klein, Judy L., and Mary S. Morgan, eds. *The Age of Economic Measurement*. Supplement to vol. 33 of *History of Political Economy*. Durham, NC: Duke University Press, 2001.

Klein, Lawrence R. *The Keynesian Revolution* (1947). 2d ed. New York: Macmillan, 1966.

Klein, Lawrence R., and Kazushi Ohkawa, eds. *Economic Growth: The Japanese Experience since the Meiji Era*. Proceedings of the Conference of the Japan Economic Research Center. A Publication of the Economic Growth Center, Yale University. Homewood, IL: Richard D. Irwin, 1968.

Koizumi Akira. "Kurain *Keinzu kakumei* no hitokōsatsu: kindai riron to marukusu riron no kōshō." *Riron* 6 (Sept. 1948): 63–70.

Kojima Katsuji. *Nihon tōkei bunka ronshū*. 4 vols. Miraisha, 1981–85.

————. *Nihon tōkei bunkashi josetsu*. Miraisha, 1972.

Komiya, Ryūtarō, ed. *Postwar Economic Growth in Japan*. Selected Papers of the First Conference of the Tokyo Economic Research Center. Translated by Robert S. Ozaki. Berkeley: University of California Press, 1966.

Komiya, Ryūtarō, and Kozo Yamamura. "Japan: The Officer in Charge of Economic Affairs." *History of Political Economy* 13, no. 3 (Fall 1981): 600–628.

Kosai, Yutaka. "The Politics of Economic Management." In Kozo Yamamura and Yasukichi Yasuba, eds., *The Domestic Transformation*, 555–92. Vol. 1 of *The Political Economy of Japan*, edited by Yasusuke Murakami and Hugh T. Patrick. Stanford, CA: Stanford University Press, 1987.

Koschmann, J. Victor, Ryūichi Narita, and Yasushi Yamanouchi, eds. *Total War and "Modernization."* Ithaca, NY: Cornell University Press, 1998.

————. "The 'New Economic Ethic' during World War II." In *The Japan Foundation Newsletter* 25, no. 2 (August 1997): 8–10.

————. *Revolution and Subjectivity in Postwar Japan*. Chicago: Chicago University Press, 1996.

Kotani Masamori and Yasuda Yoshiaki, eds. *Gendai Nihon no shōhisha mondai*. Mineruva Shobō, 1980.

Kreps, David M. "Economics—The Current Position." *Daedalus* 126, no. 1 (1997): 59–85.

Kurabayashi, Yoshimasa, and Hiroshi Matsura. "Progress of Japanese National Accounts in an International Perspective of the SNA Review." In *Developments in Japanese Economics*, edited by Ryuzo Sato and Takashi Negishi, 99–123. Tokyo: Academic Press, Harcourt Brace Jovanovich, 1989.

Kurihara, Kenneth K. "The United Nations and Full Employment." *Journal of Political Economy* 58, no. 4 (August 1950): 353–58.

Kushida Mitsuo. "Henjo." In *Nihon keizai no seichōryoku: "Shimomura riron" to sono hihan*, edited by Kin'yu Zaisei Jijō Kenkyūkai, 2–4. Kin'yū Zaisei Jijō Kenkyūkai, 1959.

Kuznets, Simon, Wilbert Moore, and Joseph Spengler, eds. *Economic Growth: Brazil, India, and Japan*. Durham, NC: Duke University Press, 1955.

Kyū Seikatsu Hogo Hō. Law no. 17 (Sept. 9, 1946). In Ōkouchi Kazuo, ed., *Rōdō*, 33. Vol. 4 of *Shiryō: sengo nijūnenshi*, edited by Tsuji Kiyoaki et al. Nihon Hyōronsha, 1966.

Leach, William. *Land of Desire: Merchants, Power, and the Rise of a New American Culture*. New York: Random House, 1993.

Lears, Jackson. *Fables of Abundance: A Cultural History of Advertising in America*. New York: Basic Books, 1994.

Maclachlan, Patricia L. *Consumer Politics in Postwar Japan: The Institutional Boundaries of Citizen Activism*. Studies of the East Asian Institute, Columbia University. New York: Columbia University Press, 2002.

Maier, Charles S. "The Politics of Productivity: Foundations of American International Economic Policy after World War II." *International Organization* 31, no. 4 (Autumn 1977): 607–33.

Makino Noboru. *Kuronikaru Nihon keizai jiten, 1945–1994*. Tōyō Keizai Shinpōsha, 1996.

Marshall, Byron K. "Academic Factionalism in Japan: The Case of the Tōdai Economics Department, 1919–1939." *Modern Asian Studies* 12, no. 4 (1978): 529–51.

Masamura Kimihiro. *Sengoshi*. 2 vols. Chikuma Shobō, 1985; Chikuma Bunko, 1990.

———. "'Seichō to kindaika' no seisaku shisō: gijutsu kakushin shita no Nihonkei Keinzushugi." In *Kindai Nihon keizai shisōshi*, part 2, edited by Chō Yukio and Sumiya Kazuhiko, 399–413. Vol. 6 of *Kindai Nihon shisōshi taikei*, series edited by Miyazawa Toshiyoshi and Ōkouchi Kazuo. Yūhikaku, 1971.

Matsumura Toshi. "Keinzu *Kōyō, rishi oyobi kahei ippan riron* no chūshin kadai." *Shisō to kagaku* 3 (Nov. 1948): 66–75.

McCloskey, Deirdre N. *If You're So Smart: The Narrative of Economic Expertise*. Chicago: University of Chicago Press, 1990.

Metzler, Mark. *Lever of Empire: The International Gold Standard and the Crisis of Liberalism in Prewar Japan*. Berkeley: University of California Press, 2006.

———. "Woman's Place in Japan's Great Depression: Reflections on the Moral Economy of Deflation." *Journal of Japanese Studies* 30, no. 2 (2004): 315–52.

———. "Ishibashi Tanzan and the 'Positive Policy' in Economics." Paper delivered at the Annual Meeting of the Association for Asian Studies, March 29, 2003.

Mezaki Kenji. "Ronsetsu: jiyū to tōsei no jintēze no keizai keikaku." In *Keizai keikaku no sho keitai*. Nihon keizai seisaku gakkai nenpō, no. 7. Nihon Keizai Seisaku Gakkai. Keisō Shobō, 1959.

Mill, John Stuart. *Principles of Political Economy, with Some of Their Applications to Social Philosophy*. New York: Longmans, Green, 1909.

Minami Ryōshin. Interview with the author, Economic Research Institute, Hitotsubashi University, Kunitachi, Tokyo, Jan. 13, 1997.

Minami Ryōzaburō. "Sengo jūnen no rōdō seisaku." In *Sengo jūnen no Nihon keizai seisaku no hensen: kaiko to hansei*. Nihon keizai seisaku gakkai nenpō, no. 4, edited by Nihon Keizai Seisaku Gakkai. Keisō Shobō, 1956.

Mirowski, Philip. *More Heat Than Light: Economics as Social Physics; Physics as Nature's Economics*. Cambridge: Cambridge University Press, 1989.

Mitchell, Timothy. *The Rule of Experts: Egypt, Techno-Politics, Modernity*. Berkeley: University of California Press, 2002.

Mitsubishi Economic Research Bureau. *Japanese Trade and Industry: Present and Future*. London: MacMillan, 1936.

Miyazawa Ken'ichi. "Keinzu no keizai junkan ron." *Keizai kenkyū* 2, no. 4 (1951): 312–17.

Mizoguchi, Toshiyuki. *Personal Savings and Consumption in Postwar Japan*. Economic Research Series, Institute of Economic Research, Hitotsubashi University, no. 12. Kinokuniya Bookstore, 1970.

Mizutani Michikazu. *Sengo Nihon keizaishi: sangyō, ryūtsū, shōhi kōzō no henka*. Dōbun Kanshutsu, 1991.

Morgan, Mary S. *The History of Econometric Ideas*. Cambridge: Cambridge University Press, 1990.

Morley, James W. "The First Seven Weeks." *Japan Interpreter* 6 (Feb. 1970): 151–64.

Morris-Suzuki, Tessa. *A History of Japanese Economic Thought*. New York: Routledge, and Nissan Institute for Japanese Studies, Oxford University, 1990.

———. *Japanese Capitalism since 1945: Critical Perspectives*. Armonk, NY: M. E. Sharpe, 1989.

Murakami Shigetoshi. *Nihon no shitsugyō to sono taisaku*. Kawade Shobō, 1955.

Najita, Tetsuo. *Japan: The Intellectual Foundations of Modern Japanese Politics*. Chicago: University of Chicago Press, 1974.

Nakamura Seiichi. "L. R. Kurain *Keinzu kakumei* no konponteki tachiba ni tsuite." *Seiji keizai ronsō* 2, no. 1 (1951): 94–98.

Nakamura, Takafusa. "Introduction 1." In Special Survey Committee, Ministry of Foreign Affairs, *Postwar Reconstruction of the Japanese Economy*, compiled by Ōkita Saburō, ix–xiv. Translation of Gaimushō, Tokubetsu Chōsa Iinkai, *Nihon keizai saiken no kihon mondai*, 1946. University of Tokyo Press, 1992.

———, ed. "Nihon keizai saiken no kihon mondai." In *Nihon keizai saiken no kihon mondai*, edited by Nakamura Takafusa and Ōmori Tokuko, 143–263. Vol. 1 of *Shiryō: sengo Nihon no keizai seisaku kōsō*, edited by Arisawa Hiromi. Tokyo Daigaku Shuppankai, 1990.

———. *Nihon no keizai tōsei: senji sengo no keiken to kyōkun*. Nihon Keizai Shinbunsha, 1974.

Nakayama Ichirō. "Han'ei e no michi." Nihon Seisansei Honbu, *Seisansei no riron to jissai*, vol. 3, 56–59. Nihon Seisansei Honbu, 1956.

———. "Keinzu no kasetsu: *Ippan riron* no kihon mondai." *Keizai* 3, no. 1 (Jan. 1949): 4–11.

———. *Sengo keizai no tenbō*. Hakunichi Shoin, 1947.

———. "Keizai minshuka no kihon mondai." *Chūō Kōron* 61, no. 1 (Jan. 1946): 20–30.

———. "Kanzen koyō no riron." *Keizai hyōron* 1, no. 5 (Aug. 1946): 4–20.

National Archives, College Park, Military Records, Record Group 331 (Allied Operational and Occupation Headquarters, World War II), Boxes 5980, 7688, 7692, 7975, 8234, 8239, 8242, 8348, 8352, and 8369.

Net National Welfare Committee, Economic Planning Agency, Economic Council of Japan. *Measuring the Net National Welfare of Japan: Report of the Net National Welfare Measurement Committee.* Printing Bureau, Ministry of Finance, 1974.

Nihon Ginkō, Hyakunenshi Hensan Iinkai. *Nihon ginkō hyakunenshi.* Vol. 5. Nihon Ginkō, 1985.

Nihon Ginkō, Kin'yū Kenkyūjo. *Nihon kin'yūshi shiryō.* Vol. 20, Shōwa zokuhen. Ōkurashō Insatsukyoku, 1990.

Nihon Seisansei Honbu. *Karuizawa toppu seminā o kaerimiru: arata na hatten o motomete.* Nihon Seisansei Honbu, 1985.

———. *Seisansei 30-nen shi.* Nihon Seisansei Honbu, 1985.

———. *Keizai kaihatsu kōshūkai sankadan hōkokusho: keizai kaihatsu no shomondai.* Productivity Report No. 20. Nihon Seisansei Honbu, 1957.

———. *Nihon seisansei shinbun,* 1956–1960.

Nihon Seisansei Honbu, Seisansei Kenkyūjo, Koyō Iinkai. *Nihon no keizai kōzō to koyō mondai.* Koyō mondai iinkai Shōwa 31-nendo hōkokusho. Nihon Seisansei Honbu, 1957.

Nihon Tōkei Gakkai. *Nihon no tōkeigaku 50-nen.* Tokyo Daigaku Shuppankai, 1983.

Nihon Tōkei Iinkai Jimukyoku, Sōrifu Tōkeikyoku. *Nihon tōkei nenkan.* Vol. 1. Nihon Tōkei Kyōkai, 1949.

Nihon Tōkei Kenkyūjo. *Nihon tōkei seido saikenshi: tōkei iinkai shikō.* 4 vols. Nihon Tōkei Kenkyūjo, 1962–63.

———, ed. *Nihon tōkei hattatsushi.* Tokyo Daigaku Shuppankai, 1960.

Noguchi Yukio. *1940 Nen taisei: saraba senji keizai.* Tōyō Keizai Shinpōsha, 1995.

Nolte, Sharon H. *Liberalism in Modern Japan: Ishibashi Tanzan and His Teachers, 1905–1960.* Berkeley: University of California Press, 1987.

Nonomura Kazuo. "Nihon no 'kiki' keizai no shoriron." In Osaka Shiritsu Daigaku, Keizai Kenkyūjo, *Sengo shakai kagaku bunken kaisetsu* (May 1947–Dec. 1947). Reprinted in Keizaigaku bunken shūmoku, 4th series. *Shakai kagaku bunken kaisetsu, 1945–1947.* 2 vols. in 1, 13–24. Bunshō Shoin, 1984.

Norgren, Tiana. *Abortion before Birth Control: The Politics of Reproduction in Postwar Japan.* Princeton, NJ: Princeton University Press, 2001.

O'Bryan, Scott P. "Economic Knowledge and the Science of National Income in Twentieth-Century Japan." *Japan Studies Review* 6 (2002): 1–19.

Ogiwara Kenji. "Ogiken no Seisansei." *Nihon seisansei shinbun,* no. 9 (Sept. 10, 1956): 6.

Ohara Keiji. "Amerika shihonshugi o sukū michi." *Keizai kenkyū* 1, no. 1 (Jan. 1950): 61–65.

———. Review of Alvin Hansen, *Monetary and Fiscal Policy. Keizai kenkyū* 1, no. 2 (April 1950): 146–51.

Okamoto Yoshihiro. "'Keinzushugi' no kisoteki shomondai." *Keizai kagaku* 1, no. 2 (Oct. 1951): 91–104.

Ōkawa Kazushi, ed. *Nihon keizai no seichō ritsu: 1878–1942 nen ni kansuru jisshōteki kenkyū.* Iwanami Shoten, 1956.

Ōkawa Kazushi, Ishiwata Shigeru, Yamada Saburō and Ishi Hiromitsu, eds. *Shihon sutokku.* Vol. 3 of *Chōki keizai tōkei: suikei to bunseki,* series edited by Ōkawa Kazushi, Shinohara Miyohei and Umemura Mataji. Tōyō Keizai Shinpōsha, 1966.

Ōkawa Kazushi and Takamatsu Nobukiyo, eds. *Kokumin shotoku.* Vol. 1 of *Chōki keizai tōkei: suikei to bunseki,* series edited by Ōkawa Kazushi, Shinohara Miyohei and Umemura Mataji. Tōyō Keizai Shinpōsha, 1974.

Ohkawa, Kazushi. *The Growth Rate of the Japanese Economy since 1878.* Hitotsubashi University, Institute of Economic Research, Economic Research Series, no. 1. Kinokuniya Bookstore, 1957.

Ohkawa, Kazushi, and Henry Rosovsky. *Japanese Economic Growth: Trend Acceleration in the Twentieth Century.* Studies in Economic Growth in Industrialized Countries. Stanford, CA: Stanford University Press, 1973.

Ohkawa, Kazushi, and Miyohei Shinohara. *Patterns of Japanese Economic Development: A Quantitative Appraisal.* New Haven, CT: Yale University Press, 1979.

Okazaki, Robert. "Economics and Economists in Japan." *Asian Survey* 4, no. 6 (June 1964): 873–79.

Okazaki, Tetsuji, and Masahiro Okuno-Fujiwara, eds. *The Japanese Economic System and Its Historical Origins.* Oxford: Oxford University Press, 1999.

Okimoto, Daniel I. *Between MITI and the Market: Japanese Industrial Policy for High Technology.* Stanford, CA: Stanford University Press, 1989.

Ōkita, Saburō. *Japan's Challenging Years: Reflections on My Lifetime.* Adapted from the Japanese by Graeme Bruce. Boston: George Allen and Unwin, 1985.

———. "Nihon keizai no seichōryoku to 'Shin chōki keizai keikaku': Shimomura Osamu shi 'Kadai seichō ron hihan' no kentō," *Kin'yū zaisei jijō* 10, no. 12 (March 16, 1959). Reprinted in *Nihon no seichōryoku: Shimomura riron to sono hihan,* edited by Kin'yū Zaisei Jijō Kenkyūkai, 31–47. Kin'yū Zaisei Jijō Kenkyūkai, 1959.

Ōkouchi Kazuo, ed. *Rōdō.* Vol. 4 of *Shiryō: sengo nijūnenshi,* edited by Tsuji Kiyoaki et al. Nihon Hyōronsha, 1966.

Okuno Sadatori. "Nihon no tōkei jijō." In Nihon Seisansei Honbu, *Seisansei no riron to jissai.* Vol. 10, 56–72. Nihon Seisansei Honbu, 1959.

Ōmori, Tokuko. "Introduction 2." In Special Survey Committee, Ministry of Foreign Affairs, *Postwar Reconstruction of the Japanese Economy,* compiled by Ōkita Saburō, xv–xxix. Translation of Gaimushō, Tokubetsu Chōsa Iinkai, *Nihon keizai saiken no kihon mondai,* 1946. University of Tokyo Press, 1992.

Oshima, Harry. "Survey of Various Long-term Estimates of Japanese National Income." *Keizai kenkyū* 4, no. 3 (July 1953): 248–56.

Ōtake Fumio, Yanagawa Noriyuji, and Noguchi Yukio. *Kenshō: ushinawareta jūnen, Heisei fukyō no ronten.* Tōyō Keizai Shinbunsha, 2004.

Ōtsuka Hisao. "The Formation of a Modern Man: The Popular Base of Democratization" (1946). Translated by Patricia Murray. *Japan Interpreter* 6, no. 1 (1970): 1–5.

Ōuchi Hyōe. *Keizaigaku gojūnen.* 2 vols. Tokyo Daigaku Shuppankai, 1959.

———. "Sengo tōkei kotohajime" (Aug. 1957). In *Tōkei jōhō.* Reprint. *Ōuchi Hyōe chosakushū,* vol. 12, 258–64. Iwanami Shoten, 1975.

Ōuchi Hyōe, Kawasaki Misaburō, Arisawa Hiromi, Kimura Kihachirō, Ōkita Saburō, and Tsuru Shigeto. "Keizai hakusho no igi," *Sekai*, no. 21 (Sept. 1947): 1–18.

———. "Raisu hakasei ikkō kangei no kotoba" (Jan. 17, 1947). In Nihon Tōkei Kenkyūjo, *Nihon tōkei seido saikenshi: tōkei iinkai shikō*, shiryō hen 2, 81–82. Nihon Tōkei Kenkyūjo, 1963.

———. "Nihon wa kongo dore hodo no jinkō o yashinaieru ka" (1946). In *Ōuchi Hyōe Chosakushū*, vol. 6, 304–16. Iwanami Shoten, 1975.

———. "Sekai shintsūka seido no kenkyū" (1946). Reprinted in *Ōuchi Hyōe Chosakushū*, vol. 6, 5–174. Iwanami Shoten, 1975.

Partner, Simon. *Toshie: A Story of Village Life in Twentieth-Century Japan.* Berkeley: University of California Press, 2004.

———. *Assembled in Japan: Electrical Goods and the Making of the Japanese Consumer.* Berkeley: University of California Press, 1999.

Patriarca, Silvana. *Numbers and Nationhood: Writing Statistics in Nineteenth-Century Italy.* Cambridge: Cambridge University Press, 1996.

Patrick, Hugh, with the assistance of Larry Meisner, eds. *Japan's High Technology Industries: Lessons and Limitations of Industrial Policy.* Seattle and London: University of Washington Press, 1987.

Patrick, Hugh T., and Henry Rosovsky. *Asia's New Giant: How the Japanese Economy Works.* Washington, DC: Brookings Institution, 1976.

Pempel, T.J. "The Tar Baby Target." In *Democratizing Japan: The Allied Occupation,* edited by Robert E. Ward. Honolulu: University of Hawai'i Press, 1987.

Poovey, Mary. *A History of the Modern Fact: Problems of Knowledge in the Sciences of Wealth and Society.* Chicago: University of Chicago Press, 1998.

Pyle, Kenneth. "Advantages of Followership: German Economics and Japanese Bureaucrats, 1890–1925." *Journal of Japanese Studies* 1 (Autumn 1974): 127–64.

Rabinow, Paul. *The French Modern: Norms and Forms of the Social Environment.* Cambridge, MA: MIT Press, 1989.

Ramseyer, J. Mark, and Frances M. Rosenbluth, *The Politics of Oligarchy: Institutional Choice in Imperial Japan.* Cambridge: Cambridge University Press, 1995.

Rice, Richard. "Economic Mobilization in Wartime Japan." *Journal of Asian Studies* 38, no. 4 (1979): 689–706.

Rice, Stuart A. "Nihon no tōkei kikō no arikata" [trans. of original] (1951). In Keizai Kikakuchō, Sengo Keizaishi Hensanshitsu, *Sengo keizaishi.* Kokumin shotoku hen. Keizai Kikakuchō, 1963.

———. "Modernization of Japanese Statistics: Summary Report of the Statistical Mission to Japan" (April 1947). In National Archives, College Park, Military Records, Record Group 331 (Allied Operational and Occupation Headquarters, World War II), Box 8352.

———. "Nihon tōkei soshiki no kindaika no hitsuyō" [trans. of original] (April 1947). In Nihon Tōkei Kenkyūjo, *Nihon tōkei seido saikenshi: tōkei iinkai shikō.* Shiryō hen, vol. 2, 83–119. Nihon Tōkei Kenkyūjo, 1962.

———. "Origin and Purpose of the Mission" (n.d.). In National Archives, College Park, Military Records, Record Group 331 (Allied Operational and Occupation Headquarters, World War II), Box 8348 (17).

————. "Outline of Second Rice Mission Report on Japanese Statistics, Draft" (n.d.). In National Archives, College Park, Military Records, Record Group 331 (Allied Operational and Occupation Headquarters, World War II), Box 7688 (22).

————. "Preliminary Report on Japanese Statistical Organization" (n.d.). In National Archives, College Park, Military Records, Record Group 331 (Allied Operational and Occupation Headquarters, World War II), Box 7975 (2).

————. "Statistical Mission: Summary Report" (n.d.). In National Archives, College Park, Military Records, Record Group 331 (Allied Operational and Occupation Headquarters, World War II), Box 8348.

Rist, Gilbert. *The History of Development: From Western Origins to Global Faith*. Translated by Patrick Camiller. New revised and expanded edition. London: Zed Books, 1999.

Rōdōshō, Shokugyō Anteikyoku Shitsugyō Taisakubu. *Shitsugyō taisaku jigyō nijūnenshi*. Rōdō Hōrei Kyōkai, 1970.

————. *Shitsugyō taisaku nenkan*. Rōdōshō, 1951.

Roll, Eric. *A History of Economic Thought*. 4th ed. London: Faber and Faber, 1979.

Ross, Kristin. *Fast Cars, Clean Bodies: Decolonization and the Reordering of French Culture*. Cambridge, MA: MIT Press, 1995.

Rostow, W. W. *The Economics of Take-Off into Sustained Growth*. Proceedings of a Conference Held by the International Economic Association. London: Macmillan St. Martin's Press, 1963.

————. *The Stages of Economic Growth: A Non-Communist Manifesto*. Cambridge: Cambridge University Press, 1960.

Ruoff, Kenneth. *The People's Emperor: Democracy and the Japanese Monarchy, 1945–1995*. Cambridge, MA: Harvard University Asia Center, 2001.

Ryū Shintarō. *Seichō keizai no yukue*. Vol. 3 of *Ryū Shintarō Zenshū*. Asahi Shinbunsha, 1968.

Sada Kaiseki. "Saibai keizairon" (1878). In *Shisō*, 307–411. Vol. 15 of *Meiji bunka zenshū*, edited by Meiji Bunka Kenkyūkai. Nihon Hyōronsha, 1955–74.

Saitō Seiichirō. *Keizai kanryō no fukken: jidai o hiraku erītotachi* (Kyoto: PHP Kenkyūjo, 1980).

Sakakibara, Eisuke. *Beyond Capitalism: The Japanese Model of Market Economics*. Lanham, MD: University Press of America, 1993.

Sapir, Michael. "Nihon no kokumin shotoku tōkei (keikaku to hyōka)" (Japanese translation of original). In Keizai Kikakuchō, Sengo Keizaishi Hensanshitsu. *Sengo keizaishi*. Kokumin shotoku hen. Keizai Kikakuchō, 1963.

Saxonhouse, Gary R., and Robert M. Stern, eds. *Japan's Lost Decade: Origins, Consequences and Prospects for Recovery*. Malden, MA: Blackwell Publishing, 2004.

Schaller, Michael. *The American Occupation of Japan: The Origins of the Cold War in Asia*. New York: Oxford University Press, 1985.

Schumacher, E. F. *Good Work*. New York: Harper and Row, 1979.

Schumpeter, Joseph A. *History of Economic Analysis*. Edited by Elizabeth Boody Schumpeter. New York: Oxford University Press, 1954.

Scott, James C. *Seeing Like a State: How Certain Schemes to Improve the Human Condition Have Failed*. New Haven, CT: Yale University Press, 1998.

Shibuya Naozō. *Sengo Nihon no koyō shitsugyō to sono taisaku*. Rōdō Hōrei Kyōkai, 1957.

Shimomura Osamu. "Seichō seisaku no kihon mondai." *Kin'yū zaisei jijō,* no. 518 (Nov. 7, 1960). Reprinted in Shimomura Osamu, *Nihon keizai seichō ron,* 3–26. Kin'yū Zaisei Jijō Kenkyūkai, 1962.

———. "Nihon keizai kichō to sono seichōryoku: kadai seichō ron hihan to seichōryoku no ginmi," *Kin'yū zaisei jijō* 10, no. 9 (Feb. 16 and 23, 1959). Reprinted in *Nihon keizai no seichōryoku: "Shimomura riron" to sono hihan,* edited by Kin'yū Zaisei Jijō Kenkyūkai, 3–29. Kin'yū Zaisei Jijō Kenkyūkai, 1959.

———. "Kinyū hikishime seisaku: sono tadashii rikai no tame ni." In *Keizai seichō jitsugen no tame ni: keizaigaku hakase Shimomura Osamu ronbun shū,* edited by Tamura Toshio, 42–70. Kōchikai, 1958.

———. "Tōmen no keizai kyokumen o tsuranuku kihon dōkō: keizai no bōchō wa hatashite genkaiten ni kita ka." In *Keizai seichō jitsugen no tame ni: Shimomura Osamu ronbun shū,* edited by Tamura Toshio, 227–50. Kōchikai, 1958.

———. "Taidan: watashi wa keizai no kichō o kō kangaeru." *Tōyō keizai shinpō,* no. 2792 (Aug. 24, 1957): 38–43.

Shinohara Miyohei. *Structural Changes in Japan's Economic Development,* Hitotsubashi University, Institute of Economic Research, Economic Research Series, no. 11. Kinokuniya Bookstore, 1970.

———. *Nihon keizai no seichō to junkan.* Sōbunsha, 1961.

———. Review of *Income, Employment and Public Policy: Essays in Honor of Alvin Hansen. Keizai kenkyū* 2, no. 1 (Jan. 1951): 72–77.

Shinohara Miyohei and Fujino Shozaburō, eds. *Nihon no keizai seicho: seichō konfarensu no hōkoku to tōron.* Nihon Keizai Shinbunsha, 1967.

Shionoya Tsukumo. "Keinzu keizaigaku." Parts 1–4. *Ekonomisuto* 31, no. 21 (1953): 47–49; 31, no. 22 (1953): 46–49; 31 no. 23 (1953): 49–51; 31, no. 24 (1953): 44–47.

———. "Marukusu ni taiketsu suru mono to shite no Keinzu." *Yomiuri hyōron* 2, no. 3 (1950): 13–17.

"Shitsugyō hoken seido yōkō" (Oct. 1945). In Ōkouchi Kazuo, ed., *Rōdō,* 69–70. Vol. 4 of *Shiryō: sengo nijūnenshi,* edited by Tsuji Kiyoaki et al. Nihon Hyōronsha, 1966.

Shitsugyō Taisaku Shingikai. *Koyō oyobi shitsugyō ni kansuru chōsa hōkokusho.* Shitsugyō Taisaku Shingikai, 1955.

———. *Koyō, shitsugyō ni kan suru tōshinsho* (April 5, 1955). Reprinted in Murakami Shigetoshi, *Nihon no shitsugyō: sono keikō to taisaku.* Kawade Shobō, 1955.

Shūsen Renraku Jimukyoku Keizaibu. "Bogudan shi no 'Nihon keizai saiken no kihon mondai' sono hoka ni kan suru dan" (June 5, 1946). In *Nihon keizai saiken no kihon mondai,* edited by Nakamura Takafusa and Ōmori Tokuko, 115–19. Vol. 1 of *Shiryō: sengo Nihon no keizai seisaku kōsō,* edited by Arisawa Hiromi. Tokyo Daigaku Shuppankai, 1990.

Smethurst, Richard. *From Foot Soldier to Finance Minister: Takahashi Korekiyo, Japan's Keynes.* Cambridge, MA: Harvard University Asia Center, 2007.

Smith, Thomas C. *Political Change and Industrial Development in Japan: Government Enterprise, 1868–1880.* Stanford, CA: Stanford University Press, 1955.

Sobashima Shōzō. "'Keinzu kakumei' wa nani yue ni kakumeiteki de aru ka." *Bankingu,* no. 80 (Dec. 1954): 10–19.

Solow, Robert M. "How Did Economics Get That Way and What Way Did It Get?" *Daedalus* 126, no. 1 (1997): 39–58.

Sōrifu. *Sōrifu V.* Vol. 5 of *Kanchō benran.* Ōkurashō Insatsukyoku, 1960.

———. "Tōkei iinkai tōkei kōshūkai junsoku." Sōrifu Kokuji no. 8 (May 23, 1947). In Nihon Tōkei Kenkyūjo, *Nihon tōkei seido saikenshi: tōkei iinkai shikō*, shiryō hen 3, 159–60. Nihon Tōkei Kenkyūjo, 1963.

Special Survey Committee, Ministry of Foreign Affairs. *Postwar Reconstruction of the Japanese Economy.* Compiled by Ōkita Saburō. Translation of Gaimushō, Tokubetsu Chōsa Iinkai, *Nihon keizai saiken no kihon mondai,* 1946. University of Tokyo Press, 1992.

State–War–Navy Coordinating Committee. "U.S. Initial Post-Surrender Policy for Japan." *Department of State Bulletin* 13, no. 326 (Sept. 23, 1945): 423–27.

Streeck, Wolfgang, and Kozo Yamamura. *The Origins of Nonliberal Capitalism: Germany and Japan in Comparison.* Cornell Studies in Political Economy. Ithaca, NY: Cornell University Press, 2001.

Studenski, Paul. *The Income of Nations: Theory, Measurement, and Analysis, Past and Present.* New York: New York University Press, 1958.

Sugihara Shirō, ed. *Kindai Nihon no keizai shisō.* Mineruva Shobō, 1971.

Sugihara Shirō. *Seiō keizaigaku to kindai Nihon.* Miraisha, 1972.

Sugihara Shirō, Sakasai Takahito, Fujiwara Akio, and Fujii Takashi, eds. *Nihon no keizai shisō no yonhyaku nen.* Nihon Keizai Hyōronsha, 1990.

Sugihara, Shirō, and Toshihirō Tanaka. *Economic Thought and Modernization in Japan.* Cheltenham: Edward Elgar, 1998.

Sugimoto Eiichi. "Kindai riron keizaigaku to Marukusu keizaigaku." *Kikan riron,* no. 1 (May 1947): 28–45.

Sugita Hiroaki. *Shōwa no ekonomisuto.* Chūō Keizaisha, 1989.

Sugiyama, Chuhei. "The Development of Economic Thought in Meiji Japan." *Modern Asian Studies* 2, no. 4 (1968): 325–41.

Sugiyama, Mitsunobu. "The World Conception of Japanese Social Science: The Kōza Faction, the Ōtsuka School, and the Uno School of Economics." Translated by Scott O'Bryan. In *New Asian Marxisms,* edited by Tani E. Barlow, 205–46. Durham, NC: Duke University Press, 2002.

Supreme Commander of the Allied Powers. *History of Nonmilitary Activities of the Occupation of Japan, 1945–1951.* Monograph no. 47, *Heavy Industry.* Washington, DC: National Archives, 1951.

———. "GHQ meirei: Nihon kōkyō jigyō keikaku gensoku" [Japanese translation] (May 22, 1946). As attachment to "Kinkyū shitsugyō taisaku hōan teian riyū setsumei" (April 23, 1949). In Ōkouchi Kazuo, ed., *Rōdō,* 125. Vol. 4 of *Shiryō: sengo nijūnenshi,* edited by Tsuji Kiyoaki et al. Nihon Hyōronsha, 1966.

Suzuki Kyōichi. *Nihon keizai to keizai keikaku.* Senbundō, 1959.

Suzuki Shūji. *Bunmei no kotoba.* Kotoba kara kangaeru Nihonjinron, no. 4. Bunka Hyōron Shuppan, 1981.

Takahashi Chōtarō. "Keizai keikaku no tame no mokei kōsei." In *Keizai keikaku no sho keitai.* Nihon keizai seisaku gakkai nenpō, no. 7. Nihon Keizai Seisaku Gakkai. Keisō Shobō, 1959.

Takahashi Kamekichi, Katsuta Teiji, Takahashi Masao, Wakimura Yoshitarō, and Minobe Tatsukichi. "Kiki zaisei to keizai antei honbu: Ishibashi zaisei no hihan to tōsei keizai seikaku kentō." *Kaizō* 27, no. 8 (Aug. 1946): 38–57.

Takahashi Korekiyo. *Zuisōroku.* Senzō Shobō, 1936.

Takahashi Taizō. "Marukusu ka, Keinzu ka." *Seikei jichō* 5, no. 3 (March 1950): 5–6.

Takaki Tatsunosuke. "Keizai hakusho happyō ni sai shite no keizai kikakuchō chōkan seimei." In Keizai Kikakuchō, *Keizai hakusho: Nihon keizai no seichō to kindaika.* Shōwa 31 nendo. Keizai Kikakuchō [unnumbered]. Shiseidō, 1956.

Takefuji Mitsuaki. "'Keikaku to jiyū' no mondai no keizai rinriteki sokumen." In *Keizai keikaku no sho keitai.* Nihon keizai seisaku gakkai nenpō, no. 7. Keisō Shobō, 1959.

Tama, Yasuko. "The Logic of Abortion: Japanese Debates on the Legitimacy of Abortion as Seen in Post–World War II Newspapers." Translated by Scott O'Bryan. *U.S.–Japan Women's Journal,* English Supplement, no. 7 (1994): 3–30.

Tamanoi Yoshirō. *Nihon no keizaigaku.* Chūkō Shinsho no. 267. Chūō Kōronsha, 1971.

Tamura Toshio, ed., *Keizai seichō jitsugen no tame ni: keizaigaku hakase Shimomura Osamu ronbun shū.* Kōchikai, 1958.

Tanaka, Kakuei. *Building a New Japan: A Plan for Remodeling the Japanese Archipelago.* English edition translated by Simul International. Simul Press, 1973.

Tōkei Hō. No. 18 (March 26, 1947). In Nihon Tōkei Kenkyūjo, *Nihon tōkei seido saikenshi: tōkei iinkai shikō,* shiryō hen 2, 67–73. Nihon Tōkei Kenkyūjo, 1963.

Tōkei Iinkai. "Chihō tōkei kikō seibi yōkō." In Nihon Tōkei Kenkyūjo, *Nihon tōkei seido saikenshi: tōkei iinkai shikō,* shiryō hen 2, 209–17. Nihon Tōkei Kenkyūjo, 1963.

———. "Chihō tōkei kikō seibi yōkō ni tsuite no hōkoku." In Nihon Tōkei Kenkyūjo, *Nihon tōkei seido saikenshi: tōkei iinkai shikō,* shiryō hen 2, 217–18. Nihon Tōkei Kenkyūjo, 1963.

———. "Tōkei hōan teian riyū setsumei (honkaigi yō)" (date unclear). In Nihon Tōkei Kenkyūjo, *Nihon tōkei seido saikenshi: tōkei iinkai shikō,* shiryō hen 2, 52. Nihon Tōkei Kenkyūjo, 1963.

———. "Tōkeihō no rippō no shui" (Feb. 12, 1947). In Nihon Tōkei Kenkyūjo, *Nihon tōkei seido saikenshi: tōkei iinkai shikō,* shiryō hen 2, 54–67. Nihon Tōkei Kenkyūjo, 1963.

———. "Tōkei iinkai junbi kaigiji gaiyō oyobi shiryō" (Dec. 20, 1946). In Nihon Tōkei Kenkyūjo, *Nihon tōkei seido saikenshi: tōkei iinkai shikō,* shiryō hen 1, 262–63. Nihon Tōkei Kenkyūjo, 1963.

———. "Tōkei tanki daigaku setchi yōkō (an)" (July 18, 1950). In Nihon Tōkei Kenkyūjo, *Nihon tōkei seido saikenshi: tōkei iinkai shikō,* shiryō hen 3, 160–63. Nihon Tōkei Kenkyūjo, 1963.

Tōkei Seido Kaizen ni kansuru Iinkai. "Tōkei seido kaizen ni kansuru iinkai no tōshin." In *Nihon tōkei seido saikenshi: tōkei iinkai shikō,* shiryō hen 1, Nihon Tōkei Kenkyūjo, 256–57. Nihon Tōkei Kenkyūjo, 1962.

Tokyo Daigaku Shakai Kagaku Kenkyūjo. *Ushinawareta 10-nen o koete.* Tokyo Daigaku Shuppankai, 2005–6.

Tokyo Keizaigaku Kenkyūjo. *Keizaigaku no shōrai.* Hirobumisha, 1946.

Toshida Seiichi. *Nihon keizai no shukudai: "ushinatta jūnen" o koete.* Daiyamondosha, 2001.

Tribe, Keith. *Strategies of Economic Order.* Cambridge: Cambridge University Press, 1995.

———. *Genealogies of Capitalism.* New York: Macmillan, 1981.

Tsunoda, Elizabeth. "Rationalizing Japan's Political Economy: The Business Initiative, 1920–1955." Ph.D. diss., Columbia University, 1993.

Tsuru, Shigeto. *Japan's Capitalism: Creative Defeat and Beyond.* Cambridge: Cambridge University Press, 1993.

———. "Economic Planning and Economic Programming in Japan." In *Essays on Economic Development.* Hitotsubashi University, Institute of Economic Research, Economic Research Series, no. 9. Kinokuniya Bookstore, 1968.

———. "Sōkan no kotoba." *Keizai kenkyū* 1, no. 1 (Jan. 1950): 2.

Tsūshō Sangyōshō, Kigyōkyoku. *Sangyō gōrika.* 2 vols. Vol. 10 of *Shōkō seisakushi.* Shōkō Seisakushi Kankōkai, 1972.

Tsutsui, William M. *Manufacturing Ideology: Scientific Management in Twentieth-Century Japan.* Princeton, NJ: Princeton University Press, 1998.

———. "W. Edwards Deming and the Origins of Quality Control in Japan." *Journal of Japanese Studies* 22, no. 2 (1996): 295–325.

Uchino, Tatsurō. *Japan's Postwar Economy: An Insider's View of Its History and Future.* Trans. Mark A. Hobson. New York: Kodansha International, 1983.

Ueno Masaji. "Keizaishigaku." In Chō Yukio and Sumiya Kazuhiko, eds., *Kindai Nihon keizai shisōshi,* part 2, 197–218. Vol. 6 of *Kindai Nihon shisōshi taikei,* series edited by Miyazawa Toshiyoshi and Ōkouchi Kazuo. Yūhikaku, 1971.

Uno Kōzō. "Keizai antei no gainen." *Hyōron* 7 (Sept.–Oct. 1946): 2–10.

———. "Shihonshugi no soshikika to minshushugi." *Sekai,* no. 5 (May 1946): 16–28.

Wada Hiroo. "Keizai kinkyū taisaku ni kansuru dai ikkai kokka enzetsu" (July 1, 1947). In Arisawa Hiromi and Inaba Hidezō, eds., *Keizai,* 55–56. Vol. 2 of *Shiryō: sengo nijūnenshi,* edited by Tsuji Kiyoaki et al. Nihon Hyōronsha, 1966.

Wakimura Yoshitarō. "Sengo sekai keizai no tenbō: tenkan no shomondai." *Sekai,* no. 6 (June 1946): 40–50.

Watabe Fukutarō. "'Keinzu kakumei' ni kansuru kōsatsu." *Shōgaku ronshū* 19, no. 1 (1950): 81–101.

Watanabe Osamu. *'Yutaka na shakai' Nihon no kōzō.* Rōdō Junpōsha, 1990.

Westney, D. Eleanor. "Emigration." In *Kodansha Encyclopedia of Japan,* vol. 2, 200–201. Kodansha, 1983.

Wiener, Martin J. *English Culture and the Decline of the Industrial Spirit, 1850–1980.* Cambridge: Cambridge University Press, 1981.

Wildes, Harry Emerson. *Typhoon in Tokyo: The Occupation and Its Aftermath.* New York: Macmillan, 1954.

Yabuuchi Takeshi. *Nihon tōkei hattatsushi kenkyū.* Gifu keizai daigaku kenkyū sōsho, no. 7. Kyoto: Hōritsu Bunkasha, 1995.

Yamada Yūzō. *Nihon kokumin shotoku suikei shiryō.* Tōyō Keizai Shinpōsha, 1951.

Yamada Yūzō and Hisatake Motohiko, eds. *Nihon no keizai keikaku,* vol. 8 of *Keizai bunseki shimupojiumu.* Nihon Hyōron Shinsha, 1957.

Yamada Yūzō and Yamada Isamu, eds. *Keizai keikaku*. Vol. 12 of *Nihon keizai no bunseki*. Shunjūsha, 1960.

Yamamoto Kiyoshi. "'Sangyō saiken' to sho seiji shutai." In Tokyo Daigaku Shakai Kagaku Kenkyūjo, *Rōdō kaikaku*, 181–244. Vol. 5 of *Sengo kaikaku*. Tokyo Daigaku Shuppankai, 1974.

Yamanaka Shirō. "Keizai antei honbu no unyō ni kansuru shiken" (March 17, 1946). In Nihon Tōkei Kenkyūjo, *Nihon tōkei seido saikenshi: tōkei iinkai shikō*, shiryō hen 1, 1–6. Nihon Tōkei Kenkyūjo, 1962.

Yano Tsuneta. *Nihon kokusei zue*. Nihon Hyōronsha, 1929.

Yasui Inomata. "Koyō riron to tenbō." *Keizai Hyōron* 1, no. 8 (Nov. 1946): 16–29.

Yoda, Tomiko, and Harry Harootunian. *Japan after Japan: Social and Cultural Life from the Recessionary 1990s to the Present*. Durham, NC: Duke University Press, 2006.

Yoshikawa, Hiroshi. *Japan's Lost Decade*. Translated by Charles H. Stewart. LTCB International Library Selection, no. 11. LTCB International Library Trust/ International House of Japan, 2001.

Yoshino Kōichi, ed. *Zen Keinosuke tsuisōroku*. Nihon Dantai Seimei Hoken Kabushiki Kaisha, 1959.

Young, Louise. *Japan's Total Empire: Manchuria and the Culture of Wartime Imperialism*. Berkeley: University of California Press, 1998.

Zen Keinosuke. "Beikoku tōkei shisetsudan shōen ni okeru sōri daijin dairi Zen kokumu daijin aisatsu" (Jan. 17, 1947). In Nihon Tōkei Kenkyūjo, *Nihon tōkei seido saikenshi: tōkei iinkai shikō*, shiryō hen 2, 79–81. Nihon Tōkei Kenkyūjo, 1963.

———. "Nihon keizai no saiken," *Nihon keizai shinbun* (Dec. 9, 1946). Reprinted in *Zen Keinosuke tsuisōroku*, edited by Yoshino Kōichi, 168–77. Nihon Dantai Seimei Hoken Kabushiki Kaisha, 1959.

Index

and Keynesianism, 100–101; "the
postwar is now over," 149; SSC on,
22, 24, 34–35, 39–40, 41. See also
*Basic Problems in the Reconstruction of
the Japanese Economy;* Occupation
Rice, Stuart A./Rice Mission,
64, 72–74, 81–86, 203n95,
207nn132,133
Rostow, W. W., 122, 123, 125, 127,
228n9
Ryū Shintarō, 3, 4, 22, 38, 172, 185n3

Samuelson, Paul, 98, 99, 102, 198n14,
202n64, 209n13, 210n22
Sapir, Michael, 82, 85–86, 203n95,
207n132
savings, 122, 212n46; promotion of, 7,
160, 168, 169–170, 171, 186n8
SCAP. *See* MacArthur, Douglas;
Occupation
science, 16, 21, 32–43, 52; scientific
management/rationalization, 31,
37–40, 48, 63–79, 98, 130, 139–140,
164–170, 176, 194n67. *See also*
statistics; technocracy
Second World War, 6, 26, 28, 106;
decision to wage, 26, 40, 47;
demobilization, 18, 88–89, 107,
144, 150; documents destroyed,
45–46, 65; economic weakness,
21–22, 40, 42–43; financing,
56–59; national accounting, 56–64;
technocracy, 15; "unscientific," 40,
42, 43. *See also* Cabinet Planning
Board (CPB) Incident; controlled
economy, wartime; mobilization
plans
Shibusawa Keizō, 18–19, 57, 70–71,
79–80, 111, 215n85
Shimomura Osamu, 94, 126–128,
134–135, 175–176, 219n24; capital-
output ratio, 220n28; debates,
126–127, 131, 135, 137, 140,
157, 219n22; Income Doubling,
158–159; Shimomura Theory, 127
Shōwa Kenkyūkai, 22, 23, 34; Shōwa
Juku, 22, 191n25

socialism, 99; and full employment,
108, 109, 111; planning, 35–36,
137, 138, 139; Socialist Party, 109.
See also Marxist economists
social science: and growthism, 5, 7,
15, 16–17, 181–182; and statistics,
73–74. *See also* science
Social Science Research Council
(SSRC), 123, 125, 218nn14,17
Soviet Union, 28, 33, 68, 139, 179;
Soviet bloc, 35, 138, 175
Special Survey Committee (SSC),
21–28, 32–43, 44, 134; analysis of
Japan's economy, 89–90; Arisawa,
23, 25, 34, 46, 114; Gotō Yonosuke,
134, 154–155; Inaba, 23, 26–27,
46; Ōkita, 23, 24, 35, 46, 65, 134,
190n20, 191n25; public works,
113; statistics, 68–69. See also *Basic
Problems in the Reconstruction of the
Japanese Economy*
standards of living, 52, 100–101, 103,
148, 160, 182, 207n131. *See also*
middle class
Statistical Research Institute of Japan
(SRIJ), 66–67, 71, 202n70, 203n91
statistics, 13–15, 17, 20, 48–56, 64–87,
95, 173, 176, 196n1, 198n13,
208n143; calculating machines,
77–78, 206n120; designated system,
74–75, 85; education, 75–77; law
(1947), 67, 74–76, 79, 205; LTES,
124–125; macroeconomic, 14, 17,
48–50, 86–87, 119, 120; statistical
and econometric revolution,
48–49, 52, 62, 63, 119–120; U.S.,
68, 72, 73–74, 77, 79–87, 201n56;
wartime, 65–67, 74. *See also* national
income accounting
Statistics Commission, 64–80, 85, 150,
203n94, 206n124
Sugimoto Eiichi, *The Basic Character of
Modern Economics,* 95–96
supply, theories, 55, 92–93, 116–117
Supreme Commander for the Allied
Powers (SCAP). *See* MacArthur,
Douglas; Occupation

About the Author

SCOTT O'BRYAN is an assistant professor of history at Indiana University, specializing in modern Japan. He has appointments at IU in the Department of History and the Department of East Asian Languages and Cultures as well as an adjunct appointment in the Cultural Studies Program. He teaches and writes on the history of social science, consumption and mass consumer culture, environmental history, urban history, and peace history and has published on topics related to the politics and epistemologies of twentieth-century forms of statistical knowledge. More recently, O'Bryan has been writing about the rise of the idea of limits in economic and environmental thought. His next book project is an environmental, urban, and cultural history that narrates a variety of schemes to reshape the built environments and human geographies of late twentieth-century Japan. O'Bryan earned his M.A. at Yale University in East Asian studies and his Ph.D. in history from Columbia University (2000).

STUDIES OF THE WEATHERHEAD EAST ASIAN INSTITUTE

SELECTED TITLES

Leprosy in China: A History, Angela Ki Che Leung. Columbia University Press, 2008

National History and the World of Nations: Capital, State, and the Rhetoric of History in Japan, France, and the United States, Christopher Hill. Duke University Press, 2008

Mediasphere Shanghai: The Aesthetics of Cultural Production, Alexander Des Forges. University of Hawai'i Press, 2007.

Kingdom of Beauty: Mingei and the Politics of Folk Art in Imperial Japan, Kim Brandt. Duke University Press, 2007.

Modern Passings: Death Rites, Politics, and Social Change in Imperial Japan, Andrew Bernstein. University of Hawai'i Press, 2006.

The Making of the "Rape of Nanjing": The History and Memory of the Nanjing Massacre in Japan, China, and the United States, Takashi Yoshida. Oxford University Press, 2006.

The Merchants of Zigong: Industrial Entrepreneurship in Early Modern China, Madeleine Zelin. Columbia University Press, 2005.

Bad Youth: Juvenile Delinquency and the Politics of Everyday Life in Modern Japan, 1895–1945, David Ambaras. University of California Press, 2005.

Science and the Building of a Modern Japan, Morris Low. Palgrave Macmillan, Ltd., 2005.

Kinship, Contract, Community, and State: Anthropological Perspectives on China, Myron L. Cohen. Stanford University Press, 2005.

Rearranging the Landscape of the Gods: The Politics of a Pilgrimage Site in Japan, 1573–1912, Sarah Thal. University of Chicago Press, 2005.

Reluctant Pioneers: China's Expansion Northward, 1644–1937, James Reardon-Anderson. Stanford University Press, 2005.

Contract and Property in Early Modern China, Madeleine Zelin, Jonathan K. Ocko, and Robert P. Gardella, eds. Stanford University Press, 2004.

Gutenberg in Shanghai: Chinese Print Capitalism, 1876–1937, by Christopher A. Reed. UBC Press, 2004.

Japan's Colonization of Korea: Discourse and Power, by Alexis Dudden. University of Hawai'i Press, 2004.

Divorce in Japan: Family, Gender, and the State, 1600–2000, Harald Fuess. Stanford University Press, 2004.

The Communist Takeover of Hangzhou: The Transformation of City and Cadre, 1949–1954, James Gao. University of Hawai'i Press, 2004.

Taxation Without Representation in Rural China, Thomas P. Bernstein and Xaiobo Lu. Modern China Series, Cambridge University Press, 2002.

The Reluctant Dragon: Crisis Cycles in Chinese Foreign Economic Policy, Lawrence Christopher Reardon. University of Washington Press, 2002.

Cadres and Corruption: The Organizational Involution of the Chinese Communist Party, Xiaobo Lu. Stanford University Press, 2000.

Japan's Imperial Diplomacy: Consuls, Treaty Ports, and War with China, 1895–1938, Barbara Brooks. University of Hawai'i Press, 2000.

China's Retreat from Equality: Income Distribution and Economic Transition, Carl Riskin, Zhao Renwei, Li Shi, eds. M. E. Sharpe, 2000.

Production Notes for O'Bryan / THE GROWTH IDEA

Interior designed by University of Hawai'i Press production staff with text in New Baskerville and display in Agenda

Composition by Lucille C. Aono

Printing and binding by The Maple-Vail Book Manufacturing Group